Evolution of a Medical Psychoanalyst

Evolution of a Medical Psychoanalyst

Reflections and Selected Papers

Myron L. Glucksman, M.D.

ISBN: 1983515140
ISBN 13: 9781983515149
Library of Congress Control Number: 2018900356
CreateSpace Independent Publishing Platform
North Charleston, South Carolina

Table of Contents

Dedication vii

Acknowledgements ix

Introduction xi

Chapter 1   Behavioral Studies in Obesity 1

Chapter 2   Biofeedback Psychotherapy 41

Chapter 3   Affect in the Therapeutic Relationship 81

Chapter 4   Elements of Clinical Change 112

Chapter 5   Dream Studies 181

Chapter 6   Psychodynamic and Psychoanalytic Education 287

Chapter 7   Psychoanalysis and Neurobiology 309

Chapter 8   Animal Assisted Therapy 368

Conclusion On Being A Psychiatrist and Psychoanalyst 379

Index 395

Dedication

For Alex, Josh, Cosy, Clio, Theo and Ava.

Acknowledgements

I wish to thank my many patients, teachers, mentors, and students for contributing to my knowledge and skill as a psychiatrist and psychoanalyst. In particular, I wish to thank Ian Alger, M.D., Irving Bieber, M.D., Walter Bonime, M.D., Paul Dince, M.D., and Marvin Drellich, M.D., who were instrumental in my development as a medical psychoanalyst. I also wish to acknowledge Arthur Epstein, M.D., Lawrence Hatterer, M.D., Jules Hirsch, M.D., and Milton Kramer, M. D., who served as role models for me as a clinical researcher. Moreover, I appreciate the encouragement of my friends and colleagues, including John Alexander, M.D., Roman Anshin, M.D., Carl Berger, M.D., Eugene Connolly, James Grashow, Mark Hinckley, Ogden Morse, Barry Primus, and Clay Whitehead, M.D.

I especially wish to thank Robert Morton for his continuing support and editorial advice; Andrea Peables for her copy-editing skills, and Darius Wantke for his technical help. Lastly, and most important, I wish to thank my wife, Leslie, for her unwavering love and forbearance while I worked on this project.

To my patients: I have disguised names, gender, age, occupation, and other identifying data in my clinical presentations.

The following journals and publishers kindly granted permission to reprint papers:

Psychosomatic Medicine, Wolters Kluwer; British Journal of Medical Psychology, John Wiley and Sons; Journal of the American Academy of Psychoanalysis and Dynamic Psychiatry, Psychodynamic Psychiatry, Guilford Publications, Inc.

Introduction

The following commentaries and papers reflect the evolution of my clinical and research career as a psychiatrist and psychoanalyst over more than six decades that witnessed significant advances in psychiatry, psychoanalysis, and neurobiology. These previously published articles with accompanying commentaries reflect the changes during the late twentieth and early twenty-first centuries that influenced my clinical practice, theoretical orientation, and research interests.

My involvement in psychiatric research began when I was a medical student at the University of Washington School of Medicine. At that time, I worked for two summers at the Western State Psychiatric Hospital in Fort Steilacoom, Washington. While there, I examined the brain amino acids of schizophrenic patients, using urine samples and paper chromatography. This was in the mid-1950s, when neurotransmitters were first identified; namely, epinephrine, norepinephrine, and dopamine. My research required me to collect urine specimens from chronic schizophrenic patients who were often confined to locked wards without access to the outside. As far as I knew, they received neither recreational therapy, vocational activities, nor psychotherapy. Major tranquilizers (e.g., Chlorpromazine) were yet to be introduced as a form of treatment. By the end of my second summer at the Western State Hospital, patients had already begun receiving Chlorpromazine. It was nothing short of miraculous to see formerly withdrawn, psychotic individuals become active and communicative. Those summer work experiences stimulated my curiosity about the world of mental disorders and psychiatry.

I became seriously interested in pursuing a career in psychiatry during my internship at the Kings County Hospital, Downstate Medical Center, in Brooklyn, N.Y. While there, I rotated through the psychiatric service and saw many patients suffering from acute psychoses, dementia, anxiety, and mood disorders. That experience solidified my determination to further my training in psychiatry. Accordingly, I began a psychiatric residency at the Payne Whitney Clinic, New York Hospital–Cornell Medical Center, following my internship. During my residency, the first generation of antipsychotic tranquilizers (e.g., Chlorpromazine, Trifluoperazine) came into common use, as did the first generation of tricyclic antidepressants (e.g., Imipramine, Amitriptyline). Minor tranquilizers, including Chlordiazepoxide, and Diazepam, also became available during that period. At that time, Lithium was still considered an experimental medication for the treatment of bipolar disorder.

During my residency, I coauthored a paper that described the treatment of a patient with Myxedema Psychosis, using L-tri-iodothyronine (Glucksman and Stokes, 1967). As far as I know, this was the first instance where L-tri-iodothyronine was used in the treatment of Myxedema Psychosis. Following psychiatric residency, I became a consultant and research investigator at The Rockefeller University. While there, I worked with Jules Hirsch, M.D., whose laboratory was involved in exploring lipid metabolism in obese individuals. My focus was on the behavior of obese subjects before, during, and following significant weight loss. Our collaboration resulted in several papers that examined the psychopathology, psychodynamics, and body image perception of obese subjects during weight loss. A major discovery by Dr. Hirsch during this period was that in both mice and humans who become obese in childhood, adipose cells increase in number and size. Despite future weight loss, hyper-cellularity of adipose tissue appeared to remain fixed.

We also found that the perception of body size remained relatively stable from adolescence onward. These findings appeared to have important prognostic implications for individuals with childhood-onset obesity, and were elaborated on in our publications.

While I worked at The Rockefeller University, I began psychoanalytic training in The Psychoanalytic Institute at New York Medical College. This was in the early 1960s, when psychoanalysis was still a popular form of therapy. At that time, to become a psychoanalyst was considered to be the ultimate goal of a well-trained psychiatrist. In addition to undergoing a training analysis, I studied the psychoanalytic literature and conducted supervised psychoanalytic treatments. After leaving the The Rockefeller University, I became chief of the Psychiatric Consultation-Liaison Service at The New York Hospital–Cornell Medical Center and carried on a part-time private practice. However, soon after completing psychoanalytic training, I was drafted into the U.S. Army at the height of the Viet Nam conflict and was assigned to the Walter Reed Army Medical Center in Washington, D.C. While there, I taught in the army psychiatric residency training program and treated patients on both the inpatient and outpatient units. That experience taught me a great deal about acute combat mental disturbances and what later became known as Posttraumatic Stress Disorder.

Following discharge from the army, I became chief of the Psychiatric Consultation-Liaison Service at the Pennsylvania Hospital in Philadelphia. During this period, my interest in the pathogenesis of somatic symptoms continued, as did my work on the psychiatric aspects of obesity. Later, I moved to Connecticut, where I was chief of the Mental Health Clinic at Danbury Hospital and joined the clinical faculty in the Department of Psychiatry at the Yale University School of Medicine. In addition, I began a private practice in general psychiatry and psychoanalysis. This was a period when state mental hospitals were closing and chronic patients were being discharged into the community. Our outpatient clinic in Danbury was overwhelmed with patients who had been discharged from the local state hospital, and out of necessity we began the first Day Hospital in our area.

Although the first generation of antipsychotic medications was already in use, I became impressed with the therapeutic benefit of a social support system in the treatment of chronic schizophrenic patients. In the meantime, as a result of my involvement in the American Academy of Psychoanalysis, I began a research project in collaboration with Albert Stunkard, M.D., a well-known authority on the psychiatric aspects of obesity. The study involved overweight individuals who were in either psychoanalysis or psychodynamic psychotherapy. We found that a significant number of patients lost weight while in treatment and also improved according to a number of psychodynamic and behavioral variables (Glucksman, M.L., Rand, C.S.W., and Stunkard, A.J., 1978). To my knowledge, this was the first and only study of a large group of overweight patients receiving psychoanalytic treatment.

During the mid-1970s, I became interested in biofeedback psychotherapy. I was already aware of the early research in biofeedback that began in the 1960s at The Rockefeller University. The chief of Consultation-Liaison Psychiatry at Yale, Hoyle Leigh, M.D., and I established a biofeedback laboratory where we investigated the effects of combined psychotherapy and biofeedback on patients with functional somatic and psychogenic symptoms. One study, in particular, involved a patient with multiple food phobias and agoraphobia. A combination of psychotherapy and biofeedback completely cured her of her phobias. Our biofeedback research led to several papers on psychophysiological changes during psychotherapy, and was the beginning of my interest in both the psychological and physiological factors that accompany clinical change during psychotherapy.

In the early 1980s, I became chair of the Committee on Programs of the American Academy of Psychoanalysis. One of the first meetings I organized was on the topic of Affect. This led to my interest in the developmental, psychodynamic, and therapeutic aspects of Affect. A book, *Affect: Psychoanalytic Theory and Practice* (Cantor, M.B., and Glucksman, M.L.; eds., 1978) contained a collection of the papers presented at that meeting. Subsequently, I began exploring the vicissitudes of affective communication between therapist and patient. In particular, I became impressed with the curative role of emotional resonance within the therapeutic relationship. The therapist's subjective experience of the patient's internal emotional state via projective identification seemed especially important and led to my writing several papers, including the role of affect in the therapeutic relationship, as well as an examination of the key elements promoting clinical change: insight, empathy, and internalization. Further exploration of the nature of love in the therapist-patient relationship led to another paper on the "special friendship," or unique type of love that may evolve between therapist and patient. I became increasingly impressed with the loving bond that may develop between patient and therapist, as well as its importance in facilitating clinical improvement. In general, I believe that an empathic understanding of the patient is essential for clinical change to occur.

In 1987, Silas Warner, M.D., and I organized a symposium devoted to contemporary dream theories and their clinical applications. The papers presented at this symposium were collected in the book, *Dreams in New Perspective: The Royal Road Revisited* (Glucksman, M.L., and Warner, S.L., eds., 1987). This sparked my longstanding interest in the function of dreams and their use in the therapeutic process. Subsequently, I collaborated with Milton Kramer, M.D., on the clinical and therapeutic functions of dreaming. In a series of papers, we examined the ways in which manifest dream content can facilitate and document clinical changes during psychotherapy. These included studies of manifest dream content at the beginning and end of treatment; the predictive value of the initial dream of treatment, and changes in manifest dream content variables during treatment (including affect, dream narrative, themes, psychodynamics, and transference). This research resulted in my book, *Dreaming: An Opportunity for Change* (Glucksman, M. L., 2007), as well as another book, *Dream Research: Contributions to Clinical Practice* (Kramer, M., and Glucksman, M., eds., 2015). More recently, we have studied manifest dream content in depressed, suicidal patients as a means of predicting suicidal behavior (Glucksman, M.L., 2014; Glucksman, M.L., and Kramer, M., 2017).

I have always been involved in teaching and supervising medical students, psychiatric residents, and psychoanalytic candidates. For a decade, I was Director of The Psychoanalytic Institute in the Department of Psychiatry at New York Medical College. Parenthetically, this was the first psychoanalytic institute in the United States that functioned as an integral part of a department of psychiatry. As such, psychoanalytic trainees in our institute are required to be physicians as well as psychiatrists. This has influenced my belief that the theory and practice of psychoanalysis is intrinsically connected with neurobiological, cognitive, and affective components of mentation as well as sociocultural forces. Unfortunately, the disciplines of psychiatry and psychoanalysis have increasingly diverged because of a dualistic attitude that views mind as a separate entity from the brain. In my opinion, mind and brain are integrated phenomena, although they need to be understood and described using different languages and concepts. Taking these issues into consideration, I wrote two papers addressing the educational challenges involved in training the contemporary psychiatrist and psychoanalyst (Glucksman, M.L., 1997; Glucksman, M.L., 2006). Two additional papers examined the synergistic possibilities between neurobiological discoveries and theories of mind (Glucksman, M.L., 1995; Glucksman, M.L., 2016). The most recent paper was motivated by the vast amount of knowledge accumulated in both neurobiology and mental functioning since Freud's *Project for a Scientific Psychology* (Freud, S., 1895), written more than a century ago.

As I reflect on my professional career, a common thread is apparent in my clinical and research endeavors; namely, an appreciation of our uniquely human capacities for self-reflection and communication in the context of our biological endowment. As a physician, psychiatrist, and psychoanalyst, I continue to be mindful of the genetic, epigenetic, physiological, and social factors that play a role in behavior and mentation. Moreover, I continue to be in awe of our capacities for emotional connectedness, imagination, and self-observation. Although the fields of psychiatry and psychoanalysis have become more divided over the past half century, I have tried to maintain my identity in both disciplines. In my opinion, the functions of mind and brain are interwoven and synonymous. I hope this collection of papers and their accompanying commentaries meaningfully reflect the evolution of my professional identity, as well as my research and clinical interests over the course of a career. In addition, I believe they may also reflect significant changes that have occurred in psychiatry and psychoanalysis over the same time period. Finally, none of my research projects and publications would have been possible without the participation of my patients and the collaboration of my colleagues. I am forever grateful to them for their support and encouragement.

Myron L. Glucksman, M.D.

Clinical Professor of Psychiatry, New York Medical College; Supervising and Training Analyst, The Psychoanalytic Institute, New York Medical College; Attending Psychiatrist, Danbury Hospital, Danbury, Connecticut.

References:

Glucksman, M.L., and Stokes, P.E., "Psychopathologic and Metabolic Changes in a Patient with Myxedema Psychosis Treated with L-tri-iodothyronine," *American Journal of Psychiatry*, Vol. 123, No. 10 (1967): 1291-1294.

Glucksman, M.L., Rand, C.S.W., and Stunkard, A.J., "Psychodynamics of Obesity,", *Journal of the American Academy of Psychoanalysis*, Vol. 6, No. 1 (1978): 103-115.

Cantor, M.B., and Glucksman, M.L. (eds.), *Affect: Psychoanalytic Theory and Practice*. New York: John Wiley & Sons, 1978.

Glucksman, M.L., and Warner, S.L. (eds.): *Dreams in New Perspective: The Royal Road Revisited*. New York: Human Sciences Press, 1987.

Glucksman, M.L, *Dreaming: An Opportunity for Change*. Lanham, MD: Jason Aronson, 2007.

Kramer, M., and Glucksman, M.L. (eds.), *Dream Research: Contributions to Clinical Practice*. New York: Routledge, 2015.

Glucksman, M.L., "Manifest Dream Content as a Possible Predictor of Suicidality," *Psychodynamic Psychiatry*, Vol. 42, No. 4 (2014): 657-670.

Glucksman, M.L., and Kramer, M., "Manifest Dream Content as a Predictor of Suicidality," *Psychodynamic Psychiatry*, Vol. 45, No.2 (2017): 147-157.

Glucksman, M.L: "Integrating Psychoanalysis and Psychodynamic Psychotherapy into a Residency Training Program," *Journal of the American Academy of Psychoanalysis*, Vol. 25, No. 4 (1997): 655-662.

Glucksman, M.L: "Psychoanalytic and Psychodynamic Education in the 21st Century," *Journal of the American Academy of Psychoanalysis*, Vol. 34, No. 1 (2006): 215-222.

Glucksman, M.L: "Psychodynamics and Neurobiology: An Integrated Approach," *Journal of the American Academy of Psychoanalysis*, Vol. 23, No. 2 (1995): 179-195.

Glucksman, M.L: "Freud's 'Project': The Mind-Brain Connection Revisited," *Psychodynamic Psychiatry*, Vol. 44, No.1 (2016): 69-90.

Freud, S: "Project for a Scientific Psychology" in J. Strachey (ed. & trans.), *The Standard Edition of The Complete Psychological Works of Sigmund Freud*, Vol. 1 (1895): 283-410, Hogarth Press, London.

## Chapter 1

Behavioral Studies in Obesity

My interest in the psychiatric aspects of obesity began when Jules Hirsch, M.D. asked me to be the psychiatric consultant for his lipid metabolism research unit at The Rockefeller University in 1963. At that time, Dr. Hirsch was exploring the metabolism and morphology of adipose cells in obese individuals before, during, and after weight loss. His need for a psychiatrist became apparent when he observed that a significant number of his obese subjects became mentally disturbed as they lost weight. Some became severely anxious and depressed, while others even displayed psy-chotic symptoms. His patient population included male and female adults with childhood-onset obesity. Most weighed in excess of 300 pounds prior to weight loss, and lost approximately half their body weight over the course of the study.

I had just completed my residency in psychiatry, and knew very little about the biological and psychiatric components of obesity. At that time, the psychiatric literature on obesity was psychoanalytically-oriented. The prevailing view maintained that individuals who become obese have suffered from psychological trauma during the oral phase of development. That is, they have been deprived of normal mother-child bonding because of a lack of appropriate affection, soothing and feeding. According to this theory, the mothers of obese children either offer or withhold food for non-nutritional reasons; for example, they use food as a substitute for other needs of the child that they cannot satisfy, or because of their own feelings of inadequacy. As a result, obese children have difficulty distinguishing between hunger, satiation, other internal somatic sensations, and their feelings. Because of their mothers' inappropriate use of food to satisfy their emotional needs, they do not develop a capacity for self-soothing; instead, they rely on food for self-soothing when feeling anxious, sad or lonely. Consequently, as adults, they overeat in order to cope with dysphoric states. Sometimes, their oral needs become displaced in the form of excessive smoking, talking, hoarding, and need for attention.

Along with the foregoing psychogenic explanation of obesity, biological factors were also invoked. A hereditary component was assumed because of the higher incidence of obesity observed in identical twins separated at birth. In addition, hyper-cellularity as well as hypertrophy of adipose cells, was observed in obese mice and humans. However, when both animals and humans lost a significant amount of weight, adipose cells were reduced in size, but not in number. An unknown feedback mechanism from adipose tissue to the brain that indicated a state of semi-starvation, leading to overeating, was postulated. Subsequently, a number of hormones have been identified, including leptin and ghrelin, that signal the hypothalamus and regulate food intake. Leptin suppresses food intake, and induces weight loss. Ghrelin induces hunger and promotes weight gain. Obese individuals appear to be leptin-resistant (Klok, et al; 2007). More recently, bariatric surgery has replaced the largely unsuccessful attempts at permanent weight loss by obese individuals. However, the complications of surgery, as well as the long-term benefits from it, remain questionable.

My research interests in obesity centered on two main areas 1. Behavioral responses to weight reduction; 2. Perception of body image before, during, and after weight loss. To my knowledge, our systematic, quantifiable assessment of behavioral variables before, during, and after significant weight loss was the first to be reported in the literature (Glucksman, M.L. et al; 1968). In that study, we described behavioral alterations in the following areas during weight loss: 1. Affective: increased symptoms of anxiety and depression during and following weight loss; 2. Perceptual: increased concern over the alteration of body size during and following weight loss; 3. Sexual: increased sexual fantasies and acting-out during and following weight loss; 4. Hunger-Food Behavior: increased hunger, as well as fantasies and dreams of food or eating during weight loss. These behavioral changes appeared to be related to the metabolic and morphological alterations that occur during semi-starvation, as well as the idiosyncratic psychodynamic meanings of weight loss and reduced body size.

In our paper "The Response of Obese Patients to Weight Reduction: The Perception of Body Size" (Glucksman, M.L., and Hirsch, J; 1969), we focused on the perception of body size before, during and after weight loss. The salient finding was that obese subjects increasingly overestimated their body size during and following weight loss. This was termed the "phantom body size" phenomenon, and was ascribed to the following causes (1) body size image that becomes relatively fixed during adolescence, and (2) psychodynamic factors that contribute to a distorted body size image during and after weight loss.

Another paper, "Obesity: A Psychoanalytic Challenge" (Glucksman, M.L., 1989), described my long-term psychotherapy with an obese woman. It focused on the psychodynamics connected with compulsive eating, weight fluctuations, body image changes, and transference phenomena that occurred during the course of treatment. This paper was an attempt to integrate psychodynamic factors along with the genetic, metabolic, morphologic, and neurochemical information available during the period of time that I treated her. On a sad and cautionary note, she later died of post-operative complications following gastric bypass surgery.

References:

1. Klok, M.D., Jakobsdottir, S., and Drent, M.L., "The Role of Leptin and Ghrelin in the Regulation of Food Intake and Body Weight in Humans: A Review", *Obesity Review*, January 8 (1): 2007, 21-34.

2. Glucksman, M.L., Hirsch, J., McCully, R.S., Barron, B.A., and Knittle, J.L., "The Response of Obese Patients to Weight Reduction", II: A Quantitative Evaluation of Behavior, *Psychosomatic Medicine*, Vol. 30, No. 4: 1968, 359-373.

3. Glucksman, M.L., and Hirsch, J., "The Response of Obese Patients to Weight Reduction: III. The Perception of Body Size", *Psychosomatic Medicine*, Vol. 31, No. 1: 1969, 1-7.

4. Glucksman, M. L., "Obesity: A Psychoanalytic Challenge", *Journal of The American Academy of Psychoanalysis*, Vol. 17, No. 1: 1989, 151-171.

THE RESPONSE OF OBESE PATIENTS TO WEIGHT REDUCTION
III. THE PERCEPTION OF BODY SIZE

MYRON L. GLUCKSMAN, M.D., and JULES HIRSCH, M.D.

Abstract:

Previous studies suggested that the perception of body size played an important role in both the obese and reduced state. In this study, a body-sizing apparatus was utilized for the measurement of body size perception. The results indicated that 6 obese subjects increasingly overestimated their own body size during and following weight loss. In contrast, 4 non-obese subjects underestimated their own body size during a period of weight maintenance. In the reduced state, the obese subjects manifested a "phantom body size" phenomenon; that is, they perceived themselves as if they had lost almost no weight. Moreover, they consistently overestimated the size of other stimuli external to themselves before, during, and following weight loss.

Disturbances of body image are often observed in obese patients. [1-6] These disturbances range from feelings of self-consciousness and contempt toward oneself to denial or distortion of one's appearance. Stunkard and Mendelson[3] suggested that three factors predisposed an obese individual to the development of a disturbed body image: the onset of obesity prior to adult life, the presence of a neurotic behavior pattern, and censure by significant family members.

The evaluation of body image has been traditionally obtained through interviews, questionnaires, and projective tests. Recently, an objective estimation of body image was developed by Traub and Orbach[7] using a body-distorting mirror. They concluded that it was a useful instrument for the quantitative measurement of body image. Studies of obese patients in this laboratory[5, 6] have indicated that body size is an important component of body image. Our definition of body size is the subjective estimation of total body girth or area. Previous data[5, 6] suggested that body size perception plays an important role in both the obese and reduced state. Some patients reported persistent feelings of obesity following weight loss. Moreover, their human figure drawings, following weight loss, contained larger waist diameters and total body areas, in contrast to their figure drawings before weight loss.

In this study, a body-sizing apparatus was utilized for the measurement of body size perception in obese patients before, during, and following weight loss.

Materials And Methods:

Six severely obese adult patients seeking weight reduction were hospitalized during the same period of time on the behavioral-metabolic unit of the University Hospital. They included 3 males and 3 females, aged from 20 to 36 years. The mean admission weight of the group was 334 lb. All the patients had been obese since childhood and unsuccessful with previous attempts at weight reduction.

The experimental program consisted of an initial 6-week period of weight maintenance (Period I), followed by a 15-week period of weight loss (Periods II and III), and a final 6-week period of weight maintenance (Period IV). The mean length of hospitalization for the group was 8 months, and the mean weight loss was 86.7 lbs. Caloric intake during each of the four periods of hospitalization has been described elsewhere.[5]

A contrast group was utilized in the study, consisting of 4 adult, non-obese, hypercholesterolemic patients. Included in this group were 3 males and 1 female, aged from 39 to 57 years. These patients were in the same hospital, lived under similar conditions, and were fed the identical diet as the obese patients.[8] However, instead of losing weight, they were maintained at their admission weights throughout hospitalization. The mean admission weight of the contrast group was 132 lb., and the mean length of hospitalization was 7 months.

Figure 1 illustrates the body-sizing apparatus used in this study. It consisted of a Hilux 102 variable anamorphic lens with a magnification of 1.0 to 2.0 times and with a regular, fixed-distance, corrector lens.*

Attached to the lens was a 16 mm. Agfa Diamator slide projector. The anamorphic lens was motorized, allowing both subject and experimenter to control it by means of manual devices. A dial, consisting of 10 equal units, was attached to the anamorphic lens, enabling the experimenter to measure the amount of distortion in two directions-obese or thin. The midpoint on this dial corresponded to an undistorted image. Thus, with the dial set at midpoint, a slide placed in the slide projector and projected through the anamorphic lens onto a screen resulted in an undistorted image. With the dial at other settings, an obese or thin image resulted. The subject was not allowed to observe the dial.

Figure 2 illustrates three different images of a female subject, when projected through the anamorphic lens (thin, undistorted, and obese).

*Projection Optics Co., Inc., Rochester, N. Y.

Subjects were tested once weekly, on the same day, and at the same hour. Each week, a few days prior to testing, a photograph was taken of each subject and converted into a 2- by 2-in. slide. Testing consisted of the following steps:

1. A slide of the subject was projected on a screen in front of the seated subject. Prior to projection on the screen, the slide was distorted in either the direction of obesity or thinness at a predetermined dial setting. The subject was requested to make the distorted screen image correspond to his or her body size, as it was perceived by the subject at that moment. The subject accomplished this by manipulating the manual device which controlled the motorized, anamorphic lens. The subject was given four trials at this task, consisting of two trials in which the screen image was initially distorted in the

direction of obesity, and two trials in which the screen image was initially distorted in the direction of thinness.

2. A slide of a symmetrical vase was presented to the subject in a manner similar to that for the previous slide. However, the subject was initially shown an undistorted image of the vase for 10 sec., instead of a distorted image. Following this, the screen image was distorted in the directions of obesity (two trials) and thinness (2 trials). During these presentations, the subject was requested to make the screen image correspond to the initial, undistorted one.

3. A slide of an anonymous average-weight male was presented in the same manner as the symmetrical vase slide.

4. A slide of an anonymous average-weight female was presented to the subject in the same manner as the two previous slides.

5. All slides and all trials were presented in a randomized fashion throughout the study.

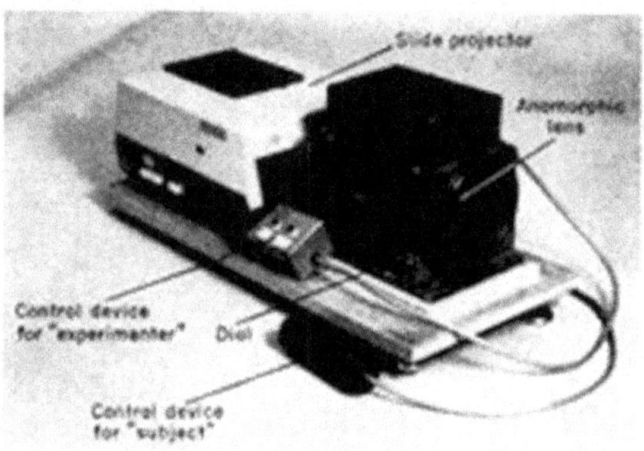

FIG. 1. Body-sizing apparatus.

The contrast or non-obese subjects were each tested once weekly for 6 successive weeks. Since they were not all hospitalized simultaneously, it was not technically possible to test each of them for 27 successive weeks, as were the obese subjects. However, the 6-week period of testing was not performed during the same phase of hospitalization for each subject. Therefore, the effects of the initial, middle, and terminal phases of hospitalization were taken into account for the non-obese group.

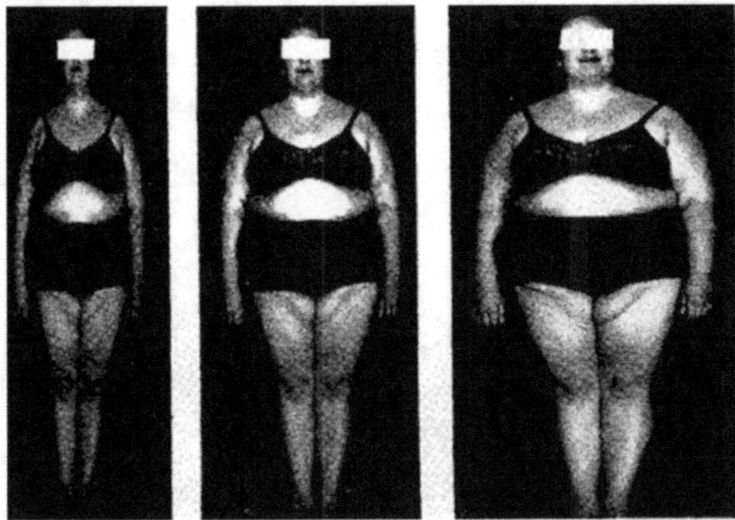

FIG. 2. Three images produced by anamorphic lens. Types of images produced are, from left to right, (1) thin, (2) undistorted, and (3) obese.

Results:

The basic unit of data was the "size estimation score." This consisted of a subject's total score for a particular stimulus in a given test during four trials. A trial score was simply the numerical value of the dial setting arrived at by the subject.

Table 1 presents the results of an analysis of variance of the periods of weight reduction and of the size estimation of stimuli by the obese subjects. Table 1 indicates that the "self" body size estimations of the obese subjects differed significantly between periods. Figure 3 illustrates that this difference consisted of an increasing overestimation of their own body size from Period I to Period IV. By contrast, their size estimations of the other three stimuli ("vase," "male," and "female") did not differ significantly between periods. There were significant differences in size estimation scores between subjects for all stimuli. Interaction between obese subjects and the periods was significant for the "self" and "female" stimuli.

TABLE 1. ANALYSIS OF VARIANCE OF PERIODS OF WEIGHT REDUCTION AND SIZE ESTIMATION OF "SELF," "VASE," "MALE" AND "FEMALE" STIMULI FOR OBESE SUBJECTS

Source of variation	df	Self Mean sq.	F	Vase Mean sq.	F	Male Mean sq.	F	Female Mean sq.	F
Periods	3	58.44	5.52*	6.19	0.95	2.30	0.40	0.35	0.06
Subjects	5	427.37	4.04*	50.07	7.68*	62.59*	10.89*	68.31	13.30*
Interaction	15	40.74	5.78*	5.64	0.86	6.34	1.10	8.67	1.85*
Residual	120	6.82		6.51		5.75		4.68	
TOTAL	143								

*$p \leq 0.05$.

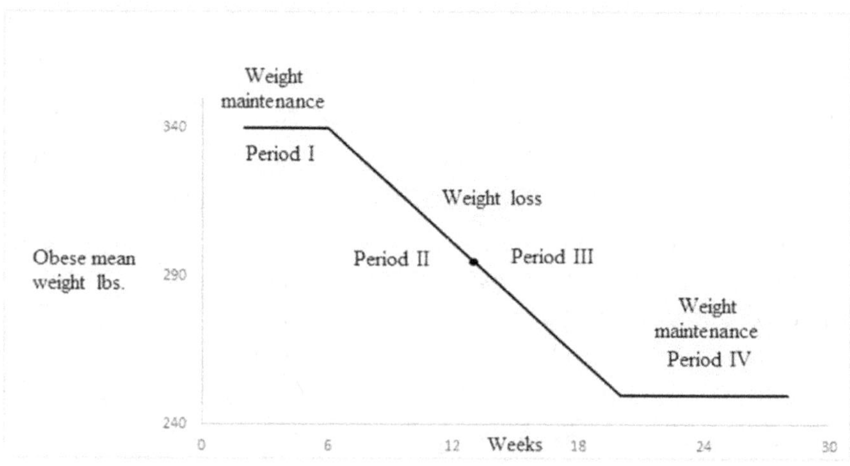

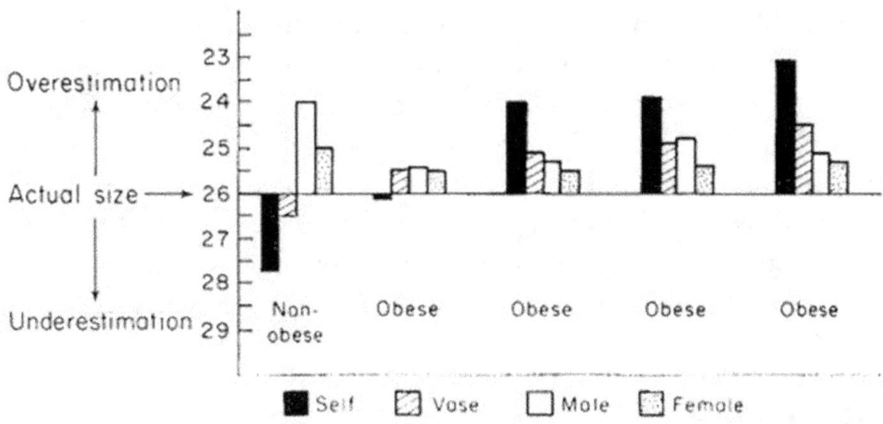

FIG. 3. Size estimation of stimuli by obese and non-obese subjects during periods of weight maintenance and weight loss.

TABLE 2. ANALYSIS OF VARIANCE OF NONOBESE SUBJECT AND SIZE ESTIMATION OF "SELF," "VASE," "MALE" AND "FEMALE" STIMULI

Source of variation	df	Mean sq.	F
Subjects	3	59.76	5.01*
Stimuli	3	60.57	5.08*
Interaction	9	30.83	3.15*
Residual	80	9.79	
TOTAL	95		

*p ≤ 0.05.

Table 2 presents the results of an analysis of variance of the non-obese subjects and their size estimation of the stimuli. There was a significant difference between subjects in their size estimations of all stimuli. Moreover, each stimulus differed significantly from the other for all subjects. Interaction between non-obese subjects and the stimuli was significant.

Obese and non-obese subjects differed, although not significantly, in their estimations of "self." The non-obese subjects underestimated their own body sizes, in comparison to the obese subjects (Fig. 3). The obese subjects overestimated and the non-obese subjects underestimated the "vase" size, although this difference was not significant. Both groups overestimated the "male" and "female" body sizes, but without a significant difference.

Discussion:

The results of this study suggest that it is possible to evaluate quantitatively the perception of body size. The anamorphic-lens technique is especially advantageous for the quantification of body size perception, because it distorts only body girth.

The most striking observation was that the obese subjects increasingly overestimated their own body size during and following weight loss (Fig. 3). Prior to weight loss (Period I), the obese group slightly underestimated their actual body size. During weight loss (Periods II and III), they overestimated their actual body size. The amount of overestimation was significantly larger than their slight underestimation of themselves during Period I. Following weight loss (Period IV), they continued to overestimate their actual body size. The amount of overestimation during Period IV was significantly larger than the amount of overestimation during Periods II and III. By measuring the screen body size (waist diameter) which the obese subjects estimated of themselves, it was possible to determine the difference between their screen body sizes from one period to the next. It was apparent that those subjects who increasingly overestimated their body size during Periods II, III, and IV were actually perceiving themselves as they had during Period I. In effect, despite their weight loss, they perceived themselves as if they had lost almost no weight. This "phantom body size" phenomenon was accompanied by supportive clinical and figure-drawing data.[6] For example, these same subjects drew progressively larger isosexual figure drawings during hospitalization. They also reported that they continued to feel obese, following weight loss.

In contrast to their progressive overestimation of "self" during and following weight loss, the obese subjects did not make the same perceptual error with regard to the "vase," "male," and "female" stimuli (Fig. 3).

Although they consistently overestimated the size of the "vase," "male," and "female" stimuli during each period of hospitalization, the amount of overestimation was not significantly different from one period to the next.

There are several possible explanations for their increasing overestimation of "self" and their rather consistent overestimation of the other stimuli from one period to the next. First, they were never shown their own actual body size but were shown the actual size of the other stimuli during testing. Thus, they never had a reference point for their own body size, in contrast to the other stimuli. Second, there may have been a significant difference in the way they perceived their own body size and the way they perceived stimuli external to themselves. This difference became more marked with weight loss because of the "phantom body size" phenomenon; that is, continued maintenance of their before-weight-loss "body size image" necessitated an increasing overestimation of their actual body size, because of their increasing weight loss. This mechanism was not necessary for the external stimuli, since the actual sizes of these were never changed during the study. One reason for the "phantom body size" phenomenon may be that, in subjects obese since childhood, the "body size image" before weight loss is relatively fixed, and cannot be altered as rapidly as the actual change in body configuration. Moreover, there may be psychodynamic determinants for the maintenance of a before-weight-loss "body size image." Of interest is the subsequent finding that 3 of the obese subjects in this study, who were retested after an additional year of weight loss, continued to overestimate their actual body size.

The greatest difference between the obese and non-obese subjects was in their perception of "self." The non-obese subjects underestimated their body size, in comparison to the obese subjects. In view of their cardiovascular pathology, the importance of remaining thin may have been an important determinant for their underestimation of body size. Entirely normal non-obese subjects might not have responded in this manner. Shipman and Sohlkhah[9] observed that normal non-obese women were accurate in their body size estimates, in contrast to obese women who estimated themselves as substantially broader than they actually were. As a group, the non-obese subjects in this study underestimated the "vase," but overestimated the "male" and "female" stimuli. It is of interest that they did not perceive stimuli external to themselves in as uniform a manner as the obese subjects. Except for their before-weight-loss "self" body size estimation, the obese subjects overestimated all other stimuli before, during, and following weight loss (Fig. 3). In view of the small number of subjects used in this study, further exploration of the perceptual differences between obese and non-obese subjects is indicated, especially now that an apparatus is available for the quantitative measurement of body size perception.

Summary:

An apparatus was constructed and utilized for the measurement of body size. Six obese and 4 non-obese (contrast) subjects were studied under similar hospital conditions. The obese subjects were studied prior to, during, and following weight loss, while the non-obese subjects were studied only during weight maintenance.

Once weekly, the subjects estimated the real size of distorted photographs projected on a screen of (1) themselves, (2) a symmetrical vase, (3) an average-weight male, and (4) an average-weight-female. The results indicated that the obese subjects increasingly overestimated their own body size during and following weight loss. They also overestimated the size of the other stimuli, but the amount of overestimation did not differ significantly, before, during, and following weight loss. Those obese subjects who overestimated their own body size during and following weight loss were perceiving themselves, in fact, as if they had lost almost no weight. A delay in the appropriate correction of the before-weight-loss "body size image," as well as psychodynamic factors, may contribute to this "phantom body size" phenomenon.

The non-obese subjects underestimated their own body size, in comparison to the obese subjects. They did not perceive the other stimuli uniformly, in contrast to the obese subjects who consistently overestimated all the stimuli external to themselves.

References:

1. BRUCH, H. *The Importance of Overweight.* Norton, New York, 1957.
2. STUNKARD, A., and MENDELSON, M. Disturbances in body image of some obese persons. *J Amer Diet Ass*, 38:328, 1961.
3. STUNKARD, A., and MENDELSON, M. Obesity and the body image: I. Characteristics of disturbances in the body image of some obese persons. *Amer J Psychiat* 123:1296, 1967.
4. STUNKARD, A., and BURT, V. Obesity and the body image: II. Age at onset of disturbances in the body image. *Amer J Psychiat* 123:1443, 1967.
5. GLUCKSMAN, M, L., and HIRSCH, J, The response of obese patients to weight reduction: A clinical evaluation of behavior. *Psychosom Med* 30:1, 1968.
6. GLUCKSMAN, M. L., HIRSCH, J., McCULLY, R. S., BARRON, B, A., and KNITTLE, J. L. The response of obese patients to weight reduction: II. A quantitative evaluation of behavior. *Psychosom Med* 30;359, 1968.
7. TRAUB, A. C., and ORBACH, J. Psychophysical studies of body image: I. The adjustable body-distorting mirror. *Arch Gen Psychiat (Chicago)* 11:53, 1964.
8. AHRENS, E. H., JR., DOLE, V. P., and BLANKENHORN, D. H. The use of orally fed liquid formulas in metabolic studies. *Amer J Clin Nutr* 2:336,1954.
9. SHIPMAN, W. G., and SOHLKHAH, N. Body image distortion in obese women. (abst.) *Psychosom Med* 29:540, 1967.

From the Rockefeller University, New York, N. Y.

Supported by Grant RO1-AM09360 of the National Institute of Arthritis and Metabolic Diseases, and Grant FR-00102, from the General Research Center Branch, Division of Facilities and Resources, U. S. Public Health Service.

We wish to express our appreciation to Dr. Bruce A. Barron of the Rockefeller University for his assistance in the statistical analyses of data in this study. We are also grateful to Mr. Richard F. Carter and Mr. Nils A. Jernberg for their help in the design and construction of the body-sizing apparatus used in this study.

OBESITY: A PSYCHOANALYTIC CHALLENGE
MYRON L. GLUCKSMAN, M.D.

Introduction:

The purpose of this paper is to examine obesity from a psychoanalytic perspective in the context of current theoretical, clinical, and biological knowledge. Obesity is usually defined in terms of body weight and includes those individuals who are 20% or more above their optimal weight, or who have 20% or more of their body weight composed of adipose tissue. Categories of obesity are based on the age of onset, types of abnormal eating patterns, and the degree of body-image disturbance. From a psychiatric standpoint, obesity is neither psychopathologically nor developmentally a uniform syndrome. Yet, the literature seems to suggest a common psychodynamic thread, especially in connection with "developmental" or "childhood onset" obesity. Those psychoanalysts who initially explored the psychogenesis of obesity linked it to disturbances in the oral phase of development (Alexander, 1934; Bychowski, 1950; Hamburger, 1951; Rascovsky et al., 1950). Freud's (1905) concept of an oral erotogenic zone promoting sexual pleasure independent of nutritional requirements was the foundation of this hypothesis. The latter held that excesses or deficiencies of oral stimulation during infancy led to partial or total "fixations" at the oral stage of development. These "fixations" were the result of either too much or too little pleasurable gratification during the oral phase. Therefore, the infant who failed to obtain an appropriate amount of oral gratification might regress to an oral level of behavior under future stressful circumstances. Examples of oral behavior include overeating, thumb sucking, smoking, drinking, and other types of orally devouring activities. Over time, the concept of oral gratification was broadened to include the infant's total kinesthetic, visual, auditory, and affective experience with the mother during the earliest stage of development. Since feeding is so central an activity during infancy, every component of the mother-child relationship can become associated with food and eating. Significant impairment of mother-child interaction, including the feeding process, can possibly lead to oral "fixation." This means that future emotional distress might result in excessive eating or other oral activities in an attempt to recreate optimal maternal care and comforting.

Levy (1934) suggested that "affect hunger" was the cause of eating disorders in adulthood. He defined "affect hunger" as the "emotional hunger for maternal love and the other feelings of being cared for in the mother-child relationship." According to Levy, obese individuals project "affect hunger" onto food as the tangible form of the mother, thereby mothering themselves in order to feel secure and to fill up their "structural emptiness." Levy's "affect hunger" appears to be closely related to Winnicott's (1953) concept of the transitional object as a "soother" or "sedative" when the mother is absent. For the obese individual, food may act as a transitional object for the purpose of defending against feelings originally connected with separation from the mother (e.g., anxiety, loneliness). Winnicott (1971) observed that feeding progresses from an initial stage of undifferentiation where the baby and breast are not perceived as separate, to a later awareness of feeding from an "other than me" source. A proper feeding experience with a "good-enough mother" promotes the development of the infant's capacity for healthy object differentiation and the ability to love. According to Winnicott (1965) and others (Kohut, 1971; Mahler et al., 1975; Spitz, 1965), satisfactory feeding experiences are a basic requirement toward the development of normal object relations and the evolution of a cohesive, stable sense of self. Anna Freud (1972) believed that food and mother became consciously separated in children by the age of two, although the unconscious equation remains intact. Bruch (1957) observed that the mothers of obese children interfere with normal developmental differentiation between self and object. According to her, the obesegenic mother maintains an overprotective, dependency-inducing attitude toward her child as if it were a prized, inanimate possession. She offers food overabundantly and inappropriately for non-nutritional reasons; for example, as a substitute for other needs of the child that she cannot satisfy or for her own dependency needs. Because of this excessive and inappropriate feeding, obese children suffer from perceptual and conceptual disturbances. Specifically, they are unable to distinguish between hunger, satiation, and other internal somatic sensations, including feelings. Bruch is in agreement with other investigators who emphasize the importance of maternal "attunement" for the infant's healthy development (Kohut, 1971, 1977; Modell, 1976; Ornstein, 1981; Tolpin, 1971). This means that the mother must differentiate the child's needs from her own in the setting of an adequate "holding environment," an atmosphere in which the mother is sensitive as well as responsive to the infant's needs, thereby promoting an internalization of the maternal soothing function. Thus, the child's capacity for self-soothing is a consequence of empathic maternal responses that create a healthy matrix of self-objects. This process enables the child to develop self-cohesion, object constancy, and the ability to tolerate separation from the mother. Goodsitt (1983) concludes that obese individuals have experienced failures in empathic mirroring leading to an inability to self-soothe when feeling anxious, depressed, or lonely. Their addictive craving for food results in temporary self-soothing, but it fails to build psychological structure or self-cohesion. According to this theory, obese persons have a limited capacity for self-soothing and overeat in order to reproduce a sensorimotor representation of the mother and her soothing activities, which have not been properly internalized.

There are two major clinical disturbances characteristic of obese individuals: (1) abnormal eating patterns, and (2) body-image pathology. Hyperphagia without the ordinary sensation of hunger is the most salient feature of their deviant eating behavior. Clinical and experimental evidence suggests that they are unable to identify the physical sensations of hunger and satiety correctly (Bruch, 1961; Stunkard and Koch, 1964). However, they compulsively overeat in association with a variety of emotional states, and in connection with a multiplicity of psychodynamic issues. Kaplan and Kaplan (1957) observed 27 affective and psychodynamic factors significantly correlated with overeating. These included anxiety, anger, guilt, depression, self-punishment, self-reward, insecurity, defiance, feeling unloved, seeking attention, avoiding competition, and the like. They point out that almost any unresolved psychodynamic conflict arising at each stage of psychosexual development can be linked to overeating. In my clinical investigations I have been impressed with the close relationship between hyperphagia and various dysphoric states associated with numerous psychodynamic issues that are the sequelae of disturbances at the oral and post-oral stages of development (Glucksman, 1968, 1972; Glucksman et al., 1978). Some investigators emphasize that overeating is primarily a means of coping with emotional distress and minimize the specific psychodynamics involved. Slochower (1983) describes several studies that suggest that obese subjects overeat in response to a variety of "uncontrollable emotional states." They are unable to cope with painful emotions because they are unable to "label them" (similar to Bruch's observations), leading to a sense of helplessness rather than mastery. Others (Castelnuovo-Tedesco and Reiser, 1988) contend that obesity and compulsive eating constitute an addictive or impulse disorder. They view overeating as a self-soothing activity that provides "substitute gratification." The latter is an attempt to replace lost or disappointing love objects, and to recreate a preverbal attachment to the mother. Addictive eating behavior is a way of coping with dysphoria, particularly empty, lonely, yearning feelings. These observations are similar to Khantzian's (1985) studies of drug-dependent individuals. He maintains that narcotic addicts choose opiates because they calm their aggressive, violent feelings, while cocaine addicts use cocaine because it relieves feelings of depression, boredom, and emptiness. Therefore, compulsive eating, similar to drug addiction, can be viewed as a form of self-medication in order to allay painful emotions. Raynes (1987) observed that overweight women manifest less well-developed internal representations of their mothers than their fathers on psychological test assessment. She hypothesizes that they overeat in response to specific distressing emotions (e.g., anxiety, loneliness) in order to compensate for inadequately internalized maternal functions, including self-soothing and "anxiety management." In general, there is substantial clinical as well as experimental evidence that overeating is a maladaptive attempt to reduce painful affects and to restore a sense of well-being by using food as a symbolic representation of maternal soothing functions.

Body image, an important component of self-image, refers to the mental representation of one's body along with the attitudes, feelings, fantasies, and conflicts associated with it. Clinically, body-image disturbances in obese patients fall into two categories: (1) Primary body-image disturbances, and (2) body-image abnormalities secondary to being obese. Primary body-image disturbances are intimately connected to problems of self-representation. For example, a large body size (fatness) can be a physical manifestation of an inner sense of worthlessness, unloveability, and inferiority. Patients who suffer from childhood-onset obesity are more likely to have primary body-image disturbances because of developmental difficulties leading to pathology of the self. Internal feelings of emptiness, vulnerability, and self-fragmentation may be defended against by perceiving oneself to be huge and impenetrable. Bruch (1957) believes that obese children need to experience themselves as big and powerful because they are compensating for the unfulfilled desires or wishes of their parents. A consistent finding in obese patients is that they have considerable difficulty in estimating their body size (Glucksman and Hirsch, 1969). They frequently overestimate their body size and believe that they are still fat even after losing a significant amount of weight. This is particularly true for patients with childhood-onset obesity, since body-size representation becomes relatively fixed during adolescence.

Secondary body-image disturbances are a consequence of being obese in a society that places a high value on thinness. Obese individuals are subject to a constant barrage from the media, advertising, and fashion that connects thinness with desirability and acceptance, while overweight is linked to unacceptability and rejection. Thus, almost all obese individuals view their bodies with some degree of self-loathing and self-derogation. These feelings are often projected onto others who are obese. Body size may also be employed defensively in a number of ways; for example, some obese patients utilize their body size to intimidate and control others, or symbolically to protect themselves from interpersonal injury (physical or psychological) Obesity may also be used as a rationalization for failure at one's career or in social and sexual relationships.

An informative study conducted under the auspices of the American Academy of Psychoanalysis examined the outcome of psychoanalytic treatment for obesity (Rand and Stunkard, 1977, 1978, 1983). It is one of the few studies carried out to date that has included control and experimental populations in order to investigate the efficacy of psychoanalytic treatment. The study consisted of 147 patients: 64 obese women, 20 obese men (experimental group), as well as 46 normal-weight women and 17 normal-weight men (control group). At the end of 4 years, 66% of the obese patients lost more than 20 pounds, and 25% lost more than 40 pounds. These results compare quite favorably with other forms of treatment for obesity (e.g., behavioral, peer support). The study clearly established that there are specific psychodynamic constellations associated with weight gain, weight loss, and deviant eating patterns for obese patients. There was also a significant reduction in the intensity of body-image disparagement that seemed to be more the result of therapy than of weight loss. Further analysis of the data in this study revealed that the psychodynamic factors could be classified under several distinct categories: (1) mood or affect, (2) self- and body image, (3) psychodynamic issues related to deprivation and gratification, (4) psychodynamic issues involved with aggression or competition, and (5) sexual conflicts (Glucksman et al., 1978). Specific psychodynamic conflicts in each of these categories were associated with weight gain, weight loss, and abnormal eating patterns with significantly greater frequency for the obese than for the normal-weight patients. Unresolved psychodynamic conflicts ("negative" psychodynamics) were more frequently observed with overeating and weight gain, while psychodynamic conflicts that had been resolved ("positive" psychodynamics) were more frequently connected with normal eating behavior and weight loss. For example, weight gain was associated with poor self-esteem and feelings of inadequacy, while weight loss was correlated with increased self-esteem and feelings of competence. The psychodynamic constellation observed with greatest frequency in the obese population involved issues of deprivation and gratification. As an example, during periods of weight gain patients often expressed feelings of being unloved and disappointed in their interpersonal relationships. However, during periods of weight loss they reported greater satisfaction in their relationships. In general, treatment enabled the obese patients to tolerate painful emotions better, particularly those connected with abandonment and separation (e.g., sadness, loneliness). They were also able to change their perception of self- and body image in the direction of greater self-esteem and less derogation of their body size.

I have treated one of the patients who participated in the Academy Study for the past 14 years. This has afforded me the opportunity to explore in much greater depth the various psychodynamics connected with obesity than the questionnaire methodology of the study permitted. In presenting this patient, I shall focus on the psychodynamics associated with compulsive eating, weight fluctuations, self-representation and body image. I shall also attempt to integrate these psychodynamic factors with current genetic, metabolic, morphologic, and neurochemical data.

Case Presentation:

The patient is a 47-year-old married professional woman who entered treatment because of obesity, dissatisfaction with her job, marital difficulties, poor self-esteem, and a pervasive sense of unhappiness. She weighed 226 pounds at the outset of therapy. Her obesity began in mid-adolescence and has continued throughout adulthood. Despite numerous diets, Weight Watchers, and appetite suppressants she was unable to lose any significant amounts of weight prior to treatment. She has three children, two sons and one daughter. Her marriage has been stable, although she has never felt fully satisfied with her husband intellectually, emotionally, or sexually. Her parents are living, but she has never felt a close bond to them, particularly to her mother. Her father became obese as an adult, but her mother and an older sister have always been thin or normal-weight. I have divided her treatment into three phases, based on weight changes and psychodynamic issues.

Phase 1:

During the initial phase of treatment she quickly formed a good working alliance and a positive transference. She felt that I was empathic and supportive, in contrast to her husband whom she portrayed as insensitive, superficial, and financially irresponsible. Their sexual relationship was sporadic and generally unsatisfying for her. Her eating pattern was characterized by binging and between-meal-eating, usually in connection with unpleasant feelings. However, she sometimes found herself overeating when –feeling neutral or even in a pleasant mood. It became apparent that she viewed herself in terms of either a thin self or a fat self. She was disgusted by her fat self and loathed her appearance. As a fat person she felt unloveable, inadequate, and sexually repulsive. On the other hand, she fantasized her thin self to be attractive, worthwhile, and sexually desirable. Yet, her actual weight precluded sexual flirtations as well as the possibility of being found attractive by men. Nevertheless, within the first year of treatment she revealed her fantasy of seducing me when she reached 150 pounds. This fantasy partly fueled a self-imposed dieting regimen during which she lost 60 pounds over the first two years of therapy. Additional details of her family history emerged over this period. She was bottle-fed as an infant and was normal-weight throughout childhood. Food was not used by her parents as a reward for accomplishments or good behavior, but she was always encouraged to "clean her plate." For as long as she could remember, her mother seemed emotionally distant, critical, and uninterested in how she felt. She could not recall her mother ever telling her she loved her. Her father was more supportive, but her mother always seemed to interfere with her attempts to be close to him. He displayed open affection for her only when he was intoxicated. She began to gain excessive weight at age 15 when the family moved to a different town where she felt lonely and socially excluded by her classmates at a new school.

At the end of 2 years of treatment she weighed 165 pounds. She decided to terminate therapy because she felt less depressed and was close to her desired weight. At the same time, she was annoyed with me for taking a "neutral" attitude in regard to her weight loss and proposed termination. The following dream occurred in this context:

> *"I was watching my EKG-my heart slowed and I asked for a pacemaker. I couldn't get one and my heart stopped. I died."*

The dream conveyed her underlying feelings about termination: she felt that she would emotionally "die" without my availability to help her understand and resolve her problems. When I did not interfere with her plans to terminate, she believed that I truly did not care about her and became enraged at me. Following our exploration of this dream she decided to continue treatment.

Phase 2:

This phase of treatment was characterized by an intensely ambivalent transference and a prolonged struggle to come to terms with the thin and fat components of her self-representation. She was alternately angry at me for failing to help her change her negative self-image, yet grateful for my acceptance of her undesirable qualities. Her fat self overshadowed her thin self, and she continually berated herself for being stupid, lazy, incompetent, and unattractive. As her fortieth birthday approached she entertained fantasies of becoming pregnant in order to prove her youthfulness and fertility. While having intercourse with her husband, she fantasized that I was impregnating her. It became clear that this was a way of incorporating me, enabling her to permanently continue her attachment to me. The baby, a displacement of myself, would provide her with my love and attention long after she terminated treatment. In addition, she could give the baby the kind of emotional closeness and loving that her mother failed to give her. Predictably, she became pregnant but had an abortion once she understood her unconscious needs for the baby, as well as the difficulties it would present at her stage of life. However, following the abortion, she became depressed and guilt-ridden. A lengthy period of grieving ensued, accompanied by a considerable increase in weight.

Oedipal themes were introduced by a dream in which she "witnessed something [she] shouldn't have." She recalled having slept in the same bedroom as her parents until age 6. Her father's genitalia were a source of curiosity and excitement for her. Memories emerged of feeling sexually aroused while sitting on his lap, hugging, and kissing him. Further dreams and fantasies centered around competitive feelings toward other women, her expectation of their retaliatory behavior, and her defenses against them. These included an avoidance of self-assertion or confrontation with female authorities and peers at work. Moreover, her obesity was a signal to other women that she posed no threat to them since there was little likelihood that men would find her attractive. Her first sexual relationship was with an older man with whom she worked at a summer job. She confided in her sister who, in turn, told her mother. A swift reproach by her mother still rings in her ears: "How could you!" She became terrified of her mother's anger in connection with any future sexual relationships.

Further exploration elicited feelings of terror and powerlessness in regard to her mother when she was a young child. According to the patient, her mother "ruled like a queen and no one was allowed to argue or disagree with her unless you were prepared to face her wrath." When the family moved and she transferred to a new school at age fifteen, she was socially rejected by her peers. Without her mother's support or understanding, she felt humiliated, sad, and alone. Eating became a source of comfort, and she began to gain weight.

As treatment progressed, dream content and fantasy material increasingly reflected pre-oedipal themes. The following dream was representative:

"I went into my childhood bedroom and saw my mother in bed. I felt sexually aroused, but she told me to take a bath before I got in bed with her. When I returned my husband was in bed instead of my mother. I was disappointed, yet went ahead and made love with him. I didn't feel anything".

She recalled how much she wanted to be loved and praised by her mother as a child, but instead was met with indifference and "perfunctory" kisses. She described having homosexual fantasies in which other women gave her the warmth, affection, and understanding she yearned for. These fantasies expressed her wish to be loved as well as understood by her mother, and functioned as a defense against heterosexual fantasies that evoked oedipally-related anxiety. Sexual intercourse with her husband was not totally satisfying because it was far more important to be held and caressed. She described a recurrent fantasy of lying in a hospital bed gravely ill, being comforted, and taken care of by me. In subsequent dreams and fantasies I played dual roles: a forbidden, incestuous love object and a comforting maternal figure. Her self-image and sexual fantasies oscillated between viewing herself as thin, successful, and sexually attractive, or as obese, worthless, and sexually repulsive. As a thin person she would seduce me, divorce her husband, and live with me. The anxiety associated with this fantasy was defended against by another fantasy where she saw herself as obese, lesbian, and in a comforting, nurturing relationship with another woman.

During this phase of therapy her weight fluctuated between 190 and 210 pounds. She resented me for not taking a more active role in supervising her attempts to diet. I responded by saying that although I understood her torment over her weight, I did not wish to become either an advocate or an opponent of any part of herself. She interpreted my response as evidence of my indifference to her weight problem, and maintained that I secretly loathed her appearance. I suggested that I reminded her of her mother who, at best, behaved indifferently toward her, and at worst, treated her with disgust. She replied: "If I were thin my mother (you) would love me . . . it's impossible to get my mother's (your) love as I am . . . why can't she (you) appreciate and love me as I am?" Toward the end of this phase of treatment she attended a weight loss spa on two occasions and cumulatively lost 25 pounds. She felt pleased with her appearance and once again entertained the possibility of termination. A pivotal dream occurred at this time:

> *"My cat was drinking from the toilet and fell in. I got so angry that I flushed the toilet in order to clean him. He jumped out - I realized that I could have killed him. I felt guilty and became aware of how much I loved him".*

She identified the cat with herself, and flushing the toilet was her wish to terminate therapy. However, she knew she couldn't terminate because she still required my help. I was apparently allowing her to terminate-"to drown"-and I seemed unconcerned. My alleged attitude enraged her and she wanted to kill me (in this case, I was the cat), yet was compelled to save both of us by having the cat jump out. She stated: "I need to come here-I need your love but that's forbidden so I have to get rid of it, flush it (you) down the toilet . . . but I want to be close to you, to have your love, respect and understanding." Further associations concerned binging, vomiting, and flushing it down the toilet. Eating voraciously (binging) was a symbolic way of incorporating me as well as her mother, and gaining our love. However, my love was forbidden and dangerous because it evoked anxiety connected with oedipal wishes. By flushing the toilet she simultaneously rid herself of the object of her in-cestuous impulses (myself) as well as her potentially punishing mother. In addition to its oedipal and pre-oedipal components, the dream portrayed various aspects of herself. The cat represented parts of herself she wished to destroy (fatness, sexual unattractiveness, social and professional inadequacy) and parts of herself she hoped to promote (normal weight, sexual attractive-ness, professional competence, social acceptance). The resolution of the "cat dream" in favor of survival and continued self-growth reflected a significant turning point in her therapy.

Phase 3:

This phase was characterized by greater self-acceptance, and a more re-alistic perception of her parents as well as of myself. Her self-esteem was enhanced when she was offered a position at work that she had fantasized about for several years. The fact that her professional ability was publicly recognized significantly buoyed her self-confidence. We continued to ex-plore the connections between her feelings, different aspects of herself, and her compulsive eating. Food enabled her to fill the emotional empti-ness she felt in her relationship with her parents and her husband. Her sessions with me helped to fill the void, but it became apparent that I had become a transitional object or "food" that she incorporated in order to feel emotionally understood and accepted. Subsequent dream and fantasy material centered around being treated and valued by me as my equal. In one dream, I came to visit her and was impressed by her books as well as other objects in her house. She took great pleasure in my appreciation of her intellect and her good taste in art. An important issue in the dream was that she appeared as her obese self and yet I still admired her: "I looked the way I am and you still liked me-it was enough for you to want to stay with me." In the following months she was gradually able to distinguish and separate her bodily self from other parts of her self-representation. During this process she realized the extent to which her obese, physical self was the externalized, reified manifestation of her internal, unacceptable qualities. Her actual weight, though still an important issue for her, received less of our attention. Her "good" and "bad' qualities, similar to her "thin" and "fat" selves, became more integrated into a cohesive, acceptable self. She gradually accepted her parents' limitations, and relinquished the fantasy of her mother giving her the overt, unqualified love and approval she longed for. Recently, her father (while sober) told her that he loved her, and acknowledged that her mother had "problems" showing affection. Her father's demonstration of his love for her as well as his validation of her mother's limitations, helped her to consolidate a sense of being worthwhile and loveable. At this point in treatment she weighed 250 pounds (her highest weight). She felt well enough of herself to participate in a hospital-sponsored weight-loss program that required 3 months on a total liquid low-calorie diet. During the initial phase of this diet she was euphoric over her rapid weight loss. However, she once again became angry at me for not complimenting her and for not fully appreciating her effort to lose weight. On the other hand, she received many compliments from friends and co-workers over her improved physical appearance. Ironically (or expectedly), her parents did not commend her for her loss of weight (50 pounds). Her fantasy of beginning a romantic relationship with me when she reached 150 pounds reemerged, although with less intensity. Her sexual fantasies about me were predominantly images of being held, comforted, and understood. Making love to me, like eating, calmed and soothed her. The following is a representative description:

> "You're soothing . . . you listen and everything's all right as long as you're here . . . I don't feel like eating when I'm with you . . . after I make love to my husband I fantasize lying next to you-I feel satisfied, comforted, and complete. I have an image of a baby with a bottle . . . it soothes all kinds of feelings-frustration, helplessness, anger, loneliness, boredom . . . it's more important than anything else"

She noted that when she had a "good" therapy session in which she felt understood and supported, she was able to leave without experiencing an impulse to eat. On the other hand, when she felt misunderstood or rejected by me, she experienced an intense desire to eat after the session. Satisfactory therapy sessions, similar to productive days at work, made her feel happy, excited, and enthusiastic. These feelings rarely evoked a compulsion to eat.

At the present time she weighs 225 pounds, which is almost exactly what she weighed at the beginning of treatment. Although her weight is the same, her feelings about herself are vastly different. She is considerably less self-derogatory about her physical appearance and places less emphasis on it. Her self-concept-is better integrated without the polarity of a thin or fat self. She views herself as professionally competent, likeable, generous, and more tolerant of her own shortcomings as well as those of others. Her relationships with men are less anxiety-producing, and she occasionally permits herself the pleasure of a heterosexual fantasy without substituting a homosexual fantasy as a defensive maneuver. Her relationship with her husband has improved, although she maintains that if she found someone more compatible and satisfying she could give up her compulsive eating entirely. This fantasy continues to include myself, although she has begun to entertain the possibility of termination again. The prospect of ending her therapeutic relationship with me still terrifies her, but she appears to have gained enough of a positive self-representation so that she can at least consider the possibility of sustaining herself without my continued availability for self-soothing.

Discussion:

I have presented this patient in order to illustrate the psychodynamics connected with compulsive eating, weight fluctuations, body image, and self-representation. I have also attempted to demonstrate the relationship of these dynamics to developmental phases and transference phenomena as they evolved during treatment. Keeping these issues in mind, I would like to briefly summarize each phase of treatment.

During the initial phase of treatment, the patient's intense positive transference fueled her efforts to lose 60 pounds. One might say that this weight loss represented a "transference cure." However, she was unable to attain her goal of 150 pounds because of the near-panic generated by approaching the weight at which she fantasized seducing me. In addition, her weight loss did little to alter her self- and body image fundamentally. She continued to view herself as fat, inferior, unloveable, and sexually undesirable- It became evident that her compulsive eating temporarily neutralized a variety of feelings: anxiety, anger, sadness, emptiness, boredom, and despair. Moreover, her large body size enabled her to avoid sexual pleasure in fantasy as well as in reality. A polarized self-representation emerged in which she defined herself in terms of a thin or a fat self. Her inability to terminate when she neared her desired weight, as well as her rage at me for failing actively to dissuade her from terminating, set the stage for the next phase of therapy.

The second phase of treatment was characterized by continued weight fluctuations in association with oscillations of transference and self-image. She perceived me as alternately uncaring, insensitive, and critical, or as warm, supportive, and understanding. The negative components of her transference were related to longstanding feelings toward her mother whom she experienced as unloving, critical, and unattuned to her needs. Her father seemed to play a less prominent role transferentially; nonetheless, she found him (and myself) ineffectual, distant, and unwilling or unable to compensate for her mother's rejection. Fantasies, dreams, and associations further illuminated oedipal and preoedipal determinants of her hyperphagia. Overeating was a symbolic expression of her oedipal wishes as well as a defense against the anxiety and guilt they generated. Her unattractive body discouraged men from finding her sexually attractive, and indicated to other women that she presented a minimal competitive threat to them. The pre-oedipal origins of her compulsive eating were connected to a deeply frustrated desire for her mother's love, acceptance, and emotional responsiveness. Moreover, her overeating was, at times, a defiant, rageful act meant as a retaliation against her mother. Her sexual inhibitions and homosexual fantasies constituted a defense against the anxiety connected with her oedipal wishes, and simultaneously reflected her strong need for an approving, caring, intuitively responsive mother. By becoming pregnant, she not only acted out her oedipal wishes, but also tried to internalize deeply longed-for qualities from her mother (love, empathy) through incorporation of myself via a baby. She continued to struggle with her thin and fat-selves, vividly portrayed by the "cat dream" in which she rescued those parts of herself she valued and hoped to expand further.

During the third phase of treatment she took significant strides toward developing an integrated, positive self-representation. She was able to place less emphasis on her bodily self and the connotations of inferiority, ugliness, and unacceptability it held for her. Consequently, she felt less critical of her own body as well as the physical appearance of other obese individuals. She gradually strengthened those parts of herself she valued: intellectual curiosity, spontaneity, humor, generosity, assertiveness, and the ability to empathize. Her ambivalent transference evolved into a more realistically based perception of myself, along with feeling respected and accepted by me. Nevertheless, she continues to harbor a fantasy of my ultimately falling in love with her, thus achieving an oedipal triumph and a reunion with an idealized mother. It has become more clearly evident that her compulsive eating is a "self-soothing" mechanism aimed at the neutralization of dysphoric states. Food remains a transitional object (including myself), providing her with emotional gratification and security. However, pleasurable moods connected with being understood or feeling competent and effective do not trigger hyperphagia. In conjunction with the development of a more cohesive, positive self-image, she has been able to lose a significant amount of weight. Termination also seems a more likely possibility now that she has achieved a reasonably stable internalized sense of being understood and valued.

I believe that resistance and countertransference issues encountered during her treatment are worthy of comment. Throughout therapy she has periodically attempted to coerce me into taking an active role in helping her to lose weight (e.g., monitoring her weight, etc.). If I were her internist I would have gladly done so. However, as her analyst, I have tried to steer a "neutral" course on this matter because I have wanted to avoid the appearance of favoring her thin self over her fat self. To have done so would have placed me in the position of rejecting or devaluing a part of herself that was unacceptable to her. In addition, I would have colluded with her magical, irrational expectations associated with weight loss. However, maintaining a "neutral" attitude on this matter has frequently subjected me to charges of being uncaring or indifferent. These criticisms have reinforced a frequent sense of never quite giving enough of myself to her. Occasionally, I have reacted defensively by becoming over-solicitous, withholding, or annoyed. In general, I have tried to be empathic without intervening, as far as dieting and weight loss are concerned. I believe that my attempt to accept unqualifiedly both her thin and fat selves has served a self-object function that she has successfully internalized. Moreover, I believe that understanding and empathizing with her emotional deprivations rather than focusing exclusively on their irrational aspects, has enabled her gradually to accept rather than condemn her entire self. Similar to other patients suffering from psychophysiological disorders or chronic physical illness, I have repeatedly told her that she is struggling with biological forces that may be beyond her control and that place limitations on the ultimate weight she might attain. At the risk of appearing pessimistic, I believe that this approach has helped somewhat to lessen her conscious sense of guilt over not losing enough weight.

In part, I have considered her preoccupation with her weight and physical appearance as forms of resistance that have had to be explored patiently in order to comprehend and interpret their unconscious sources. On the other hand, I have grown to appreciate how exquisitely painful it has been for her to possess a body that others have overtly or covertly devalued, rejected, or ridiculed. As a result, I have come to admire her courage in continuing to effect internal changes, despite a relatively refractory external appearance. As far as her repeated attempts to terminate are concerned, I have basically viewed them as tests of my emotional availability and commitment to help her. Although her lengthy treatment might be viewed as a continuing effort on her part to hold me as a transitional object, I believe that she has also required that amount of time to internalize and consolidate my maternally-soothing qualities successfully.

The observations I have made from this single case study appear to support the conclusions of the Academy study in regard to the treatment of obesity. Namely, treatment improves self- and body image, while psychodynamic issues are clearly associated with hyperphagia and weight changes. In the Academy study, psychodynamic issues connected with emotional gratification and deprivation were predominant (Glucksman et al., 1978). For this patient, a profoundly disturbed relationship with her mother seemed to be the crucial factor in her failure to develop a well-internalized sense of self capable of effective self-soothing. Nevertheless, it is difficult, if not impossible, to ascribe her obesity to disturbances in her early feeding experiences. There is insufficient data either from anamnesis or direct observations to conclude that her oral phase of development was poorly negotiated. We can only infer from her memories, fantasies, and dreams that she experienced a qualitatively deficient amount of maternal nurturing during the oral phase. The clinical material clearly demonstrates that her abnormal eating pattern and impaired self-image are etiologically connected to conflicts at the pre-oedipal, oedipal, and post-oedipal developmental stages. In view of this, her compulsive eating and self-pathology can be considered the sequelae of a long-standing, severely disturbed total relationship with her mother (and to a lesser extent her father) that adversely affected each phase of development.

Perhaps, only long-term prospective studies of maternal-infant interaction (including feeding) will provide us with the necessary data in order to understand more fully the relationship between inadequate maternal care-giving during the initial months of life and the development of obesity.

Although her weight has fluctuated within a range of nearly 100 pounds over the course of treatment, she has had virtually no net loss of weight. The Academy study demonstrated significant net losses of weight after 4 years of treatment; this patient has been in treatment for a considerably longer duration. Taking into consideration the undeniable relationship between compulsive eating, weight gain, weight loss, and psychodynamic issues, what other factors might have contributed to her inability to maintain a significantly lower weight? Obviously, hereditary, metabolic, morphologic, and neurochemical influences must be taken into account. Recent studies suggest the presence of a significant genetic component to obesity. Stunkard et al. (1986) observed a strong relationship between the weights of adoptees and the body-mass index of their biological parents. Conversely, there was no correlation between the weights of adoptees and the body-mass index of their adoptive parents. This genetic influence was not confined to the obesity weight class alone, but was displayed across the entire range of body fatness-from very thin to very fat. On the basis of this as well as other studies (Borjeson, 1976) there appears to be little doubt that genetic factors play an important role in the predisposition to obesity. Two studies recently published demonstrate that reduced energy expenditure is an important factor contributing to obesity among infants born to overweight mothers and also among certain southwestern American Indian families (Ravussin et al., 1988; Roberts et al., 1988). These findings indicate a genetic influence that predisposes certain individuals and families to lower rates of energy expenditure and a higher risk of becoming obese. There is also evidence that abnormalities of fat cell morphology (hypertrophy and hyperplasia) in children and adults who become obese may play a role in determining the extent to which permanent weight loss is possible (Hirsch and Knittle, 1970). Because of these genetic, metabolic and morphologic factors, it may be extremely difficult for obese individuals (including the patient I have presented) to maintain a significantly lowered body weight over a prolonged period of time, effective psychotherapy notwithstanding.

Some obese individuals seem to crave carbohydrate-rich foods while others do not. Studies have shown that obese carbohydrate-cravers report feeling less depressed, calmer, and more relaxed following the ingestion of carbohydrate-rich meals (Lieberman et al., 1986; Wurtman and Wurtman, 1986). Changes in serotonergic neurotransmission may be partially responsible for the affective change following carbohydrate consumption. Carbohydrate ingestion raises brain tryptophan levels, thereby accelerating the synthesis and release of serotonin. The latter is intimately involved in mood alteration and exerts antidepressant effects. Therefore, certain obese individuals, similar to the drug addicts described by Khantzian (1985), may select carbohydrate-rich foods in order to self-medicate when they experience painful feelings, particularly those in the depressive spectrum. Many obese patients, including the one I have discussed, often report sad, empty, yearning, lonely feelings. Although these feelings are often linked to preoedipal dynamics, (e.g., inadequate maternal care-giving), they may be soothed and diminished temporarily through the ingestion of foods high in carbohydrate content. The addictive-like eating patterns of this group of obese individuals may be partially explained on the basis of the neurochemical sequence activated by carbohydrate ingestion.

Summary:

In summary, although therapy can be effective in promoting positive changes in self and body-image for obese patients, it may not be as effective in bringing about a permanently lowered body weight. The Academy study, as well as my case illustration, clearly document a relationship between compulsive eating, weight fluctuations, emotions, body image, self-representation, and specific psychodynamic issues. The latter appear to be the product of disturbances throughout childhood and

adolescent development, particularly in the area of mother-child interaction. Inappropriate or deficient maternal emotional attunement and
responsivity seem to play an especially crucial role. However, there is insufficient data to implicate the feeding process during the oral phase of
development as a primary etiological factor. Although hyperphagia and
weight fluctuations definitely articulate with psychodynamic processes,
there are underlying genetic, metabolic, morphologic, and neurochemical phenomena that exert a profound influence on body weight over an
extended period of time. Similar to other psychophysiological disorders,
obesity appears to be the final common pathway resulting from a complex
interaction between critical developmental experiences and genetically determined biological processes.

References:

Alexander, F. (1934), The influence of psychological factors upon gastrointestinal disturbances, *Psychoanal. Quart., 3*, 501-539.

Borjeson, M. (1976), The aetiology of obesity in children: A study of 101
twin pairs, *Acta Pediat. Scand., 65*, 279-287.

Bruch, H. (1957), The Importance of Overweight, W. W. Norton, New
York.

Bruch, H. (1961), Conceptual confusion in eating disorders, *J. Nerv. Ment.
Dis., 133*, 46-54.

Bychowski, G. (1950), On neurotic obesity, *Psychoanal. Rev., 37*, 301-319.

Castelnuovo-Tedesco, P., and Reiser, L. W. (1988), Compulsive eating:
Obesity and related phenomena, panel report, *J. Am. Psychoanal. Assoc.,
36*, 163-171.

Freud, A. (1972), The psychoanalytic study of infantile feeding disorders,
in S. Harrison and J. McDermitt (Eds.), *Childhood Psychopathology*,
International Universities Press, New York.

Freud, S. (1905), Three essays on the theory of sexuality, *Standard Edition*,
Hogarth Press, London.

Glucksman, M. L. (1968), The response of obese patients to weight reduction: A clinical evaluation of behavior, *Psychosom. Med., 30*, l-ll.

Glucksman, M. L. (1972) Psychiatric observations on obesity, *Adv. Psychosom. Med., 7,* 194-216.

Glucksman, M. L., and Hirsch, J. (1969), The response of obese patients to weight reduction: III. The perception of body size, *Psychosom. Med., 31,* l-7.

Glucksman, M.L., Rand, C. S.W., and Stunkard, A. J. (1978), Psychodynamics of obesity, *J. Am. Acad. Psychoanal., 6,* 103-115.

Goodsitt, A. (1983), Self-regulatory disturbances in eating disorders, *Int. J. Eating Disorders, 2,* 51-60.

Hamburger, W. W. (1951), Emotional aspects of obesity, *Med. Clin. N. Amer., 35,* 483-499.

Hirsch, J., and Knittle, J. L. (1970), Cellularity of obese and non-obese human adipose tissue, *Fed. Proc., 29,* 1516-1521.

Kaplan, H. I., and Kaplan, H. S. (1957), The psychosomatic concept of obesity, *J. Nerv. Ment. Dis., l25,* 181-201.

Khantzian, E. J. (1985), The self-medication hypothesis of addictive disorders: Focus on heroin and cocaine dependence, *Am. J. Psychiatry, 142,* 1259-1264.

Kohut, H. (1971), *The Analysis of the Self,* International Universities Press, New York.

Kohut, H. (1977), *The Restoration of the Self,* International Universities Press, New York.

Levy, D. (1934), Primary Affect Hunger, *Am. J. Psychiatry, 94,* 643-652.

Lieberman, H. R., Wurtman, J. J., and Chew, B. (1986), Changes in mood after carbohydrate consumption among obese individuals, *Am. J. Clin. Nutr., 44,* 772-778.

Mahler, M. S., Pine, F., and Bergman, A. (1975), *The Psychological Birth of the Human Infant,* Basic Books, New York.

Modell, A. (1976), The "holding environment" and the therapeutic action of psychoanalysis, *J. Am. Psychoanal. Assoc., 24,* 285-307.

Ornstein, A. (1981), Self-pathology in childhood: Developmental and clinical considerations, *Psychiatric Clinics of North America, 4*, 435-453.

Rand, C. S. W., and Stunkard, A. J. (1977), Psychoanalysis and obesity, *J. Am. Acad. Psychoanal., 5*, 459-497.

Rand, C. S. W., and Stunkard, A. J. (1978), Obesity and psychoanalysis, *Am. J. Psychiatry, 135*, 547-551.

Rand, C. S. W, and Stunkard, A. J. (1983), Obesity and psychoanalysis: Treatment and four-year follow-up, *Am. J. Psychiatry, 140*, 1140-1144.

Rascovsky, A., DeRascovsky, M. W., and Schlossberg, T. (1950), *Int. J. Psycho-Anal., 31*, 144-149.

Ravussin, E., Lillioja, S., Knowler, W. C., Christin, L., Freymond, D., Abbott, W G. H., Boyce, V., Howard, B. V., and Bogardus, C. (1988), Reduced rate of energy expenditure as a risk factor for body-weight gain, *N. Eng. J. Med., 318*, 467-472.

Raynes, E. (1987), The effects of developmental relationships on eating behavior in adult women, Ph.D. dissertation, Yeshiva Univ., New York.

Roberts, S. B., Savage, J., Coward, W. A., Chew, B., and Lucas, A. (1988), Energy expenditure and intake in infants born to lean and overweight mothers, *N. Eng. J. Med., 318*, 461-466.

Slochower, J. A. (1983), *Excessive Eating: The Role of Emotions and Environment*, Human Sciences Press, New York.

Spitz, R. (1965), *First Year of Life*, International Universities Press, New York.

Stunkard, A. J., and Koch, C. (1964), The interpretation of gastric motility: I. Apparent bias in the reports of hunger by obese persons, *Arch. Gen. Psychiatry, 11*, 74-82.

Stunkard, A. J., Sorensen, T. I. A., Hanis, C., Teasdale, T. W., Chakraborty, R., Schull, W J., and Schulsinger F. (1986), An adoption study of human obesity, *N. Eng. J. Med., 314*, 193-198.

Tolpin, M. (1971), On the beginnings of a cohesive self, *Psychoanal. Study Child, 26*, 316-352.

Winnicott, D. W. (1953), *Transitional Objects and Transitional Phenomena, Int. J. Psycho-Anal., 34*, 89-97.

Winnicott, D. W. (1965), *The Maturational Processes and the Facilitating Environment*, International Universities Press, Madison, CT.

Winnicott, D. W. (1971), *Playing and Reality*, Basic Books, New York.

Wurtman, R. J., and Wurtman, J. J. (1986), Carbohydrate craving, obesity and brain serotonin, *Appetite, 7*, 99-103.

Myron L. Glucksman is a Clinical Professor, Department of Psychiatry, New York Medical College and an Associate Clinical Professor, Department of Psychiatry, Yale University School of Medicine.

Journal of the American Academy of Psychoanalysis, 17(1), 151-171, 1989.

## Chapter 2

Biofeedback Psychotherapy

I first became aware of the use of biofeedback when I was working at The Rockefeller University. At that time, Neal Miller demonstrated that rats could be conditioned to alter their heart rate and blood pressure with biofeedback (Miller, N.E., 1973). These experiments gradually expanded to include human subjects. A number of voluntary and autonomic nervous system modalities were studied, including blood pressure, muscle tension, heart rate, electrical skin conductance, respiration, and skin temperature. As a result, biofeedback became a mode of treatment for a variety of psycho-physiological disorders, including migraine and muscle tension headaches, hypertension, cardiac arrhythmias, and asthma. Simultaneously, a small group of psychodynamically oriented clinicians began experimenting with biofeedback while treating patients with anxiety and somatizing disorders (Adler, C.S., and Morrissey-Adler, S., 1979; Rickles, W.H., Onoda, L., and Doyle, C.C., et al.; 1979). They observed that autonomic and voluntary nervous system changes often accompany significant memories, conflicts, fantasies, and affects. They termed this application of biofeedback "biofeedback psychotherapy" or "psychotherapy with physiological monitoring." It appeared to be particularly helpful for patients who had difficulty recognizing their inner feelings, or who experienced their emotions as vague physical sensations. In addition, it enabled patients with such disorders as tension headaches and hypertension to recognize the relationship between their conflicts or feelings with perturbations in muscle tension and blood pressure.

I initially used biofeedback instrumentation while treating patients with psychophysiological disorders, including migraine, tension headaches, and hypertension. Subsequently, I employed it as an adjunct to psychotherapy with patients who suffered from anxiety, phobias, obsessions, and conversion symptoms. During the 1970s, I supervised residents on the Psychiatric Consultation-Liaison Service at the Yale University School of Medicine. Along with a colleague, Hoyle Leigh, chief of the Psychiatric Consultation-Liaison Service, we began to systematically study biofeedback psychotherapy with suitable patients. One of the subjects we chose to study was a patient who was phobic of many different foods. In addition, she was phobic of frequenting public places, including stores, movie theaters, and restaurants. One of her twice-weekly therapy sessions took place in the laboratory where several modalities, including skin conductance response, heart rate, skin temperature, and muscle tension were monitored throughout each session. Laboratory sessions consisted of psychodynamic psychotherapy, and in-vivo desensitization to the various foods to which she was phobic. Our paper, "Skin Conductance Changes and Psychotherapeutic Content in the Treatment of a Phobic Patient" (Glucksman, M.L, Quinlan, D.M., and Leigh, H., 1985), describes her skin conductance responses during treatment. Changes in her skin conductance response correlated with her phobic symptoms, sense of mastery, and intensity of feelings. Another paper, "Physiological Changes and Clinical Events during Psychotherapy" (Glucksman, M.L., 1985), describes biofeedback psychotherapy with several patients suffering from hypertension and functional pain. It illustrates how their physiological responses corresponded with feelings, conflicts, memories, and fantasies.

At the time that these biofeedback psychotherapy studies were carried out, the current techniques of measuring anatomical and physiological changes in the brain were unavailable. Biofeedback monitoring was the only way of evaluating central and autonomic nervous system responses. During recent decades, numerous studies utilizing fMRIs, CTs, and PET scans have measured brain function in various psychopathological disorders (schizophrenia, depression, anxiety, OCD, etc.) as well as before, during, and after treatment. Although they are informative, these newer imaging techniques are still unable to tell us the content or quality of thoughts, memories, and dreams. In particular, they cannot describe the qualitative nuances of various moods or feelings. Despite our technological advances, we still require verbal communication between patient and therapist for a fuller understanding of internal, subjective, psychological, and physical experience. Biofeedback psychotherapy was (and still is) a method of using both instrumentation and human interaction to understand the relationship between physiological responses and psychological phenomena. Hopefully, future studies will improve our knowledge of the interface between functional changes in the brain and subjective phenomena, including thoughts, feelings, memories, and perceptions. Moreover, this may lead to a fuller understanding of the interplay between brain, mind, and body.

References:

Miller, N.E., "Biofeedback: Evaluation of a New Technique," *New England Journal of Medicine*, 290 (1973): 684-685.

Adler, C.S., and Morrissey-Adler, S., "Strategies in General Psychiatry" in *Biofeedback and Clinical Medicine*, J. Basmajian, ed., Baltimore: Williams & Wilkins, 1979, Chapter 13, 180-196.

Rickles, W. H., Onoda, L., and Doyle, C.C., "Biofeedback as an Adjunct to Psychotherapy,", Task Force on Biofeedback and Psychotherapy Report, Biofeedback Society of America Study Section #9: 1979, Denver, CO.

Glucksman, M.L., Quinlan, D.M., and Leigh, H., "Skin Conductance Changes and Psychotherapeutic Content in the Treatment of a Phobic Patient," *British Journal of Medical Psychology*, 58 (1985): 155-163.

Glucksman, M.L: "Physiological Changes and Clinical Events during Psychotherapy", Integr. Psychiatry, 3:1985, 168-184.

SKIN CONDUCTANCE CHANGES AND
PSYCHOTHERAPEUTIC CONTENT IN THE TREATMENT OF A
PHOBIC PATIENT
MYRON L. GLUCKSMAN, DONALD M. QUINLAN AND
HOYLE LEIGH

Abstract:

This study examined the relationship between skin conductance response (SCR) and psychotherapeutic content in a single case study. Four SCR conditions of one minute's duration each, reflecting maximal increase (amplitude) and least amount of change as well as one-minute periods preceding these criterion conditions, were measured for each psychotherapy session across 12 consecutive sessions. Psychotherapeutic content corresponding to these SCR conditions was evaluated according to 14 categories by five judges. There were significant relationships between SCR conditions and four psychotherapeutic content categories. Increases in SCR corresponded to a decreasing sense of mastery, increased symptom experience, increased symptom occurrence, and increased negative affects. This study suggests that there was a relationship between a responsive physiological measure and relevant psychotherapeutic content categories in an individual patient.

Introduction:

The interaction between physiological and psychological variables during psychotherapy and structured interviews has been demonstrated by a number of investigators (Laswell, 1935; Malmo et al., 1950; Shagass & Malmo, 1954; Lacey, 1959; Toomin & Toomin, 1975; Werbach, 1977; Adler & Morrissey-Adler, 1979; Rickles et al., 1979). For example, affective arousal during psychotherapy has been clearly associated with increased autonomic and voluntary nervous system activity, while affective tranquility has been correlated with autonomic and voluntary nervous system quiescence (Mittelmann & Wolff, 1943; McCurdy, 1950; Oken et al., 1962; Roessler et al., 1975). Other variables such as the quality of interaction between patient and therapist have also been associated with physiological changes for both participants. Specific phenomena in the therapeutic relationship including empathy, permissiveness, praise, criticism, antagonism and cooperativeness have been examined with reference to accompanying physiological responses (Coleman et al., 1956; DiMascio et al., 1957; Dittes, 1957; Malmo et al., 1957: Kaplan, 1963; Kaplan et al., 1963). In general, these studies have shown that there is less autonomic nervous system arousal in both patient and therapist when they have psychological rapport than when their relationship is conflictual.

Lacey (1959), in his review of psychophysiological research in psychotherapy, emphasized the importance of response specificity when examining the relationship between autonomic nervous system activity and clinical material. With this in mind, we studied the relationship between a responsive autonomic nervous system modality and psychotherapeutic content. In studies of this nature the psychotherapeutic content to be examined is usually selected prior to measuring corresponding physiological responses. In this study, we selected predefined physiological changes (skin conductance response) and subsequently evaluated the corresponding psychotherapeutic content in a single patient over 12 sessions. This approach provided a more stringent test of any association between psychotherapeutic content and skin conductance response, since the latter may be responsive to a wide range of stimuli during psychotherapy. For purposes of this study, we chose a patient with well-defined symptomatology who was in psychotherapy. The hypothesis investigated was that periods of increased skin conductance response would be associated with categories of psychotherapeutic content relevant to the patient's psychopathology.

Case History:

The patient who participated in this study was a 37-year-old married female who sought treatment for multiple phobias and anxiety symptoms. For two years prior to treatment she was unable to frequent public places such as stores, theatres and restaurants without developing severe anxiety symptoms (hyperventilation, tachycardia, flushing, light-headedness). She was phobic of many different foods (meats, fish, vegetables) because she believed that she would develop an anaphylactic reaction if she ate them. Her food phobias were so pervasive prior to treatment that she was reduced to eating only toast and drinking fluids. She weighed 92 pounds, whereas her usual adult weight had been 110 pounds. Her sleep pattern and appetite were within normal limits, and there was no evidence of depression. She experienced neither a distortion of her body image nor a need to maintain a lowered body weight. Amenorrhea, compulsive dieting and other signs of anorexia nervosa were absent.

The patient grew up in an upper middle-class family and was a college graduate. According to the patient, she had had a close, affectionate relationship with her father, who died of a myocardial infarction five years prior to her entering treatment. She reported that her mother was alcoholic, phobic, emotionally repressed and very concerned about superficial appearances. She had a younger sister who suffered from allergies and functional colitis. The patient felt that her mother paid more attention to her sister because of the latter's allergies, which began in childhood. When the patient left home for college she developed typical anxiety symptoms, which were interpreted as allergic phenomena (although she had no allergies until then). Following graduation from college and her break-up with a boyfriend, she once again developed anxiety symptoms and consulted an allergist who began her on a desensitization program. She subsequently saw a psychiatrist and remained in therapy for almost a year until her marriage. Her relationship with her husband was rewarding and stable, although she sometimes felt that he was too involved in his work and not emotionally responsive enough toward her.

The patient was engaged in twice weekly psychoanalytically oriented therapy with one of the investigators (M.L.G.) for several months prior to her participation in this study. During that time her pathological dependency and ambivalent feelings toward her mother became evident. It also became clear that her mother had been unable to allow the patient and her sister to separate fully from her. Through various manipulations she kept the patient closely attached to her; any kind of self-assertive, independent behavior on the patient's part was invariably criticized and linked with potential disaster. The patient developed a fear of being alone as a child, along with the conviction that she could never cope adequately apart from her mother. Moreover, her mother emphasized the importance of external appearances and conventionally proper behavior. As a result, the patient constantly suppressed her spontaneous feelings, and displayed an outer facade of congeniality and pleasantness no matter how she felt inwardly. The positive aspects of her self-image came largely from her father who encouraged her socialization and academic interests. The patient's motivation to participate in this study was in part due to her desire to receive systematic desensitization to her food phobias in the laboratory. She was informed as to the general nature of the inquiry, and was eager to collaborate with her therapist in a research project (at this point she had developed a strong positive transference). The research protocol required her to have one of her two-weekly sessions in the laboratory. These sessions resembled those in the therapist's office in terms of structure and orientation; however, they differed in that systematic desensitization to her food phobias was carried out during the last 15 minutes of each session. This consisted of having her eat each food which she had previously avoided. She was initially self-conscious over being physiologically monitored and tape-recorded, but rather quickly adapted to this novel situation.

During the portion of therapy in which this study was carried out she continued to explore her conflicts with her mother. The origins of her phobic symptoms began to emerge; these included partial identifications with her mother and sister as well as a belief that she would become ill or die if she attempted to act independently of her mother. Thoughts or fantasies of successful individuation resulted in strong feelings of isolation, helplessness and panic. She became aware of her fear of losing control over certain feelings, particularly anger toward her mother and sister. Moreover, she acknowledged her rivalry with them for her father's affection, along with her fear of their retaliatory aggression. She ultimately made the connection between her fear of death and her death wishes toward them. During this phase of treatment she overcame all of her food phobias, and experienced considerably less anxiety in public places and social situations. It was firmly established that she was not allergic to any particular food, since she was eventually able to eat everything she had previously avoided without becoming symptomatic. Whereas she initially required her husband or a friend to accompany her to and from the laboratory, she was able to come and go by herself toward the end of the study.

Following the laboratory phase of treatment, she continued in therapy for another year. During the termination phase of therapy her husband changed jobs, necessitating a geographic relocation. She experienced a brief exacerbation of her phobic symptoms and recalled that her mother once told her that her sister had an anaphylactic reaction in the context of moving from one place to another. At the time of termination she was asymptomatic and functioning well. Her weight had increased to 108 pounds. Follow-up visits up to two years after termination revealed that she was continuing to function effectively and was relatively free of symptoms.

Method:

After giving informed consent, the patient came to the laboratory once weekly for a total of 12 successive visits. During the laboratory therapy sessions she was seated opposite the therapist. A partition separated the patient from the monitoring equipment. Prior to the session, a female technician applied the electrodes attached to each of the modules used in this study. The physiological modalities monitored included: skin conductance response, heart rate, muscle tension, and skin temperature. All modalities were ink-recorded on a Beckman RB polygraph. The sessions were tape-recorded and time-synchronized with the polygraph record at 30-second intervals; therapy sessions were 45 minutes in duration. Skin conductance response (SCR) was chosen for specific study because it was the patient's most responsive physiological variable during and across sessions, as determined by inspection of the polygraph record without knowledge of the corresponding session content. A BFT Model 701 Galvanic Skin Response unit was used for this purpose. Electrodes were attached to the distal phalanges of the second, third and fourth digits of the patient's left hand.

The polygraph recordings were analyzed by a technician who had no knowledge of the patient or of the purpose of the study. Scoring of the polygraph recordings was carried out in the following manner. The largest skin conductance increase (that is, the SCR of greatest amplitude) during each session was identified. A one-minute segment was measured from the beginning of this increase in addition to a one-minute segment prior to this increased response. These constituted the 'activation' and 'pre-activation' conditions respectively. The least responsive portion of the skin conductance record was also identified (that is, where there were minimal or no changes in SCR). One-minute segments were measured in the same manner as they were for the largest skin conductance increase. These constituted the 'non-activation' and 'pre-non-activation' conditions. Thus, four skin conductance conditions were identified for each therapy session (activation, pre-activation, non-activation and pre-non-activation).

The verbal content corresponding to each of the four conditions for all 12 therapy sessions was identified and obtained from the tape-recordings. Thus, a total of 48 tape-recorded segments were typed and given without any other identifying clues to five judges (four psychiatrists and a clinical psychologist) who examined them independently of one another. The judges were asked to rate each segment according to a number of psychotherapeutic content categories which were considered relevant to psychotherapy in general, and to this patient in particular. These included: (1) *Mastery* - the patient's sense of inner control over her thoughts, feelings and impulses. (2) *Direction of mastery* - evidence of increasing or decreasing inner control over her thoughts, feelings, etc. (3) *Threatening material* - her perception of real or imagined physical and psychological threats. (4) *Defenses* - assessment of the effectiveness or ineffectiveness of defenses, e.g. denial, intellectualization, etc. (5) *Involvement with the therapist* - concerns, thoughts, feelings or fantasies toward the therapist; these were categorized as positive, negative, ambivalent or neutral. (6) *Separation - isolation* themes - presence of thoughts, feelings or fantasies referring to any type of separation, sense of aloneness, isolation or abandonment. (7) *Symptom experience* - reference to or actual occurrence of physical and/or psychological symptoms. (8) *Affect* - intensity of feelings, emotions or moods; these were categorized as either positive (happiness, well-being), negative (anger, sadness) or mixed. The judges were given a detailed guideline for rating each of these categories.

Results:

1. *Reliability of ratings:*

   The 48 segments (12 sessions by 4 conditions) were rated by the five judges. Individual pairwise comparison of items by judges by the kappa coefficient yielded consistently low non-significant reliabilities between one rater and the other four. The remaining four judges' ratings yielded consistently significant kappas for all but one item. The ratings of the one judge were discarded, and the mean ratings of the remaining four judges were computed for further analysis. Reliability of the composite ratings of the four judges was computed using Cronbach's alpha via the SPSS Reliability subprogram (Hull & Nie, 1979). The alpha coefficients were the mean of all possible split-half reliability coefficients, corrected for attenuation. The alpha coefficients are presented in Table 1.

Table 1: Inter-rater reliability alpha coefficients (four raters, 48 segments)

Category	Alpha coefficient
Mastery: positive	0.84
Mastery: negative	0.88
Direction of mastery*	0.66
Threatening material present	0.66
Defenses present	0.83
Involvement with therapist present	0.84
Type of involvement	0.16
Separation/isolation themes	0.80
Symptom experience (a or b)	0.90
(a) Symptom: talking about	0.88
(b) Symptom: actual experience	0.71
Affect present (a or b)	0.58
(a) Positive affect	0.82
(b) Negative affect	0.76

*Only three judges rated this category.

Except for the rating 'type of involvement' (positive, negative, ambivalent, neutral) all reliabilities were statistically significant. Most also showed moderate to high degrees of agreement (greater than 0.70), in spite of the high levels of inference required for judgements. The rating for 'type of involvement' was deleted from further analyses.

In addition to the separate ratings, each judge made an attempt to 'guess' the condition from which each segment was drawn. None of the judges was able to guess the condition at a level higher than chance. When the conditions were collapsed to activation vs. non-activation, and to pre-activation/non-activation vs. activation/non-activation segments, again none of the judges exceeded chance agreement. Thus, the four conditions were not distinguishable by whatever gross or subtle criteria the judges employed. The absence of significant rates of successful guessing suggests that subsequent results were not due to obvious but unrated differences among conditions.

2. *Psychotherapeutic content and skin conductance response:*
    The ratings of the four types of conditions (pre-activation, activation, pre-non-activation and non-activation) were analyzed in a 2 x 2 analysis of variance design, collapsed across sessions. Of the 13 categories with sufficient reliability for further testing, only one had an effect for pre-activation/non-activation vs. activation/non-activation conditions, and one had an interaction for the two factors. This number of results does not exceed what would occur by chance for the number of main effects and interactions.

Table 2. Psychotherapeutic content category ratings for skin conductance response activation and non-activation conditions

Category	Skin conductance response activation		Skin conductance response non-activation		F test
	Mean	SD	Mean	SD	d.f. = 1,44
Direction of mastery	1.56	(0.56)	2.10	(0.61)	8.60**
Symptom experience	1.62	(0.40)	1.38	(0.41)	4.31*
Actual symptoms	1.18	(0.28)	1.02	(0.10)	5.67*
Negative affect	1.72	(0.30)	1.47	(0.38)	5.50*

*P<0.05   **P<0.01

Note. Scores are mean rating by 4 judges over 12 sessions, Range: (0-4).

F ratios for the pre-activation/non-activation vs. activation/non-activation main effects and interactions are not presented.

SD Standard Deviation.

Table 3. Correlations among significant psychotherapeutic content categories

	Actual Symptoms	Negative affect	Direction of mastery
Symptom experience	0.39**	0.34*	- 0.18
Actual symptoms	-	0.30*	- 0.21
Negative affect	-	-	- 0.52***

P<0.05   ** P<0.01   *** P<0.001   d.f. = 46.

There were, however, four significant effects for the comparison of activation vs. non-activation: direction of mastery, symptom experience (i.e. talking about symptoms), actual symptoms, and negative affect. The means for these categories are presented in Table 2.

Neither ratings of positive mastery (feeling in control) nor negative mastery (feeling out of control) reached statistical significance, but the direction of change of mastery was significantly different. Mastery content was more often in the decreasing direction during activation, and was more often in the increasing direction during non-activation segments.

The patient's reference to symptom(s) and the actual occurrence of symptom(s) were significantly higher for activation than for non-activation segments. Negative affect demonstrated a significant main effect for activation/non-activation; there were significantly higher levels of negative affect for activation than for non-activation segments.

Table 3 presents correlations between the psychotherapeutic content categories which were significantly associated with skin conductance conditions. Moderately significant correlations were observed between symptom experience, actual symptoms and negative affect. There was a highly significant negative correlation between direction of mastery and negative affect.

Discussion:

These data suggest that skin conductance response (SCR) can be used as a physiological measurement corresponding to specific psychotherapeutic content categories during psychotherapy for a patient responsive in this modality. Moreover, this study demonstrates that judges rating psychotherapeutic content independently of each other can discriminate among highly complex categories with significant inter-rater reliability. The lack of significant agreement on 'type of involvement with the therapist' was perhaps due to a lack of clarity in the definition of this category. It may also reflect the difficulty an observer uninvolved in the actual therapeutic process may have in evaluating the vicissitudes of the patient-therapist relationship from an examination of isolated one-minute verbal segments. Moreover, the judges did not have the benefit of non-verbal information (e.g. facial expression, body posture, etc.) to aid them in rating the categories. Generally speaking, the significant degree of inter-rater reliability in this study indicates that psychotherapeutic content categories relevant to the therapeutic process can be objectively measured as discrete clinical entities using verbal content alone. It should be noted that the psychotherapeutic content categories were selected on the basis of the patient's clinical presentation. Other categories may have been present and relevant, but were not rated.

Those psychotherapeutic content categories which were significantly associated with the two different conditions of skin conductance response (activation and non-activation) all showed effects in consistent directions. Direction of mastery decreased in those segments associated with skin conductance activation. Conversely, direction of mastery increased in those segments connected with skin conductance non-activation. That is, when the patient experienced a progressive lack of control over her thoughts, feelings or behavior, she manifested a significant increase in skin conductance. On the other hand, when she felt in progressively greater control, her skin conductance either decreased or did not change. The presence or absence of the sense of mastery itself was not significantly associated with the two different SCR conditions. Thus, for this patient, it was change in the sense of mastery rather than absolute level of mastery that influenced SCR. Therefore, the direction of change in one's sense of mastery appears to be a more meaningful variable from a psychophysiological viewpoint. Mittelmann & Wolff's study (1943) supports this finding in that they observed a correlation between finger temperature and mastery. Those patients who experienced a lack of emotional mastery and whose defenses were not functioning effectively had a decrease in finger temperature, while those who felt in control and had a sense of mastery demonstrated an increase in finger temperature. The sense of mastery or control over one's intrapsychic state is a common goal of all psychotherapies (Lefcort, 1966; Gillis & Jessor, 1970; Strupp, 1970; Frank, 1971). Liberman (1978) emphasized the role of a sense of mastery in maintaining behavioral changes following psychotherapy. He and his colleagues demonstrated that subsequent to termination of psychotherapy, those patients who attributed their improvement to an internal sense of mastery maintained their clinical improvement more successfully than those who felt their improvement was due to external factors (e.g. medication). The following statements reflected this patient's sense of decreasing and increasing mastery: (1) *Decreasing mastery* - 'I was angry, but that makes me feel like I don't have any control over what I'm doing.' (2) *Increasing mastery* - 'I really have been leaving my life and decisions up to circumstances...and not really taking charge...[now] the anxiety reactions are under control... I'm creating them...there is no reason to do it anymore.' For this patient, the achievement of a sense of inner control was crucially important in her struggle to overcome her pathological dependency on her mother. From clinical observations, her increasing sense of mastery played a major role in the amelioration of her phobias and anxiety symptoms.

The occurrence of actual symptoms as well as the patient's verbal reference to them were significantly correlated with the activation conditions. For the most part, the symptoms which occurred during her therapy were phobic ideation and anxiety. Luborsky et al. (1973) documented the occurrence of specific psychological antecedents prior to symptom formation during psychoanalysis. These included helplessness, resentment, frustration, depression and anxiety. Luborsky's findings are inferentially supported in this study in that symptom experience, actual symptoms, decreasing mastery and negative affect were all significantly correlated with the activation conditions. Moreover, these psychotherapeutic content categories were significantly correlated with one another (Table 3). Negative affects most often experienced by the patient included helplessness, anxiety, anger, resentment and guilt. Further analysis would be necessary to validate the temporal sequence between symptom formation and the affective antecedents described by Luborsky. Positive affects (e.g. happiness, well-being) were associated with neither the activation nor the non-activation conditions. There is general agreement in the literature regarding the relationship between skin conductance and affect. Most investigators agree that skin conductance is positively correlated with affective intensity, whether or not it is overtly manifested (McCurdy, 1950; Lacey, 1959; Roessler et al., 1975).

Kaplan et al. (1963) observed a more specific correlation between galvanic skin response (GSR) activity and negative affects; that is, affects such as hostility, fear and embarrassment were associated with greater GSR activity. Although there is some evidence that specific affects are associated with distinct patterns of physiological response (Schwartz et al., 1981), other findings suggest that physiological response is not affect specific (Roessler et al., 1975). The results of this study tend to confirm the positive correlation between skin conductance and intensity of affect. As far as negative affect alone is concerned, there was a clear-cut correlation between higher levels of negative affect and activation conditions, while non-activation conditions were associated with lower levels of negative affect. In view of the fact that the patient subjectively experienced and expressed her negative affects more intensely than her positive ones, this finding supports the general consensus that intensity of affect is associated with increased skin conductance.

There were no significant differences in the levels of content categories between the pre-activation and activation, as well as between the pre-non-activation and non-activation, conditions. It remains for further study to determine the duration of the activation and non-activation conditions in terms of their association with relevant psychotherapeutic content. Nevertheless, the study did succeed in identifying for this patient a physiological response (SCR) that was associated with relevant psychotherapeutic content.

Conclusion:

This study demonstrates that specific psychotherapeutic content categories can be discretely measured with significant inter-rater agreement among blind independent judges. Four of the 13 reliably rated psychotherapeutic content categories were significantly associated with different SCR conditions in this patient. These results suggest that the selection of a responsive physiological measure is a promising methodological approach in exploring the relationship between clinical content and physiological phenomena during psychotherapy. No doubt, a more sophisticated and perhaps continuous monitoring of clinical and physiological data would be even more informative. Clearly, SCR proved to be a sensitive physiological indicator for changes in psychotherapeutic content in this particular patient. Other patients might have shown physiological responsivity in other modalities corresponding to relevant psychotherapeutic content. The question remains as to whether the same relationships exist between SCR and psychotherapeutic content for other patients as they do for this one. Although this is a single case study, the findings suggest that the use of a responsive physiological measure and the selection of clinically relevant content categories can lead to a more meaningful understanding of the relationship between physiological responses and the psychotherapeutic process.

Acknowledgements:

We wish to thank Vincenta Leigh, RN for her help in carrying out this study.

References:

Adler, C. S., & Morrissey-Adler, S. (1979). Strategies in general psychiatry. In F. Basmajian (ed.), *Biofeedback in Clinical Medicine*, pp. 180-196. Baltimore: Williams & Wilkins.

Coleman, S. S., Greenblatt, M. D., & Solomon, H. C. (1956). Physiological evidence of rapport during psychotherapeutic interviews. *Diseases of the Nervous System,* 17, 71-77.

DiMascio, A., Boyd, R. W., & Greenblatt, M. (1957). Physiological correlates of tension and antagonism during psychotherapy. A study of interpersonal physiology. *Psychosomatic Medicine,* 19, 99-104.

Dittes, J. E. (1957). Galvanic skin response as a measure of patient's reaction to therapist's permissiveness. *Journal of Abnormal Social Psychology,* 55, 295-303.

Frank, J. D. (1971). Therapeutic factors in psychotherapy. *American Journal of Psychotherapy,* 25, 350-361.

Gillis, J. S., & Jessor, R. (1970). Effects of brief psychotherapy on belief in internal control: An exploratory study. *Psychotherapy: Theory, Research, and Practice,* 7. 135-137.

Hull, C. H., & Nie, N. H. (1979). *SPSS Update.* New York: McGraw-Hill.

Kaplan, H. B. (1963). Social interaction and GSR activity during group psychotherapy. *Psychosomatic Medicine,* 25, 140-145.

Kaplan, H. B., Burch, N. R., Bloom, S. W., & Edelberg, R. (1963). Affective orientation and physiological activity (GSR) in small peer groups. *Psychosomatic Medicine.*25, 245-252.

Lacey, J. I. (1959). Psychophysiological approaches to the evaluation of psycho therapeutic process and outcome. In E. A. Rubinstein & M. D., Parloff (eds), *Research in Psychotherapy,* pp. 160, 208. Washington, DC: National Publishing Co.

Laswell, H. D. (1935). Verbal references and physiological changes during the psychoanalytic interview: A preliminary communication. *Psychoanalytical Review,* 23, 10-24.

Lefcort, H. M. (1966). Belief in personal control: Research and implications. *Journal of Individual Psychology,* 25, 185-195.

Liberman, B. L. (1978). The role of mastery in psychotherapy: Maintenance of improvement and prescriptive change. In J. D. Frank, R. Hoehn-Saric, S. D. Imber, B. L. Liberman, & A. R. Stone (eds), *Effective Ingredients of Successful Psychotherapy*, pp. 15-'12. New York: Brunner/Mazel.

Luborsky, L., Docherty, J. P., & Penick, S. (1973). Onset conditions for psychosomatic symptoms: A comparative review of immediate observation with retrospective research. *Psychosomatic Medicine, 35*, 187-204.

Malmo, R. B., Shagass, C., & Davis, F. H. (1950). Symptom specificity and bodily reactions during psychiatric interview. *Psychosomatic Medicine, 12*, 362-376.

Malmo, R.B., Boag, T.J., &Smith, A.A. (1957).Physiological study of personal interaction. *Psychosomatic Medicine, 19*, 105-119.

McCurdy, H. G. (1950). Consciousness and the galvanometer. *Psychological Review, 57*, 322-327.

Mittelmann, B., & Wolff, H. G. (1943). Emotions and skin temperature: Observations on patients during psychotherapeutic (psychoanalytic) interviews. *Psychosomatic Medicine, 5*, 211-231.

Oken, D., Grinker, R. R., Heath, H. A., Herz, M., Korchin, S. J., Sabshin, M., & Schwartz, A. B. (1962). Relation of physiological response to affect expression. *Archives of General Psychiatry, 6*, 336-351.

Rickles, W. H., Onoda, L., & Doyle, C. C. (1979). Biofeedback as an adjunct to psychotherapy. Task Force on Biofeedback and Psychotherapy Report, Biofeedback Society of America Study Section 9, Denver.

Roessler. R., Bruch, H., Thum, L., & Collins, F. (1975). Physiologic correlates of affect during psychotherapy. *American Journal of Psychotherapy, 29*, 26-36.

Schwartz, G. E., Weinberger, M. P., & Singer, J. A. (1981). Cardiovascular differentiation of happiness, sadness, anger, and fear following imagery and exercise. *Psychosomatic Medicine, 43*, 343-364.

Shagass, C., & Malmo, R. B. (1954). Psychodynamic themes and localized muscular tension during psychotherapy. *Psychosomatic Medicine, 16*, 295-313.

Strupp, H. H. (1970). Specific vs. nonspecific factors in psychotherapy and the problem of control. *Archives of General Psychiatry, 23,* 393-401.

Toomin, M. K., & Toomin, H. (1975). GSR biofeedback in psychotherapy: Some clinical observations. *Psychotherapy: Theory, Research and Practice, 12,* 33-38.

Werbach, M. R. (1977). Biofeedback and psychotherapy. *American Journal of Psychotherapy, 31,* 376-382.

Received March 1984; revised version received August 1984.

British Journal of Medical Psychology (1985), 58, 155-163 Printed in Great Britain.

© 1985 The British Psychological Society.

Requests for reprints should be addressed to Myron L. Glucksman, One Medical Center Drive, Danbury, CT 06810, USA. (68 Marchant Road, Redding, Ct. 06896).

Donald M. Quinlan and Hoyle Leigh are at the Department of Psychiatry, Yale University School of Medicine.

PHYSIOLOGIC CHANGES AND CLINICAL EVENTS DURING PSYCHOTHERAPY
MYRON L. GLUCKSMAN, M.D.

Summary:

Physiologic monitoring provides some understanding of the continual and, at times, dramatic interplay between clinical events and physiologic responses. The responses can be especially helpful in signaling or validating significant material during psychotherapy and can graphically portray for patients how certain impulses, thoughts, memories, conflicts, and affects can alter physiologic responses (e.g., blood pressure, muscle tension). In turn, they may aid the therapist in identifying the earliest stages of an illness (e.g., hypertension) and may lead to specific treatment interventions, including medication or alteration of psychotherapeutic technique. Psychotherapy provides unlimited opportunities to observe, explore, and utilize relationships between psychologic and physiologic phenomena-information which, judiciously employed, can benefit both patient and therapist.

Introduction:

Psychiatrists have been concerned with the relationship between somatic symptoms and psychopathology since Freud (1) began his early explorations into the causes of conversion phenomena. Alexander (2), Wolff (3), and others (4-7) continued this work in their studies of specific personality factors, psychodynamic conflicts, affects, and other behavioral variables in connection with certain physiologic responses and psychosomatic illnesses.

Over the past 50 years, a large number of investigators have explored the relationship among psychodynamic processes, symptoms, affects, aspects of the therapist-patient relationship, and normal as well as pathologic physiologic responses during dyadic and group interactions (8- 14). A number of central nervous system modalities have been studied (blood pressure, respiration, heart rate, skin temperature, skin conductance, muscle tension).

In general, these studies have demonstrated that there is a close relationship between clinical events and physiologic responses during interviews and various types of psychotherapy. For example, affective arousal during psychotherapy has been clearly associated with increased autonomic and voluntary nervous system activity, whereas affective tranquility has been correlated with autonomic and voluntary nervous system quiescence.

Some of these studies have focused on the patient-therapist relationship, examining such variables as empathy, permissiveness, praise, criticism, antagonism, and cooperativeness between patient and therapist (15-18). Observations from these studies indicate that there is less autonomic nervous system arousal for both patient and therapist when they have psychologic rapport than when their relationship is antagonistic. The relationship between symptom exacerbation or improvement and physiologic responsivity has also been studied. For example, the systematic desensitization of phobias has been associated with decreasing autonomic nervous system activity (19). Changes in physiologic activity have also been correlated with the improvement of psychotic symptoms (20), the lessening of depression (21), and the reduction of anxiety symptoms (22).

Decreased autonomic nervous system activity has been linked to greater degrees of psychologic resistance and defensiveness, as well as to genuine states of relaxation and internal security (23, 24). On the other hand, a decreased sense of mastery or internal control has been associated with increased autonomic nervous system responsivity (24). In a comprehensive review, Lacey (25) emphasized that although physiologic changes can be an excellent monitor of psychologic events taking place in therapy, they must always be interpreted with full knowledge of the clinical data. Individuals have idiosyncratic patterns of autonomic nervous system responsivity, so that there is little uniformity of response to similar clinical phenomena. For example, one patient who experiences anxiety may have tachycardia, whereas another may not. A wide range of physiologic responses occurs within normal limits in connection with psychotherapeutic events; e.g., talking itself can significantly increase mean arterial blood pressure in normotensive individuals, whereas silence does not (26). During any psychotherapy session, there are continuous fluctuations in physiologic activity that can be understood only in terms of the patient's idiosyncratic response patterns and the vicissitudes of the psychotherapeutic process.

Use of Biofeedback:

During the past decade, biofeedback has emerged as a method of treatment for various psychophysiologic and psychiatric disorders. These include migraine and muscle contraction headaches, hypertension, cardiac arrhythmias, asthma, Raynaud syndrome, anxiety states, and phobias. Biofeedback essentially helps the patient modify both voluntary and involuntary nervous system activity through direct feedback of certain physiologic functions. For example, a patient may modify blood pressure response by means of continuous and direct feedback of information on systolic and diastolic blood pressure levels. Biofeedback has usually been used as an adjunct to behavioral therapy (e.g., systematic desensitization, progressive relaxation, autogenic training).

However, a few psychodynamically oriented therapists have used the biofeedback instrumentation not only in conjunction with behavioral techniques, but also as a monitor of physiologic responses during psychotherapy (27-29). They have observed that autonomic and voluntary nervous system responses occur in conjunction with significant conflicts, fantasies, memories, affects, and changes in the therapist-patient relationship. Physiologic variables such as skin conductance response, blood pressure, skin temperature, muscle tension, and heart rate can provide meaningful feedback for both the patient and therapist during psychotherapy. This physiologic information can be used in a similar fashion to that of visual feedback in videotherapy. Several terms have been introduced to describe this form of treatment, including "biofeedback-psychotherapy" (27), "psychophysiologic therapy" (30), and "psychotherapy with physiologic monitoring" (13).

Biofeedback-psychotherapy can be especially helpful for patients who find it difficult to connect somatic sensations or symptoms with their feelings. A certain group of these patients, described as "alexithymic" (31), are unable to differentiate one emotion from another, cannot verbalize their feelings, and frequently experience their emotions as vague somatic sensations. For these patients, biofeedback-psychotherapy can be helpful in enabling them to reinterpret their somatic experiences into meaningful feelings. Other patients who have psychophysiologic disorders can be helped to identify specific conflicts and affects that play an important role in symptom formation (hypertension, asthma, migraine). For example, an individual with hypertension can directly observe the relationship between blood pressure fluctuations and relevant psychodynamic conflicts, fantasies, and feelings. Patients with well-circumscribed symptoms, such as phobias and free-floating anxiety, can monitor corresponding physiologic changes, with exacerbations and reductions in their symptomatology. Although biofeedback-psychotherapy may add a beneficial dimension to the treatment of certain patients, it may be too intrusive, distracting, and even disruptive for others. For example, paranoid patients may be too threatened by the biofeedback apparatus. Depressed, borderline, and psychotic patients may be unable to cognitively organize and interpret the feedback data made available to them. When used judiciously, biofeedback can provide us with an opportunity for the immediate observation of normal and pathologic physiologic reactions during psychotherapy.

Illustrative Cases:

The following clinical examples illustrate the use of biofeedback-psychotherapy:

(A) A 35-year-old male business executive came to therapy for anxiety symptoms and labile hypertension for which he was not receiving medication. He exhibited an obsessive-compulsive character structure and had a strong tendency to deny and isolate his feelings. His interpersonal relationships were marked by neurotic competitiveness and a need to control others. During one therapy session, he described a meeting at work where a fellow employee had attempted to obstruct one of his proposals. As he was talking, his blood pressure increased dramatically from a normotensive level. While exploring his feelings toward this individual, he finally acknowledged how angry he was at him. Further associations led to his feelings of intense rivalry and hatred toward a younger brother. This information enabled the patient to understand the connection between his sibling rivalry, his need to dominate others, angry feelings when thwarted, and elevations of his blood pressure.

(B) A 40-year-old married woman came to treatment for muscle contraction headaches and low back pain. During the course of treatment, it became evident that she invariably developed either a headache or backache on the days following sexual relations with her husband. She had been raised by extremely religious, puritanical parents who instilled in her excessive guilt in connection with her sexuality. During the course of one therapy session, she recalled a childhood experience in which she engaged in mutual genital exploration with a male cousin. As this memory came into sharper focus, there was a dramatic increase in her skin conductance response and muscle tension level. She reported that she was reexperiencing her feelings of terror at the time, believing that "my mother would hang me," and "my father would kill me" if she and her cousin were discovered. As a result of this observation, as well as others, it became clear to the patient how her feelings of anxiety, guilt, and fear of lethal punishment in connection with her sexual impulses and behavior were related to her headaches and back pain.

(C) A 55-year-old married male corporate executive entered treatment because he was dissatisfied with his interpersonal relationships. His wife criticized him for not communicating his feelings directly, and his peers and subordinates felt that he was remote and vague during business meetings. The patient was hypertensive and stabilized on medication. He held his feelings under tight control and never expressed them directly, particularly annoyance and anger. He was raised in a family where feelings were never shared or discussed. Confrontations were avoided and he never heard his parents argue. During treatment, it became apparent that he avoided confrontations with his wife, friends, and business associates at all costs. This resulted in chronic feelings of resentment and anger. During one session, there was a significant increase in his blood pressure from a normotensive level, as well as a sudden increase in his skin conductance response, as he was calmly describing his daughter's boyfriend. Further exploration led to his admission of feelings of distrust and anger toward the boyfriend because the patient believed him to be irresponsible and exploitative. On another occasion, he reported an impending evaluation he was about to conduct with one of his surbordinates. As his blood pressure increased, he became aware of how enraged he was with this man because of the latter's mistakes and generally poor job performance. He had never confronted him directly about these problems, even though he had considered firing him for some time. These clinical observations allowed us to make a connection between suppressed feelings of resentment, anger, or even rage, and elevations of his blood pressure. It was striking how, in the course of a single session, his blood pressure returned to normotensive levels once he had identified and expressed these feelings.

I have presented these patients to illustrate the relationship between physiologic changes and relevant clinical events during treatment. In some instances, the physiologic response corresponding to the patient's productions reached pathologic proportions (e.g., elevated blood pressure). In other instances, the physiologic response, though not pathologic, was indicative of psychodynamically meaningful material (e.g., increased skin conductance). In the majority of studies concerned with psychophysiologic phenomena during psychotherapy, observations have been made either empirically by the therapist (similar to the clinical material I have just presented) or they have been based on specific physiologic responses in connection with pre-selected clinical variables. For example, a specific affect or therapeutic intervention has been selected for study and the corresponding physiologic responses evaluated. A few well-controlled studies have required judges to rate psychotherapeutic content independently according to specific clinical variables during symptomatic, as well as asymptomatic, events in the course of therapy (32-33). These "double-blind" studies have provided a more rigorous approach to an examination of the relationship between clinical events and physiologic responses during psychotherapy.

In a recent study by myself and two colleagues (34), the relationship between skin conductance response and several psychotherapeutic variables was examined in a patient undergoing psychoanalytically oriented psychotherapy. (Skin conductance response is a measure of electrodermal activity, which in turn is an exquisitely sensitive indicator of sympathetic nervous system responsivity and emotional arousal).

The patient was a 37-year-old married woman who manifested phobic and anxiety symptoms. Perhaps the most salient finding from this study was that increases in skin conductance response (SCR) corresponded to the patient's decreasing sense of mastery or control over her feelings, thoughts, and behavior. Conversely, decreases in SCR corresponded to an increasing sense of mastery or inner control. Another important observation was that increases in SCR also corresponded to symptom manifestation (phobic ideation, anxiety). Conversely, no change in SCR corresponded to the absence of symptomatology. Increases in SCR also correlated with affective intensity. "Negative" affects, in particular, corresponded to increases in SCR. The "negative" affects most frequently experienced by the patient included anxiety, helplessness, guilt, resentment, and anger.

The connection between SCR and emotional arousal during psychotherapy is well known (8,10,11,13). Other voluntary and involuntary nervous system responses, including muscle tension, heart rate, blood pressure, skin temperature, and respiratory function, have also been correlated with affective intensity, symptom occurrence, and changes in the patient-therapist relationship during psychotherapy (9,12,15-18,24,32). The data from these studies indicate that a variety of significant physiologic responses occur during therapy. These correspond to specific clinical events, including affective arousal and expression, the emergence of meaningful conflicts into conscious awareness, and the recall of significant memories. Physiologic changes are also connected with symptom formation, vicissitudes in the patient-therapist relationship, and the perception of real or imagined threats that lead to a temporary failure of psychologic defenses along with a decreased sense of inner control and feelings of relative helplessness. Voluntary and involuntary nervous system changes within a normal range of reactivity correspond to these clinical phenomena.

Pathological Responses:

In some patients, however, the same clinical events are accompanied by physiologic responses of pathologic proportions. Frequently, these pathologic responses reflect the presence of an existing disease, such as hypertension (e.g., the business executives described earlier). Most clinicians have observed symptom exacerbation in patients with asthma, ulcerative colitis, migraine, rheumatoid arthritis, duodenal ulcer, etc., during psychodynamically meaningful periods of therapy. Frequently, symptoms apparently unconnected with a particular illness or syndrome occur within a given therapy session. Pain, nausea, vertigo, gastric discomfort, and various motor or sensory phenomena are often reported. Occasionally, these turn out to be conversion symptoms because they are primarily symbolic in function and representation. Sometimes, they are the result of an abnormally intense or prolonged physiologic response (e.g., gastrointestinal hypermotility or muscular contraction). They may subsequently become secondarily invested with symbolic meaning. These symptoms may or may not represent the initial stages of a developing illness (e.g., labile blood pressure preceding fixed hypertension).

When somatic symptoms or illness do occur in the course of psychotherapy, they are most likely the result of a complex interplay among hereditary, biologic, social, and psychodynamic factors. For example, it is not unusual for patients to become symptomatic or even ill on the anniversary of the death of a loved one, or when exploring other significant object losses. In recent years, there has been an accumulation of data emphasizing the importance of object loss, separation, bereavement, and such affects as grief, despair, hopelessness, and depression in the development of physical illness (35-40). Of particular interest is the "giving up-given up" complex described by Engel and Schmale (37). They have concluded that real, threatened, or fantasied object loss provides the most frequent setting in which the "giving up-given up" complex occurs. The latter is a clinical state characterized by two major affects-helplessness and hopelessness. The helplessness reflects a loss of ego autonomy connected to feelings of deprivation or lack of gratification from "other-than-self" objects. The hopelessness reflects feelings of despair resulting from an awareness that the self can no longer provide gratification. In the "giving up" phase, there is a failure of psychologic defenses and an awareness of the inability to receive object gratification. In the "given up" phase, self-representations are no longer perceived as sources of gratification or supplies. Thus, the "giving up-given up" complex is a state in which the self and objects no longer provide the necessary gratifications. During this state, there is a tendency to experience feelings and memories, as well as to engage in behavior apparently connected to past events that evoked similar ego alterations. This complex is neither synonymous with depression and grief, nor is it necessarily followed by somatic illness; nonetheless, it appears to be a contributing factor in the emergence of somatic illness, provided other hereditary or biologic factors are also present.

The "Symptom-Context" Method:

The vast majority of studies concerned with the role of antecedent psychologic factors in the onset of somatic symptoms or illness have been carried out in a retrospective manner. That is, patients or experimental subjects have been evaluated by means of psychologic tests, interviews, reviews of the development of their illnesses, etc., after they had developed particular symptoms or illnesses. Even those studies that have examined clinical data prior to the onset of a particular symptom or illness during psychotherapy have been carried out in a retrospective fashion. Only a small number of these studies have been based on the immediate observation of the onset of symptoms or frank illness, that is, when the therapist or observer was present when the symptoms or illness first became apparent.

Luborsky et al. (41) compared the psychologic conditions preceding somatic symptoms by using a review of "immediate observation" research and "broad context" or retrospective research. They could find only 23 studies clearly based on the immediate observation of the onset of symptoms. The latter included petit-mal seizures, stomach dysfunctions, headaches, hay-fever, asthma, colon dysfunction, backache, nasal dysfunction, and Raynaud syndrome. Of these clinical entities, only five were studied in the context of ongoing psychotherapy; these included stomach pain, headaches, petit-mal seizures, asthma, and Raynaud syndrome. They noted that the most frequent psychologic antecedents cited in the immediate observation studies were: (A) resentment or hostility, (B) frustration secondary to being thwarted, (C) anxiety secondary to the perception of threat, (D) helplessness, and (E) a change in the relationship with the therapist or experimenter.

Luborsky and Auerbach (33) further refined the process of analyzing antecedent factors connected to the occurrence of symptoms during psychotherapy sessions. They termed this the "symptom-context method." In brief, there are two approaches to this method: (A) the immediate context: the patient's productions (thoughts, fantasies, affects, etc.) are examined immediately before and after the emergence of a symptom; (B) the broad context: the entire session or group of psychotherapy sessions surrounding the critical point at which the symptom occurs are evaluated.

Using the symptom-context method, Luborsky and Auerbach (33) explored the antecedent factors connected with momentary forgetting, stomach pain, and migraine headaches. The psychologic factors most frequently observed just prior to the onset of stomach pain and headache were related to the feeling of helplessness; this feeling was connected to a concern over the loss of supplies, a lack of inner control, and the perception of being blocked or frustrated by the therapist. Direct reference to the therapist was an antecedent factor for symptoms of momentary forgetting and headaches. These references were ones that were threatening to the patient and reflected increasing transferential involvement. Knapp and associates (32) carried out an elegant study that examined the context of asthmatic symptoms manifested by a patient in psychoanalysis. In their study, two psychoanalyst judges achieved some success in predicting asthmatic exacerbations from the psychotherapeutic material. Their predictions were based on factors including psychosocial stress, emotional arousal, and defensive disruption.

Illustrative Cases:

The following clinical presentations are examples of the symptom-context approach to understanding the development of somatic symptoms during psychotherapy. The first patient to be described illustrates the "broad context approach" in delineating the psychodynamic antecedents of an acute physical illness that occurred during psychoanalysis. The patient was a middle-aged married professional man who entered psychoanalysis for depressive symptoms, episodic excessive drinking, and anxiety. Just prior to entering treatment he had voluntarily given up his job as manager of a professional partnership. He was depressed over the loss of this position, even though it was customary to rotate it among the partners. He was also preoccupied with growing older and concerned over the possible loss of his professional skills. The patient was outwardly aggressive and competitive with his peers, appeared confident, and behaved with a certain sense of bravado in social situations. However, he felt inwardly weak, vulnerable, and terrified of failure.

His father, who had died several years earlier, was a critical, unaffectionate man who often physically abused the patient during his childhood. His mother, who was still alive, was a domineering, possessive woman, frequently capricious in her expressions of affection for him. An older brother, with whom he had had an extremely competitive relationship, had died of myocardial infarction several years prior to the patient's entering analysis.

At the time the patient began treatment, his marriage was in serious difficulty. For the previous 10 years, he had been partially impotent and had engaged in several extramarital relationships. Having had a strict religious upbringing, he was guilt-ridden over them and anticipated punishment in the form of professional failure, illness, or death. His sexual difficulties were clearly connected to unresolved oedipal issues. Unconsciously, he viewed his wife as a "madonna" who was a forbidden love object. He identified her with certain qualities of his mother and older sister (protective, loving, and nurturing). He was able to have successful sexual relations only when he fantasized his partner to be a whore, or viewed her in some other degrading role.

His relationships with his male peers and friends were characterized by intense competitiveness and the need for total control over them. At the same time, he was frightened of being overwhelmed and injured by them.

His transference to me evolved along several lines; at one level, I was a male rival to be dominated and defeated; at another, I was a benevolent father to whom he could confess and receive forgiveness. At yet another level, I represented his mother, who could be either loving, accepting, and protective or controlling, arbitrary, and rejecting. The patient was in analysis for approximately 1.5 years prior to the development of his physical symptoms. Approximately 6 weeks prior to his illness, he had a series of dreams that portrayed myself and other men as indifferent, uncaring, and castrating. He viewed himself as relatively helpless in his relationship with me, his father, and his professional partners. He was caught between his wishes to be omnipotent and totally dominant over his male competitors, and his fear of being castrated by them in the form of rejection, betrayal, and criticism. He became consciously aware of his murderous impulses toward male rivals and his consequent fears of likewise being killed by them.

At this point in the analysis, I was about to leave for my summer vacation. Shortly before I left, the patient had a dream in which he was helping his father water the lawn of the house in which he grew up. The water began flooding the house, and he tried to sweep it away but couldn't control it.

He yelled to his mother for help, but she did not answer. His associations led to his feelings of powerlessness and helplessness in the face of his father's anger, criticism, and brutality. Moreover, he felt that his mother never protected him from his father's wrath, and abandoned him emotionally as well as physically. These fears articulated with his fantasies of losing control and becoming psychotic during my absence. According to the patient, I was capable of injuring him whenever and in whatever way I wished (similar to his father), and I offered him no help or protection (similar to his mother).

Shortly after I returned from my vacation, he was about to observe his 55th birthday-the same age at which his brother had died. In fact, the date of his brother's death was only 2 months away from the time at which we resumed treatment. He began exploring his competitive, murderous feelings toward his brother, and his guilt over outliving him. He verbalized fantasies of being asked to leave his job by his professional partners and of my terminating the analysis if he expressed his full rage toward me. At this time, his wife threatened to leave him if he did not give her more attention and affection. In addition, one of his partners told him that he saw no improvement in his behavior and was disappointed in him. The patient felt on the verge of being abandoned by me, his wife, and his partners. He wanted to escape, but felt trapped and helpless. It was in this setting that he developed a sudden hemorrhagic gastritis for which he was hospitalized. Although he had engaged in episodic drinking over the previous few years, he had never been ill or symptomatic from it, except for the occasional hangover.

During his hospitalization the patient reported that he felt he was being punished for his past "sins" (sexual acting-out and destructively aggressive behavior toward other men). He identified with his older brother who had died at almost the exact time of year that he was hospitalized. Psychodynamically, there was a confluence of several issues just prior to his illness. My departure for vacation and his wife's threat to leave him had reactivated fears of abandonment that were connected to earlier losses of his mother's protection, which had left him vulnerable to his father's brutality. Approaching the age at which his brother had died reinforced feelings of guilt and castration anxiety associated with sibling rivalry and murderous impulses toward his brother and father. His ego state at this time corresponded to Engel's "giving up-given up" complex; he perceived a loss of gratification from both self and other-than-self objects, with no hope of rescue. His usual defenses were no longer effective in coping with his fears of impending abandonment and castration. The clinical data suggest that his illness was a pathologic consequence of the interplay between his feelings of terror, helplessness, and hopelessness and the concurrent gastric mucosal changes aggravated by alcohol.

The following clinical vignette illustrates the "immediate context" approach in examining the development of a somatic symptom within a psychotherapy session. The patient was a 3S-year-old married woman who had been in psychoanalytically oriented psychotherapy for several years. She originally entered treatment for obesity and marital problems. She frequently complained of abdominal pain and discomfort, which her internist attributed to either gastrointestinal hypermotility or esophageal spasm. These symptoms occasionally occurred during therapy sessions, and the following is an example of the immediate context in which an episode of esophageal spasm occurred.

During a session, the patient associated to a dream in which she found herself in an apartment outside of which there were several strange men whom she thought might harm her if she went out. Her husband entered and went into the bathroom, which appeared quite messy. She went into the bathroom with him and saw an open door leading into another apartment in which there were other people. She found herself wondering how to close the door in order to make her apartment safer. She associated to her husband's lack of organization and responsibility, typified by his messy desk and financial indebtedness. Further associations led to her son's girlfriend, whom she had discovered cleaning the bathroom. This in turn, led to her fear that her son would eventually leave her and marry his girlfriend. She finally acknowledged her own sexual attraction to her son, and her anxiety over sexual fantasies involving other men. She connected this to the danger the strange men in the dream posed for her. She was already well aware of the fact that one of the defensive functions of her obesity was to make her unattractive to men, which in turn protected her from the possibility of a sexual flirtation or even a friendly relationship with a man other than her husband. She was less well aware of the role her anxiety over incestuous impulses played in her jealousy of her son's relationship with his girlfriend and in the various ways in which she rejected her husband (including her sexual inhibitions). She associated the closed door and safety of the apartment to her reluctance to explore her sexual fantasies and incestuous feelings for her son any further. At this point in her associations she remarked: "There are some issues I don't want to face." Almost instantaneously, she complained of a burning pain in her epigastrium, characteristic of previous episodes of esophageal spasm.

In this patient, the somatic symptom occurred as she was struggling to defend against the anxiety resulting from a growing awareness of her sexual and incestuous impulses. Closing the door in the dream symbolized her need to repress them. At a critical point during her associations, her usual defenses of denial and repression were no longer effective. She became overwhelmed by feelings of anxiety, a relative sense of helplessness, and a desire to escape psychologically. The somatic symptom resulted from vagal arousal corresponding to a temporary failure of her usual psychologic defenses.

These clinical presentations illustrate both the immediate and broad context approach toward understanding the psychodynamic setting in which somatic symptoms occur during psychotherapy. In each patient, there was a complex interplay between physiologic and psychodynamic factors. The latter were characterized by conflicts with specific psychogenetic origins, a current stress or stresses articulating with these conflicts, and a temporary failure of ordinarily effective defenses to cope adequately with associated impulses and affects.

In the first patient, the current stresses were threatened object losses and castration fears, which reactivated memories and affects connected with earlier ones. His usual defenses (acting-out, denial, projection) no longer effectively neutralized his fears of being abandoned or killed. Self and other-than-self objects were no longer a source of gratification, resulting in feelings of helplessness and hopelessness. Over a period of several months, these psychotherapeutic events, the gastric mucosal changes corresponding to them, and the direct effect of alcohol precipitated his illness.

In the second patient, the current stress was her growing awareness and anxiety over incestuous impulses emerging from the manifest dream content. Her usual defenses (repression, denial, overeating) were unavailable for neutralizing the anxiety associated with her sexual impulses. Feelings of anxiety and helplessness, along with parasympathetic nervous system arousal, resulted in the esophageal spasm. This was a transient somatic symptom that subsided when her usual defenses of denial and repression once again restored her ego integrity.

Both patients illustrate how somatic symptoms can occur in connection with psychotherapeutic phenomena over the course of months or minutes. Psychotherapy itself is neither a cause nor a required element in the pathogenesis of somatic symptoms or illness. Nevertheless, it can facilitate their occurrence and clearly provides us with a magnification of the psychodynamic context in which they take place.

Conclusion:

In this article, I have attempted to explore the numerous connections between normal, as well as pathologic, physiologic responses and psychotherapeutic events. Specific components of the psychotherapeutic process that appear to be involved include: the awareness or expression of certain affects (particularly negative ones); the emergence of threatening impulses, memories, thoughts, or fantasies into conscious awareness; transient loss of effective psychologic defenses; and impairment of ego integrity, namely, a loss of the sense of internal mastery or control with a corresponding feeling of helplessness. The development of somatic illness during psychotherapy appears to require the added dimensions of threatened or actual object loss connected to psychodynamic conflicts at different levels of psychogenetic development, temporary defensive failure, and the corresponding affects of helplessness and hopelessness. The latter "giving up-given up" complex may be associated with prolonged or intensive voluntary and involuntary nervous system activity, as well as other biologic, immunologic, and morphologic changes leading to frank illness. I wish to emphasize that these are, at best, partial and tentative explanations, based on the available experimental and clinical data.

I have also described how physiologic monitoring during psychotherapy provides us with some understanding of the continual and, at times, dramatic interplay between clinical events and physiologic responses. The latter can be especially helpful in either signaling or validating significant material during psychotherapy. Moreover, they can provide patients with a graphic portrayal of how certain impulses, thoughts, memories, conflicts, and affects can alter physiologic responses (e.g., blood pressure, muscle tension). In turn, they may aid the therapist in identifying the earliest stages of an illness (e.g., hypertension) and may lead to specific treatment interventions, including medication or alteration of psychotherapeutic technique. Clearly, the psychotherapeutic process provides us with unlimited opportunities to observe, explore, and utilize the relationships between psychologic and physiologic phenomena. If used judiciously, this information can benefit both patient and therapist during psychotherapy.

References:

1. Freud, S. *On the Psychical Mechanism Of Hysterical Phenomena: preliminary Communication*, Vol. II, The Standard Edition. London: Hogarth Press, 1955, pp 1-181.
2. Alexander, F. *Psychosomatic Medicine*, New York: W.W. Norton & Co., 1950.
3. Wolff, HG. *Stress and Disease.* Springfield, IL: Charles C Thomas, 1953.
4. Engel, G, Reichsman F. *J AM Psychoanal Assoc* 1956;4:428-452.
5. Weiner, H, et al. *Psychosom Med* 1957;19:1-10.
6. Graham, DT, et al. *Psychosom Med* 1962;24:257-266.
7. Holmes, TH, Wolff HG. *Psychosom Med* 1952;14:18-33.
8. Laswell, HD. *Psychoanal Rev* 1935;23:10-24.

9. Shagass, C, Malmo RB. *Psychosom Med* 1954; 16:295-313.

10. Dittes, JE. J *Abnorm Soc Psychol* 1957; 54:187-191.

11. Kaplan, HB, et al. *Psychosom Med* 1963;25:245-252.

12. Heim, E, et al. *J Psychosom Res* 1968;12:261-274.

13. Roessler, R, et al. *Am J Psychother* 1975;29:26-36.

14. Rickles, WH, et al. *Biofeedback as an Adjunct to Psychotherapy, Task Force on Biofeedback and Psychotherapy Report, Biofeedback Society of America, Study Sec. No. 9,* Denver, 1979.

15. Coleman, R, et al. *Dis Nerv Syst* 1956;17:71-77.

16. Dittes, JE. J *Abnorm Soc Psychol* 1957;55:295-303.

17. Malmo, RB, et al. *Psychosom Med* 1957;19:105-119.

18. DiMascio, A, et al. *Psychosom Med* 1957;19:99-104.

19. Marks, I, et al. *Psychol Med* 1971;1:299-307.

20. Fenz, WD, Steffy RA. *Psychosom Med* 1968;30:423-436.

21. Schwartz, GE, et al. *Psychosom Med* 1978;40:355-360.

22. Mowrer, OH, et al. In *Psychotherapy: Theory and Research.* New York: Ronald Press, 1953, pp. 546-640.

23. Oken, D, et al. *Arch Gen Psychiatry* 1962;6:20-35.

24. Mittelmann, B, Wolff HG. *Psychosom Med.* 1943;5:211-231.

25. Lacey, JI. In: Rubenstein EA, Parloff MB (eds). *Research in psychotherapy.* Washington, DC: National Publishing Co., 1959.

26. Lynch, JJ, et al. *Psychosom Med* 1981;43:25-33.

27. Adler, C, Adler SM. In Basmajian J. (ed), *Biofeedback in Clinical Medicine.* Baltimore: Williams & Wilkins, 1979, pp. 180-196.

28. Toomin, MK, Toomin H. *Psychother Theory Res Pract* 1975;12:33-38.

29. Werbach, MR. *Am J Psychother* 1977;31:376-382.

30. Stroebel, CF. *Psychiatr Opin,* 1979 (June):13-17.

31. Sifneos, PE. *Psychother Psychosom* 1975:26:65-70.

32. Knapp, PH, et al. *Psychosom Med* 1970;32:167-188.

33. Luborsky, L, Auerbach AH. *J Am Psychoanal Assoc* 1969;17:68-99.

34. Glucksman, ML, et al. *Br J Med Psychol* (in press).

35. Green, WA. *Annals NY Acad Sci* 1966; 125:794-801.

36. Schmale, A, Iker H. *Annals NY Acad Sci* 1966;125:807-813.

37. Engel, GL, Schmale AH. *J Am Psychoanal Assoc* 1967;15:344-365.

38. Morillo, E, Gardner LL *Psychosom Med* 1979;41:545-555.

39. Shekelle, RB, et al. *Psychosom Med* 1981;43:117-125.

40. Ackerman, SH, et al. *Psychosom Med* 1981;43:305-310.

41. Luborsky, L, et al. *Psychosom Med* 1973;35:187-204.

*From the Departments of Psychiatry, Yale University School of Medicine, New Haven, CT, and New York Medical College, Valhalla, NY.

Based, in part, on a presentation to the American Psychiatric Association Annual Meeting, Toronto, Canada, May 17, 1982.

## Chapter 3

Affect in the Therapeutic Relationship

My interest in the subject of Affect began when I organized a meeting devoted to that topic for the American Academy of Psychoanalysis in 1980. By then, psychoanalytic theories of Affect had undergone considerable revision since Freud's original concept of emotion as a manifestation of instinctual discharge. The words "affect," "feeling," and "emotion" are used interchangeably in the literature, although they are often distinguished from one another by some authors. "Mood" is usually characterized as a prolonged state of a particular feeling or emotion. In contrast to mood, feelings are more transient and accompanied by behavioral and physiological reactions. In any event, there is a general consensus that an affect or feeling is a behavioral event, subjectively experienced, and often accompanied by physiological changes. Affects are assumed to be undifferentiated in the first few months of life, except for gradations of pleasure and unpleasure. They begin to differentiate somewhere between the fifth to eighth months of life when the infant becomes aware of the presence or absence of its primary caregiver. The terms "stranger" or "separation" anxiety refer to the major emotion experienced by the infant around six to eight months of age, whenever the primary caregiver disappears. The subsequent capacity to differentiate affects depends on a number of factors, including parental mirroring or communication of various emotions (affective resonance), the learning of language to signify specific feelings, as well as defensive patterns and character structure.

The failure or impaired ability to experience, differentiate, and communicate feelings is termed "alexithymia" (Sifneos, P.E., 1973., Nemiah, J.C., 1977). Individuals with alexithymia frequently experience their emotions as vague somatic sensations and often manifest somatic symptoms. During the course of development, affects become associated with ideas, beliefs, fantasies, perceptions, and memories. Therefore, feelings are intimately connected with cognition, perception, and language. Verbal and nonverbal communication conveys essential meaning only when accompanied by emotions or feelings. In particular, affects serve as exquisitely sensitive signals providing meaningful information during the course of interpersonal communication. In fact, the quality of our human connectedness depends on the capacity to convey and experience our feelings with, and for, one another.

All forms of psychotherapy involve the communication of affect between therapist and patient. Empathy on the part of the therapist is a basic requirement for any type of therapy to be effective. If a therapist lacks empathy, a trusting therapeutic alliance cannot develop, and therapy will most likely fail. The empathic process involves understanding the affective-cognitive-perceptual internal experiences of the patient. This activity requires the therapist to transiently introject and identify with the patient's feelings and projections. Clinical change is facilitated by the therapist's ability to understand and communicate back to the patient the latter's inner emotional experience. With certain patients, the therapist may experience different ego states, including boredom, depersonalization, and emptiness. The first paper, "Altered States of Consciousness in the Analyst" (Glucksman, M.L., 1998), describes the various emotional states that may be evoked in the therapist during the empathic process. The second paper, "Affect Dysregulation: Defense or Deficit" (Glucksman, M.L., 2000), examines the various ways that patients defend against painful or intolerable affects. It also explores how individuals fail to differentiate and experience affects, resulting in deficits of self-representation that include inner blankness or emptiness. In addition, the paper describes the neurobiological substrate of emotional regulation. This involves components of the limbic system, including the amygdala, hippocampus, anterior cingulate, medial, and lateral prefrontal cortex. In the course of development, repeated experiences lead to cognitive-affective schemata of feeling, thinking, and behavior that correspond to different neuronal pathways or networks. The latter are mediated by a number of neurotransmitters that facilitate qualitative differences among affects. Both of these papers focus on affective phenomena in the therapeutic relationship and are connected to the next chapter, which examines the process of clinical change.

References:

Sifneos, P.E., "The Prevalence of 'Alexithymic' Characteristics in Psychosomatic Patients," *Psychotherapy and Psychosomatics*, 22 (1973): 255-262.

Nemiah, J.C., "Alexithymia: Theoretical Considerations," *Psychotherapy and Psychosomatics*, 28 (1977): 199-206.

Glucksman, M.L., "Altered States of Consciousness in the Analyst," *Journal of the American Academy of Psychoanalysis*, Vol. 26, No. 2 (1998): 197-207.

Glucksman, M.L., "Affect Dysregulation: Defense or Deficit?", *Journal of the American Academy of Psychoanalysis*, Vol. 28, No. 2 (2000): 263-273.

ALTERED STATES OF CONSCIOUSNESS IN THE ANALYST
MYRON L. GLUCKSMAN, M.D.*

Introduction:

In this article, I explore altered states of consciousness evoked in the analyst during treatment. These altered states include dissociation, depersonalization, feelings of unreality, inattentiveness, boredom, sleepiness, and emptiness (the latter consists of a lack of self-experience affectively, cognitively, and perceptually). In general, altered states of consciousness in the analyst are either defensive in function, or represent a form of identification with the patient. They can be considered part of the wide array of cognitive, affective, perceptual, somatic, and behavioral responses that are countertransferential in nature. For purposes of this inquiry, I am referring to the "totalistic" concept of countertransference, which includes the analyst's empathic, identificatory, and idiosyncratic responses to the patient (Racker,1957, Tansey and Burke, 1989). Freud (1912) suggests that the optimal state of consciousness for the analyst is one of "evenly suspended attention" (p. 111). In this mental state, the analyst's unconscious becomes a "receptive organ" toward the transmitting unconscious of the patient. Freud's description of the relationship between the analyst's and the patient's unconscious connotes an interactive process in which conscious as well as unconscious information is transmitted by the patient, received and retransmitted by the analyst (the converse is also true). In our moment-to-moment communication with patients, we are subjected to an enormous number of stimuli consisting of language, ideation, imagery, feelings, and behavior. This sensory input continually influences the level and quality of our state of consciousness. The latter consists of a continuum ranging from alertness and attentiveness to inattentiveness and sleepiness. As part of the empathic process, we attempt to understand the affective-cognitive-perceptual inner experiences of our patients. This activity involves transient or trial introjections and identifications in response to our patients' productions and projections. Grotstein (1994) defines empathy as the analyst's trial introjective identifications in response to the patient's projections. Grotstein views projection and projective identification as closely related processes, since from the object relations' point of view, "one cannot project without the availability of an object to contain the projective identities" (p. 716). In projective identification, the analyst's identification with the patient's projected identification constitutes introjective identification. According to Grotstein, introjective identification may lead to projective counter identification (e.g., what the analyst counterprojects into the patient either intrapsychically or interpersonally), which is a manifestation of the initial stage of countertransference. This may evolve into countertransference proper, which derives from the analyst's idiosyncratic personality structure, and is not directly evoked by the patient's projections. As a group, altered states of consciousness in the analyst are clinically meaningful phenomena that can be considered part of the empathic, identificatory, and idiosyncratic aspects of the countertransferential process.

A number of investigators have explored both the defensive and identification aspects of the analyst's response in regard to altered states of consciousness. Geller (1994) points out that there is a continuum of interest that therapists experience with patients. Under optimal conditions, the therapist is attentive, curious, and engaged in goal-directed listening. At the lower level of the interest continuum, the therapist becomes inattentive, alienated from the patient, and bored. McLaughlin (1975) views boredom as a defense against the affective deprivation experienced by the analyst with patients who deny, repress, or isolate their affects; on the other hand, it may serve as a defense against those patients who assault the analyst with intense negative affects (rage, terror, despair, etc.). Altschul (1977) believes that the therapeutic process in general, and certain patients in particular, promote narcissistic depletion in the therapist, leading to inattentiveness and boredom. He suggests that boredom protects the therapist from the rage and sadism evoked by his/her unmet narcissistic needs. Brown (1977) examines those patients in whom a whole or part of the self is dissociated, and by means of projective identification, impel the analyst into feeling depleted, depersonalized, or "half-alive." Giovacchini

(1989) distinguishes between the analyst's experience of emptiness as either a countertransferential response to the patient's defensiveness against intolerable ego states, or an ego deficit in the patient that is projected into the analyst. In the latter situation, the patient's deficient self-representation, experienced as an emptiness or blankness, is projected into the analyst who, by means of introjective identification, experiences a similar inner state of emptiness or blankness. Levy (1984) believes that emptiness, depersonalization, and boredom are closely related, and may occur when there is a failure by the patient to maintain stable self-objects and self-integration. On the other hand, he points out that emptiness or the absence of mental content can also be a defense against frightening or intolerable affects and their associated ideas, fantasies, and memories. Taylor (1984) emphasizes the communicative style of certain patients (obsessional, narcissistic and schizoid) who evoke boredom and sleepiness in the analyst. These patients can be characterized by an absence of symbolic thinking, as well as an inability to reveal fantasies, childhood memories, feelings, and dreams. In therapy, they tend to dwell on concrete events, details of daily living, symptoms, and are unable to describe their inner fantasies and emotions. Using Bion's (1977) frame of reference, Taylor observes that these individuals lack the ability to transform primitive sensations and feelings or "beta elements" into mental processes that can be dreamt about or expressed as thoughts and feelings (alpha elements). During normal development the child projects primitive, unverbalizable feelings (beta elements) onto the mother who transforms them back to the child as alpha elements in the form of feelings, imagery, thoughts, and language. It is by means of this process that the child acquires autonomous alpha functioning. If this interactive process between mother and child is disturbed, the child will develop defective alpha functioning along with a diminished capacity to symbolize, imagine, and express feelings. As an adult, the individual will have a restricted fantasy life, little imagination, and difficulty identifying or communicating feelings. Such individuals are affectively dysfunctional and may become alexithymic. As patients, they are more likely to evoke boredom and sleepiness in their therapists. Taylor views the analyst's task with these patients as having to metabolize their projected beta elements, and to transform them into feelings, thoughts, and words that can be reinterpreted to the patient.

Case Examples:

The following clinical examples illustrate how altered states of consciousness in the analyst may represent either a defensive reaction and/or a form of identification with the patient:

Kathryn

Kathryn is married and holds a responsible executive position. She has a daughter, age 12, who is being treated for a malignant brain tumor. Kathryn's husband is frequently away because of his job, drinks excessively, and is not emotionally supportive. Kathryn feels isolated, unhappy, and trapped. In a recent session, she was telling me about her frustration with her manager's inflexibility. As she spoke, her voice became quiet and monotonic. I found myself becoming inattentive and bored. She remarked that I did not appear interested in her problem. I acknowledged my inattentiveness, and wondered if her tone of voice was consistent with how she truly felt. She responded that she felt a sense of futility, but was afraid to tell me because I might give up on her. She continued, describing her hopelessness about her marriage, job, and her daughter's poor prognosis. As she spoke, her voice became more expressive and I felt much more alert and engaged. In this interchange, Kathryn was defending against unbearable feelings of futility and hopelessness about her life. Her monotonic voice reflected her suppression of these feelings. In turn, I felt affectively deprived, and defended myself against this uncomfortable state by dissociating, which was manifested by my inattentiveness and boredom.

Laura

Laura was the victim of sexual abuse from ages 9-15 by several older men. Her mother, who was diabetic and often bedridden, died when Laura was 15. Her father remarried shortly after her mother's death, and Laura felt excluded by her stepmother and a younger stepsister. She felt ignored by her father and was frequently the target of his anger and criticism. In this context, she gradually became more withdrawn, depressed, and suicidal. From ages 18-21 she became pregnant several times; these pregnancies were terminated by abortions. Feelings of shame and guilt connected to her sexual promiscuity and the abortions led to several suicide attempts and hospitalizations. Subsequently, she suffered from recurrent depressions characterized by intense guilt, shame, self-directed rage, and self-mutilation. During therapy sessions, she frequently becomes depersonalized and experiences an inner "numbness" or lack of feelings. In a recent session, she told me the following dream: "I was running away from someone, but the harder I ran, the harder whomever it was following me, also ran. I knew I would eventually have to turn around and face whomever it was; I was scared, and then I woke up." Laura associated her assailant to one of the men who sexually abused her. She hated him for molesting her, and hated herself for acquiescing. As she spoke, she became affectless and distant. I felt disconnected from her and somewhat sleepy. I asked her what she was feeling and she replied that she was feeling nothing, 'Just numb and unreal." I wondered if she had felt any emotion just before entering this feelingless state. She recalled that as she was relating the dream she felt frightened, followed by intense self-loathing. A stream of familiar self-recriminations ensued: "I'm a slut, a murderer, dirty,-I don't deserve to live." It became clear that her pursuer in the dream was not only the man who sexually abused her, but was also her harsh self-condemnation, which she realized she eventually would have to confront and resolve. Transferential implications of the dream were also apparent, but not addressed at this time. During this interaction, Laura dissociated from her fearful, self-persecutory feelings by depersonalizing. I introjectively identified with her projected internal state, and became depersonalized as well as feelingless. My transient sleepiness was most likely a defense against this uncomfortable inner state of depersonalization and feeling- lessness.

Bill

Bill is an attorney who entered treatment at the urging of his girlfriend, who feels that he is often insensitive and unresponsive to her feelings. He is extremely successful at his work, largely because of his logical, meticulous approach to legal issues. He is aware, however, that others find him boring, unspontaneous, and lacking a sense of humor. During therapy sessions, Bill speaks in a sober, bland, controlled tone of voice. He complains of an inner constrictedness that prevents him from experiencing any kind of intense feeling, ranging from joy to sadness. His responses to my questions are carefully measured and obsessively qualified. Bill's father, an engineer, is emotionally distant and highly critical of Bill's mistakes. His mother is subservient to his father, and rarely expresses an opinion of her own. Bill approaches therapy as though it were a serious, burdensome task to be carried out in a business-like, error-free manner. He transferentially perceives me as his critical father who will reprimand him for his slightest mistake. During therapy sessions, I often find myself carefully planning out my responses before speaking. I am also aware that I lack my usual spontaneity, sense of humor, and emotional expressiveness. Sometimes, I feel inattentive, bored, and sleepy. These changes in my usual behavior reflect my introjective identification with Bill's projected inner state of emotional inhibition and self-censorship. A complex transference-countertransference enactment occurs between us by means of Bill's projective and my introjective identification, in which I am simultaneously Bill's critical, emotionally detached father as well as his frightened, inhibited son. My inner dullness, boredom, and sleepiness are defensive reactions to my frustration and rage at being deprived of my usual sense of an alive, spontaneous, feeling self. Our exploration of Bill's inner states of inhibition and emotional constriction has helped us to understand their origins, enabling Bill to become emotionally freer and more spontaneous.

Carol

Carol is a recently divorced woman with depressive symptoms who frequently experiences inner emotional emptiness. She recalls that her parents never communicated feelings when she was growing up; instead, they discussed only facts and events. Her father suffered from rheumatoid arthritis and was bedridden for many years. He was a kind man, yet emotionally remote. Her mother, who never hugged or kissed her, was strict and critical. For many years, Carol felt trapped and emotionally abused in her marriage. Her husband, who had an explosive temper, was critical and oblivious to her feelings. Similar to her parents, he would only discuss concrete facts and circumstances. Carol constantly tried to please her husband so that he would not become angry at her or their children. Socially, she always acted in a way that she assumed others expected her to behave. She feels that she is unaware of a part of herself, often experiencing an inner emptiness. During therapy sessions, she frequently becomes emotionally flat, expressionless, confused, and unable to complete a thought sequence. On these occasions, she reports that she feels "in a fog", "empty," and "disconnected" from me. I, in turn, feel emotionally distant from her, perplexed, and my mind becomes vacant. In this context, I sometimes fantasize screaming at or shaking her. I find myself questioning her vigorously in an attempt to ellicit some type of feeling. At those times when we are able to identify Carol's feelings, she invariably expresses profound hurt, sadness, and loneliness. I believe that Carol's "empty," "disconnected" state represents a dissociated defensive process that protects her from these feelings of hurt, sadness, and isolation. Moreover, her inner emptiness reflects an affective void in her sense of self. This affective self-deficit most likely originated in the absence of parental emotional attunement to her needs and feelings. Because her parents never acknowledged or expressed unpleasant emotions, Carol finds it impossible to identify and communicate feelings such as fear, sadness, or anger. Instead, she experiences either emptiness, pressure in her head, or vague pains in her chest and abdomen. Her somatic symptoms and inability to identify or describe her feelings are characteristic of alexithymia, which is consistent with the arrested development of her affective self-representation (Sifneos, 1975).

Through Carol's projective and my introjective identification, I frequently experience internal states similar to Carol's: emptiness, dissociation, and depersonalization. This appears to be a transference-countertransference enactment of the emotionally barren relationship between Carol and her parents, in which I am simultaneously the emotionally unresponsive parent as well as Carol's affectively negated sense of self. My aggressive fantasies represent defensive as well as projective counteridentification responses. I defend myself against my inner state of emotional emptiness with angry, aggressive fantasies. In turn, I projectively counteridentify these fantasies in an attempt to force Carol out of her emotional detachment and emptiness. My major task in treatment is to make sense out of Carol's amorphous inner states, and then reinterpret them to her as feelings and words that are consistent with meaningful experiences and interpersonal interactions in her life (similar to Taylor's concept of the therapist re-interpreting the patient's beta elements into alpha elements). Through this process, Carol and I are gradually reconstructing her inadequately developed affective sense of self.

Sally

Sally is married and entered treatment for anxiety episodes and dysthymia. Sally's mother was hospitalized several times for depression when Sally was between 6 and 12 years of age. Her parents were divorced when she was 14; subsequently, Sally and her two younger sisters lived with her father who had gained custody of them. Her father remarried when Sally was 16, and she was sent off to boarding school. She never returned to live with either parent, and both have died since Sally began treatment. In a recent session, Sally complained bitterly about her husband's drinking and emotional detachment from her. They had recently moved to a new community where she felt alone and without supportive friendships. She recalled the loneliness and sadness she felt as a child when her mother was hospitalized, and later, when her parents were divorced. She continued to talk about her feelings of rejection and sadness when her father remarried and sent her away to boarding school. Her associations led to her grief over her parents' deaths. At this point, she became overwhelmed with sadness and began to cry. She wondered whether she had the strength to survive the despair she felt over these abandonments and losses. As she spoke and wept, I recalled my own mother's death when I was an adolescent, and the sadness I felt at that time. I associated to the subsequent deaths of my father, several close friends, and relatives. I proceeded to think about certain personal and professional disappointments. A growing sadness enveloped me, and I began to think about a recent illness and my own mortality with increasing anxiety. Sally asked me even more insistently if I thought she could survive her current crisis without becoming more depressed and nonfunctional. She spoke rapidly, and her voice grew louder with an increasing sense of desperation. I became aware that I was emotionally detaching from her; my sadness and anxiety receded as I became more dissociated. At this point, I told Sally that I felt her despair and that it seemed unbearable; she readily agreed. I added that I would remain emotionally available to help her survive this crisis, and would not abandon her. In turn, she became considerably less agitated and despondent. During this interchange, I introjectively identified with Sally's projected sadness, vulnerability, and despair. As her feelings intensified, I became progressively enveloped by them until I defended against my own dysphoria by dissociating. Moreover, I counteridentified with personal associations involving losses, disappointments, illness, and mortality. My interpretation regarding her unbearable despair, as well as my continued availability, enabled her to become less anxious, and facilitated my emergence from a dissociated state.

Discussion:

These clinical vignettes illustrate that altered states of consciousness in the analyst may be primarily defensive, or may reflect the patient's projective and the analyst's introjective identification. The analyst's use of introjective identification is a key element in the empathic process. The analyst may also react by counter- and/or projectively counteridentifying with the patient's internal state, however. The latter two mechanisms are central components of countertransference, and in turn, may be defended against by altered states of consciousness. As defensive functions, inattentiveness, boredom, sleepiness, dissociation, and depersonalization protect the analyst from either the discomfort of an absence of affect and meaningful communication, or from the pain of an overly intense affective state in the patient. In the case of the former, patients may be silent, monotonic, emotionally impoverished or concrete. They do not convey feelings, ideation, fantasies, memories, dreams, and other elements of human experience that bring meaning and richness to the verbal and nonverbal communication between patient and analyst. As a result, the analyst is deprived of the opportunity to introject a cognitive-emotional-perceptual schema of the patient, which is an essential requirement for an appropriate empathic response. On the other hand, some patients flood the analyst with a torrent of unpleasant emotions that are too painful for him/her to tolerate. They may also inundate the analyst with trivial, repetitive productions that may evoke disinterest and boredom. The entire spectrum of emotional and cognitive communication from the patient" including affective/ideational deprivation as well as affective/ideational flooding, may result in various alterations of consciousness that reflect defensive reactions within the analyst. Affective/ideational deprivation as well as affective/ideational flooding may constitute, within a particular context, resistance on the part of the patient. Conversely, altered states of consciousness that are defensive in nature, may function as resistance within the analyst.

Altered states of consciousness may also reflect the analyst's introjective identification with the patient's projected internal state. The patient's internal state may include one or more of the following: (a) Dissociation, depersonalization, or feelings of unreality. These internal states defend the patient against intolerable impulses, thoughts, feelings and memories. (b). An alexithymic condition, characterized by an absence of feelings, fantasies, memories, and dreams, as well as the tendency to focus on concrete events, somatic symptoms, and the superficial details of daily living. (c) Self-deficits or lacunae of self-representation, manifested by the experience of inner emptiness, blankness, vagueness, and impoverishment of thought or feeling. These internal states may be verbalized or unverbalized via the patient's projective and the analyst's introjective identification. The analyst may subsequently defend himself/herself against these introjected internal states by means of denial, isolation, inattentiveness, boredom, dissociation, depersonalization, and sleepiness. Moreover, the analyst may also counteridentify and projectively counteridentify with his/her own thoughts, fantasies, and feelings in response to the patient's projected internal state. For purposes of this discussion, I am using Grotstein's (1994, 1995) concept of projective identification. That is, in order for projective identification to occur, the analyst must introjectively identify with what the patient projects. Projective counteridentification is, in turn, what the analyst projects into the patient and is introjected by the latter. I believe that an intermediate step of counteridentification also takes place, consisting of the analyst's idiosyncratic associations, fantasies, memories, and feelings in response to his/her introjective identification with the patient's projections. Counteridentification precedes or may be simultaneous with projective counteridentification. Counteridentification and projective counteridentification are part of the countertransference process, and articulate with the analyst's personal developmental history, conflicts, self- and object representations. If the analyst can recognize and understand his/her defensive, introjective, counteridentification and projective counteridentification responses, successful empathic attunement occurs. Otherwise, treatment may result in empathic failures, impasses, and premature termination. Therefore, ongoing mutual exploration by analyst and patient promotes greater cognitive-affective attunement to each other, resulting in less frequent defensive or projective-introjective alterations of consciousness. If the analyst repeatedly experiences alterations of consciousness with a particular patient, anticipation and identification of prodromal changes in consciousness (early warning signals) is vitally important. These sensory cues, which precede definitive alterations of consciousness, may alert the analyst to the presence of either a defensive reaction and/or a projective-introjective process occurring within himself/herself. In turn, this enables the analyst to closely monitor and examine his/her internal responses so that an alteration of consciousness can be either interrupted or prevented. Alterations of consciousness are ubiquitous in every treatment and take place within the analyst as well as the patient. If the analyst recognizes and dynamically understands alterations of consciousness within him/herself, the treatment process can be facilitated, thereby providing a more meaningful and constructive therapeutic experience for both patient and analyst.

References:

Altschul, V. A. (1977), The so-called boring patient, *Am. J. Psychotherapy,* 3, 533-545.

Bion, W. R. (1977), *Seven Servants*, Jason Aronson, New York.

Brown, D. G. (1977), Drowsiness in the countertransference, *Int. Rev. Psychoanal.,* 4, 481-492.

Freud, S. (1912), Recommendations to physicians practicing psychoanalysis, *Standard Edition, Vol. 12*, pp. 109-120.

Geller, J.D.(1994), The psychotherapist's experience of interest and boredom, *Psychotherapy, 31,* 3-16.

Giovacchini, P. (1989), *Countertransference Triumphs And Catastrophes*, Jason Aronson, Northvale, NJ.

Grotstein, J. S. (1994), Projective identification reappraised, part I, *Contemp. Psychoanal., 30,* 708-746.

Grotstein, J. S. (1995), Projective identification reappraised, part II: The countertransference complex, *Contemp. Psychoanal., 31,* 479-511.

Levy, S. T. (1984), Psychoanalytic perspectives on emptiness, *J. Am. Psychoanal. Assoc., 32,* 387-404.

McLaughlin, J. T. (1975), The sleepy analyst: Some observations on states in the analyst at work, *J. Am. Psychoanal. Assoc., 23,* 363-382.

Racker, H. (1957), The meanings and uses of countertransference, *Psychoanal. Q., 26,* 303-357.

Sifneos, P. (1975), Problems of psychotherapy of patients with alexithymic characteristics and physical disease, *Psychother. Psychosom.*, *26*, 65-70.

Tansey, M. J., and Burke, W. F. (1989), *Understanding Countertransference*, The Analytic Press, Hillsdale, N.J.

Taylor, G. J. (1984), Psychotherapy with the boring patient, *Can. J. Psychiatry*, *29*, 217-222.

Dr. Glucksman is Clinical Professor of Psychiatry, New York Medical College; Supervising and Training Analyst, The Psychoanalytic Institute, New York Medical College.

Presented at the 41st Winter Meeting of The American Academy of Psychoanalysis, New York, NY, January 1998.

Journal of The American Academy of Psychoanalysis, 26(2), 197-207, 1998.

AFFECT DYSREGULATION: DEFENSE OR DEFICIT?
MYRON L. GLUCKSMAN, M.D.

Introduction:

The purpose of this article is to explore both psychodynamic and neurobio-logical phenomena in those individuals who have either a limited or total absence of affective experience and expression. Affect is a major component of the sense of self as well as a fundamental means of communication with others. Disorders of affect are found across virtually the entire psychopatho-logical spectrum, including bipolar, personality, anxiety, depressive, and dis-sociative disorders. A definition of affect involves three interrelated process systems: (a) neurophysiological, including autonomic, neuroendocrine, and neurotransmitter activity; (b) motor or behavioral-expressive, including fa-cial expressions, body movements, posture, tone of voice; and (c) cognitive-experiential, including ideational activity, subjective awareness, and verbal expression of feeling states (Taylor, Bagby, and Parker, 1997). The terms "feeling" and "emotion" are used interchangeably in this paper and refer to the behavioral-expressive and cognitive-experiential components of affect, although the neurobiological processes are implicit.

Affective phenomena have been the focus of psychoanalytic theory and practice since Freud (1894) first defined affect as a "sum of excitation which possesses all the characteristics of a quantity . . . spread over the memory-traces of ideas." Freud (1895) originally used the terms affect and anxiety in-terchangeably and believed that they resulted from inadequately discharged "somatic sexual excitation" or libido. In his paper "Inhibitions, Symptoms and Anxiety" (1926), Freud altered his conception of anxiety, viewing it as a signal of a "danger-situation." According to this model, anxiety ini-tiates defensive processes that remove the ego from the danger-situation. In Freud's view, significant developmental danger-situations included ob-ject loss, castration, and fear of the super-ego (Freud, 1926). Freud (7917, 1926) also considered mourning to be an affect, signaling object loss. Anna Freud (1936) subsequently expanded the range of affects activating the defensive process to include "love, longing, jealousy, mortification, pain, hatred, anger, and rage." Brenner (1992) later elaborated on the role of depressive affect, noting its function as a signal that a "calamity" has occurred, while anxiety signals that a calamity is impending. Although others (Basch, 1976; Emde, 1988; Jones, 1995; Tomkins, 1962) have attempted to modify Freud's theory of the role of affects, the concept that affects serve as signals that mobilize defensive and adaptive measures aimed at protecting the individual from perceived psychological or physical danger (including affects themselves) remains central to contemporary psychoanalytic schools of thought (Jacobson, 1994).

The construct of affect regulation has evolved from clinical, developmental, and neurobiological studies. Affect regulation is a process involving reciprocal interactions between the neurophysiological, motor-expressive, and cognitive-experiential affective systems (Taylor et al., 1997). Social interaction (including emotional feedback between individuals), language, fantasies, dreams, play, facial expressions, defense mechanisms, autonomic, neurochemical, and musculoskeletal activity collectively influence emotional regulation. Most developmental observers agree that the behavioral-expressive manifestations of affects constitute the infant's main vehicle of communicating needs, desires, satisfaction, and displeasure to the caregiver. During infancy, the subjective-experiential component of affect consists of relatively undifferentiated precursor states of contentment and distress (Hesse and Cicchetti, 1982). Freud (1916-1917) believed that mental activity is continually directed toward achieving pleasure (contentment) and avoiding unpleasure (distress) in accordance with the pleasure principle. In the course of development, affects evolve from these primitive states of pleasure and unpleasure into a range of specific emotions (Krystal, 1988). This involves language and ideation that facilitate the construction of symbolic representations of various emotions in order for them to be identified and verbalized (Brenner, 1992; Krystal, 1974; Schur, 1955). Affect development and regulation are intimately connected to the caregiver-child relationship. By means of imitation, mirroring, and affective attunement, the mother enables her infant to organize and regulate its emotional experience (Stern,

1985). Normal affective development and regulation fails when the mother is unable to understand or read her infant's emotional cues. According to Bion's (1962, 1965) frame of reference, the mother functions as a "container" for receiving the infant's primitive feelings and sensations ("beta elements"). Her task is to cognitively process and transform these beta elements into meaningful affects and other aspects of experience that can be communicated back to the infant ("alpha elements"). It is in this fashion that the mother acts as an external regulator of the infant's internal affective states. As the child develops language skills, it is gradually able to attach words and meanings to various feelings. Verbalization of feelings further helps the child to organize, integrate, and tolerate affective experiences (Bretherton, Fritz, Zahn-Waxler, and Ridgeway, 1986). Transitional objects (Winnicott, 1953) also serve as self-soothing regulators of affect. They are the precursors of imaginal activities such as fantasies, dreams, and play, which function as regulators of affect throughout life. If the developmental sequences of mirroring, affective attunement, and parental processing of the child's inner affective life are deficient, a deficit of emotional experience and expression may result. Such disturbances of affect development and regulation may lead to several clinical syndromes characterized by an absence or limitation of affect. These disorders include alexithymia and as-if personality.

The term "alexithymia" was introduced by Sifneos (1973) and Nemiah (1977) to describe an affect-deficit syndrome that includes the following features: (a) difficulty identifying feelings and distinguishing them from bodily sensations connected with emotional arousal; (b) difficulty describing feelings to others; (c) a limitation of imaginal activities, including fantasies and dreams; and (d) a tendency to focus on concrete events and somatic symptoms. Some investigators (Haviland, MacMurray, and Cummings, 1988) view alexithymia as a defensive operation utilizing repression, denial, reaction formation, and externalization. Others (Lane and Schwartz,19871, Wilson, Passik, and Faude, 1990) argue that it is a manifestation of developmental deficits in affective regulation, cognition, and self-representation. To some extent, alexithymia resembles the "as-if 'personality (Deutsch, 1942), which is characterized by a lack of individuality, a sense of inner blankness, and a proneness to adopt the behaviors and standards of others. Giovacchini (1972) distinguishes between "pseudo" as-if personalities who use inner blankness as a defense against intolerable feelings and "true" as-if personalities whose inner blankness represents a deficit of self-representation. Dissociation, particularly depersonalization, may be confused with alexithymia and as-if personalities. Depersonalization is characterized by an inner sense of unreality as well as a disconnectedness from self and others. Depersonalization of nonorganic etiology appears to be a defensive reaction in response to severe trauma (physical, psychological, sexual) and the painful affects associated with it (Steinberg, 1991). In general, those syndromes that exhibit an impairment of the experience and expression of affect appear to fall into two categories: (a) Defensive, that is, affects are viewed as signals of danger or threat (including certain affects themselves), requiring neutralization by means of various defensive operations; and (b) Deficit, that is, developmental disturbances result in deficits of self-representation (inner blankness, emptiness) as well as an inhibition or absence of affective experience and expression.

Clinical Presentation:

The following clinical presentation illustrates some of the theoretical, clinical, and neurobiological issues involved in disorders characterized by a limitation or absence of the experience and communication of affect.

Susan began treatment with me for depressive symptoms as well as an inner sense of emotional emptiness. She had an almost total amnesia for her childhood up to prepubescence. Feelings were never openly expressed in her family, and she recalled being told that crying was unnecessary. Her father, who was wheelchair-bound for many years because of rheumatoid arthritis, seemed kind but emotionally remote. Her mother was strict, impersonal, and neither hugged nor kissed her. She could not recall her parents ever praising her, comforting her, or telling her they loved her. Family discussions centered around events, facts, and tasks, but never on feelings. For many years, Susan felt trapped and emotionally abused in her marriage.

Her husband was critical, demeaning, oblivious to her feelings, and had an explosive temper. Similar to her parents, he discussed only concrete facts and events. She constantly tried to please him so that he would not become angry at her or their children. Susan reported that she always behaved socially according to what she assumed others expected of her. However, her self-identity seemed amorphous and empty. During therapy sessions, she often communicated in a monotonic, expressionless fashion. When asked what she was feeling, she frequently reported that she experienced an inner "numbness," "fogginess," or "emptiness." She often complained of somatic symptoms, including vague chest, back, and abdominal pains. These symptoms seemed to correlate with what ought to have been emotional responses. The first several years of treatment were focused on helping her identify and express certain basic feelings, such as fear, anger, and sadness. Her husband was resistant to marital therapy and tried to undermine her treatment in various ways (e.g., "the psychiatrist is only interested in your money"; "he'll addict you to medication"). When she eventually divorced him, he accused her of having an affair with me. Unfortunately, her son, who was strongly identified with his father, refused to let her see her grandchildren after the divorce. Periodically, her despondency over this situation led to suicidal ideation, although she never considered acting on these fantasies. Because of her depressive symptoms, she was prescribed an antidepressant (Fluoxetine) that somewhat lessened her hopelessness and suicidal fantasies. At times during sessions, she fleetingly felt sadness, anger, or loneliness in connection with not being allowed to see her grandchildren. However, she invariably "lost" or felt "disconnected" from these feelings, experiencing an inner numbness and sense of unreality ("they go inside-I know they're in there, but I don't know the exact words to use to get them out"). At other times, she described an inner emptiness or void, when thoughts and feelings were totally absent ("I feel empty, like a shell - nothing inside, just air"). She differentiated between these two affectless states; the former began with a feeling that quickly disappeared, while the latter occurred without a prior feeling. We were gradually able to identify a prodromal sequence to the former state, characterized by an internal reprimand that told her, "You shouldn't feel that - it's wrong." She identified this internalized criticism as coming from either her husband or her mother. On the other hand, her empty, vacant states were often present from the time of awakening and tended to last longer. If they occurred during a therapy session, she could sometimes avoid them by focusing on me - "If I keep looking at you I can hold on better to the conversation-I feel like I'm someone, a person." These two qualitatively different affectless states predated the onset of her depression and persisted following the decrease in her depressive symptoms. Over the course of treatment, she began to remember her dreams, which were often colorless and without affect. Her associations led to the recovery of a number of childhood memories, many of which were connected to a sense of isolation and aloneness. For example, she recalled frequently playing by herself in a closet with her dolls and carrying on an active dialogue with them. Until the present, she has not been able to recall an incident of either physical or sexual abuse. More to the point, if she suffered from any type of abuse, it was the lack of emotional feedback and attunement on the part of her parents. During sessions, I have frequently experienced internal states similar to Susan's: fogginess, vagueness, and blankness. In turn, I have reacted with fantasies of screaming at her or shaking her violently. My internal states appear to be manifestations of her projective and my introjective identification with her internal experience. I believe that my aggressive fantasies represent a defense against my experience of inner fogginess or blankness, as well as a projective counteridentification aimed at forcing Susan out of her empty, blank states. My major task in treatment has been to understand her amorphous inner states and to re interpret them to her in affectively meaningful terms (similar to Bion's concept of reinterpreting beta elements into alpha elements). Through this arduous process, Susan and I have been slowly expanding her affective repertoire.

Discussion:

This clinical presentation illustrates the psychopathological and psychodynamic features of a patient with profound difficulties in identifying and expressing her feelings. Diagnostically, she manifests features of depression, depersonalization, alexithymia, and as-if personality. The most challenging task has been that of distinguishing between her dissociative, as-if personality and alexithymic symptoms. At first she seemed to exhibit the salient criteria for alexithymia: inability to identify and express her feelings, somatization, and a limitation of her fantasy and dream life. However, as treatment progressed, dissociative phenomena in the form of depersonalization became more apparent. Transient conscious awareness of feelings was quickly followed by depersonalization (inner numbness, disconnectedness, unreality). I gradually began to distinguish between my internal states, which corresponded with hers, via her projective and my introjective identifications. When she depersonalized, I felt numb and unreal. On the other hand, when she reported an inner void or emptiness, I experienced a mental blankness. Although I was able to qualitatively distinguish between these internal states, there was frequently an admixture of both. Over time, it became clear that her depersonalization was a defensive response to feelings that she believed were wrong and unacceptable. These included anger, sadness, loneliness, and sexual arousal. Although she rarely felt satisfaction or pleasure, these feelings were somewhat more tolerable. When they did occur, she was less likely to depersonalize, although open acknowledgement of these feelings was also inhibited. Her defensive response to both negative and positive feelings was historically connected to her parents, who never permitted the expression of dysphoria (crying, anger, sadness) and discouraged her from openly expressing joy or pride. Issues concerning love, sexuality, and relationships were never discussed in her family. Of major developmental importance was the impact of a lack of emotional communication between her parents and herself. Affect becomes an integral part of self-representation as a result of emotional attunement between parent and child. With the development of language and symbolic thought, feelings are identified and endowed with meaning within the self-representational framework. If this does not occur, there are lacunae of self-representation along with deficiencies of corresponding affects. According to Giovacchini (1972), blankness or emptiness within the self-representation of the as-if personality is a result of the internalization of a maternal introject that is also blank or empty. Susan's parents do not appear to have had a sufficient amount of internal emotional vitality for her to introject. I believe that Susan's amnesia for her childhood as well as her inner sense of emptiness or blankness reflected the paucity of emotional attunement and communication she received from her parents. Her depressive symptoms appeared to be largely connected to the loss of her grandchildren, and were more easily distinguishable than her dissociative, and as-if personality features were from one another.

At the present time, there is a substantial amount of information that can be helpful in understanding the neurobiological substrate of emotional dysregulation. Specific components of the limbic system, including the amygdala, hippocampus, anterior cingulate, and medial prefrontal regions appear to generate affective states (LeDoux, 1999; Panksepp, 1999). In addition, the neocortex, particularly the lateral prefrontal cortex, is involved in modulating emotions by means of thinking and reasoning (LeDoux, 1999). Repeated experiences in the form of events and social interactions lead to the development of stable cognitive-affective schemata or programs of feeling, thinking, and behavior with corresponding neuronal pathways and networks (Ciompi, 1991). These schemata are important components of memory, and function as internal systems of reference that influence the perceptual and cognitive processing of future experiences (Taylor et al., 1997). Panksepp (1999) observes that there are many specific and nonspecific neurochemical processes involved in these cognitive-affective schemata. He hypothesizes that the quantitative dimension of affect is mediated by a number of neurotransmitters, including norepinephrine, serotonin, acetylcholine, and glutamate, while the neuropeptides are more influential in facilitating the qualitative differences among affects. On the other hand, Gamma-aminobutyric acid (GABA) is an inhibitory neurotransmitter, and exerts inhibitory control over affective-behavioral responses. LeDoux's experiments (1994, 1996, 1999) demonstrate that emotional learning, specifically fear conditioning, takes place through two pathways, one cortical and the other subcortical. The latter is a direct route from the thalamus to the amygdala and is useful in circumstances requiring a rapid appraisal and response, particularly in danger situations. The former is a longer pathway from the thalamus and hippocampus to the neocortex, and from there to the amygdala; it allows higher cognitive systems to perform a more detailed evaluation of the situation based on past experience and leads to a more regulated emotional response. LeDoux's (1999) concept of working memory involves both pathways; the thalamic-amygdala circuit plays a significant role in implicit or unconscious memory, while the thalamic-hippocampal-neocortical-amygdala pathway is more involved in explicit or conscious memory. Emotions (particular fear) are experienced through activation of both pathways, although the primary one utilized depends on the degree of threat or urgency in a given situation. Current evidence suggests that the right hemisphere plays a dominant role in the processing and regulation of emotions (Taylor et al., 1997). While the right hemisphere is dominant for the subjective experience of emotions, the left hemisphere seems to be more involved in the inhibition and regulation of emotional expression. Schore (1999) proposes that early attachment experiences are stored in the maturing right hemisphere and that these working models of the attachment relationship encode strategies of affect regulation. According to this hypothesis, affective communication between mother and child, including facial expressions, prosody, and gestures, are processed and stored in the right brain for future use. A number of investigators have proposed that alexithymia represents a dysfunction of the right hemisphere or a deficit in interhemispheric communication (Hoppe and Bogen, 1977; Voeller, 1986; Weintraub and Mesulam, 1983). However, in view of the fact that affective regulation, imaginal activity, and cognitive processing involve both hemispheres, it seems more likely that alexithymia results from bilateral hemispheric dysfunction associated with disturbances of early attachment and affective attunement. Our understanding of affect dysregulation, particularly those disorders characterized by limited affective experience and expression, has been augmented by these neurobiological findings. In Susan's case, a lack of parental affective attunement and communication beginning in infancy most likely led to a deficit of cognitive-affective schemata. As a result, the implicit or unconscious component of her working memory failed to provide her with spontaneous affective responses since these were not appropriately encoded during her formative years of development. Furthermore, her dissociative defenses (depersonalization), characterized by transient conscious internal reprimands, suggest that parental prohibitions of certain feelings (anger, sadness, joy) became incorporated into her working memory at the hippocampal-neocortical (explicit or conscious) level. On the other hand, the automatic preconscious nature of her dissociative defenses (depersonalization) indicate the involvement of a thalamic-amygdala or implicit memory component as well. This would be consistent with studies of childhood trauma, which demonstrate that the process and content of dissociated states are associated with implicit memory. Nevertheless, under certain conditions (flashbacks, dreams) traumatic experiences may subsequently be retrieved and transformed into explicit memory (Brenneis, 1996). From a neurobiological point of view, Susan's affective impairment can be viewed as a continuum consisting of a deficit of affective encoding mediated by implicit emotional memory at the subcortical level as well as a dysfunctional defensive response (depersonalization) mediated by both implicit and explicit memory at the subcortical and neocortical levels. Obviously, this explanation is highly speculative in nature and based only on the available experimental and clinical data. Fortunately, treatment has provided Susan with another opportunity to learn how to identify and express her feelings. Schore (1999) suggests that the role of the therapist is to act as an external affect regulator of the patient's dysregulated states so that more mature affect regulation can develop. This is similar to Bion's model in which the therapist empathically processes and transforms the patient's poorly differentiated internal states into meaningful affective experiences. Recent findings suggest that the prefrontal limbic cortex exhibits the plastic capacities of early development more than other parts of the cerebral cortex (Barbas, 1995) and that the right hemisphere cycles into growth phases throughout life (Thatcher, 1994). Kandel (1983, 1998). Observations that learning, including psychotherapy, can produce enduring functional and structural changes in the brain strengthen the concept that treatment can improve disorders of affect regulation.

Summary:

In summary, affect dysregulation, particularly the impaired capacity to identify, subjectively experience, and express feelings, originates in a parent-child matrix of inadequate emotional attunement. This leads to defective learning and encoding of emotions mediated by the appropriate subcortical and neocortical neuronal pathways. In turn, both implicit and explicit affective memory fails to provide a repertoire of cognitive-affective schemata that enable the individual to respond in an emotionally meaningful and appropriate fashion. The clinical manifestations of this developmental disturbance may include defensive dysfunction (depersonalization) as well as self-representational deficits (alexithymia, as-if personality). During psychotherapy, the therapist acts as an external regulator and interpreter of the patient's dysfunctional or absent internal affective states. This provides the patient with an opportunity to learn and encode feelings so that they can be identified, experienced, and communicated in a healthier, more effective way. Hopefully, further advances in our understanding of the psychodynamic and neurobiological phenomena associated with affect dysregulation will enable us to improve our treatment of patients with disorders consisting of an absence or limitation of the experience and expression of affect.

References:

Barbas, H. (1995), Anatomic basis of cognitive-emotional interactions in the primate prefrontal cortex, *Neuroscience and Biobehavior Review, 19*, 499-510.

Basch, M. F. (1976), The concept of affect: A re-examination, *Journal of the American Psychoanalytic Association, 24*, 759-777.

Bion, W. R. (1962), *Learning from Experience*, Heinemann, London.

Bion, W. R. (1965), *Transformations*, Heinneman, London.

Brenneis, C. B. (1996), Memory systems and the psychoanalytic retrieval of memories of trauma, *Journal of the American Psychoanalytic Association, 44*, 1165-1187.

Brenner, C. (1992), A psychoanalytic theory of affects, in T. S. Shapiro, and R. N. Emde(Eds.), *Affect: Psychoanalytic Perspectives*, International Universities Press, Madison, CT, pp. 305-314.

Bretherton, I., Fritz, J., Zahn-Waxler, C., and Ridgeway, D. (1986), Learning to talk about emotions: A functionalist perspective, *Child Development, 57*, 529-548.

Ciompi, L. (1991), Affects as central organizing and integrating factors: A new psychosocial/biological model of the psyche, *British Journal of Psychiatry, 159*, 97-105.

Deutsch, H. (1942), Some forms of emotional disturbances and their relationship to schizophrenia, *Psychoanalysis Quarterly, 11*, 301-321.

Emde, R. N. (1988). Development terminable and interminable: I. Innate and motivational factors from infancy, *International Journal of Psychoanalysis, 69*, 23-42.

Freud, A. (1936), *The Ego and the Mechanisms of Defense*, International Universities Press, New York.

Freud, S. (1894), *The neuropsychoses of defense*, in J. Strachey (Ed.), *The Standard Edition of the Complete Psychological Works of Sigmund Freud*, vol. 3, Hogarth Press, London, pp. 45-61.

------. (1895), On the grounds for detaching a particular syndrome from neurasthenia under the description 'anxiety neurosis,' *Standard Ed., 3*, 90-115.

------. (1917a), Introductory lectures on psychoanalysis: Part III. General theory of the neuroses, *Standard Ed., 16*, 339-357.

-----. (1917b), Mourning and melancholia, *Standard Ed., 4*, 243-258.

-----. (1926), Inhibitions, symptoms and anxiety, *Standard Ed., 20*, 87-174.

Giovacchini, P. L. (Ed.), (1972), *Tactics and Techniques in Psychoanalytic Treatment*, Jason Aronson, Inc., New York.

Haviland, M. G., MacMurray, J. P., and Cummings, M. A. (1988), The relationship between alexithymia and depressive symptoms in a sample of newly abstinent alcoholic inpatients, *Psychotherapy and Psychosomatics, 49*, 37-40.

Hesse, P., and Cicchetti, D. (1982), Perspectives on an integrated theory of emotional development, in D. Cicchetti, and P. Hesse (Eds.), *New Directions for*

Child Development: Emotional Development, Jossey-Bass, San Francisco, pp. 3-48.

Hoppe, K. D., and Bogen, J. E. (1977), Alexithymia in twelve commissuo-rotomized patients, *Psychotherapy and Psychosomatics, 28,* 148-155.

Jacobson, J. G. (1994), Signal affects and our psychoanalytic confusion of tongues, *Journal of the American Psychoanalytic Association, 42,* 15-42.

Jones, J. M. (1995), *Affects as Process: An Inquiry into the Centrality of Affect in Psychological Life*, Analytic Press, Hillsdale, NJ.

Kandel, E. R. (1983), From metapsychology to molecular biology: Explorations into the nature of anxiety, *American Journal of Psychiatry, 140,* 1277-1293.

Kandel, E. R. (1998), A new intellectual framework for psychiatry, *American Journal of Psychiatry, 155,* 457-469.

Krystal, H. (1974), The genetic development of affects and affect regression, *Annals of Psychoanalysis, 2,* 98-126.

Krystal, H. (1988), *Integration and Self-healing: Affect, Trauma, Alexithymia, Analytic Press,* Hillsdale, NJ.

Lane, R. D., and Schwartz, G. E. (1987), Levels of emotional awareness: A cognitive developmental theory and its application to psychopathology, *American Journal of Psychiatry, 144,* 133-143.

LeDoux, J. E. (1994), Emotion, memory and the brain, *Scientific American,* 50-57.

LeDoux, J. E. (1996), *The Emotional Brain: The Mysterious Underpinnings of Emotional Life*, Simon and Schuster, New York.

LeDoux, J. E. (1999), Psychoanalytic theory: Clues from the brain, *Neuro-Psychoanalysis, 1,* 44-49.

Nemiah, J. C. (1977), Alexithymia: Theoretical considerations, *Psychotherapy and Psychosomatics, 28,* 199-206.

Panksepp, J. (1999), Emotions as viewed by psychoanalysis and neuroscience: An exercise in consilience, *Neuro-Psychoanalysis, 1,* 15-38.

Schore, A. N. (1999), Commentary on emotions: Neuro-psychoanalytic views, *Neuro-Psychoanalysis, 1,* 49-55.

Schur, M. (1955), Comments on the metapsychology of somatization, *Psychoanalytical Study of the Child, 10,* 110-164.

Sifneos, P. E. (1973), The prevalence of "alexithymic" characteristics in psychosomatic patients, *Psychotherapy and Psychosomatics, 22,* 255-262.

Steinberg, M. (1991), The spectrum of depersonalization: Assessment and treatment, in A. Tasman, and S. M. Goldfinger (Eds.), *Dissociative Disorders: Review of Psychiatry,* American Psychiatric Press,*10,* pp. 223-247.

Stern, D. N. (1985), *The Interpersonal World of the Infant,* Basic Books, New York.

Taylor, G. J., Bagby, R. M., and Parker, J. D. A. (1997), *Disorders of Affect Regulation, Alexithymia in Medical and Psychiatric Illness,* Cambridge University Press, Cambridge, UK.

Thatcher, R. W. (1994), Cyclical cortical reorganization: Origins of human cognitive development, in G. Dawson, and K. W. Fischer (Eds.), *Human Behavior and the Developing Brain,* Guilford Press, New York, pp. 232-266.

Tomkins, S. S. (1962), *Affect/Imagery/Consciousness. Vol. 1: The Positive Affects,* Springer, New York.

Voeller, K. S. (1986), Right-hemisphere deficit syndrome in children, *American Journal of Psychiatry, 143,* 1004-1009.

Weintraub, S., and Mesulam, M. M. (1983), Developmental learning disabilities of the right hemisphere, *Archives of Neurology, 40,* 463-468.

Wilson, A., Passik, S. D., and Faude, J. P. (1990), "Self-regulation and its failures", in J. Masling (Ed.), *Empirical Studies of Psychoanalytic Theories,* vol. 3, Analytic Press, Hillsdale, NJ, pp. 149-213.

Winnicott, D. W. (1953), Transitional objects and transitional phenomena, *International Journal of Psychoanalysis, 34,* 89-97.

Dr. Glucksman is Clinical Professor of Psychiatry and Director of The Psychoanalytic Institute, Department of Psychiatry and Behavioral Sciences, New York Medical College, Valhalla, New York.

This paper was presented at the 43rd Winter Meeting of the American Academy of Psychoanalysis, New York City, January 8, 2000.

Journal of the American Academy of Psychoanalysis, 28(2), 263-273, 2000.

## Chapter 4

Elements of Clinical Change

The factors that facilitate clinical change during psychodynamic psychotherapy or psychoanalysis have interested me since residency training. My various supervisors and mentors emphasized different aspects of the treatment process. Some focused on altering the patient's irrational beliefs and expectations. Others stressed the importance of the therapeutic relationship, namely transference and counter-transference phenomena. Still others emphasized sociocultural forces influencing the patient's self-esteem, values, and relationships. In addition, the framework of treatment has been an endless source of controversy. What is the optimal frequency of sessions? Is it better for the patient to sit up or lie down? How active or passive should the therapist be? What are the criteria for clinical improvement? What are the indications for termination? These and other issues have been, and continue to be, the focus of ongoing clinical research.

Many studies have attempted to document clinical change during psychoanalysis and psychotherapy. In general, they have demonstrated that different psychotherapies can facilitate clinical improvement although the type of therapy may not be as important as the therapist who conducts it. In regard to the latter, it appears that the empathic process is a central component of successful treatment. The therapist's capacity to introject and identify with the patient's internal psychic experience is vital. Moreover, the patient's ability to internalize the therapeutic relationship is equally important. This is a complex process involving the patient's acquiring insight and working through distorted perceptions of the therapist.

The first paper, "Insight, Empathy, and Internalization: Elements of Clinical Change" (Glucksman, M.L., 1993), explores two major areas that contribute to clinical change. These include the patient's acquiring insight or understanding, as well as the quality of interaction between therapist and patient. The former involves recognizing and changing irrational beliefs, perceptions, defenses, and behavior through insight and interpretation. The latter involves working through transference distortions and experiencing the relationship with the therapist as a different and healthier one than others in the patient's past. In effect, clinical change results from the sum of interactions between therapist and patient, including insight, interpretation, realistic and distorted perceptions of the therapist, as well as the patient's internalization of the beneficial aspects of the therapeutic relationship.

A second paper, "Is Love Curative?" (Glucksman, M.L., 2010), explores the role of love in the therapeutic relationship. The terms "transference love" and "erotic transference" have been used interchangeably in the psychoanalytic literature. It is generally accepted that romantic and sexual feelings for the therapist are connected to earlier successful or unsuccessful love relationships; moreover, they are facilitated by the intimacy of the therapeutic setting, idealization of the therapist, as well as the latter's non-judgmental, empathic attitude. The major task of the therapist is to understand and interpret the past and current meanings of the patient's sexual or romantic fantasies and behavior. Projective identification, counter-identification, and counter-projective identification are key elements in this process. Therapists need to avoid acting out their fantasies and feelings that are an inherent part of this interaction with patients. At the same time, a realistic, unique type of relationship may develop between therapist and patient in the course of treatment. It is characterized by emotional resonance, trust, respect, caring, and the sublimation of sexual gratification. This new or different object relationship between therapist and patient has been termed a "special friendship" or "transformative relationship." It involves mature, mutually loving feelings without the enactment of sexual impulses or fantasies. In essence, it is a deeply felt sense of emotional and psychological inter-connectedness. Moreover, it can facilitate the patient's capacity for intimacy and love in other relationships.

A third paper, "Case Presentation: Long-Term Treatment" (Glucksman, M.L., 2013), describes the psychodynamic psychotherapy of a depressed, chronically suicidal, self-mutilating female patient. The patient was sexually abused by her father from ages six to fourteen. Her mother failed to protect her from her father's sexual molestation. The patient acted out her feelings of guilt and rage connected to her incestuous relationship by self-punitive cutting and suicidal behavior. Her longstanding defenses included repression, depersonalization, displacement, projection, and acting out. An initial, prolonged negative transference evolved into an ambivalent, and subsequently, positive one. During the course of treatment, she gradually internalized the reparative elements of our relationship: safety, empathy, understanding, trust, and stability. Serendipitously, my dog, Joe, served as a benign, transitional object with whom she developed a trusting, loving relationship. As she developed insight into the determinants of her self-destructive behavior, her cutting and suicidal fantasies subsided. Her initial self-representation as an unworthy, unlovable person transformed into a perception of herself as a worthwhile, loving mother and grandmother. Supplemental psychotropic medication helped to stabilize her mood and reduce the severity of her symptoms. This long-term treatment illustrated the curative elements of insight and the therapeutic relationship. In addition, it emphasized the value of long-term psychotherapy with certain patients. A thoughtful commentary on long-term psychotherapy follows the paper (Friedman, R.C., 2013).

References:

Glucksman, M.L., "Insight, Empathy, and Internalization: Elements of Clinical Change," *Journal of the American Academy of Psychoanalysis*, Vol. 21, No. 2 (1993): 163-181.

Glucksman, M.L., "Is Love Curative?" *Journal of the American Academy of Psychoanalysis and Dynamic Psychiatry*, Vol. 38, No. 1 (2010): 159-180.

Glucksman, M. L., "Case Presentation: Long-Term Treatment," *Psychodynamic Psychiatry*, Vol. 41, No. 3 (2013): 385-392.

Friedman, R.C., "Commentary on 'Case Presentation: Long-Term Treatment," *Psychodynamic Psychiatry*, Vol. 41, No. 3 (2013): 393-395.

INSIGHT, EMPATHY, AND INTERNALIZATION: ELEMENTS OF CLINICAL CHANGE
MYRON L. GLUCKSMAN, M.D.*

The fundamental goal of all psychotherapies is the promotion of clinical change. However, the criteria for improvement or cure vary considerably, and range from symptom removal to alterations of personality structure. Psychoanalysts do not speak in terms of "cure," but rather focus on changes in specific parameters, including: symptom reduction, affective regulation, resolution of intrapsychic conflict, improved self-integration, modifications of pathological defenses, more realistic perceptions of the analyst and others, as well as greater conscious awareness of unconscious processes —"where id was, there ego shall be" (Freud, 1933, p. 80). These intrapsychic changes are expected to result in interpersonal ones as well: the capacity for more trusting, self-revealing, emotionally spontaneous relationships, and the ability to maintain long-term, intimate, loving relationships with important others. Moreover, we anticipate that these intrapsychic and interpersonal changes will continue to be maintained long after treatment is formally terminated.

By and large, two major areas have been identified that contribute to clinical change. These include: (1) insight or understanding; that is, the acquisition of knowledge or some type of rationale that helps the patient explain his or her symptoms or problems; (2) the therapeutic relationship; that is, the quality and nature of the interaction between patient and therapist. Historically, the development of insight has been regarded as the primary factor in promoting change.

Freud (1917a) stated that "By means of the work of interpretation, which transforms what is unconscious into what is conscious, the ego is enlarged" (p. 455). His emphasis on interpretation and the achievement of insight remained the centerpiece of psychoanalytic treatment, notwithstanding the evolution of his metapsychological theories. Strachey (1934) elaborated on the curative role of mutative interpretation, defining it as that type of interpretation which facilitates the conscious awareness of id impulses and which usually occurs within the context of transference. As far as he and others were concerned, suggestion, reassurance, and abreaction were also agents of clinical change, but were considered to be of lesser importance than insight. Greenson (1967) succinctly sums up the requirements of the analyst in giving interpretations: "he must decide what he shall tell the patient, when he shall tell it, and how he shall do it" (p. 372). In this statement, Greenson emphasizes the importance analysts have attached to the specificity, timing, and language used in making interpretations. On the basis of their research, Weiss and Sampson (1986) conclude that the fundamental task of therapy is to help the patient change his or her pathogenic beliefs by means of interpretation and the development of insight. Bieber (1980) also contends that psychoanalysis is primarily a cognitive process aimed at uncovering and changing irrational beliefs, as well as the affects and defenses associated with them. In general, interpretations are intended to provide the patient with an awareness of how or why symptoms, fantasies, perceptions, feelings, and behavior are consciously or unconsciously determined. This cognitive-affective understanding (insight) plays an important role in bringing about clinical improvement.

Although insight has been traditionally viewed as the central component of change, recent research suggests that the therapeutic relationship may exert an even greater curative influence (Luborsky et al., 1975). Historically, the therapeutic relationship has been divided into two components: (1) transference, and (2) non-transference. The term, transference, was first used by Freud in "The Psychotherapy of Hysteria" (1895), and later elaborated on in the well-known Dora case (1905). Freud's (1905) definition of transference has withstood the test of time and is well-worth repeating: "what are transferences? They are new editions or facsimiles of the impulses and fantasies which are aroused and made conscious during the progress of the analysis; but they have this peculiarity, which is characteristic of their species, that they replace some earlier person by the person of the physician" (p. 116). According to Freud (1912), the resolution of transference is the key curative element in psychoanalytic treatment: "it is on that field (transference) that the victory must be won-the victory whose expression is the permanent cure of neurosis" (p. 108).

From the classical point of view, the acquisition of insight through interpretation and the resolution of transference are mutually linked. In order to understand this linkage, we must refamiliarize ourselves with the "Drive-Conflict" model of neurosis (Burke and Tansey, 1991); namely, that sexual and aggressive drives or impulses lead to anxiety because of ego and superego prohibitions. Various defenses are employed to alleviate or neutralize anxiety, and perhaps other affects such as anger, shame, or depression. If these defenses prove inadequate or are utilized to a pathological degree, symptom formation occurs. The analyst, by virtue of his or her neutral or "opaque" stance, evokes transference reactions in which repressed instinctual impulses become activated and facilitate the patient's distorted view of the analyst. For example, a hostile, competitive transference might be ultimately connected to incestuous impulses and murderous wishes associated with an unresolved oedipal conflict. Uncovering, interpretation, and insight into these underlying impulses and behavior toward the analyst presumably results in a more realistic perception of the analyst, as well as more appropriate interpersonal relationships. A more contemporary understanding of transference minimizes the role of instinctual drives and their interpretation; however, I shall elaborate on this viewpoint later.

A number of clinicians have paid considerable attention to the non-transference or "real" relationship between analyst and patient (Greenson, 1967; Rogawski, 1987; Stone, 1967; Zetzel, 1956). Greenson (1967) distinguishes the real relationship from transference on the basis of its being the undistorted, realistic, genuine part of the therapeutic relationship. Although transference is also genuinely felt, it is the unrealistic, distorted part of the therapeutic relationship. It is often difficult, if not impossible, to distinguish between transferential and real aspects of the therapeutic relationship. In clinical practice, a particular sequence of events frequently includes both elements. For example, a therapist answers the telephone during a session and speaks briefly. The patient remains silent for several minutes following the interruption of the session. When the therapist explores the patient's silence the latter initially denies that the telephone conversation bothered him, but then explodes with anger at the therapist. He recalls that his father, a successful businessman, frequently interrupted conversations with him, in order to make or receive telephone calls. In this example, the patient's angry response consists of both transferential and real elements. The intensity and inappropriateness of his anger has transferential origins connected to his father's behavior. However, his annoyance over the interruption is appropriate and understandable, based on the therapist's actual or real behavior.

Ferenczi (1933/1949) was the first analyst to recognize that the real relationship could have a significant curative influence. Differing from Freud (who had abandoned his earlier seduction theory), Ferenczi observed that many of his patients actually did experience childhood traumas, including physical, sexual, and emotional abuse. As a result, they suffered from injuries and deficits of the self. Ferenczi believed that it was necessary for the analyst to actively use his or her personal qualities of caring and acceptance in order to help the patient experience a new or different kind of relationship in order to repair the damaged self. Ferenczi was ostracized from the mainstream of psychoanalysis over this issue because Freud believed that there might be no limit or boundary to the therapeutic relationship once the analyst actively introduced real aspects of his or her personality. Freud's letter to Ferenczi (Lum, 1988) brought matters to a head when he warned Ferenczi that his technique of "motherly affection," including kissing his patients would likely lead to further sexual acting-out. Ferenczi argued that boundaries could be maintained if the analyst was fully aware of his or her countertransference. Despite Freud's disapproval, Ferenczi's emphasis on the curative role of the real relationship influenced a number of his successors, including Balint, Thompson, Winnicott, and Kohut. They, along with others, formulated the Developmental-Arrest model of psychopathology (Object Relations, and Self Psychology schools) (Burke and Tansey, 1991). This viewpoint holds that childhood physical and emotional traumas lead to injuries and deficiencies of self-functions. These include a lack of self-cohesiveness, diminished self-esteem, impaired self and object representation, unstable object constancy, and primitive defense mechanisms (splitting, projective identification). As a result, relationships with others are tenuous, prone to distortion, and easily ruptured. The curative element in the Developmental-Arrest model involves empathy and reinforcement of the healthy, unique aspects of the patient's self. During the course of treatment, the patient gradually internalizes qualities of the analyst's personality as well as reparative interactions with the analyst that promote healing and growth of the injured self. Interpretation and insight, although still an important part of this process, are not necessarily primary.

In contrast to the Developmental-Arrest model, the Drive-Conflict model positions the analyst as an old or childhood object on whom instinctual impulses are projected and defended against. Cure is largely accomplished by interpretation and insight into this process. According to the Developmental-Arrest model, the analyst inevitably becomes the source of empathic failures that resonate with earlier parental ones. However, through empathic responsivity and explanation, the analyst provides a new or different object to be internalized by the patient. Looked at another way, this process is analogous to the developmental experience. Loewald (1960) points out that analysis is "an intervention designed to set ego development in motion, be it from a point of relative arrest, or to promote what we conceive of as a healthier direction and/or comprehensiveness of such development" (p. 224). Loewald believes that the analyst-patient relationship provides another developmental opportunity for the patient to find a "new way of relating to objects as well as of being and relating to oneself" (p. 225).

The Relational-Conflict or Interpersonal model of psychopathology (Burke and Tansey, 1991) combines elements of both the Drive-Conflict and Developmental-Arrest models. Moreover, it focuses primarily on transactions in the here and now between patient and therapist. This theory holds that the patient unconsciously attempts to arrange the therapeutic interaction along the same transactional patterns that he or she has found so painful, yet predictable, in the past. The patient overtly and covertly coerces the therapist to join in recreating the patient's familiar past cast of characters. The therapist therefore becomes a key player in the unfolding therapeutic drama, and of necessity, must be an active participant-observer who uses his or her own experience in transactions with the patient to reshape them into healthier ones. In turn, the patient experiences the therapist as a new object through the process of mutual collaborative effort in analyzing their joint participation in old object relationships.

These three models of psychopathology illustrate the change in emphasis on what is considered to be curative within the therapeutic relationship. This shift has centered on the changing role of the therapist from a passive, "neutral" observer and interpreter on whom old object relationships are projected, to a more involved participant-observer who acts as a player in the recreation of old object relationships and as a facilitator of new and healthier object relationships. In the process, core conflicts and irrational beliefs or expectations can be resolved, whereas injuries and deficits of the self are simultaneously repaired.

Obviously, there are potential difficulties with this contemporary model of the therapeutic relationship and its curative elements. First, it requires the analyst to be constantly aware of the patient's idiosyncratic projections (old objects) and of his or her own projections (countertransference) onto the patient. Second, the analyst must also be aware of the degree to which his or her actual or real behavior and characteristics (new objects) influence the patient and vice versa. This requires an almost superhuman ability on the part of the analyst to distinguish between and constructively utilize these different phenomena. Clinically, there is usually an admixture of transference, countertransference, and real elements within the therapeutic relationship that facilitate change.

Case Example:

Mrs. G. entered treatment several years ago with complaints of depression and severe headaches. As therapy progressed, it became clear that she was unhappily married to a man who had a fierce temper and who was extremely critical of her. The patient grew up in a large family with a father who drank heavily and was often violent. Her mother was overwhelmed with raising her children and rarely, if ever, played with the patient. Neither parent gave her physical affection nor told her they loved her. The patient's transference varied from being distrustful and wary (expecting me to erupt with anger at any time, similar to her father and husband), to idealizing me in the form of romantic and sexual dreams or fantasies. To some extent, her idealization of me was based on very early memories of sitting on her father's lap and playing affectionately with him, or being held lovingly by her mother. During the course of treatment, she divorced her husband and concentrated on developing her own career. My countertransference alternated between feeling frustrated and annoyed with her when she was silent or detached from me, to having protective and sexual fantasies about her. I recognized that my negative countertransference was partially connected to my relationship with my mother who was sometimes unavailable and emotionally detached because of a chronic illness. My positive, eroticized countertransference resonated with happy, playful times I experienced with my mother, as well as sexual feelings I felt toward her and my sister. Simultaneous with these transference and counter-transference reactions was the development of a real, relatively undistorted relationship between the patient and myself. She experienced me as different from her father and husband; for the most part, she felt I was attentive, understanding, and non-hurtful. These qualities partially contributed to her idealized transference, but also enabled her to become realistically more trusting, emotionally expressive, and self-revealing. On the other hand, my occasional annoyance, impatience, or lack of sensitivity led her at those times to become appropriately distrustful and reluctant to engage with me. As she gradually succeeded in her struggle to change, I developed genuine feelings of respect and caring for her unique qualities and her commitment to the therapeutic process. Moreover, I felt validated and effective as her therapist. My feelings, in turn, further reinforced her sense of worthwhileness, self-confidence, and affection for me.

This clinical illustration demonstrates the complex interplay between transference, countertransference, and the real relationship that synergistically promoted clinical change. Both the patient and myself projected onto each other old objects that required resolution. At the same time, we experienced one another as new or different objects, which beneficially contributed to modification of our respective self and object representations. An important component of the patient's perception of me as a new object was my empathic responsivity toward her.

Emde (1990) explores the relationship between empathy and the developmental process during therapy, drawing parallels between the early caregiver's and the therapist's empathic roles. Similar to the relationship between mother and child, the therapist is empathically available to the patient, thereby facilitating the patient's development of affective self-regulation as well as healthy self and object representations. This requires the therapist to have what Emde refers to as "developmental empathy." This kind of empathy requires that the therapist, like the mother, be capable of transient identifications; that is, to have a "temporary sense of oneness with the other, followed by a sense of separateness" (p. 885). An acceptable description of empathy may be helpful in exploring this topic further. The following is Buie's (1981) definition: "empathy occurs in an interpersonal setting between persons who remain aware of their separateness, yet in essence it is an intrapsychic phenomenon based in a human capacity to know another person's inner experience from moment to moment" (p. 282). Differing with the common belief that empathy means to experience another person's feelings, Buie and others (1981) emphasize that it involves cognitive, perceptual, and affective components. Buie (1981) and Basch (1983) both agree that the child's capacity for empathy does not begin until approximately 14-18 months of age. Although the infant is capable of experiencing primary emotions (pleasure, fear, anger) prior to this stage, it is only upon the attainment of the ability to recall and maintain the image of an object without the help of external reminders (evocative memory) that empathy can occur. Buie disagrees with those who trace the capacity for empathy to the earlier stage of symbiotic unity, and instead suggests that the child must already have available self and object representations. These are necessary because they provide the "memory configurations of self and others that can be compared and could correspond to observed cues about another person's thoughts and feelings" (Buie, 1981, p. 289). According to Buie, there are four types of empathy:

conceptual, self-experiential, imaginative imitation, and resonant. Each of these modes involves the empathizer (analyst) comparing the object's (patient's) behavioral cues with referents from his or her own self and object representations.

Stern (1985) notes that a precursor to empathy occurs in infants at approximately nine months of age. At this stage, infants become more aware of the congruence between their own affective state and the emotional expression on someone else's face. He terms this affective matching "interaffectivity" or "affect attunement." This process is synonymous with mirroring or empathic responsiveness. In order for this to occur, the parent must be able to ascertain the infant's feeling state from its overt behavior. Then, the parent must perform a behavior that corresponds to the infant's behavior (a movement, sound, look). In turn, the infant "reads" the parental response as corresponding to its internal feeling state. However, Stern cautions us not to equate interaffectivity or affective attunement with empathy. The latter requires the cognitive elements of comparing memory traces (representations) of self and others that correspond to the observed ideation, feelings, and behavior of another individual.

Empathy, similar to the real relationship, was traditionally viewed as a nonspecific curative factor in therapy. It remained for Kohut (1971) to elaborate on the role of empathy as a major curative force in psychoanalytic treatment. In order to understand Kohut's use of the empathic process, it is necessary to define the "self-object" relationship. A self-object refers to another person who performs a necessary function(s) or gratifies particular needs of the patient. The self-object is experienced as an inner part of the self. The child experiences two kinds of self-objects during development: those that respond to and confirm the child's "innate sense of vigor, greatness and perfection" (mirroring self-objects), and those the child perceives as images of "calmness, infallibility, and omnipotence" (idealized self-objects) (Kohut and Wolf, 1978). Disturbed interaction between the child and caregiver (physical or emotional abuse, faulty interaffectivity) results in an impaired self-object relationship, and a damaged sense of self. The analytic situation presents the patient with another opportunity to form a constructive self-object relationship, which will facilitate further healing and growth of the self. According to Kohut, the key to a therapeutically successful self-object relationship is the establishment of an empathic bond with the patient. This consists of two phases: (1) understanding the patient, (2) explaining or interpreting to the patient. This may be a sequential or simultaneous process, but if successful, leads to healthier, more mature self-objects and increased self-esteem. Kohut (1984) stresses that psychoanalytic cure does not enable the self to be free or independent of self-objects. Rather, "it increases the self's ability to use self-objects for its own sustenance, including an increased freedom in choosing self-objects" (Kohut, 1984, p.77). In other words, the successfully analyzed patient, like the mature, self-confident adult, develops the capacity to continually seek out mirroring and idealized self-objects. Kohut described the process whereby functions and characteristics of the self-object are taken in by the individual and become part of his or her own repertoire of internalized representations and behavior as "transmuting internalization."

Kohut, of course, did not invent the concept of internalization. Freud (1915, 1917b) was the first to explore the two major components of internalization: introjection and identification. In fact, he borrowed the term "introjection" from Ferenczi in describing how objects that are sources of pleasure are taken into the ego (Freud, 1915, p. 136). Freud (1917b) subsequently introduced the term "identification" in Mourning and Melancholia to explain how the lost object becomes part of the ego: "Thus, the shadow of the object fell upon the ego, and the latter could henceforth be judged by a special agency, as though it were an object, the forsaken object" (p. 2a\. Freud (1938) subsequently hypothesized that identification was the central mechanism utilized in the formation of the super-ego.

According to Schafer (1968), introjection and identification are the major processes involved in internalization. He defines internalization as "all those processes by which the subject transforms real or imagined regulatory interactions with his environment, and real or imagined characteristics of his environment, into inner regulations and characteristics" (p. 9). Schafer describes an introject as "an inner presence with which one feels in a continuous or intermittent dynamic relationship. The subject conceives of this presence as a person, a physical or psychological part of a person (e.g., a breast, a voice, a look, an affect)" (p. 72). The introject may exist within the confines of either the mind or body (or both), but is not experienced as a part of the subjective self. For example, a patient tells me that when she's confronting a serious problem, she imagines me talking to her in a soothing tone of voice. She further fantasizes how I would approach and explore various aspects of the problem. In this instance, the patient introjects both physical and psychological characteristics of mine, but realizes they are separate from her subjective self.

Identification, on the other hand, involves a subjective experiencing of qualities and interactions with an object that has become egosyntonic. According to Schafer (1968)

> *the subject modifies his motives and behavioral patterns, and the self-representations corresponding to them, in such a way as to experience being like, the same as, and merged with one or more representations of that object; through identification, the subject both represents as his own one or more regulatory influences or characteristics of the object that have become important to him and continues his tie to the object. (p. 140)*

Schafer suggests that insofar as identification is integrated into self-representation, it reflects a higher degree of internalization than does introjection.

Geller and colleagues (1981-1982) point out that all psychotherapies provide patients with the opportunity to internalize their interactions and experiences with the therapist. Loewald (1960) believes that the analyst-patient relationship, similar to that between parent and child, involves the internalization of interactions that promote ego development and structural change. To the degree that the analyst facilitates healthier modes of thinking, feeling, and behaving, the patient internalizes these therapeutic interactions or the "therapeutic dialogue," despite various resistances.

Clinical Presentations:

The following are two clinical presentations that illustrate the interaction of insight, transference, the real relationship, empathy, and internalization in promoting clinical change.

Example 1:

Mrs. L. originally consulted me when she was a college student. At that time, she was forced to withdraw from school because of disorganizing anxiety and feelings of being out of control. Her parents were divorced, and both had remarried. During the early months of treatment she frequently experienced feelings of self-disintegration, and at these times, would beg me to physically hold her so that she could feel "safe" and "connected" to someone. Since early childhood she believed that her father basically disliked her. He often told her that she was ugly, an "airhead," and would never find a husband. During her adolescence, he criticized her for dressing like a "slut" and for being sexually provocative. Her mother was submissive to her father; although she took care of the patient's essential needs, she did not give her a sense of being genuinely loved. She developed a negatively toned self-representation, believing that she was stupid, unattractive, unlovable, and different from other girls. Treatment was punctuated with outbursts of rage at me when she felt that I was critical or devaluing (like her father) or uncaring and unaffirming (like her mother). At other times, she idealized me and experienced me as warm and protective-her "teddy bear." Over the course of several years of treatment she gradually became more integrated and less prone to episodes of rage, panic, and self-fragmentation. She was able to hold a job and eventually married. Her husband wanted a baby but she was terrified of pregnancy and childbirth. A recurrent theme in her dreams and fantasies was of unbearable pain during childbirth, along with being ripped apart and bleeding to death. This was connected to her expectation of punishment for openly displaying her sexuality by enjoying intercourse and becoming pregnant. If that occurred, her father's charge that she was a worthless slut would be validated, and she firmly believed I would feel the same way about her. Moreover, she anticipated being an incompetent mother, incapable of loving her child. Throughout this phase of treatment, I empathized with her feelings of terror, guilt, and shame. I continued to explore and interpret the origins of her fantasies. All the while, I conveyed to her my belief that her sexual feelings were acceptable, and that she would prove to be a worthy, loving mother.

Recently, she reported the following dream:
I decided that I wanted to have a baby, but I never told you. I'd had a session with you that made it possible for me to decide to have one-something clicked inside me and I knew I wanted a baby. It was an internal feeling-not that I was trying to please you or my husband. But I didn't want to tell you because I didn't want pressure on myself of having to do it now.

Her associations to the dream were the following:
when I woke up I knew I wanted a baby-that it was something I wanted for myself. My decision to have the baby happened the same way I decided to marry Bill-it's because I feel safe with you, I feel accepted, and know you really care about me. You've restored my faith in people-that they do give a damn. There are jerks in the medical profession, but I know I'll be able to trust some of them and they will help me get through the pregnancy and delivery. I'll be able to communicate with them because I can talk to you. I believe I can take the risk of having a baby.

When I asked the patient what I said or did that helped her decide to take the risk of having a baby, she replied:
Because you\e given me confidence in myself. You believe in me and make me feel that I'm a loving person, that I can love a baby and be a good mother. I used to feel guilty that I couldn't do that, and you wanted me to. Now, I feel it inside myself-I believe in myself and that I can do it. You give me what fathers should give to daughters-confidence

and positive thoughts about myself. I don't hear that I'm basically sick from you. My father never gave me confidence that I could be a good mother, a good lawyer, or a successful person. You're not my father, but you're my "good" father. My own father was a confidence-buster. I wasn't good enough for him. You're human and steady- I see affection and acceptance in your eyes. What helped me to survive and not kill myself was that you cared about me-you understood me and believed I could make something of myself. I missed that with my father. You give me a feeling in my chest-that you really love me. I get that feeling every time I'm here, even if we have a bad session. My father never really loved me for myself. You do.

In this clinical vignette, I have attempted to distill the treatment process into its essential components. My empathic stance with this patient facilitated both mirroring and idealized transferences as well as an appreciation of our real relationship. On the other hand, there were prolonged periods of negative transference in which I represented old objects, including her critical father and unaffirming mother. As she gradually worked through her negative transference, she began to experience me as a new and different object. That is, she internalized the positive aspects of our real relationship. Unlike the transferentially determined old objects, (bad parents), I was perceived as a reality-based new object or good parent. Her internalization of my acceptance, understanding-even love-changed her self-representation from a negatively to a positively toned one. As a result, she came to view herself as likeable, worthwhile, and capable of being a loving, competent mother. Her dream reflected her internalization of these qualities to the extent that her self-representation enabled her to make an autonomous decision to have a baby.

Example 2:

Mrs. C. entered treatment for acute anxiety and depressive episodes. Just prior to seeing me, she had made a geographic move, her former therapist had died, and her son was hospitalized for schizophrenia. In addition, she had experienced multiple losses earlier in her life. Her mother was hospitalized many times for depression from the time the patient was five years old, and finally left her and her two younger sisters when the patient was 11. She remained with her father to whom she was extremely attached until she was 12, when he remarried. At this time, she was sent off to boarding school where she met her first husband whom she married while both were in college. Her husband began abusing drugs and became psychotic after their son was born. The patient divorced him and remarried her present husband 3 years later. Throughout her second marriage, she engaged in serial extramarital relationships, each of which she terminated. During the early phase of treatment her dreams were replete with themes of abandonment, loss, and reunion with her mother and first husband. A recurrent fantasy involved her expectation that her present husband would leave her for another woman. While in analysis with me, her father died, and she eventually reconciled with her mother whom she had seen only infrequently since age 11. Her salient dynamics included the belief that her mother abandoned her because she was jealous of the patient's relationship with her father, and wanted to punish her. She recalled conscious sexual feelings for her father after her mother left, but denied any overt sexual contact with him. Her extramarital affairs represented an acting-out of her oedipal wishes, including ultimate rejection of her lovers (father figures) with the goal of appeasing her mother and hoping for her return. They also served to protect her from anticipated abandonment by her husband (who represented her father who had left her for her stepmother and sent her away to boarding school). Moreover, her husband also represented her mother who had originally abandoned her. During the initial stage of each affair she experienced intense feelings of excitement, "bliss," and a surge of creativity. These feelings resonated with the ones she had with her father shortly after her mother left, and also reminded her of the happy, playful times with her mother prior to age five. Thus, her affairs symbolized a reenactment of her oedipal triumph, as well as a reunion with her loving, creatively inspiring mother (pre-oedipal). During the early phase of treatment, I was transferentially perceived as her abandoning, rejecting mother and her adoring, seductive father. Later, she experienced me as her betraying, unloving father and her attentive, playful mother. Despite these shifting transferences, she simultaneously and realistically viewed me as someone who cared about her welfare, tried to understand her, and behaved in a trustworthy, reliable manner.

Recently, she described an episode that vividly portrayed how her introjection of me helped her to allay an anxiety attack:

I was driving and suddenly became anxious, like my skin was coming off and my insides were flying apart. It was the same feeling I had when my mother left me. Then, I thought of you sitting with me in your office. I knew I could call you or see you if the anxiety became intolerable - it was so excruciating; I felt like I could die. I imagined you being with me, understanding me. It lasted a few minutes and subsided. I need to have myself understood and accepted-it gives me self-affirmation. When my mother was with me and I could talk with her, I felt she was really there for me. I felt enormous affection, humor, insight, support, and energy from her - it gave me tremendous confidence in myself.

This clinical example demonstrates how she internalized me as a positive, soothing, maternal introject in order to contain her anxiety.

In another session, she described how her use of insight helped her to withstand periods of depression and anxiety:

The concepts I've learned with you have helped me get through my periods of depression and anxiety. When I'm depressed I feel grief, desolation, and abandonment. Then I realize it's in the past and I can let it go. When I feel anxious I recall my sexual feelings toward my father when my mother left. When I feel successful-for example, giving a lecture or having a responsive class, I get anxious and sexually stimulated. Then I feel guilty over my closeness with my father and the fantasy that I pushed my mother out of her marriage. I expect retribution-that my students won't like me, that my colleagues will reject me, or I'll fail at my writing-but then I realize it's not the same situation as when my mother left, that it's not relevant now-it's not the same situation as when I was really abandoned by my mother and felt guilty for having my father for myself. These are simple concepts-they may not even be correct, but they're helpful and they came out of our relationship.

In this instance, the patient demonstrates how her internalization of insights gained from treatment enabled her to work through periods of depression and anxiety.

Perhaps she describes the process of internalization most clearly in her own words:

When I am away from you, I continue our dialogue. This is a complex process and one that has been modified over time. When I am separated from you, my friends, and family, or when I am contemplating a separation, I am most prone to acute anxiety. When I am in a period of stress and am away from you, my dialogue takes on the following pattern: the first step is usually to picture you just as you are in your chair in the office. In the earlier stages of therapy and occasionally now I would assure myself that you were there and that if the anxiety became too acute I could go to a phone booth and call you or somehow make contact. In conjuring up your image I would assure myself that you would be able to grasp the problem I was having, listen to me, and help me. In the earlier stages of therapy this step did not come as easily and I would "get through" the situation by reassuring myself that I would soon be back in your physical presence. Although this still happens, I am more apt to be reassured simply by bringing you up in my mind: that you are there for me, are interested, and will make the effort to understand me.

Although creating an image of you is reassuring, I usually need to do further work to allay the anxiety. After a decade of therapy, it still amazes me how my mind will set up a resistance to what it knows about itself. But I often have to push for insight to allay anxiety about the task at hand whether it be driving a car, delivering a paper, or separating from someone close. Sometimes I accomplish this by mentally talking to myself; often by writing.

An example was my most recent stay at a writers' colony. I initially suffered acute anxiety because of separation from my husband. When I arrived, a clique of writers had already established itself and I felt left out. The combination of inner and outer stress in strange circumstances created anxiety that gave me the desire to be in touch with you. I conjured up your image several times during the initial part of the stay and assured myself that you would be available were I to call you. Nonetheless, I felt challenged to work out the anxieties on my own. For several days, I monitored my feelings and worked on some of the principles that I had uncovered in therapy.

For example, some of the rage, helplessness, and grief I felt at initially feeling alone in the group could be traced back to early separations from my mother. I was forced to overcome my grief and anxiety in order to make friends in the totally new environment of my grandparents' house. Similarly, the anxiety created by my separations from home could be traced to earlier separations from both my mother and father. Once I identified the intense overwhelming feelings of separation as stemming from childhood experience, I began to get relief. By the end of the first week, I had worked on my problems mostly internally, resolved a number of them, and happily integrated myself into the colony.

As far as I can tell, the process of dialogue when I am away from you began a number of years ago: first, the visualizing of you and then reassuring myself of your qualities and commitment; second, the attempt to work out the principles that underly my anxiety. Over time, I seem to have internalized your presence and the principles of analysis more fully so that I am able to work more out when not in your actual presence. And yet, even now, the imaging of you and the knowledge of your availability and commitment is extremely important.

This patient illustrates, largely in her own words' how the interplay of transference, the beneficial influence of our real relationship, my empathic responsivity, her internalization of my physical presence and specific qualities of mine, as well as the insights gained from treatment, collectively facilitated clinical change. Her coincidental choice of the terms "dialogue" and "internalized" echoes the observations of several other investigators.

Viederman (1991) suggests that the successful outcome of analysis results from the internalization of the dialogue between analyst and patient which, though guided by a theoretical model, is powerfully influenced by the special quality of their relationship" (p. 487). In a study of the self-analytic function following the termination of analysis, Kantrowitz et al. (1990) noted that patients who engaged in self-analytic work did so by "analysis of dreams, imaginary conversations with the former analyst, and use of free association in which the patient might, or might not, picture another person listening to the process" (p. 643). This self-analytic dialogue resulted in both the acquisition of insight and the achievement of greater affective comfort. Those patients who reported that they had benefited from analysis found emotional comfort when they fantasized the presence of someone (the analyst) who understood them when they were under stress, whereas others were helped by the acquisition of a belief system that enabled them to make sense out of previously unintelligible thoughts, feelings, and behavior. For some, it was a combination of those factors. Kantrowitz and her colleagues (1989) further observed that the analytic process may be facilitated when the patient internalizes particular characteristics of the analyst previously inhibited, deficient, or absent in themselves. Meissner (1991) points out that interpretations become meaningful and are accepted depending on the patient's perception of the analyst as a trustworthy, reliable, empathic individual. In other words, insight can only occur when transference distortions are sufficiently worked through in the context of an empathically responsive, real relationship. Weiss and Sampson (1986) believe that clinical improvement is brought about by a process in which the patient unconsciously tests or acts out irrational beliefs in relation to the analyst (transference), and benefits by new experiences with the analyst, along with the accumulation of insight gained from the analyst's interpretations. Geller et al.'s (1981-1982) research suggests that an internal dialogue consisting of cognitive, affective, visual, tactile, and auditory personifications of the therapist continues long after the termination of treatment. He hypothesizes that the internalization of the therapeutic relationship in the form of evocative memories provides the patient with a model for continuing the work of therapy.

In summary, recent research findings as well as the clinical experiences of myself and others suggest that improvement or change results from the synergistic interaction of several key processes. These include the following: (1) Working through distorted perceptions of the analyst (and patient) as old objects (transference and countertransference resolution); (2) experiencing the analyst (and patient) as new or different objects (real "bilateral" relationship); (3) internalizing by means of introjection and identification meaningful physical and psychological characteristics of the analyst, as well as the therapeutic dialogue, including mutually arrived at insights. I believe that these processes, individually and collectively, are facilitated by the formation of an empathic bond between analyst and patient. This requires the analyst to form an internal cognitive-affective schema of the patient and to effectively communicate this empathic understanding to the patient.

In conclusion, I would suggest that it is the totality of our interactions with patients-projections, realistic perceptions, and internalizations that bring about clinical change. Perhaps, Guntrip (1975) described this process most poignantly:

> *to find a good parent at the start is the basis of psychic health. In its lack to find a genuine "good object" in one's analyst is both a transference experience and a real-life experience. In analysis, as in real life, all relationships have a subtly dual nature. All through life we take into ourselves both good and bad figures who either strengthen or distract us, and it is the same in psychoanalytic therapy: it is the meeting and interacting of two real people in all its complex possibilities. (p. 67)*

References:

Basch, M. F. (1983), Empathic understanding: A review of the concept and some theoretical considerations, *J. Am. Psychoanal. Assoc., 31,* 101-126.

Bieber, I. (1980), *Cognitive Psychoanalysis,* Jason Aronson, New York.

Buie, D. H. (1981), Empathy: Its nature and limitations, *J. Am. Psychoanal. Assoc., 29,* 281-307.

Burke, W. F., and Tansey, M. J. (1991), Countertransference disclosure and models of therapeutic action, *Contemp. Psychoanal., 27*(2), 351-384.

Emde, R. N. (1990), Mobilizing fundamental modes of development: Empathic availability and therapeutic action, *J. Am. Psychoanal. Assoc., 38,* 881-913.

Ferenczi, S. (1933/1949), Confusion of tongues between adults and the child, *Int. J. Psychoanal., 30,* 225-230.

Freud, S. (1895), The psychotherapy of hysteria, *Standard Edition,* Vol. 2, pp. 255-305.

Freud, S. (1905), Fragment of an analysis of a case of hysteria, *Standard Edition,* Vol.7, pp.7-122.

Freud, S. (1912), The dynamics of transference, *Standard Edition,* Vol. 12, pp. 99-108.

Freud, S. (1915), Instincts and their vicissitudes, *Standard Edition,* Vol. 14, pp. 111-140.

Freud, S. (1917a), Introductory lectures on psychoanalysis, *Standard Edition,* Vol. 16.

Freud, S. (1917b), Mourning and melancholia, *Standard Edition,* Vol. 14, pp. 239-258.

Freud, S. (1933), New introductory lectures on psychoanalysis, *Standard Edition,* Vol. 22, pp. 5-182.

Freud, S. (1938), An outline of psychoanalysis, *Standard Edition,* Vol. 23, pp. 144-207.

Geller, J. D., Cooley, R. S., and Hartley, D. (1981-1982), Images of the psychotherapist: A theoretical and methodological perspective, *Imagination, Cognition and Personality,* *1*(2), 123-146.

Greenson, R. R. (1967), *The Technique and Practice of Psychoanalysis,* Vol. 1, International Universities Press, New York.

Guntrip, H. (1975), My experience of analysis with Fairbairn and Winnicott (how complete a result does psychoanalytic therapy achieve?), in K. A. Frank (Ed.), *The Human Dimension in Psychoanalytic Theory,* Grune and Stratton, New York, pp. 49-68, 1977.

Kantrowitz, J. L., Katz, A. L., Greenman, D. A., Morris, H., Paolitto, F., Sashin, J., and Solomon, L. (1988), The patient-analyst match and the outcome of psychoanalysis: A pilot study, *J. Am. Psychoanal. Assoc., 37*(4), 893-929.

Kantrowitz, J. L., Katz, A. L., and Paolitto, F. (1990), Followup of psychoanalysis five to ten years after termination: II. Development of the self-analytic function, *J. Am. Psychoanal. Assoc., 38*(3), 637-654.

Kohut, H. (1971), *The Analysis of the Self,* International Universities Press, New York.

Kohut, H. (1984), How does analysis cure?, in A. Goldberg (Ed.) with the collaboration of P. Stepansky, University of Chicago Press, Chicago.

Kohut, H., and Wolf, E. S. (1978), The disorders of the self and their treatment: An outline, *Int. J. Psychoanol., 59,* 413-425.

Loewald, H. W. (1960), On the therapeutic action of psychoanalysis, in *Papers on Psychoanalysis,* Yale University Press, New Haven, pp. 221-256, 1980.

Luborsky, L., Singer, B., and Luborsky, L. (1975), Comparative studies of psychotherapies: Is it true that everybody has won and all must have prizes?, *Arch, Gen. Psychiat., 32,* 995-1008.

Lum, W. B. (1988), Sandor Ferenczi (1873-1933)—the father of the empathic-interpersonal approach, Part II: Evolving technique, final contributions and legacy, *J. Am. Acad. Psychoanal., 16*(3), 317 -347.

Meissner, W. W. (1991), *Whatis Effective in Psychoanalytic Therapy,* Jason Aronson, Northvale, NJ.

Rogawski, A. S. (1987), Reality in the patient-analyst relationship, *J. Am. Acad. Psychoanal.*, *17*(3), 415-426.

Schafer, R. (1968), *Aspects of Internalization*, International Universities Press, Madison, CT.

Stern, D. N. (1985), *The Interpersonal World of the Infant*, Basic Books, New York.

Stone, L. (1967), The psychoanalytic situation and transference, *J. Am. Psychoanal.*

Assoc., *15*, 3-58.

Strachey, J. (1934), The nature of the therapeutic action of psychoanalysis, *Int. J. Psychoanal.*, *15*, 127-159.

Viederman, M. (1991), The real person of the analyst and his role in the process of psychoanalytic cure, *J. Am. Psychoanal. Assoc.*, *39*(2), 451-489.

Weiss, J., and Sampson, H. (1986), *The Psychoanalytic Process*, Guilford, New York.

*Clinical Professor of Psychiatry, New York Medical College; Supervising and Training Analyst, The Psychoanalytic Institute, New York Medical College.

Presented at the Annual Meeting of the American Academy of Psychoanalysis, May 1992.

Journal of The *American Academy of Psychoanalysis*, 21(2), 163-1 81, 1993.

IS LOVE CURATIVE?
MYRON L. GLUCKSMAN

Abstract:
This article explores the phenomenon of love in the therapeutic relationship and its role as a curative factor. Since Freud's (1915) description of transference love, a major goal of treatment is to understand its developmental antecedents. Most analysts agree that transference love is no different than ordinary love, except that it is overdetermined and requires the patient to view it as simultaneously real and illusory without reciprocity from the analyst. Non-transferential, realistic elements of the therapeutic relationship also play an important role in treatment. An important outgrowth of the therapeutic process is the development of a new object relationship between analyst and patient. This special or transformative friendship is a new object relationship characterized by genuine feelings of mutual respect, trust, caring, and even love. It facilitates the patient's capacity to form and maintain other loving relationships. Two case presentations are illustrative.

"Essentially, one might say, the cure is effected by love." With these words, in a 1906 letter to Jung, Freud began an exploration of the role of love in psychoanalytic treatment that continues to the present day (McGuire, 1974, pp. 11-13). In the letter, Freud meant that transference love was a powerful force that once understood, could facilitate cure. According to him, transference love was a mixture of pre-oedipal and oedipal object relations, including romantic, erotic feelings, projected and displaced onto the analyst (Freud, 1912). If these unconscious determinants could be made conscious and their influence on the patient's neurotic behavior and symptoms understood, cure (or at least, improvement) occurred. Freud later realized that certain obstacles stood in the way: some patients were unable to experience their love for the analyst as unrealistic, thereby creating resistance to the treatment; some analysts were unable to tolerate their patients' love; others became complicit and engaged in a mutual love relationship. Famous examples were Breuer's discontinuation of treatment with Anna O.

and Jung's transgression of sexual boundaries with Sabina Spielrein (Tansey, 1994). Freud's solution to this problem was to advise the analyst to regard the patient's love as unreal and to trace it back to its unconscious origins. Nevertheless, he remained tentative about the nature of the patient's love and stated that "Transference love has perhaps a degree less of freedom than the love that appears in ordinary life and is called normal" (Freud, 1915, p. 168). As for the erotic or loving feelings experienced by the analyst, they were to be carefully self-contained and kept out of the treatment. This approach led to his ultimate disapproval of Ferenczi's (1933) emphasis on actively using the analyst's empathic, loving feelings for the patient in order to repair the deficit of love suffered in childhood. Ferenczi's technique of mutual analysis, including personal revelations and physical acting-out (e.g., hugging, kissing), forced Freud to admonish him and sever their relationship. This theoretical and technical disagreement between Freud and Ferenczi set the stage for subsequent divergent views on the curative role of love in the analyst- patient relationship.

Overview

Before further examination of the role of love in the therapeutic relationship, an exploration of the concept of love might be useful. The ancient Greeks divided love into several categories: Agape, or non-erotic brotherly love; this form of love encompasses parental, filial, and love between friends. Eros, or sexual, romantic love. Philein, or the love of truth and knowledge; this refers to spiritual, altruistic, and idealistic forms of love (Coen, 1994). Plato believed that sexual impulses can be transformed into "higher and desexualized" forms of love (Bergmann, 1982, p. 109). Freud (1921), apparently influenced by Plato, observed that erotic impulses can be sublimated into affectionate, tender love that is more enduring than sexual love. From a psychoanalytic perspective, love consists of a dynamic continuum involving pre-oedipal and oedipal longings for total affirmation, acceptance, exclusivity, security, and sexual gratification. Mature love consists of mutual empathy, attachment, tenderness, respect, trust, affection, and sincere wishes for the other's happiness and fulfillment (Balint, 1948; Bergmann, 1980; Kernberg, 1974, 1977). A distinction can be made between mature love and falling in love. The latter is characterized by projection of the ego ideal onto another; intensification of pre-oedipal needs, particularly the re-finding of symbiotic bliss; and the expression of prohibited, oedipally derived sexual feelings (Bergmann, 1980; Kernberg, 1994). Bergmann (1980) emphasizes that mature or enduring love involves the re-finding of an early love object, improvement over earlier object relations, and an element of mirroring that is transmuted into "a feeling of being understood in a special way by the beloved" (p.75). Ogden (1986) describes a continuous interplay of projective identifications that enable the lover to perceive, understand, and experience the beloved. In psychodynamic terms, mature, romantic love appears to be a complex cognitive, emotional state, based on earlier object relations, idealization, uninhibited expression of sexual feelings, and the ability to negotiate ongoing mutual projective identifications in a satisfactory way (Gabbard, 1996b; Ogden, 1986). Long-term, intimate, loving relationships (e.g., marriage) are most likely dependent on the successful integration of these elements.

Having explored both philosophical and psychoanalytic concepts of love, an examination of the significance of love in the therapeutic relationship is in order. Historically, psychoanalysts have largely focused on the role of transference love in the treatment process. In theory, there was general agreement that the patient's resolution of pre-oedipal, oedipal, irrational projections, and displacements onto the analyst led to more realistic, mature loving relationships outside of treatment. Erotic transference and its various manifestations was the dominant focus of attention beginning with Freud's (1915) description of this phenomenon. Person (1985) observes that the terms erotic transference and transference love have been used interchangeably by clinicians. Unfortunately, this has placed excessive importance on the role of sexual feelings and fantasies in transference love rather than loving, caring ones. In this article, transference love and erotic transference are used interchangeably, although distinctions between these terms and their associated phenomena will be further explored and clarified. Erotic transference can be transient, chronic, delusional, and acted-out (e.g., displacement onto others, stalking). Because transference always has ambivalent elements, erotic transference can be transformed into equally hateful feelings (negative transference) as a result of perceived rejection, criticism, or indifference by the analyst. However, the primary purpose of this article is to focus on the possible curative effect of love in the therapeutic relationship, notwithstanding the fact that hate, rage, and aggression are frequent components of transference love. In any event, Freud's (1915) emphasis that the role of the analyst is to analyze and understand all the past and current meanings of the patient's love has remained a central focus of treatment. On the other hand, the tenacity and intensity of the patient's love has often been a major obstacle or resistance to the analyst's efforts. Freud offered no suggestions regarding the analyst's sexual feelings and fantasies for the patient except to suggest that "The course the analyst must pursue . . . is one for which there is no model in real life" (Freud, 1915, p. 766). It remained for others, beginning with Ferenczi, to address that issue (Lothane, 1998). Over time, the definition of transference gradually expanded to include the totality of the patient's experience with the analyst. Balint (1952) believes that the analyst provides the patient with a new relational experience in order to repair developmental traumas. Silverberg (1948) points out that in addition to transference distortions and unrealistic expectations, the patient also harbors a wish for the relationship with the analyst to become a different and more successful one than previous relationships. Loewald (1960) and Schafer (1977, 1993) note that in the course of analyzing transference love, the patient has the opportunity to not only work through old, unsatisfactory object relations, but can also learn newer, healthier ways of loving through the new object relationship with the analyst. Loewald (1970) emphasizes the analyst's love and respect for the patient's attempts to correct previous developmental failures, stating that "in our best moments of dispassionate and objective analyzing we love our object, the patient" (p. 297). Kohut (1959, 1971), though never using the term love, focuses on empathic listening, mirroring, and idealizing in order to repair earlier narcissistic injuries, thereby promoting self-object cohesiveness. There is an implication that this process helps the patient develop a better capacity to love and beloved. As the conceptualization of transference broadened, attention gradually shifted toward the interaction between patient and analyst within the framework of transference love. Modell (1997) emphasizes the paradoxical nature of transference love in that it is simultaneously both real and illusory. Sexual and loving feelings may be experienced as authentic for both patient and analyst, but they occur in the context of an asymmetrical, nonreciprocal relationship. The analyst maintains the capacity to shift between different levels of reality and the patient learns to do so by observing and internalizing the analyst. Bergmann (1982) refers to transference love as... "a special hothouse variety of love that makes fewer demands" on patient and analyst than love outside the analytic setting (p. 107). It is intensified by the lack of opportunity for reciprocity between analysand and analyst. Person (1988) suggests that the analytic situation itself facilitates erotic transference and the propensity to fall in love. It is an intimate, secluded setting where there are no demands from everyday life on the patient. All attention is focused on the analysand while the analyst is nonjudgmental, empathic, shares the patient's secrets, and is sworn to confidentiality. Joseph (1993) states that "the characteristic nature of the patient's way of loving will inevitably be enacted in the relationship with the therapist" (p. 107). She emphasizes the enormous pressure exerted by the patient on the analyst to enact transference love. Nevertheless, despite the myriad forms of love manifested by the patient, the major task of the analyst is to explore and understand its various meanings. Joseph refers to Freud's (1915) famous statement regarding the analyst's responsibility: "The psychoanalyst knows that he is working with highly explosive forces and that he needs to proceed with as much caution and conscientiousness as a chemist" (p. 170). Hoffer (1993) makes no distinction between love within and outside the analytic setting, except that the relationship between analyst and patient is unequal and not mutual in the ordinary sense. Gabbard (1996b) reminds us that the patient's love for the analyst must be understood for its current and historic meanings; it is real because it involves the actual relationship with the analyst, and unreal because it contains elements of past object relationships that have been reactivated in the therapeutic dyad. Some analysts have attempted to divide the therapeutic relationship into that which is real or undistorted, and that which is unreal or distorted. Zetzel (1956) refers to the "therapeutic alliance" (p. 370) as the realistic, cooperative part of the relationship, as differentiated from transference. Greenson (1967) distinguishes the "working alliance" and "real relationship" from transference (pp. 190-224). The working alliance refers to the patient's motivated, reasonable ego and the analyst's empathic, observing ego. The real relationship encompasses the realistic, genuine aspects of the relationship between analyst and patient. Lipton (1977) describes the "personal relationship" (p. 265) that is based on the "unobjectionable element of the transference on the part of the patient" (p. 265), and the analyst's realistic perception of the patient. Hoffman (1983) and Gill (1982, 1993) also emphasize the importance of the realistic components of the interaction between analyst and patient. Whether considered real or unreal, distorted or undistorted, there is general agreement that it is the entire spectrum of love in the analytic relationship that needs to be understood in terms of its past and current meanings.

Recently, increasing attention has been given to the analyst's feelings and behavior in response to the patient's love. The subjective perceptions of analyst and patient, including the interactions between them, have become an important focus of inquiry (Stolorow & Atwood, 1992). Accordingly, transference love cannot be understood without paying attention to countertransference love. Together, they "form an intersubjective system of reciprocal mutual influence" (Stolorow, Brandchaft, & Atwood, 1995, p. 42). Countertransference love or erotic countertransference describes the analyst's reciprocal response of sexual, romantic feelings for the patient (Gabbard, 1991, 1994). When the analyst loses a sense of the "as-if," asymmetrical nature of the therapeutic relationship and believes that his feelings are real or unique, acting-out and boundary violations are likely to take place (Gabbard, 1994b). According to Kernberg (1994), intense erotic countertransference occurs in three types of clinical situations: male analysts treating masochistic female patients who evoke strong rescue fantasies; analysts of either sex with unresolved narcissistic features; female analysts with masochistic tendencies treating narcissistic male patients. Erotic countertransference may also be a defense against either the patient's or the analyst's hostility and contempt (Gabbard, 1997, 1994a; Searles, 1979). The termination phase of treatment, in particular, promotes intense sexualized countertransference as a defense against grief and loss (Gabbard, 1994a). Searles (1959) comments on his own erotic and romantic desires to marry certain patients during the termination phase of analysis. He attributes this to the fact that the nearer termination approaches, the more the patient becomes "a likeable, admirable, . . . loveable, human being from whom the analyst will soon become separated" (p. 300). He connects these feelings to the ungratified love that both parent and child experienced in the oedipal phase, as well as to the reality of the situation. Erotic countertransference enactments are likely to occur when the patient's self and object representations are projected into the analyst and find a "good fit" (p. 261) n the analyst's internal world (Gabbard, 1996a). Loving, lustful feelings and needs projected into the analyst may articulate with the latter's unresolved developmental issues, poor self-esteem, or damaged object relations, leading to countertransference enactments. Divorce, death of a loved one, ageing, and illness may make the analyst particularly vulnerable to the patient's romantic, sexual projections. Schafer (1993) points out that there may be several defensive reasons for a male analyst to develop an erotic countertransference; these include a need to avoid a female patient's aggression, to bolster his own flagging self-esteem, to enliven an "emotionally dead" (p. 86) analysand, and to avoid recognition of a maternal transference. Gabbard (1994b) adds that sexualization of the countertransference may defend against feelings of love which many analysts find more difficult to tolerate than lustful, sexual feelings.

While there is uniform agreement that working through transference-countertransference love is beneficial to the treatment process, there are some clinicians who claim that it can be distinguished from mature, genuine, undistorted loving feelings between analyst and patient (Hirsch, 1994). In fact, the power and therapeutic value of "analytic love" (p. 252) of this sort is thought to enhance and further the therapeutic process (Shaw, 2003). Thompson (1998) suggests that a unique type of friendship develops between the analyst and patient who survive feelings of loving and hating in the course of treatment. This special friendship can be characterized by emotional intimacy, trust, forgiveness, endurance of frustration, generosity of time and spirit, and the sublimation of sexual gratification. He cites Freud (1921) who describes friendships as an outgrowth of "sexual impulsions that are inhibited in their aims which achieve such lasting ties between people" (p. 115). In particular, the longevity, devotion, and self-sacrifice of a strong friendship are compensation for the non-gratification of sexual impulses as well as the freedom from the emotional upheavals of a sexual relationship. Novick and Novick (2000) observe that meaningful and lasting change occurs "in the context of the analyst's reality-based respect, admiration, and love for the patient" (p. 215). Suttie (1935) feels that the goal of psychoanalytic treatment is "the overcoming of the barriers to loving and feeling oneself loved" (pp. 53-54). Loewald (1960) states that analysts must have "love and respect for the individual and individual development" in order for the treatment to be successful (p. 20). Coen (1994) believes that out of the crucible of passionate feelings, including love and hate, a transformative love evolves between analyst and patient that is not necessarily curative, but facilitates change. Shaw (2003) points out that the analyst's dedication to the growth and safety of the analysand is in itself an act of love and respect. After exploring a full range of feelings toward one another, analyst and patient eventually experience mutual "respect, understanding, acceptance, empathy, admiration, caring, and a sincere wish for the other's happiness, fulfillment and love" (p. 270). Davies (1998) ventures further, suggesting that following successful working-through of transference-countertransference love, analyst and analysand, similar to the post-oedipal parent and child, may acknowledge and contain healthy sexual and romantic feelings for each other in the safe-enough environment of therapy. In summary, a number of clinicians believe that within the context of exploring and understanding transference-countertransference issues (including transference love), genuine, realistic feelings of respect, caring, and even love, can develop between analyst and patient. These feelings are especially promoted by the intimate nature of the relationship, free from outside influences. A special kind of friendship develops, albeit asymmetrical and nonreciprocal, which is confined to the boundaries governing the therapeutic relationship. The caring, respectful, loving elements of this friendship are thought to facilitate the patient's growth and change.

Case Presentations:

The following are two case presentations that illustrate the complex nature of transference-countertransference phenomena, especially transference-countertransference love, and the unique type of friendship between analyst and patient that can develop in the context of treatment:

1. Katherine originally sought treatment because she was unhappy with her second husband's reluctance to have a child. Her first marriage was childless and ended in divorce. Her second husband was 15 years older and already had two adult daughters from his first marriage. While in therapy, she became pregnant, gave birth to a daughter and terminated treatment. At age 10, her daughter was diagnosed with a brain tumor which was surgically removed. Unfortunately, this procedure left her with residual brain damage, hormonal dysfunction, and learning difficulties. Katherine's husband developed impotency after their daughter was born and became disinterested in sex. His employment was sporadic, and Katherine became the family breadwinner. She held a responsible job and was extremely competent at her work. Her husband drank excessively and was often emotionally distant. She returned to therapy depressed, trapped in a sexless marriage, and burdened with a sick child. She also developed physical problems of her own, including severe migraine headaches. At the beginning of treatment, she revealed that a major reason for having left therapy the first time

was because she felt that I seemed indifferent to her feelings. She connected this perception to her first husband's lack of emotional attunement and his extramarital affairs. Moreover, her father, although a kind man, was neither emotionally expressive nor overtly affectionate. Her mother, though nurturing, was not overtly demonstrative. Nevertheless, she believed that both parents loved her.

As therapy progressed, Katherine began looking forward to her sessions and felt that the time spent with me was her only opportunity for being understood and valued. She responded well to an antidepressant (sertraline 100-400 mg. per day), and her general functioning improved. As her trust in me deepened, she stated that she could express herself openly and honestly, without fear of criticism or rejection. She respected the way I thought about her problems and conflicts, idealizing my intellect and knowledge. Gradually, she revealed her romantic and sexual fantasies about me. Ultimately, she told me she was in love with me and wanted to have a relationship outside of treatment. Although she recognized the boundaries of our relationship, she continued to pressure me in various ways to enact her transference love. Even though I was not initially physically attracted to her, I began to have sexual fantasies about her. My fantasies included elements of rescuing her, feeling affirmed, comforted, and masculine. In retrospect, I realized that I was responding to her projections of wishing to be taken care of, valued, and soothed. I also felt a pull to reveal some of my own travails to her, including a recent illness and ageing. Her idealization of me, as well as my narcissistic needs, impelled me to counterproject my vulnerable feelings. As treatment progressed, Katherine became more aware of the connection between her unfulfilled needs for love and emotional attunement in childhood, both marriages, and her subsequent projections toward me. Although her sexual and romantic fantasies about me gradually diminished, they were never entirely extinguished. Together, we struggled with her daughter's developmental problems, her own illnesses, work stresses, financial difficulties, and disappointment in her marriage. Over time, her capacity to persevere in the face of enormous challenges, as well as her commitment to therapy, encouraged my respect and admiration for her. The sexual fantasies and narcissistic needs I counter-projected toward her were replaced by genuine wishes for her well-being, personal growth, and success. Likewise, she accepted the realistic limitations of our relationship, and her idealization of me subsided. Indeed, our shared experiences, emotions, and insights during the therapeutic journey forged a mutual bond of trust, caring, and loving feelings toward each other. These feelings were relatively realistic and undistorted in the context of the boundaries of the therapeutic relationship.

2. John entered treatment several years after his previous analyst died. He had been in therapy off and on since suffering acute anxiety in college. Although married, the father of four children, and a successful businessman, he was plagued by self-doubts and insecurity. His father was a physician, emotionally distant, prone to fits of temper and demeaning outbursts. His mother was submissive to his father and did not protect John from his rages. He recalled hiding a kitchen knife under his pillow at night in order to defend himself because he believed his father might try to kill him. In early adolescence, an older male cousin fondled him and he recalled feeling sexually aroused. Subsequently, he felt attracted to other boys and began having homosexual fantasies. He dated girls and had sexual relationships with them during and after college. His wife was sexually naïve when he met her and made few demands on him as a lover. At the time he entered treatment, their sexual relationship was almost nonexistent. John's sexual fantasies were primarily homosexual, although he had never acted on them.

He claimed that his previous analyst strongly suggested that he never give in to them. During the initial phase of therapy, John was wary of me and eager to please to the point of being obsequious. He was fearful of male authority figures, socially inhibited, and afraid of confrontation. His dreams were replete with other men attacking or trying to kill him. In early transference dreams, I was cast in the role of a critical, threatening, male authority. He had no close male friends, and derived erotic gratification from either visiting gay internet sites or fantasizing about other nude men at the sauna in his gym. He was especially attracted to men who had ample bodily hair and uncircumcised penises (similar to his father). In his fantasies about these men, he was the one who performed fellatio, feeling loved and safe during the act. He denied having sexual fantasies about me, claiming that I was a father figure and that it would be incestuous. I did not experience sexual fantasies toward him during sessions, even though I attempted to transiently identify with him when he described his homosexual activities. Kernberg (1994) suggests that analysts should tolerate the development of sexual feelings and fantasies for their analysands, both homosexual and heterosexual, in order to better understand their patients' transference love dynamics. Although I did not experience sexual fantasies or feelings toward him, I did feel protective and supportive of him. In addition, I was envious of his material success, and sometimes annoyed at his passive-aggressive behavior. The latter included complaints about my fee, requests to change appointments, and references to his successful investments. My countertransference was characterized, by a counter-projective response to his projections of a need for love and safety, as well as his competitiveness toward me. It became clear from his dreams and fantasies that John's homosexual longings were connected to the love and approval he craved, but never received from his father. For him, sexual intimacy was synonymous with love and emotional attunement. Because his wife was sexually inhibited and emotionally constricted, there was little possibility for him to change their relationship. On the other hand, with my tacit approval, he sought out discrete relationships with other men. However, his sexual liaisons only temporarily satisfied his needs for love, soothing, and safety. Nevertheless, the more contact he had with other men, including a heterosexual friend, the greater comfort and security he felt with them. His dream imagery gradually changed from playing a passive role with threatening men to being more assertive and effective. He assumed a leadership role in a men's group at his church, and became more self-confident at business meetings. Gradually, he was able to understand the difference between sexual intimacy and genuine caring, loving feelings for another man. However, he was unable to develop the same level of emotional intimacy with his wife. Moreover, he was neither able to leave her, nor willing to come out of the closet because of concern that his children would lose respect for him. In retrospect, he realized that the only individuals he had ever fully trusted were his previous analyst and me. While exploring this issue, he acknowledged that not only did he trust and respect me, but he also loved me, although without conscious sexual feelings. Moreover, there was no evidence in his manifest dream content of a sexualized transference. For my part, I felt a deep affection and respect for his ongoing struggle to find intimacy and security. At this point in therapy, we had weathered many crises together, including our respective health problems, hospitalizations, and surgeries. In addition, we contended with John's troubled marriage, conflicts with his children, business problems, and his ongoing search for a sexual identity. From the crucible of our transference-countertransference projections and needs, there gradually emerged a mutual bond of realistic, respectful, loving feelings for each other.

Discussion:

These case presentations illustrate the complex admixture of negative trans-ference/ transference-countertransference phenomena (including transfer-ence-countertransference love), and realistic, mature loving feelings between analyst and patient. Katherine discontinued therapy because of a negative transference toward me that was partly connected to her first husband and father. Her resumption of treatment was partly motivated by her daughter's illness and an unsatisfactory, sexless marriage. In addition, she may have unconsciously wished to experience a more intimate, loving relationship with me than she had with her father and husbands. I believe that her erotic transference was, in part, a projection and displacement of her yearning for her father's love as well as for emotional and sexual intimacy with her husband. My empathic, understanding role further fueled her romantic, sexual fantasies toward me. Her idealization of my intellectual abilities and therapeutic skills articulated with my narcissistic needs for affirmation of my professional competence. In addition, my feelings of vulnerability be-cause of ageing and a recent illness prompted me to counterproject sexual fantasies toward her that consisted of feeling potent, valued, and comforted. Perhaps, my unresolved needs for love and protection because of the death of my mother when I was an adolescent resonated with her unsatisfied needs for love and nurturing from her mother when she was a child. Moreover, her projected wishes to be rescued from an untenable marriage stirred my needs to be rescued from the inevitability of physical decline and death. These projections and counter-projections were intensified by the protected intimacy of the therapeutic setting unencumbered by outside realities. It could be inferred that these interactions between Katherine and me, in-cluding idealization, projection, and counter-projection of ungratified needs from earlier object relations, along with mutual sexual stimulation, fit the criteria for falling in love (Bergmann, 1980; Kernberg, 1994; Ogden, 1986). As Freud (1915) observes, transference (and countertransference) love is no different than normal love except that it occurs in the context of treatment. On the other hand, while Katherine and I were working through these ide-alizations and projections, another equally, if not more important, process was taking place concurrently. I believe that she realistically perceived certain aspects of our relationship that were new or different than her previous relationships. My empathic attunement and exploration of her unconscious motivations constituted a unique experience for her. She identified with and internalized my exploratory approach to problems, as well as my tolerance for ambiguity, conflict, and emotional discomfort. As others have commented, her relationship with me could be viewed as a novel mode of experience and a different kind of relating with a new object (Horner, 1987; Loewald, 1960; Schafer, 1977, 1993). A natural corollary of our evolving relationship included her realistic feelings of respect, trust, and affection for me. From my perspective, I developed genuine feelings of respect, admiration, and affection for her commitment to growth and change. Altogether, our reciprocal feelings of trust, affection, and concern for the other's well-being constituted a mature, realistic, loving relationship admixed with transference-countertransference love.

The early phase of John's treatment was characterized by a negative transference in which he projected and displaced his distrust and fear of his father onto me. John's father was in the army during World War II, and away from home during the first 3 years of his life. During this period, he had his mother's undivided attention as the youngest child. However, when his father returned home, his world abruptly and traumatically changed. He was terrified by his father's rages and beatings of his older brother and himself. His mother, frightened and submissive, did not protect him from his father's brutality. For much of his childhood, he was afraid that his father might actually kill him. A vivid memory was of his hirsute, uncircumcized father walking around the house naked. Another recollection was of his father, a physician, about to perform a tonsillectomy on him when he was 10. A terrifying image of his father in surgical mask and gown applying an ether mask over his face remained with him throughout his life. With neither affection nor love from his father, he developed a "crush" on a male elementary school classmate in the absence of sexual feelings. In early adolescence, an older male cousin fondled him, resulting in his first homosexual arousal. John's dreams were replete with threats of being injured or killed by other men. Consciously, he felt anxious in social or business settings where men were present. His fantasies consisted of hugging, kissing, or engaging in fellatio with men who were hairy and uncircumcised. It was only in these fantasies that he felt safe and loved. Although he could be sexually aroused by women, he was not as physically attracted to them as he was to men. It became evident to us that John's homosexual fantasies were partly derived from his unsuccessful attempts to gain his father's love and approval. As therapy progressed, he gradually became more trusting and candid with me about his fantasy and dream life. However, his conscious fears of being cheated by business partners or audited by the Internal Revenue Service, stimulated my fears of being sued for malpractice or criticized by my professional peers. His projections of being injured by male authority figures and rivals evoked my counter-projections involving fear of injury by men, particularly my older brother, when I was growing up. A turning point in treatment occurred when John permitted himself to have a sexual liaison with another man. He had my tacit approval, and did not feel the guilt and shame he anticipated. On the other hand, the actual experience fell short of the love and intimacy he imagined in his fantasies. Although the compulsive urge to act on his fantasies did not abate, he came to realize that his sexual relationships with other men could not repair the lack of love from his father. Nevertheless, he developed friendships with several men and gradually became less intimidated by other males. Because his mother failed to protect him from his father's violence, he maintained a distrust of women and their dependability. This belief was reinforced by his wife's unpredictable responses to his overtures for affection and her disinterest in sex. Moreover, she was resistant to therapy and not supportive of his treatment. Her behavior only served to reinforce his ambivalence toward women and his attraction to men. As John became less threatened by other men, he became more assertive in business meetings and less inhibited socially. His dreams changed from those containing imagery of violent encounters with other men, to ones centered on problem-solving situations. Although his sexual fantasies continued to involve men with uncircumcised penises, he became more interested in establishing emotional intimacy in his actual relationships. He began to perceive me as a trusted confidante with whom he could share his deepest fears and wishes. In my counter-projective response, I imagined him as a friend with whom I could share common interests and personal problems. During the course of exploring his growing trust in me, he acknowledged strong feelings of affection, even loving feelings for me. This was the first time in his life that he experienced loving feelings for anyone, except his children. In doing so, he realized that he could have a loving, intimate relationship with a man without a sexual component. At this point in treatment, I felt realistic admiration, respect, and affection for John's capacity and commitment for change. A mutual bond of sincere caring for each other's well-being, even loving feelings, had formed between us in the context of shifting transference-countertransference projections.

The foregoing case presentations have explored the manifestations, meanings, and impact of love in the therapeutic relationship. Transference-countertransference issues, particularly love, characterized by projections, counter-projections, idealization, pre-oedipal and oedipal object relations, as well as sexual excitation, were an integral part of the treatment process. Negative transference, including distrust, anger, disappointment, and competitiveness also played a significant role in each patient's therapy. An equally important, perhaps more significant phenomenon, was the simultaneous development of a new or different relationship between each patient and myself. This has been described by others as a new object relationship, special type of friendship, or transformative relationship (Coen, 1994; Loewald, 1960; Schafer, 1993; Thompson, 1998). It is characterized by relatively realistic, mature feelings of respect, caring, affection, trust, and even love between patient and analyst. It can be differentiated from what is termed the therapeutic alliance (Zetzel, 1956), real relationship (Greenson, 1967), or personal relationship (Lipton, 1977). The latter terms refer to the relatively undistorted perceptions that patient and analyst have of each other that are not necessarily synonymous with a new object relationship. The new object relationship or special type of friendship appears to be an outgrowth of the hard work of the treatment process; that is, working-through of negative transference-countertransference, resistance, transference-counter-transference love, sexualization, attainment of insight, and the exploration of emotions, fantasies, as well as real events in the lives of both patient and analyst. Altogether, these experiences forge an intimate bond between analyst and analysand. Nevertheless, a critical question remains: to what extent, and how is this new object relationship curative?

There is little doubt that successful resolution of transference-countertransference phenomena, including transference-countertransference love, facilitates clinical change. Patients gain insight into the pre-oedipal, oedipal, and post-oedipal origins of their fears, deprivations, losses, conflicts, and narcissistic injuries that have led to their difficulties with loving and being loved. The manifestations of transference love encountered by the analyst are formidable; they range from declarations of love, sexual attraction, flattery, demands for attention, flirtation, and seductive behavior to delusional ideation, suicidal threats, sexual harassment, and stalking. Or they may hide behind silence, withdrawal, anger, hyper-independence, and acting out with lovers (transference displacement). Whatever their manifestations, the analyst is coerced into enacting a complicated drama with the patient that repeats the story of the latter's developmental traumas and disappointments with love. The analyst's countertransference is a crucial informative guide as to the meanings of the patient's behavior. Exploration, understanding, and interpretation of projections, counter-projections, projective identifications, and counter-projective identifications enable analyst and patient to gain insight and mastery into the puzzle of transference-countertransference issues (Grotstein, 1994, 1995; Natterson, 1991; Tansey & Burke, 1989). In Katherine's case, we were able to connect her romantic, sexual fantasies about me with her lack of sufficient emotional, loving responses from her father. My sexual fantasies of being affirmed and comforted by her informed us of her unsatisfied needs for maternal nurturing as a child. In John's case, an early negative transference helped us to understand the link between his father's brutality, and his fear of me as well as other men. My feelings of protectiveness and tenderness toward him enabled us to understand his frustrated craving for love and security from his father. In both cases, transference-countertransference working-through helped Katherine and John gain insight and a sense of mastery over their maladaptive behaviors that originated in their developmentally damaged capacity to love and be loved. However, in my view, this was still not sufficient enough for either of them to actually experience a genuine, healthy feeling of being loved or being able to love. How did Katherine and John reach a point in treatment where they were able to achieve this?

I believe that for each of these patients, as transference-countertransference issues were being worked through, a simultaneous process was taking place that enabled them to genuinely experience loving feelings. In the context of working through projective and counter-projective phenomena, they introjected, identified with, and internalized countless verbal and nonverbal interactions with me. To the extent that these interpersonal transactions conveyed empathy, emotional attunement, respect and caring, they developed a capacity to love and feel loved. In other words, they were provided with another opportunity to experience the attachment process in a healthier way than they had in their early development (Bowlby, 1958; Loewald, 1960, 1970; Stern, 1985; Winnicott, 1960). Bowlby (1958) describes five infant behaviors that constitute attachment behavior: sucking, clinging, following, crying, and smiling. Loewald (1960) suggests that the parent-child relationship serves as a model for the analyst-patient relationship. In the former, the child internalizes different aspects of the way it is related to by the mother, emotionally and physically. Self and object representations are gradually formed from a multiplicity of interactions: touching, feeding, playing, vocalizing, mirroring, affirming, and affective attuning. The same holds true for the analyst-patient relationship by means of a safe, predictable, holding environment that includes empathic attunement, respect, understanding, and caring. Gill (7979) and Hoffman (1983) point out that it is through the analysis of transference that a new interpersonal experience develops. Bolognini (1994) describes the development of this new relationship as the "affectionate transference" (p. 83), which results from understanding, trust, intimacy, and openness between analyst and patient. It is akin to Thompson's (1998) special or transformative friendship, characterized by forgiveness, generosity, understanding, and tolerance for frustration. The new object relationship that evolved between Katherine, John, and me fulfilled the criteria for mature love: mutual empathy, tenderness, respect, trust, affection, and sincere wishes for the other's well-being. Perhaps, it was analogous to that form of love the ancient Greeks termed "Agape," or love between friends. Nevertheless, residual elements of transference-countertransference remained because this new object relationship was built upon the scaffolding of previous ones that continued to exert an influence. Katherine still harbored sexual and romantic fantasies about me, albeit contained, rooted in her childhood needs for nurturing and affection. John continued to have a measure of distrust and ambivalence toward me connected to his father's anger and rejection. Was this new object relationship, or special friendship, that developed between Katherine, John, and me curative? I believe it facilitated cure, to the extent that we were eventually able to experience genuine, loving feelings for one another admixed with lingering transference-countertransference elements. At the very least, our realistic, mutual loving feelings promoted their capacity to change, as Coen (1994) suggests. Each of them was strongly motivated to achieve the capacity for giving and receiving love. Using the parent-child model, their internalization of our mutually loving relationship will hopefully serve as a building block for more fulfilling relationships with others. Of course, the capacity to love and be loved is not an essential requirement for every patient. Some already possess this ability, while others have more pressing therapeutic priorities. Moreover, many individuals are so developmentally damaged that their character structure is too fragile and unstable to successfully internalize a new object relationship. Others lack the observing ego, "as-if" capacity to explore their love for the analyst, believing it to be real and unambiguous, outside the scope of investigation. Some authors believe that optimal success in treatment cannot occur without the analyst developing authentically loving, respectful feelings for the patient (Gerrard, 1999; Rabin, 2003; Shaw, 2003). However, I do not concur with this viewpoint, and believe that mutual loving feelings are not a necessary requirement for clinical improvement. The new object relationship that develops during treatment may be characterized by many qualities, but it does not necessarily include the capacity to love and be loved. On the other hand, meaningful change is not likely to occur without genuine empathy, respect, caring, and understanding by the therapist. By the same token, the patient needs to trust, respect, and feel understood by the therapist in order to make significant strides in treatment.

Conclusion:

Is it necessary to actually communicate affectionate, loving feelings to the patient? This is a highly controversial issue; some (Gabbard, 1996a, b; Gorkin, 1987) believe that self-disclosure of sexual or loving feelings is often counter-productive and detrimental to the treatment. Gabbard, in particular, holds that self-disclosure of these feelings may be defensive, and only partially true given the shifting nature of transference-countertransference perceptions. It might also threaten the patient's sense of safety and imply action rather than the maintenance of boundaries. On the other hand, Davies (1994, 1998) contends that self-disclosure of sexual feelings for a patient who has a sound sense of the boundary between the real and the illusory might be of benefit. In particular, patients who begin treatment with sexual inhibitions or impairment of their sexual self-image, and have successfully worked through these issues might feel meaningfully affirmed if the analyst acknowledges their sexual attractiveness in a safely contained way. In general, I believe that self-disclosure of sexual feelings for a patient can be more damaging than therapeutic, because it implicitly threatens therapeutic boundaries and arouses incestuous anxiety. Furthermore, sexual feelings and fantasies usually indicate a sexualized transference-countertransference that represents significant unresolved developmental issues and conflicts. Continued exploration is necessary in order to understand the unconscious meanings for both patient and analyst. I prefer to use the term sexualized transference rather than erotic transference in order to distinguish it from transference love. The latter refers to romantic, affectionate, caring feelings, while the former refers to sensual, lustful, erotic feelings. Although this distinction is often difficult to make in the clinical setting, it may help toward clarifying the confusion between erotic transference and transference love. Communication of affectionate, even loving feelings, for patients who have developed a new object relationship with the therapist, and understand the limitations and boundaries of that relationship, may be validating. This is a clinical decision that depends on the degree of resolution of transference-countertransference love, as distinguished from sexualized (erotic) transference-countertransference. If the analyst decides to self-disclose loving feelings, it usually occurs at a point when the patient expresses realistic feelings of appreciation, affection, or love after a significant amount of therapeutic work has been accomplished. In doing so, the analyst needs to be fully aware of countertransference motives, especially gratification of narcissistic needs, or neutralization of the patient's aggression and anger. Moreover, both patient and analyst need to keep in mind the ambiguous, "as-if" nature of their relationship, and to maintain the capacity to contain their feelings as well as continue the task of analyzing. When one tells a friend, "I love you," in the context of mutual honesty and emotional intimacy, it is the most basic expression of a healthy, human attachment. In the case of a social or nonromantic friendship, although sexual impulses may be present, their containment is usually assured by the nature and history of that relationship. I believe this was true between Katherine, John, and me at the point in treatment when an exchange of mutual loving feelings occurred. In each instance, considerable working-through of transference-countertransference love and sexualization had taken place. In addition, each of them had developed a new object relationship (transformative or special friendship) with me that was characterized by mutual respect, trust, caring, and affection. My sincere, non-seductive communication of loving feelings was meant to be affirming and beneficial. I believe it helped each of them to feel worthy of being loved, and furthered their capacity to love another person. Loving feelings do not necessarily need to be spoken; they can be communicated nonverbally with a smile, affirmative nod, or gesture. Bolognini (1994) suggests that it may be therapeutic during the termination phase of treatment for the analyst to acknowledge loving feelings for the patient while respecting the limits and boundaries of the relationship. He states: "every good father should at least dance a waltz with his daughter . . . so that she can feel appreciated, valued and admired" (p. 82). He points out that analogous to the oedipal relationship, sexual and romantic fantasies need to be recognized and then renounced in order for the patient to find a new object relationship that is possible in reality. Bolognini (1994) defines the "affectionate transference" (p. 83) as an internalization of the analyst-patient relationship involving gratitude, appreciation, affection, and the capacity for another reality-based, loving relationship. I believe he is referring to the transformative or special friendship described earlier (Coen, 1994; Thompson, 1998), and to the mutually loving feelings that evolved in my treatment of Katherine and John. A central, though not always achievable, feature of this new object relationship is that it serves as a laboratory for the patient to experience and communicate mature love, which if not curative, promotes the capacity for intimacy and love in other relationships. Once again, we return to the controversy between Freud and Ferenczi on the role of love in the analytic relationship. Although they differed in their theoretical and technical approaches to using the power of love for clinical change, both understood its importance as a facilitator of cure.

References:

Balint, M. (1948). On genital love. *International Journal of Psychoanalysis, 28*, 34-40.

Balint, M. (1952). On love and hate. *International Journal of Psychoanalysis, 33*, 355-362.

Bergmann, M.S. (1980). On the intrapsychic function of falling in love. *Psychoanalytic Quarterly, 49*, 56-77.

Bergmann, M.S. (1982). Platonic love, transference love, and love in real life. *Journal of the American Psychoanalytic Association, 30*(1), 87-111.

Bolognini, S. (1994). Transference: Erotized, erotic, loving, affectionate. *International Journal of Psychoanalysis, 75*, 73-86.

Bowlby, J. (1958). The nature of the child's tie to his mother. *International Journal of Psychoanalysis, 39*, 350-373.

Coen, S. I. (1994). Barriers to love between patient and analyst. *Journal of the American Psychoanalytic Association, 42*(4), 1107-1135.

Davies, J.M. (1994). Love in the afternoon, a relational reconsideration of desire and dread in the countertransference. *Psychoanalytic Dialogues, 4*(2), 153-170.

Davies, J.M. (1998). Between the disclosure and foreclosure of erotic transference-countertransference, can psychoanalysis find a place for adult sexuality? *Psychoanalytic Dialogues, 8*(6), 747 -766.

Ferenczi, S. (1933). Confusion of tongues between adults and the child. *International Journal of Psychoanalysis, 30*, 225-230.

Freud, S. (1912). The dynamics of transference. In J. Strachey (Ed. & Trans.), *The standard edition of the complete psychological works of Sigmund Freud* (Vol. 12, 99-108). London: Hogarth Press.

Freud, S. (1915). Observations on transference-love. In J. Strachey (Ed. & Trans.), *The standard edition of the complete psychological works of Sigmund Freud* (Vol. 12, pp. 159-171). London: Hogarth Press.

Freud, S. (1921). Group psychology and the analysis of the ego. In J. Strachey (Ed. & Trans.), *The standard edition of the complete psychological works of Sigmund Freud* (Vol. 18, pp.69-143). London: Hogarth Press.

Gabbard, G. O. (1991). Psychodynamics of sexual boundary violations. *Psychiatric Annals, 21*, 651-655.

Gabbard, G.O. (1994a). Sexual excitement and countertransference love in the analyst. *Journal of the American Psychoanalytic Association, 42*(4), 1083-1106.

Gabbard, C.O. (1994b). On love and lust in erotic transference. *Journal of the American Psychoanalytic Association*, 42(2), 385-403.

Gabbard, G.O. (1996a). The analyst's contribution to the erotic transference. *Contemporary Psychoanalysis, 32*(2), 249-273.

Gabbard, G.O. (1995b). *Love and hate in the analytic setting.* Northvale, NJ, and London: Jason Aronson.

Gerrard, J. (1999). Love in the time of psychotherapy. In D. Mann (Ed.), *Erotic transference and countertransference: Clinical practice in psychotherapy* (pp. 21-41). London: Routledge.

Gill, M. M. (1979). The analysis of the transference. *Journal of the American Psychoanalytic Association, 27*, 263-288.

Gill, M. M. (1982). *Analysis of transference. Vol. 1: Theory and technique.* Madison, CT: International Universities Press.

Gill, M. M. (1993). One-person and two-person perspectives: Freud's "observations on transference-love." In E.S. Person, A. Hagelin, & P. Fonagy (Eds.), *On Freud's "observations on transference-love"* (pp. 114, 129). New Haven, CT: Yale University Press.

Gorkin, M. (1987). *The uses of countertransference.* Northvale, NJ: Jason Aronson.

Greenson, R. R. (1967). *The technique and practice of psychoanalysis* (Vol. 1, pp. 190-224). New York: International Universities Press.

Grotstein, J.S. (1994). Projective identification reappraised. *Contemporary Psychoanalysis, 30*(4), 708-746.

Grotstein, J.S. (1995). Projective identification reappraised. *Contemporary Psychoanalysis, 31*(3), 479 -511.

Hirsch, I. (1994). Countertransference love and theoretical model. *Psychoanalytic Dialogues, 4*(2), 171-192.

Hoffer, A. (1993). Is love in the analytic relationship real? *Psychoanalytic Inquiry, 13*, 343-356.

Hoffman, I. Z. (1983). The patient as interpreter of the analyst's experience. *Contemporary Psychoanalysis, 19*, 389-422.

Horner, A. J. (1987). The "real" relationship and analytic neutrality. *Journal of the American Academy of Psychoanalysis, 15*(4), 491-501.

Joseph, B. (1993). On transference love: Some current observations. In E.S. Person A. Hagelin, & P. Fonagy (Eds.), *On Freud's "observations on transference-love"* (pp. 102-113). New Haven, CT: Yale University Press.

Kernberg, O. F. (1974). Mature love: Prerequisites and characteristics. *Journal of the American Psychoanalytic Association, 22*, 743-768.

Kernberg, O. F. (1977). Boundaries and structure in love relations. *Journal of the American Psychoanalytic Association, 25*, 81-114.

Kernberg, O. F. (1994). Love in the analytic setting. *Journal of the American Psychoanalytic Association, 42*(4), 1137 -1157.

Kohut, H. (1959). Introspection, empathy, and psychoanalysis. *Journal of the American Psychoanalytic Association, 7*, 459-483.

Kohut H. (1971). *The analysis of the self.* New York: International Universities Press.

Lipton, S. D. (1977). The advantages of Freud's technique as shown in his analysis of the rat man. *International Journal of Psychoanalysis, 58*, 255-273.

Loewald, H. W. (1960). On the therapeutic action of psychoanalysis. *International Journal of Psychoanalysis, 41*, 16-33.

Loewald, H. W. (1970). Psychoanalytic theory and the psychoanalytic process. In *Papers on psychoanalysis* (pp. 277-301). New Haven, CT: Yale University Press.

Lothane, Z. (1998\. The feud between Freud and Ferenczi over love. *The American Journal of Psychoanalysis, 58*(7), 21-39.

McGuire, W (Ed.). (1974). *The Freud/Jung letters: The correspondence between Sigmund Freud and C. G. Jung.* R. Manheim & R. F. C. Hull (Trans.) (pp. 11-13). Princeton, NJ: Princeton University Press.

Modell, A. H. (1991). The therapeutic relationship as a paradoxical experience. *Psychoanalytic Dialogues, 1*, 13-28.

Natterson, J. (1991). *Beyond countertransference.* Northvale, NJ: Jason Aronson.

Novick, J., & Novick, K. K. (2000). Love in the therapeutic alliance. *Journal of the American Psychoanalytic Association, 48*(l), 188-218.

Ogden, T. H. (1986). *The matrix of the mind: Object relations and the psycho-analytic dialogue.* Northvale, NJ: Jason Aronson.

Person, E. S. (1985). The erotic transference in women and in men: differences and consequences. *Journal of the American Psychoanalytic Association, 13,* 159-180.

Person, E. S. (1988). *Transference love and romantic love.* In *Dreams of love and fateful encounters* (pp. 241-264). New York: W. W. Norton and Co.

Rabin, H. M. (2003). Love in the countertransference, controversies and questions. *Psychoanalytic Psychology, 20*(4), 677 -690.

Schafer, R. (1977). The interpretation of transference and the conditions for loving.
Journal of the American Psychoanalytic Association, 25, 335-362.

Schafer, R. (1993). Five readings of Freud's "observations on transference-love." In E. S. Person, A. Hagelin, & P. Fonagy (Eds.), *On Freud's "observations on transference-love"* (pp. 86, 75-95). New Haven, CT: Yale University Press.

Searles, H. F. (1959). Oedipal love in the countertransference. In *Collected papers on schizophrenia and related subjects* (pp. 284-303). New York: International Universities Press.

Searles, H. F. (1979). *Countertransference and related subjects: Selected papers.* New York: International Universities Press.

Shaw, D. (2003). On the therapeutic action of analytic love. *Contemporary Psychoanalysis, 39*(2), 251-278.

Silverberg, W. V. (1948). The concept of transference. *Psychoanalytic Quarterly, 17,* 303-321.

Stern, D. N. (1985). *The interpersonal world of the infant.* New York: Basic Books.

Stolorow, R. D., & Atwood, G. E. (1992). *Contexts of being, the intersubjective foundations of psychological life.* New York: Analytic Press.

Stolorow, R. D., Brandchaft, B., & Atwood, G. E. (1995). *Psychoanalytic treatment, an intersubjective approach* (p. 42). New York: Analytic Press.

Suttie, I. (1935). *The origins of love and hate* (pp. 53-54). New York: Julian Press.

Tansey, M.J. (1994). Sexual attraction and phobic dread in the counter-transference. *Psychoanalytic Dialogues, 4*(2), 139-152.

Tansey, M. J. and Burke, W. F. (1989). *Understanding countertransference, from projective identification to empathy.* Hillsdale, N.J.: Analytic Press.

Thompson, M. G. (1998). Manifestations of transference, love, friendship, rapport.

Contemporary Psychoanalysis, 34(4), 543-561.

Winnicott, D. W. (1960). The theory of the parent-infant relationship. In *The maturational processes and the facilitating environment: Studies in the theory of emotional development* (pp. 37-55). New York: International Universities Press.

Zetzel, E. (1956). Current concepts of transference. *International Journal of Psychoanalysis, 37,* 369-376.

The personal clinical material in this article has been disguised and was reviewed and approved by the patients for publication.

This article was presented, in part, at the 53rd Annual Meeting of the American Academy of Psychoanalysis and Dynamic Psychiatry, May 17, 2009, San Francisco, CA.

Myron L. Glucksman, M.D., Clinical Professor of Psychiatry, New York Medical College, and Training and Supervising Analyst, The Psychoanalytic Institute, New York Medical College, Valhalla, NY.

Journal of the American Academy of Psychoanalysis and Dynamic Psychiatry, 38(1) 159-180, 2010.

CASE PRESENTATION: LONG-TERM TREATMENT
MYRON L. GLUCKSMAN

Abstract:

The long-term (14 years) psychodynamic psychotherapy and pharmaco-therapy of a depressed, suicidal, self-mutilating female patient is described. Her diagnoses included Chronic Posttraumatic Stress Disorder, Borderline Personality Disorder, and Recurrent Major Depression. Treatment was punctuated with repeated hospitalizations for self-mutilation (cutting) and suicidal ideation. A major determinant for her psychopathology was sexual abuse by her father from ages 6 to 14. This resulted in feelings of guilt and rage that she repressed and acted out through self-mutilating and suicidal behavior. A prolonged negative transference gradually became ambivalent, then positive. This was associated with her internalization of the healing qualities of the therapeutic relationship. She also gained insight into the reasons for her need to punish herself. Her initial self-representation as unworthy and bad was transformed into perceiving herself as a worthwhile, loving person. This case illustrates the role of long-term treatment for a complex, life-threatening, psychiatric disorder.

Introduction:

The following case presentation describes the long-term psychodynamic psychotherapy of a severely disturbed, chronically self-mutilating, suicidal woman who began treatment at age 52. Sessions varied from twice weekly during the initial phase of treatment, to once weekly, once bi-weekly, and once monthly during the termination phase. Diagnostically, she suffered from Chronic Posttraumatic Stress Disorder secondary to childhood sexual abuse, as well as Borderline Personality Disorder with Recurrent Major Depression. Her lengthy treatment was due to a number of factors, including: (1) severe childhood trauma resulting in a pernicious negative introject of her father, and an ambivalent introject of her mother; (2) intense feeling of guilt and rage that were turned inward with self-punitive cutting and suicidal ideation; (3) extreme distrust of me, as well as other men, whom she expected to hurt and sexually violate her as her father had done; (4) long-standing, well-established defenses, including repression, depersonalization, displacement, projection, and acting out; (5) an initial, prolonged negative transference that evolved into one that was ambivalent, and subsequently positive. As treatment progressed, the patient gradually internalized the healing aspects of our relationship: trust, safety, stability, understanding, and caring. In doing so, she regulated her guilt, rage, and self-destructive impulses more effectively. This process was facilitated by the serendipitous presence of my dog, Joe, who served as a benign, transitional object. His beneficial influence during treatment has been discussed elsewhere ("The Dog's Role in the Analyst's Consulting Room," Glucksman, 2005). Over the course of treatment, she also developed insight into the determinants of her need for abuse and self-punishment. Her initial self-representation as unworthy, bad, and unlovable, incrementally changed to that of a worth-while, good, loving mother and grandmother. The judicious use of psycho-tropic medication stabilized her mood and helped reduce the severity of her symptoms. This case illustrates the role of long-term psychodynamic psychotherapy and pharmacotherapy in the treatment of a patient with a complex, life-threatening, psychiatric disorder.

Case Presentation:

Margaret* was a 52-year-old divorced woman who was referred to me by her youngest daughter, whom I had previously treated. A major portion of the daughter's treatment concerned the negative impact of her mother's chronic depressive symptoms on her. Margaret gave a history of longstanding de-pression, recurrent suicidal ideation, depersonalization, and self-mutilation. Prior to seeing me, she had never sought treatment. When we first met, she lived with her daughter and was employed as a factory clerk. She had divorced her husband at age 31, after nine years of marriage, because he was alcoholic and abusive. Following her divorce, she raised and supported three daughters, one of whom was already married with two daughters of her own. Margaret's mother died of breast cancer at age 67, when Margaret was age 31. Her father died of a ruptured aortic aneurysm at age 73, when she was age 43. She had one older sister and two younger twin sisters, all of whom were married with children of their own. An older brother was in prison for pedophilia.

In the course of her first few visits, Margaret was preoccupied with suicidal thoughts and reported that she continually cut her arms with a razor. Her self-mutilation began several years earlier, accompanied by suicidal urges. However, she denied ever making a serious suicide attempt. She described herself as "numb" inside, and wanted to die so that she could rejoin her mother. Her voice was monotonic, and she spoke in a detached manner. I was so concerned about her safety that I persuaded her to be voluntarily hospitalized. She was given the following psychotropic medications as an inpatient: Paroxetine 40 mg/day, Risperdal 2 mg/ day, Trazodone 50 mg/ day, and Clonazepam 0.5 mg as needed. Following her discharge after two weeks on a psychiatric inpatient unit, she attended a day hospital for several weeks, and saw me twice weekly. The first dream she reported to me was the following: "A man attacked me and tried to cut my back with a knife. The cops couldn't catch him, and he got away with it." Margaret associated the man to her father who frequently belittled her, and beat her with his belt. Her husband often berated her when he was drunk, and sometimes hit her. She admitted that she was afraid of me, and expected me to hurt her in some way. Margaret continued to have dreams where either her father or another man was trying to kill or injure her. A typical dream was the following: "I was with my brother and sister in a movie theater. My father ordered us killed, and a man shot us with a machine gun." Her associations were to her father's punitive, sometimes brutal behavior. Once again, she reported cutting her arm repeatedly, hoping to die. Because I believed she was unable to control her suicidal impulses, I re-hospitalized her on a voluntary basis.

Following a one-week hospitalization, Margaret related the following dream to me: "I saw a little girl crying and went over to her. It was me. Then I was standing in front of my father yelling at him for what he did to the little girl." This dream occurred approximately two years after she began therapy. Margaret proceeded to tell me that she harbored a long-standing secret. With much hesitation and great difficulty, she revealed to me that her father forced her to perform fellatio beginning at age six. She told her paternal grandmother, who yelled at her father and scolded Margaret for it. However, she never told her mother because her father threatened to kill her if she did. At some point, her father initiated sexual intercourse with her that continued until she was 14. He stopped when she began having her periods. Revealing her father's sexual abuse was a turning point in Margaret's treatment because it reflected her growing trust in me, as well as her nascent positive transference. However, following her revelation, Margaret cut and scratched her arms and legs with increasing frequency. She expressed intense guilt, and it became evident that her self-mutilation was a way of punishing herself for her incestuous behavior. Cutting and bleeding also helped to rid her of the rage she felt toward her father. Moreover, the act of cutting itself enabled her to feel her hatred and guilt, instead of her usual inner emotional numbness. She felt that she deserved to die, and once again I hospitalized her for a brief period. Her medication regimen was changed to Mirtazapine 30 mg per day, Bupropion 300 mg per day, and Clonazepam 0.5 mg as needed. After her discharge, she confided that I was the only person who could "protect" her from her father, and that my office was a place where she felt safe. On the other hand, she fantasized that I might rape or beat her. If this were to occur, she could have me prosecuted and vicariously exact revenge on her father. According to Margaret, her paternal great-grandfather, grandfather, and brother were sexual predators. However, her brother never tried to sexually abuse her. Her ex-husband was the only man (except for her father) with whom she had ever had sexual relations. She did not derive pleasure from sex with her husband, and avoided dating men after her divorce. Because she confused her father's sexual abuse with affection when she was a child, sex with me would at least mean that I cared about her. Margaret also recalled that she sometimes experienced pleasure during sexual intercourse with her father, exacerbating her feelings of guilt and self-loathing. Her vacillating perception of me as either an abuser or a protector continued for many months. Moreover, her ambivalence toward me evoked ambivalent feelings on my part toward her. I often felt angry and exasperated when she alluded to suicidal fantasies, but she kept me guessing as to whether or not she would act on them. I occasionally entertained retaliatory fantasies (reprimanding her, or referring her to another therapist), but realized that I was being coerced into behaving like her abusive father via projective identification. That is, I identified with her projections of an internalized punitive, cruel father. At times, she behaved like a frightened, helpless little girl toward whom I felt fatherly and protective. As I struggled with these transference-countertransference fantasies and feelings, I steadfastly tried to maintain a supportive, empathic role with her.

In her third year of treatment, Margaret was found to have a suspicious cyst in her right ovary. She hoped that it would be malignant so that she could die from cancer, as her mother did. Moreover, it would be just punishment for betraying her mother by having sex with her father. She visited her mother's grave on Mother's Day, and felt simultaneous love and hate for her. She reasoned that if her mother really loved her she would have protected her from her father. In another dream, she watched her mother slowly die along with a little girl who was also dying. Margaret felt that when her mother died, the "child part" of her also died. Her mother was her "lifeline," but failed to help her, leaving her with no hope and vulnerable to her father's abuse. While at the cemetery, she also visited her father's grave and had a fantasy of cutting herself to the point of bleeding to death on his grave. In doing so, she could "place guilt on his soul." Her self-mutilating behavior increased following her visit to the cemetery, and she was hospitalized once again after she showed me letters that she wrote to me, her daughters, and granddaughters, expressing explicit suicidal fantasies. On Father's Day of the following year, she visited her father's grave and told him he was a "son-of-a-bitch." Then, she poured her urine over it and stabbed the gravesite with a knife. Several months after this event, she reported the following dream: "I'm in a room in a mental hospital with a little girl about six years old. A man comes in and tries to take her away. I told him 'you can't have this little girl,' and he let go of her. The little girl moved closer to me." Margaret felt that the dream meant she had gained more power over her internalized father. The little girl was herself, and that as an adult she was re-claiming, as well as protecting, her abused childhood self.

During the fourth year of treatment, I moved my office from a medical building to a small cottage adjacent to my house. My dog, Joe, a Labrador retriever, serendipitously began attending sessions with those patients who acquiesced to his presence. Over time, I realized that many patients felt soothed and comforted by him. Margaret took a liking to Joe, and felt reassured by his calm demeanor. She often brought him biscuits and petted him during sessions. I assumed that her relationship with Joe was a transference displacement. She often arrived early for her sessions, and frequently asked me if Joe could stay with her in the waiting room. Eventually, she confided that she told Joe certain things that she withheld from me. In particular, she whispered to him about her urges to cut or kill herself. At the beginning of sessions, it became a routine for me to ask Joe, in a playful manner, what Margaret had told him in the waiting room. Sometimes, she reluctantly informed me that she had told Joe about her self-destructive urges. I also observed that she acted out her mixed transference to me through her behavior with Joe. For example, she often told him what a good dog he was, while she petted him. On the other hand, she sometimes scolded him for growling or grabbing a biscuit out of her hand. At one point, Margaret asked if she could have a photo of Joe to keep at home. After interpreting that this was a way of always having me close to her, I gave her a photo of him. On one occasion, she reported that she was feeling suicidal and about to cut herself at home when she noticed Joe's photo. She picked it up and stroked it until her suicidal urge subsided. As we explored her actions, she realized that my presence, personified by Joe's photo, prevented her from acting on her self-destructive impulses. This reflected her increasing internalization of my life-affirming, self-protective function. Joe's therapeutic influence on Margaret, as well as with other patients, has been described in a separate article cited in the Introduction.

During the next few years of treatment, Margaret continued to struggle with hatred toward her father, guilt over the incest, and anger at her mother for not protecting her. Her repetitive cutting and suicidal ideation led to additional brief hospitalizations. The manifest content of her dreams frequently contained themes of violence, mutilation, and death when she felt suicidal. A typical dream was the following: "I died and was placed in a casket. I saw that my face was all torn up." During her seventh year of treatment, a lesion was discovered in her right breast. She wished it would turn out to be malignant so that she could join her mother, whom she hoped would forgive her. However, it was found to be benign, to which she responded with disappointment and relief. Mother's Day continued to be an especially difficult time of year for her, evoking ambivalent feelings toward her mother as well as suicidal urges. Significantly, prior to Mother's Day in her eighth year of treatment, she voluntarily gave me a packet of razor blades that she had saved. By doing so, she indicated that she had formed an alliance with me to protect her from herself.

In her ninth year of treatment, she turned 61, the age at which her mother died. Although she felt guilty about outliving her mother, she was grateful to be alive for her grandchildren. She also revealed that she trusted me more and felt that I genuinely cared for her. In this context, she confided her fantasy of having sex with me in a loving way. On the other hand, she continued to have fantasies of being raped and beaten by me. Her longstanding belief that being abused was evidence of being loved was increasingly challenged by her actual experience with me. Contrary to her father and husband, she felt that I was consistently empathic and understanding toward her. In turn, she gradually began to feel more worthwhile and less self-destructive. She felt in better control of her urges to cut herself and enjoyed spending more time with her grandchildren. In addition, she became increasingly self-assertive, and even hired an attorney to represent her for what she believed to be wrongful termination of her job. We reduced the frequency of her sessions to once weekly, and decreased the dosage of Bupropion to 100 mg per day.

During the 11th year of treatment, we began to meet once every two weeks. She found another job as a sales clerk and moved into subsidized housing. Her cutting and suicidal thinking stopped altogether. Margaret remarked in one of her sessions that "I actually have a future that I want and don't dread." The Bupropion was discontinued, and Mirtazapine was lowered to 15 mg per day. She felt "more at peace" with herself; her feelings of guilt and rage became almost nonexistent. At the beginning of her 14th year of treatment, we agreed to meet once monthly, and to terminate altogether at the end of the year, if all went well. The decision to terminate under these conditions was a mutual one, although Margaret initially raised the possibility of termination. Several months prior to termination she reported the following dream: "My brother and I were talking about certain possessions that belonged to our parents that I have. He wanted to know why I kept them, and I told him: 'daddy gave them to me.' He wanted to come over and take them, but I said he couldn't because I wanted to keep them." Although her brother had died several years earlier, her nephew expressed a wish to have her brother's bible, which he had given to Margaret before he died. She realized how much she loved her brother when they were growing up together. Ironically, he was also sexually abused by an older man when he was a child. She felt that her use of the word "daddy," as well as her wish to keep the things her father gave her, meant that her profound hatred toward him had significantly diminished. She neither felt the need to punish herself, nor to have me protect her from her self-destructive urges. Three months prior to termination, we discontinued the Mirtazapine. At that time, she celebrated her 66th birthday, having outlived her mother by five years. At her last session, Margaret told me she had adopted a dog that she loved. I interpreted this as a transitional or replacement object for both Joe and myself. She also reported a dream in which black mice were biting her, but she was able to rid herself of them. Margaret believed that the mice represented her angry, self-punitive feelings which she was finally able to control. Two years have passed since Margaret terminated treatment, and during that time we had no contact. Interestingly, a small balance remained on her bill that she did not pay. This was unlike her, because she always paid her portion of the fee not covered by insurance. My assumption is that her debt symbolizes a continuing connection to me. Perhaps, it also represents the remnants of her negative transference. In any event, I have assumed that it is more likely the former than the latter, and have not pursued it further with her.

Margaret's lengthy treatment was due to a number of factors that were summarized in the Introduction to this case presentation. However, I believe it is worth emphasizing the salient elements that contributed to her long-term treatment. A central factor was her profound distrust of her father, other men, and me. Changing her perception of men via her transference and "teal" relationship with me necessitated countless interactions between us over hundreds of hours. In effect, I served as a "new object" that gradually replaced the internalized "old object" of her father. This was an entirely different kind of experience for her that involved empathy, understanding, limit setting, interpretive comments, and consistency on my part. For Margaret, it meant taking incremental risks in trusting a male stranger whom she perceived as extremely threatening, and with whom she felt in constant mortal danger. Another contributing factor to the duration of treatment was the tenacity of her long-standing defenses, including repression, depersonalization, and acting out of her feelings connected to the sexual abuse. This required a lengthy process in which she learned to identify, experience, and process her emotions, enabling her to express and cope with them in more constructive ways. In addition, the gradual reduction of her self-mutilating and suicidal behavior necessitated continuous internalization of my self-regulatory, self-protective functions. Margaret's deeply negative self-representation was another obstacle that contributed to the length of treatment. The change in her self-image from that of an unworthy, unlovable, guilty individual, to someone who viewed herself as worthwhile, lovable, and valued required an untold number of positive interactions with me and other caregivers. In retrospect, the success of her treatment involved the totality of our interactions: projections, counter-projections, realistic perceptions, dreams, fantasies, interpretations, introjections, and internalizations. Above all, it required mutual commitment, honesty, trust, and endurance.

References:

Glucksman, M. L. (2005). The dog's role in the analyst's consulting room. *Journal of the American Academy of Psychoanalysis and Dynamic Psychiatry, 33*(4), 611-618.

Myron L. Glucksman, M.D., Clinical Professor of Psychiatry, New York Medical College, Valhalla, NY; Supervising and Training Analyst, The Psychoanalytic Institute, New York Medical College.

Psychodynamic Psychiatry, 41 (3) 385-392, 2013.

Commentary on "Case Presentation: Long-Term Treatment," by Myron L. Glucksman Richard C. Friedman, Editor

The thoughtful research review by Leichsenring, Abbass, Luyten, Hilsenroth, and Rabung is followed in this issue of *Psychodynamic Psychiatry* by a case report of a successful long-term treatment. Leichsenring, Abbass, Luyten et al. point out that there is no universally accepted definition of long-term psychodynamic psychotherapy. A commonly accepted criterion is continuous psychotherapy for at least one year or 50 sessions, although other criteria have been used by some authors. The clinical discussion by Glucksman is a report of a treatment conducted over 14 years, not one year or 50 sessions. Although Glucksman's approach certainly qualifies as psychodynamic psychotherapy it also included interaction with his dog who served as a helpful co-therapist. This in itself directs attention to the variance that exists in clinical treatment situations as they occur naturalistically in the community.

The researchers observed that short-term psychotherapy may not be adequate treatment for patients with complex mental disorders including personality disorders. Specific aspects of what is meant by "complexity" as revealed in the life story of Dr. Glucksman's patient, Margaret, are painful to read. When she began treatment, Margaret was a 52-year-old divorced woman who had classical symptoms of severe depression and borderline personality disorder. It was not until two years of psychotherapy had been completed, however, that Margaret's history of sexual abuse emerged. This patient's father regularly forced her to participate in fellatio beginning at age 6. Although she revealed this to her paternal grandmother, the abuse continued and included sexual intercourse which occurred throughout her later childhood stopping only when her menstrual periods began. This patient was unable to seek protection from her mother because her father threatened to kill her if she revealed their sexual relationship. Childhood sexual abuse is far more common than is generally realized even by psychotherapists, but the type of abuse that Margaret experienced was extra-ordinary by any measure.

It is not necessary to review the entire history and course of therapy here. The point I wish to emphasize concerns the "appropriate" duration of psychotherapy. The present cost-conscious and insurance-based environment emphasizes the need to offer the most highly effective psychotherapeutic interventions in the shortest time and with the least economic cost. How does one assess the appropriate duration of a psychotherapeutic treatment for a patient like Margaret? The complex origins of Margaret's psychological difficulties emerged only in the context of years of psychotherapy. If Margaret's assessment was based on an intake interview, treatment of the most severe component of her depression with drugs and/ or cognitive behavior therapy might take a fairly brief time. If self-mutilation was expressed during that treatment or was reported in the assessment interviews, time-limited dialectical behavioral therapy might be added to the regimen. One might conceptualize Margaret's depression and self-mutilation at a neuro-biological level and some might conclude that she suffered from a "brain disorder" manifested by severe symptoms of mood dysregulation. How does one factor into a model of this patient's "disorder," however, the fact that she was repeatedly forced to have oral sex and sexual intercourse with her father beginning at age 6, and that he threatened to murder her if she told her mother? Her paternal grandmother, who Margaret did confide in, did not intervene in such a way as to end the abuse.

Eight years in the life of a child is not equivalent to 8 years in the life of an adult. Even if it were, the duration of psychological stress does not translate directly into the duration of psychological treatment. In any case, the experience of time is different for adults and children and cascading effects on mood regulation, personality integration, cognitive and social development are especially profound when chronic stress occurs during childhood. Contrary to present trends, the duration of a treatment should not be assessed in comparison to other commonly used treatments for "most" or "many patients", but rather in relation to the psychological needs of the person who requires treatment. Typical models of treatment do not factor in that a woman who was sexually abused by her own father is not likely to trust a therapist. It might seem that mistrust might be greatest of a male therapist, but the impotence and collaboration of the female authority figures in the patient's childhood suggest that Margaret was likely to be mistrustful of women and men alike although for different reasons. The fact that this particular therapist was able to engage in productive therapeutic work with this particular patient is a testament to unique capacities of both. Not only was Dr. Glucksman able to establish a working alliance that facilitated honest communication, he skillfully managed an erotic transference that many therapists might have found daunting. Could therapeutic work like this have been carried out by following a manual? It is difficult to see how. The work required an interactive flow of communication that ultimately helped Margaret develop a sense of trust. Could any reasonably well-trained therapist have carried this work out? It seems unlikely! One imagines that *some* therapists, perhaps women as well as men, might have achieved a comparably successful therapeutic result with Margaret. What percentage of possible psychotherapists might this be however? There is no way of knowing. It seems on face value that the type of therapeutic work discussed in this treatment vignette requires a fair amount of clinical experience, training, sensitivity, and someone whose personal life rests on a sound foundation. The issues in this admittedly partial discussion of the complexity of Margaret's case are not to be found in the Fifth Edition of the *Diagnostic and Statistical Manual of Mental Disorders* of the American Psychiatric Association nor should they be. Diagnostic manuals are not meant to be text books of psychiatry. The discipline of psychiatry is built on many types of evidence. Often there are no randomized controlled studies whose results indicate the best type(s) of treatment interventions. The *variance* of factors influencing patient needs and potential treatment responses and therapist characteristics is substantial. Straightforward modes of treatment that can be manualized are appropriate for research purposes and are often valid and practical, clinically. Such approaches address only part of patient-therapist variance that occurs in the general community, however.

Although it is perhaps anxiety provoking, it is important to acknowledge that complex problems often require complex and labor- intensive solutions. These solutions may be imperfect, and not all sensitive, thoughtful therapeutic work leads to outcomes as positive as Glucksman reports in his vignette. This is true of medical therapeutics generally, and as financiers, politicians, military planners, and statesmen often discover, may also be true of well-intended interventions in other areas of life as well.

## Chapter 5

Dream Studies

Until Freud's publication of *The Interpretation of Dreams* (1900), dreams were considered to be mystical, supernatural, and even prophetic. They were part of the folklore of various cultures and were believed to have meaning not only for the dreamer but also for the society in which the dreamer lived. An example is the biblical description of the pharaoh's dream, which Joseph interpreted as predictive of a future famine in Egypt. Freud recognized that dreams are a part of normal mental functioning and developed a methodology for understanding them. He concluded that dreaming was a form of censorship over aggressive and sexual impulses or wishes, which occurred during sleep. According to him, dreaming allowed the dreamer to remain asleep; hence, he referred to dreams as "the guardians of sleep." Freud termed his method for understanding the meaning of a dream "free association." The latter required the dreamer to verbalize whatever memories, feelings, wishes, and conflicts the dream imagery evoked. Since Freud believed that the dream was a form of censorship, he viewed the dream imagery as a defensive phenomenon. The latter included several basic defensive maneuvers that Freud termed "dreamwork": symbolism, displacement, and condensation. In his view, these mechanisms simultaneously defended against, as well as represented, unconscious mentation, or primary process thinking. By means of free association, the underlying wishes or impulses that were defended against by these mechanisms could be identified and interpreted.

Since the mid-twentieth century, sleep and dream researchers have demonstrated that dreaming occurs throughout the sleep cycle on a regular basis. It is characterized by periodic neuronal excitations that spread from the midbrain to the cortex accompanied by rapid eye movement (or REM) sleep. Dreaming is essential for mental homeostasis; for example, dream deprivation results in anxiety, irritability, and mental disorganization. Laboratory studies indicate that dreams are associated with memory processing, learning, and problem-solving. Creative artists and scientists frequently use their dreams for inspiration and solutions to challenging problems. Dreams often contain intense emotions that may not be consciously experienced. There is evidence that a major function of dreaming is to neutralize intense feelings experienced prior to sleep. Dreams often reflect conflicts and dilemmas that require resolution. Sometimes they vividly portray ourselves and others. In other instances, they replay traumatic experiences with the same emotional impact as the original events.

The contemporary view of dreaming differs from Freud's theory; the latter posits that dreamwork represents censorship of instinctual wishes or impulses. Our current understanding is that the dream imagery associated with the dreamwork is not so much a censoring mechanism as it is a metaphorical portrayal of the issues, conflicts, and wishes that are addressed in the dream. The dream imagery, or manifest content, requires interpretation in order to understand its essential meaning or latent content. This can be viewed as analogous to understanding the underlying meaning or message in an abstract painting or poem. Dream imagery often incorporates events and experiences that occurred on the day or days prior to the dream (day residue). In a sense, dreaming is analogous to a daily diary composed during sleep that records the dreamer's experiences, feelings, conflicts, and wishes.

Dreams can provide the clinician with important information regarding diagnosis, psychodynamics, emotional states, impending crises (including suicidality), relationships, and self-representation. These elements can be used to assess progress, or lack of progress, during treatment. Resolution of problems and conflicts as well as impending decisions can also be reflected in dream imagery. In general, dreams can be arbitrarily characterized according to their manifest imagery. For example, anxiety dreams contain frightening or terrifying imagery. Other dreams may be primarily concerned with conflicts or problems. Still others may be about relationships or self-identity. Special categories include nightmares, posttraumatic stress disorder, and anniversary dreams.

In order to be therapeutically useful, the underlying meaning or latent content of a dream needs to be understood. This is usually accomplished by the process of free association. The latter involves a dialogue with oneself or others concerning various components of the dream imagery. This requires paying attention to the central theme or narrative, predominant feelings, context or surroundings, activities, people, and portrayals of self. There may be more than one interpretation or understanding of the dream imagery. Equally important to an understanding of the dream are the memories, connections, new perspectives, and insights that accompany the free association process. To paraphrase Freud, dreams provide us with a unique window into the unconscious workings of the mind.

My paper, "The Use of Successive Dreams to Facilitate and Document Change During Treatment" (Glucksman, M.D., 1988) grew out of my continuing interest in the elements that promote clinical change during therapy. In my work with patients, I was impressed with how their dreams reflected their central conflicts, wishes, feelings, relationships, and self-portrayals. In particular, I became aware of changes in dream imagery that correlated with their clinical progress. This paper describes the changes in both manifest and latent content of the dreams of three patients, each of whom I treated over a period of several years.

The first patient was a nun who was referred to me by the Mother Superior of her religious order. She was severely depressed, withdrawn, and unable to perform her regular duties in her community. At first, she was reluctant to talk, but she gradually began to tell me about herself. She entered the convent following an attempted date rape in her sophomore year of college. Her experiences with men were extremely limited prior to that event. Moreover, her mother never discussed sex with her, nor did she explain menstruation to the patient when it occurred. The convent sponsored a private school, and the patient was a teacher on its faculty. For a number of years, she functioned quite well at her job, but she grew increasingly frustrated with the circumscribed social life of the convent. A few years prior to entering treatment with me, she had begun having sexual fantasies about a male caretaker at the convent. She became extremely guilt-ridden over her fantasies as well as more socially withdrawn. Her work performance began to decline, and she received an unsatisfactory evaluation from her Mother Superior. Following this, she became increasingly depressed. Her sequential dreams during therapy reflected her core psychodynamic conflicts as well as their resolution. Over time, she became more functional, less guilty in regard to her sexuality, and better able to express her feelings. Ultimately, she left the convent, lived independently, continued to teach, and began dating men. Eventually, she married a man with whom she had developed a sexually intimate, trusting relationship.

The second patient was a married, male attorney who presented with symptoms of generalized anxiety. He was extremely competitive with his peers, fearful of losing a case and of being humiliated during court proceedings. His father was authoritarian, critical, and ill tempered. On the other hand, his mother was loving and supportive. He often felt that his father was jealous of his close relationship with his mother. As a boy, he fantasized that his father might physically injure or kill him. His early transference to me was marked by fear and distrust. Over the course of treatment, his oedipal rivalry with his father was reflected in his dreams and behavior. During sexual intercourse, he often fantasized that his wife was a whore, in order to defend against his incestuous wishes. Gradually, his transference changed into viewing me as caring and helpful. By the same token, his relationships with his colleagues became more friendly and cooperative. Dream imagery during treatment resonated with his intrapsychic and interpersonal psychodynamic changes.

The third patient was a single, female writer who became depressed following her mother's death in a house fire. She was guilt-ridden over her mother's demise, believing that if she had been at home when it occurred, she might have prevented it. Her mother was an alcoholic, and the patient had an ambivalent relationship with her. Her parents were divorced, and she barely spoke with her father. The latter was a successful businessman who left her mother for another woman. The patient had a history of breaking off relationships with boyfriends and believed that most marriages were doomed to failure. Her mother was a talented artist, but never achieved professional success. She came from an upper-class family while the patient's father was from a poor Hispanic background. The patient had several siblings, but felt that she was her father's favorite. Her self-identity was split between identifying with her mother's intelligence and aristocratic background, as well as with her father's charm and ethnic pride. The patient believed that her mother was envious of her professional success and relationships with men. However, she experienced episodes of disinterest in her work and unsuccessful romantic relationships. During treatment, it became clear that she was afraid of evoking her mother's wrath by surpassing her professionally and romantically. Her dream content reflected her fear of retaliation or injury from other women for her successes at work and with men. The patient's predominant transference was manifested in dreams containing oedipal themes where romantic contact between us was often interrupted by another woman. Over time, the patient resolved her conflicted relationship with her mother and reconciled with her father. She became less threatened by other women and more secure in her relationships with men. Her work inhibitions became less frequent and her self-identity became more integrated. Her successive dreams reflected these psychodynamic and behavioral changes.

A second paper on this subject, "Using Dreams to Assess Clinical Change during Treatment" (Glucksman, M.L., and Kramer, M., 2004), examines the relationship between the manifest content of selected dreams during the initial and later phases of treatment. The dreams of twelve patients who had completed either psychoanalysis or psychodynamically oriented therapy were selected from the initial and terminal phases of treatment. Clinical improvement was evaluated by two independent observers and based on the following criteria: (1) Symptom Reduction; (2) Resolution of Central Conflicts; (3) Level of Functioning; (4) Ego Strength; (5) Interpersonal Relationships; (6) Transference Resolution; (7) Affect Regulation; and (8) Self-Analytic Capacity. In general, the dream manifest content from the initial phase of treatment compared to the last stage of treatment demonstrated clinical progress.

The third paper, "The Clinical and Predictive Value of the Initial Dream of Treatment" (Glucksman, M.L., and Kramer, M., 2011), examines the clinical significance of the first dream reported by a patient in treatment. Various analysts have suggested that the initial dream of treatment reflects the patient's central psychodynamic conflicts and may predict the future course of treatment. In order to test this hypothesis, my coauthor (Milton Kramer) and I collected the initial dreams of sixty-three patients who were either currently in psychoanalytic or psychodynamically oriented therapy, or had already terminated treatment. Each initial manifest dream report was rated by one or both of us, depending on whether familiarity with the patient precluded one of us from doing so because of bias. Manifest dream content was rated according to variables relevant to the treatment process. These included (1) Affect and Affect Valence of manifest content; (2) Associations to manifest content; (3) Psychodynamic Theme of manifest content; (4) Psychodynamic Theme as a Predictor of Core Psychodynamic Issues; (5) Transference in manifest content; (6) Gender suggested by manifest content; (7) Psychodynamic Theme Category of manifest content; and (8) Clinical Progress.

The results indicated that Affect or feelings occurred in almost half of the initial dream reports; of these, negative affect was evident in 32% of the initial dream reports, while positive affect was present in only 11% of them. Negative affect occurred in 70% of Associations to the manifest content of initial dream reports, and Positive affect in only 4% of Associations to the manifest content of initial dream reports. These observations were consistent with our findings in an earlier study where initial dreams contained significantly more negative than positive affect (Kramer, M., and Glucksman, M. L., 2006). This observation reflected the dysphoria experienced by patients when they first entered treatment. The Psychodynamic Theme of manifest content was consistent with the core psychodynamic issues that emerged during treatment in 94% of the initial dream reports. Transference was evident in 44% of the initial dream reports; it was negative in 61% and positive in 32% of them. Evidence of negative transference reflected initial feelings of distrust and fear toward the therapist at the beginning of therapy. Gender of patients was judged correctly in 62% of the initial dream reports (by the rater who was not their therapist). This finding suggested that manifest content may indicate the gender of the dreamer. The most frequent Psychodynamic Theme Categories of the initial dream reports were Relational (43%) and Injury (36%). That is, interpersonal conflicts and fears of physical or psychological injury were the predominant themes of initial dream imagery. The majority of patients made clinical progress in treatment, regardless of their Psychodynamic Theme category. In summary, the initial dream of treatment was a valuable source of information regarding the valence of Affect, Psychodynamic Theme, and prediction of Core Psychodynamic Issues that emerged during treatment. Although this study focused only on manifest content of the initial dream of treatment, it also pointed out the clinical importance of latent content in connection with a fuller psychodynamic understanding of the patient.

A fourth paper, "Initial and Last Dream Reports of Patients in Psychodynamic Psychotherapy and Combined Psychotherapy/ Pharmacotherapy" (Glucksman, M.L., and Kramer, M., 2012), was a systematic attempt to assess clinical improvement through dream imagery in a group of patients who had either terminated treatment or were making satisfactory progress in therapy. The initial and last manifest dream reports of each patient were collected and rated independently by two observers, according to the following variables: (1) Affect and Affect Valence of manifest content; (2) Affect Valence of Associations to manifest content; (3) Direction of Associations to manifest content (positive or negative); (4) Narrative in manifest content (phenomenological description of imagery); (5) Psychodynamic Formulation (generic psychodynamic formulation of manifest content); (6) Transference; and (7) Dream Theme of manifest content.

The results demonstrated that there was a decrease in Negative affect between the first and last manifest dream reports, and an increase in Positive affect between the initial and last dream reports of treatment. This finding suggested that patients were more dysphoric at the beginning of treatment, and less so toward the end. Likewise, there was a decrease in Negative affect and an increase in Positive affect between the initial and last associations to manifest dream content. By the same token, there was a decrease in Negative association themes, and an increase in Positive association themes between the initial and last manifest dream reports. Dream narratives, or the stories conveyed by the dream imagery, changed from negative to positive between the initial and last manifest dream reports. Generic psychodynamic formulations of manifest content changed from negative to positive between initial and final manifest dream reports. The change in dream narratives and psychodynamic formulations suggested clinical improvement over the course of treatment. Evidence of Transference appeared in almost half of manifest dream reports, and changed from negative to positive between initial and last dream reports. This suggested that negative feelings and perceptions of the therapist in the early stage of treatment changed into more positive ones at a later stage. Relational themes in manifest content became more frequent in the last dream reports than in the initial ones. This suggested that patients felt less threatened and more comfortable in their interpersonal relationships toward the end of treatment. Likewise, themes of Injury became less frequent between the initial and last manifest dream reports. In conclusion, the changes in each of these manifest dream variables reflected clinical improvement during treatment.

The preceding four papers illustrate the usefulness of manifest dream content in evaluating clinical change from the beginning to the end of treatment. In view of the current emphasis on evidence-based research, it is important to point out that manifest dream content can be objectively evaluated by independent observers. Conversely, latent dream content is dependent on the observers' subjective interpretation of the data. Objective data-gathering notwithstanding, the therapist's subjective experience remains an important component toward an empathic understanding of the patient's internal mental landscape. The findings in these papers not only support the effectiveness of psychodynamically oriented and psychoanalytic therapy, but also provide an objective methodology for evaluating therapeutic outcomes. Equally important is the information provided by dreams regarding salient psychodynamics, feelings, wishes, self-image, and relationships. What patients may not be able to consciously appreciate or articulate can often be poignantly expressed through dream imagery. Consequently, dreams are a unique and valuable source of information for both patient and therapist.

References:

Freud, S., "The Interpretation of Dreams" in J. Strachey (Ed. & Trans.), *The Standard Edition of the Complete Psychological Works of Sigmund Freud*, Vols. 4 and 5 (1900): London: Hogarth Press, 1953.

Glucksman, M.L., "The Use of Successive Dreams to Facilitate and Document Change During Treatment," *Journal of the American Academy of Psychoanalysis*, Vol. 16, No. 1 (1988): 47-70.

Glucksman, M.L., Kramer, M., "Using Dreams to Assess Clinical Change during Treatment," *Journal of the American Academy of Psychoanalysis and Dynamic Psychiatry*, Vol. 32, No. 2 (2004): 345-358.

Glucksman, M.L., and Kramer, M., "The Clinical and Predictive Value of the Initial Dream of Treatment," *Journal of the American Academy of Psychoanalysis and Dynamic Psychiatry*, Vol. 39, No. 2 (2011): 263-283.

Kramer, M., and Glucksman, M.L., "Changes in Manifest Dream Affect," *Journal of The American Academy of Psychoanalysis and Dynamic Psychiatry*, Vol. 34, No. 2 (2006): 249-260.

Glucksman, M.L., and Kramer, M., "Initial and Last Manifest Dream Reports of Patients in Psychodynamic Psychotherapy and Combined Psychotherapy/Pharmacotherapy", *Psychodynamic Psychiatry*, Vol. 40, No. 4 (2012): 617-634.

THE USE OF SUCCESSIVE DREAMS TO FACILITATE AND
DOCUMENT CHANGE DURING TREATMENT
MYRON L. GLUCKSMAN, M.D.

Introduction:

The universally accepted goal of most therapies is the promotion of intra-psychic and interpersonal change. Psychoanalysis, in particular, aims for structural as well as dynamic change: the strengthening of ego functions, greater self-cohesion, modification of super-ego demands, successful resolution of unconscious conflicts and transference reactions, as well as the replacement of pathological defenses and destructive interpersonal practices with healthier ones. The data for evaluating clinical change comes from a variety of sources: overt behavior, the relationship with the analyst and others, the manifest and latent content of the patient's productions and the quality of the patient's affective communications.

The dream holds a special place among the patient's productions as an invaluable source of information in connection with personality structure and dynamics. Since dreams reflect virtually every aspect of the dreamer's experience, it seems reasonable to assume that clinical changes during the course of treatment will be incorporated into dream content. A number of knowledgeable clinicians have observed changes in both dream content and structure as treatment progresses (Alexander, 1961; Bonime, 1962; Dewald, 1972; Saul, 1972; Warner, 1983). These include an increase in successful resolutions of neurotic conflicts, greater congruence of manifest and latent content, as well as less disguise and distortion. Warner (1983) reported changes in the manifest content of dreams during treatment, particularly in the area of increased self-esteem. The dreams of his patients changed from initial ones which reflected masochistic or self-punitive themes, to later dreams which contained a greater "self-soothing capability" and more self-gratifying themes. Warner (1987), Greenberg (1987), and Fossahage (1987) emphasize that the manifest content can be viewed as a metaphorical presentation of various intrapsychic issues rather than exclusively as a censoring process aimed at disguising underlying instinctual drives and wishes. They point out that manifest imagery is a communication of the patient's attempts at problem or conflict resolution, self-portrayal, affective regulation and the maintenance of intrapsychic organization. Thus, manifest content itself can be an important index of clinical change during treatment.

Bonime (1986) has convincingly described how collaborative work between analyst and patient in connection with dreams promotes insight and facilitates behavioral change. His clinical vignettes demonstrate that dreams not only provide a wealth of information concerning the genesis of psychopathology, but they also validate evolving health in the areas of self-concept, affect and interpersonal relationships. I have been particularly interested in how successive dreams reflect change in regard to self-representation, defensive operations, interpersonal relationships, as well as the resolution of specific conflicts and transference reactions. In this paper, I shall describe the treatment of several patients whose dreams provided invaluable data which contributed toward an understanding of the determinants of their pathological functioning. I shall attempt to demonstrate how their successive dreams facilitated and documented clinical change in connection with self-concept, defenses, core conflicts, transference reactions, relationships and affective communications.

Clinical Illustrations:

Sister Theresa:

Sister Theresa was a forty-year-old nun referred to me by her Mother Superior because she had become increasingly depressed, withdrawn and unable to perform her expected duties in her religious community. She had entered the convent twentyone years previously, and seemed destined to become one of its leaders until she became symptomatic. She came to her initial sessions reluctantly and spoke very guardedly. The first dream she related was the following:

"I'm in a strange room with strangers, I cannot communicate with them. I feel panicked that I don't fit in".

Her associations centered around her feelings of alienation from the other sisters in the community, particularly her inability to speak openly with them about her inner thoughts and feelings. She often felt misunderstood and unappreciated by her superiors. Withdrawal, silence and immersion in her books were her main defenses against these painful experiences. However, her sense of alienation was not confined to the religious community. As she described her childhood, it became clear that she felt alienated within her own family. Neither parent expressed his or her real feelings, so that there was an absence of emotional communication in the home. Her mother always seemed critical and made her feel unworthy or never "good enough." When her mother was angry she became cold and silent. Her father was remote and unavailable emotionally. She felt loved in a vague way, but her parents never displayed physical affection toward her or each other. She described herself as shy, socially immature and prudish as an adolescent. Boys frightened her and she did not date in high school. Her parents never discussed sex with her, nor did her mother provide her with information about menstruation. However, she once cautioned the patient about the unpleasantness of a pelvic examination. Several months after entering treatment, she reported the following dream:

"I was in a hospital for dry hands. I was bleeding from my vagina".

This dream afforded her the opportunity to explore the sexual fantasies and feelings which resulted in constant guilt during her entire time in the convent. She recalled that in her sophomore year of college, she dated a young man who, on one occasion, became very aggressive in his demands for sexual contact with her. She was terrified and fled from him. He pursued her, but she managed to fend him off and subsequently ended their relationship. A short time later, she entered the convent. In retrospect, she realized that she had escaped from any further relationships with men. Her associations to sexual intercourse included fantasies of pain, mutilation, bleeding and punishment. Nevertheless, she acknowledged that she masturbated, but always with enormous guilt. The rules of communication in the convent were very strict, and the expression of any unpleasant feeling, such as anger, was implicitly forbidden. Any discussion of sexual feelings was absolutely prohibited. Once, she tried to talk with one of her superiors about her guilt over masturbation and was told that sisters recited psalms or prayed instead. A Mother Superior once told her she had "rough hands," which she thought might be connected to her masturbation. However, the dream encompassed more than her sexual conflicts. She felt that she was "emotionally bleeding to death" in the convent. Her inability to communicate her feelings with the other sisters reminded her of the emotionally restrictive atmosphere within her own family. About a year prior to entering treatment, she was severely criticized by her Mother Superior for not performing her job satisfactorily. She felt that the criticism was extremely unfair since she had received neither training nor supervision for that particular job. She was ultimately relieved of her duties and transferred to another facility affiliated with the community. She experienced her demotion as a devastating rejection, and gradually began her descent into the depression which necessitated treatment. A year after she began treatment, the following dream occurred:

"I was with Dave and his wife having lunch. She was pouting, crying and uncommunicative. I began touching his genitals and exciting him in front of her".

Her associations focused on a caretaker at the convent whose wife had recently left him. She frequently fantasized having sex with him, and was consumed with guilt over it. She admitted to masturbating with these fantasies, and eventually revealed that she masturbated to fantasies about me. She was secretly glad that Dave's wife had left him, and acknowledged feelings of rivalry toward her, as well toward my wife. The pouting, crying, uncommunicative wife in the dream was also herself-sad, isolated, wishing for, but unable to have an intimate relationship with anyone, particularly a man. During the ensuing months, successive dreams and her associations were replete with Oedipal material. She was gradually able to discuss her sexual fantasies more openly with me and felt less guilty about them. Her depression lifted, and she became more involved in the community's activities. She was more communicative with her peers, although feelings such as resentment, annoyance and anger were still impossible for her to verbalize. She believed that she would either destroy the person toward whom these feelings were directed, or would be destroyed herself as a consequence of their retaliation. During her second year of therapy she related the following dream:

> *"I was with a group of kids and got lost in a museum. I wanted to buy a necklace with a Unicorn on it but I didn't. I gave up, disappeared into the crowd and felt lost"*.

The patient taught in a school sponsored by her religious community, and had been on a recent visit to a museum with her class. While in the museum she felt a strong urge to leave the convent, but became terrified of the idea and suppressed it. She associated to the unicorn as a symbol of virginity, purity and her vows of chastity. She also recalled that the unicorn's horn, according to mythology, was ground up and eaten to enhance potency. She realized that the dream raised several important issues: could she ever become uninhibited enough to enjoy her sexual fantasies, masturbation, and even sexual intercourse, without fearing divine or parental (especially her mother's) punishment? Would it ever be possible for her to express her feelings, pleasant or unpleasant, without fear of criticism and retaliation? Was it possible that she might feel confident enough someday to actually leave the convent? In the dream, she was indecisive and gave up. Withdrawal, avoidance, and giving up were her chief defenses since childhood. In doing so, she protected herself from her mother's criticism and her father's remoteness. By remaining silent, she avoided expressing the anger she harbored against her parents; if she did so, she was certain of their retaliatory response which would leave her feeling even more isolated. Through the years, the religious community had protected her from the possibility of sexual relationships, angry confrontations, as well as a host of other threatening feelings and situations which the secular world presented. During our sessions she would often "stonewall" me by lapsing into silence, or deftly changing the subject whenever she wished to avoid a painful feeling or unacceptable fantasy.

At this juncture, I suggested that she join a therapy group, in addition to her individual sessions. I believed that a group would afford her the opportunity to explore relationships with both sexes-something that was not possible in her community. I also hoped that the group would diminish her sense of isolation, and reduce her guilt over her sexuality. Moreover, I anticipated that the group melieu would encourage her to express her feelings and make it more difficult for her to retreat. After several months of group therapy, she reported the following dream:

> *"I was in group therapy; they wouldn't let me leave until I defined a word. I shouted: "I can't do it." They shouted: "Yes, you can." The word "was masturbate."*

This dream occurred while the group was discussing the sexual conflicts of various members, including hers. It was a novel experience for her to talk about her sexual feelings in the presence of men and women who neither criticized nor punished her for having them. The group was extremely supportive, but at the same time did not allow her to escape into her defensive silences or other distancing maneuvers when she felt threatened. She gradually felt more comfortable with the men in the group and was able to talk about her feelings more openly. A subsequent dream reflected her growing self-confidence:

> *"I was conducting a class of adults in sexual instruction. Both men and women were in the class".*

At this point, she believed that she was a valued, contributing member of the group. She often took the initiative in exploring certain themes and was much less anxious when she asserted herself. Her guilt over masturbation and her sexual fantasies continued to subside. She began to express her angry feelings, often displaying a delightful quality of feisty spontaneity. In her fourth year of treatment she had the following dream:

"A man brought me presents and flowers. I was asleep when he brought them, but then I woke up".

She associated the man to me, and her gratefulness for my help. Her "asleep-self" corresponded to her state of despair, inhibition, and unawareness prior to treatment. Her "awake self" reflected her current feelings of vitality, hopefulness and the insights she had gained through treatment. Her transference to me was less eroticized, and she perceived me in a less idealized, more realistic fashion. She felt much less intimidated by her Mother Superior and was more assertive with her. She enrolled in a course for certification as a swimming instructor at the YMCA and expanded her social contacts outside of the community. In her fifth year of treatment she disclosed the following dream:

"I was with Sister Irene. There were some fish out of their tank gasping. I put them back in the tank and posed for a photographer in a bathing suit. I felt guilty and made him take the picture of me in a habit. Then I went on an eating binge and was not in the convent".

She associated to the dream as follows: "I've made the decision to leave the community-I can't have intimate relationships with the people in there. Yet, it offers security, safety and predictability. But, it's dull and constricted. I love to swim-it feels free and unconstricted. I don't feel self-conscious in a bathing suit now. I like wearing civilian clothes and having my hair free. I feel like I'm leading a double life; I'm having a lot of sexual fantasies-long, love-making scenes either with you or other men. I don't binge eat anymore-I'm substituting reading instead. I used to binge out of defiance, rage or resignation. I feel guilty over my deviousness and my double life. Sister

Irene is the only person I can confide in-but I have to be devious if I want friends who live outside the community. I feel comfortable with men in my swimming class-there's a lot of physical contact-l couldn't have done that a couple of years ago."

This dream poignantly illustrated her struggle to arrive at the decision to leave the convent, as well as her anxiety over her ability to survive outside the religious community. She vacillated between feeling free and feeling constricted sexually, affectively and interpersonally. She finally resolved her conflict in the direction of freedom and self-dependence at all levels. Several months after she had this dream, she informed her Mother Superior that she planned to leave the community. Since her departure she has lived independently, held a responsible teaching position, increased her circle of friends, and dated several men. She was able to have sexual intercourse, which she found pleasurable. A year ago, she met a man with whom she developed a loving, intimate relationship, and they were recently married.

The dreams of this patient sequentially illuminated her dynamics and her progressive changes during treatment. Initially, she was depressed and alienated from her community, her family and herself. Through her dreams and the exploratory work they generated, she became aware of the sources of her guilt and inhibitions in connection with her sexuality and the ability to express her feelings. She gradually came to realize that although the convent originally fulfilled her needs for a caring, supportive family, it actually reinforced her guilt over her sexuality and contributed to further suppression of her feelings. Her fantasy of finding the loving, accepting mother she longed for could not be actualized within her religious family. Successive dreams during treatment enable her to identify and resolve her sexual conflicts, work through transference distortions, improve her self-esteem, alter her defensive responses, and express her feelings more directly.

Tom:

Tom was a thirty-five-year-old attorney who entered analysis for relief from his anxiety symptoms. He was married and the father of two children. His anxiety symptoms were mainly connected with his work. He obsessed over the viability of his law practice, and felt threatened by his professional peers. Early in treatment, he related the following dream:

"I was going to work. There was a giant black fish in the subway system and everybody was afraid of it. It started devouring people. Everybody panicked. I warned several women of the danger and they went to a friend's house, but l stopped at a dirty bookstore first".

Tom's associations centered around his difficulties at work: for example, his constant fear of losing a case, or of being criticized by a judge and humiliated in court. The friend in the dream was a male school chum who was the first in his crowd to "get laid." He recalled how shy and inhibited he was with girls during adolescence. He began having sexual relations in college, often fantasizing that his partner was a whore. Sometimes, he imagined that his wife was a prostitute when he had sexual relations with her. He acknowledged a long-standing habit o of picking up prostitutes and frequenting porno shops. Then he realized it was his mother's birthday, and he'd forgotten it. He wondered if his memory lapse might have something to do with his father's jealousy when he paid special attention to his mother. She was loving and supportive, while his father was authoritarian, critical, competitive and ill-tempered. He often felt that he could never do anything well enough to please his father. The giant black fish reminded him of how frightened he was of sharks when he swam at the family's summer cottage. I pointed out to him that the giant black fish might represent his father and the men who threatened him so much at work. He agreed and wondered if I, too, would be critical and punitive during the analysis. A month later, he reported the following dream:

'I was part of Hitler's entourage in a cold, desolate country. He had a violent temper with fits of rage. I felt sorry for his wife. We were in a

war with bloody battles, trenches, bayonets, and people having their limbs cut off. I couldn't decide which side I was on".

He associated Hitler to his father, who often behaved like a dictator with fits of rage. The household frequently seemed like a battlefield when his father was angry. He recalled his terror-filled fantasies of being physically hurt, or even killed by his father. His mother was sometimes the object of his father's tirades, causing him to feel sorry for her but unable to protect her. However, it was Tom's older brother who usually took the brunt of his father's rage. His brother did poorly in school, and Tom realized that he could avoid his father's anger by excelling in his schoolwork. However, this made him feel guilty, augmented by the fact that his brother had a partially paralyzed arm due to a childhood accident. Tom avoided winning at competitive games with his father and brother, even though he knew he was capable of doing so. He was afraid of incurring his father's wrath (the latter became infuriated when he lost) and felt sorry for his brother. Thus, he was conflicted between his wish to excel in order to placate his father, and a desire to lose in order to avoid his father's anger, as well as to feel less guilty toward his brother. He acted out this conflict at work by never performing up to his full potential, fearing that if he succeeded he would either feel guilty or invite the hostile envy of his colleagues. He found it difficult to assert himself and expressed his anger indirectly through sarcasm or banter. His early transference to me was marked by distrust, fear and doubts over my sincerity in wanting to help him. On the other hand, he was a "good" patient, never missed a session and associated diligently to his dreams.

Several months later he had the following dream:

"Four of us came ashore in Argentina' It was a hostile environment and we tried to figure out how to get out. An older man offered us his boat. We couldn't figure out why he was giving us his boat. He wanted us to pay $75 for it. We got up early next morning, got into the boat and headed out for sea. But we didn't know what to do next".

Tom felt that the four people in the dream represented himself and his three siblings who lived in a totalitarian regime controlled by their father. Father's Day was approaching, and he was apprehensive about visiting his father. He identified me with the older man who offered to rescue them, and the $75 was my analytic fee. His feelings toward me at this point were decidedly ambivalent; on the one hand, he was frightened of my possible criticism or even outright rejection. He fantasized that I might tell him he was "unanalyzable," as a previous analyst had. On the other hand, I seemed to understand him and to be making a genuine effort to help him. However, the future course of treatment was uncertain, and he wasn't sure he could change. Subsequent sessions revolved around his mixed transference to me. He wished he could incorporate my warmth, confidence and directness; yet, he continued to anticipate being hurt by me and secretly wanted to defeat me by not changing. A few months later he presented the following dream:

"I was travelling in Europe with a group and had to report to somebody. Then I was with you and everything was going well. I had a peaceful feeling".

This dream occurred shortly after my return from a vacation abroad. It's most striking aspect was the "peaceful feeling" he experienced. While I was away, he had fantasies of travelling with me as a son might with a kind, loving father. It would be pleasant and peaceful. He felt that our recent sessions had been productive and that we were engaged in a cooperative effort. His trust in me had grown and he viewed me as his ally. Europe, however, reminded him of two world wars, mutilation and death. Our work continued to focus on his irrational fears of the consequences of competition with other men. In order to protect himself from injury, he avoided confrontations, almost never asserted himself, and rarely expressed overt anger toward another man. After months of working on these issues he dreamt the following:

"I was swept off my feet by a beautiful woman. Being in love with her was like walking through clouds-it was magic. Then it was years later

and I was a dancer wearing a colorful red cape. She's there, but doesn't recognize me. I ask another woman what's going on with my old girlfriend, and she tells me that she's the star of the show and is dating the lead male dancer. I dance with another woman who's beautiful and available. But I'm crushed that my old girlfriend doesn't recognize me. The woman I'm dancing with asks me to join her and my old girlfriend after the show. I'm looking forward to it and to the new relationship with the woman who's available".

Tom associated the old girlfriend to his mother, and the new, available woman to his wife. At the time of the dream, his parents were moving to Florida. He felt that the lead male dancer was his father who was taking his mother away with him. Prior dreams and associative material had made him cognizant of the linkage between his sexual feelings for his mother and his expectation of punishment from his father (which frequently occurred in the form of criticism or ridicule). He realized that his need to fantasize about his former girlfriends and his wife as whores during intercourse, as well as his habit of picking up prostitutes, defended him from incestuous wishes and paternal retaliation. At this stage of treatment he felt comfortable in relinquishing his mother to his father, who had mellowed considerably over the years. This dream was a milestone in his analysis because it clearly demonstrated a successful resolution of his Oedipal conflict. Another dream during the same month was the following:

"I was playing basketball very intensely and was in the thick of the game. Our team may have lost by a point but it didn't matter. We were evenly matched and I found the game intense, competitive, but enjoyable".

Tom recalled a recent meeting during which he participated in a vigorous discussion with some of his colleagues. He felt competent and effective during the meeting, and actually enjoyed it. Work was no longer a dangerous battlefield for him, but rather a place where he could assert himself with a sense of security and acceptance. Approximately two months prior to termination of treatment he had the following dream:

"You and I live near each other overlooking the water. It's early morning and I'm in bed with Jean. You're in bed with an older woman whom I don't know. I want to make love to Jean. The older woman gets up and asks me if we'd like to go to the theater. You and I go out onto the deck and Billy M. comes out to get his car. I ask if you'd like to meet him. I tell you about Billy and his wealthy father".

Tom associated to a recent vacation during which he and his wife visited his parents in Florida. While there, he had fantasized vacationing with my wife and myself as two couples who were friends and equals. His father seemed less domineering and more affectionate. In turn, he felt less antagonistic and more tolerant of him. Billy was a college friend who had a very dependent, competitive relationship with a wealthy, autocratic father. Tom realized how much his relationship with his father, myself and other men had changed since he began treatment. Billy represented his former self, in contrast to his current self. Tom felt that he was able to express his love for his wife and children more freely now. He was also developing a closer friendship with one of his male colleagues. His feelings toward me had changed from distrust and fear at the beginning of the analysis to his present feelings of trust and friendliness. At the end of the session he warmly thanked me for the help I had given him.

Tom's dreams accurately portrayed his central conflicts, and documented their resolution during the course of treatment. At the beginning of analysis, he saw himself in mortal combat with other men. He felt constantly threatened, vulnerable, ineffectual and unable to realize his full potential. His major defenses were avoidance, passivity and isolation of his feelings. His successive dreams helped us to determine the etiology of his irrational fears in relationships with other men. As he worked through his conflicts, he became more assertive and effective at work. His dreams progressively illustrated his changing transference toward me from someone whom he feared and distrusted to a caring, helpful friend in whom he could confide. Transference resolution correlated with the development of less competitive, more affectionate feelings toward his father and myself. He was able to befriend a male colleague and was generally more expressive of his loving feelings toward his wife and children.

Carol:

Carol entered treatment in a depressed state following her mother's death. Her parents had been separated for several years when her mother was killed in a fire that destroyed the family home. Carol was enraged with her father who had left her mother for another woman, and she blamed him for her mother's death. Her mother was alcoholic, and the fire was apparently due to a cigarette she failed to extinguish when she fell asleep. Carol had ambivalent feelings toward her mother; she respected her intellectual and creative abilities, but was terrified of her anger and criticism. Her mother seemed to favor her older brother, and Carol felt deprived of her affection. On the other hand, Carol felt that she was her father's favorite, although he teased and ridiculed her instead of showing his love directly. Carol's mother was a painter who never achieved public acclaim, while her father was a well-known, financially successful photographer. Carol was a journalist, but suffered from frequent writing blocks. Her parents were from different ethnic backgrounds, and Carol's self-identity was strongly influenced by this. Her mother came from a wealthy, politically influential "Wasp" family, while her father's parents were poor Mexican-Americans. Carol identified with her mother's verbal facility, intelligence and aristocratic background, as well as with her father's charm, humor and strong sense of family. However, she felt split between her "Wasp" self (intellectually superior, well-spoken) and her "Mexican" self (dark complexioned, passionate). A dream reported early in treatment was one she had dreamt prior to therapy:

"My mother died and insisted on haunting me".

This dream preceded her mother's death and conveyed the central theme of treatment. Carol was guilt-ridden over her mother's death, and believed that had she been at home the night of the fire she might have prevented it. She realized that part of her hated her mother, and wished for her death on numerous occasions. Her mother's death represented not only the actual fulfillment of her wishes, but also precluded a successful resolution of her ambivalent relationship with her while she was still alive. She was barely on speaking terms with her father and refused to have anything to do with his girlfriend.

Carol was single and involved in a relationship with a male colleague, John. Eighteen months after she began treatment she related the following dream:

> *"I was in Italy with my mother and Steve. Then I was in a cabin kissing Steve and he wanted to make love, but my mother walked in"*

Carol recalled that John wanted to make love the night of the dream, but she had refused. She realized that she was angry at him for spending too much time at work, and not paying enough attention to her. Steve was a former boyfriend whom she had left, which was a pattern she had followed with other men. She did not want to get married because she felt most marriages were doomed to failure. Moreover, her mother had repeatedly warned her that men were irresponsible and unfaithful, similar to her father. Her mother's interruption of her lovemaking in the dream reminded Carol of her fear of losing her boyfriends to other women. In order to avoid this possibility, she often broke off a relationship when she sensed her partner's interest in another woman, or vice versa. Carol realized the extent to which her mother's hostility toward her father and men, generally, had interfered with her heterosexual relationships. She distanced herself from men by criticizing and dominating them. In addition, she chose men who were socially, intellectually, and occupationally inferior to her, thus guaranteeing a lack of respect for them as well as a justification for leaving them. Several months later, she had the following dream:

> *"I was with my father and not feeling well. He wanted to stroke me and I let him. But I fled when he wanted to have intercourse. Then I went*

through the same thing with my brother, Bob, but I forgave him and had warm feelings for him".

Carol associated to her mixed feelings of discomfort and excitement when her father hugged or kissed her. But she hated him for his flirtatious behavior with women and for his extramarital relationships. She couldn't recall any childhood sexual contact with her father or her brother, but she and her brother discussed sex with each other during adolescence, and she was aware of her sexual attraction to men who resembled him. However, she was repelled by the idea of intercourse with her father or brother. Some months later she dreamt the following:

"You and I were sitting in a big house on the floor. Then you grabbed my hand and led me into a bedroom. There was a portrait of a blond woman who was your wife. You wondered if someone else was in the house".

Carol acknowledged that she'd been having fantasies of sexual intercourse with me which made her extremely anxious. She was frightened of my wife's jealousy and possible retaliation. Finally, she recalled that her mother was blonde and concluded that I represented her father in the dream. This was the first of many transference dreams with Oedipal themes. Their manifest content invariably contained sexual activity between us which was usually interrupted by a woman. Several months later she reported the following dream:

"A Japanese woman jumped on me and tried to kill me. I was so scared I couldn't scream".

Carol associated to a Japanese friend of her mother's who was a successful painter. Her mother was envious of her friend's success. In fact, Carol believed that her mother didn't really want her to succeed: "She didn't want me to do better than her-I'm convinced she didn't even want me." In subsequent sessions, Carol expressed her belief that her mother would react with envy and murderous rage if she surpassed her professionally, or in her relationships with men. It became apparent how threatened she was by her female colleagues at work. One woman in particular, who was very aggressive, evoked terror and rage in Carol. Unable to confront her directly, Carol related to her with sarcasm, condescension, or by total avoidance. Our sessions focused on the various ways in which her fear of female rivals led to her inability to maintain intimate relationships with men, as well as to acts of self-sabotage at work. It became clear that her fear of envy and retaliation by other women for her success at work was a major inhibiting force contributing to her writer's block. Blonde, intelligent "Wasp" women were especially threatening to her because they reminded her of her mother and her childhood schoolmates who excluded her from their social cliques because she was "Mexican." Consequently, she viewed herself as unacceptable and inferior, which she defended against by overachievement, a superior attitude and a caustic wit. Although she had several close female friends, she could never place her entire trust in them, believing that they might eventually betray or reject her.

During this phase of treatment Carol oscillated between feeling affectionate and trusting toward me, or believing that she was rejected and unloved. Each spring, she became depressed when the anniversary date of her mother's death approached. She mourned not only for her dead mother, but also over the impossibility of ever receiving-her unqualified love and approval. During these periods, themes of loss and abandonment were predominant. She attempted to reconcile with her father, although she still blamed him for betraying her mother. Moreover, she felt devalued by him because he never complimented her on her physical appearance, reinforcing her feelings of unattractiveness. His frequent absences from home and inability to directly express his love for her intensified her feelings of being unloved and abandoned.

Carol eventually left John and began a relationship with Jim, who was divorced and considerably older than her. He was a successful artist who possessed many of the combined qualities of her parents. Jim was brilliant, talented, humorous and passionate. However, he continued to be involved with his ex-wife, as well as with a former girlfriend who tenaciously pursued him. Carol's dreams continued to portray themes of being violently attacked by another woman for stealing her boyfriend or husband. She identified with her father's girlfriend (Sandra) when she told me: "I'm alive and my mother's dead. I'm doing exactly what Sandra did to my mother-taking her husband away. I'm the apple of my father's eye, but I've committed a terrible crime. I've transgressed and everybody looks down on me." About a year after beginning her relationship with Jim, in the context of continued working-through of her Oedipal conflict, she reported this dream:

> "I was in Jim's apartment and it was under siege. Someone shot out a large picture window and Mary burst in with her friends. She was charming. I was very nervous and tried to stay out of it. She wanted me to take a walk with her and I did. We looked at horses and she finally left".

Although Carol remained frightened of a violent confrontation with Jim's ex-girlfriend, Mary, she felt less guilty and more confident. She associated horses to her resumption oi horseback riding which she enjoyed, having excelled in riding competitions as a teenager. She equated her competence at riding with a renewed ability to write creatively. She felt less intimidated by her female colleagues and expressed her feelings more candidly. Another dream, a short while later, added confirmation to the resolution of her Oedipal conflict:

> "You and Leslie finally decided to get married after twenty years. I was happy about it and the wedding was very touching".

Carol, who had previously met my wife (Leslie) on a social occasion, acknowledged, "I'm finally letting go of you-I can let Leslie have you." She was simultaneously more accepting of her father's girlfriend, Sandra, and finally had reconciled with her father. Shortly after this dream, Carol won a sizeable grant which enabled her to take a leave of absence from work in order to devote more time to her writing. Then she dreamt the following:

"I was sitting in the kitchen talking with someone about how many people were going to be at my house. My father said he might wind up spending more time there than anybody. A ghost appeared outside and watched me. It disappeared and then reappeared. It approached a basketful of stuffed animals and two stuffed bears extended their arms to it. The ghost was very skinny- I thought it was sick or dying and felt sorry for it".

Carol connected the ghost to her mother and their unresolved relationship which had haunted her since her mother's death. She recalled recently reading an article about exorcizing the devil from cabbage patch dolls. The stuffed animals in the dream once belonged to her mother, who had given them to Carol. She described her own struggle to exorcize her mother's destructive influence over her:

"My mother's ghost tells me not to be happy or successful. I'm spending more time with my father-I'm going with him to the opera and to his photography exhibit this weekend. But I feel my mother doesn't want us to be happy together. I have to be unhappy to please her... I'm trying to kill off my mother's ghost but I feel guilty over that."

Carol sensed that her mother's power over her was diminishing, allowing her to feel happier with her work and closer to her father. She even felt compassion and pity for her, realizing how vulnerable, unhappy and unfulfilled she actually was. During her leave of absence, Carol worked on a novel about the Mexican side of her family. She experienced a wave of creativity and confidence that she had never had before. In fact, she was able to ask another woman who was a friend and writer to critique her work. The friend's opinion, which was very favorable, motivated Carol to show it to a woman journalist who was one of her chief "rivals." She gave Carol some helpful suggestions and was very supportive. These events and Carol's growing insight helped her to feel more secure and trusting in her relationships with her female colleagues.

Carol ended her relationship with Jim because he would not commit himself to marriage or having children with her. Although she grieved over the loss, she nevertheless felt confident that her reasons for leaving him were healthy rather than neurotic. She subsequently met a man who was closer to her in age, and her commitment to him has grown. The possibility of terminating treatment in the near future has become a central issue, and she recently reported this dream:

"I was at the edge of a small lake. I was supposed to cross it. Dr. S. tossed me flippers to help me cross it instead of using a leaky boat. But I felt I could cross without the flippers although they made it a lot easier".

Carol associated Dr. S. (her family physician) to me. Crossing the lake without flippers was herself functioning without my help. The leaky boat symbolized the problems she had not fully resolved and her continuing vulnerability. Carol ended the session, saying, "I think I'll survive-you've given me the tools to make it without therapy-thank you for the help you've given me."

Carol's treatment has been long and arduous. Yet, her dreams have served as beacons, illuminating her dynamics and validating changes in her self-concept, conflicts, feelings, defenses and relationships. Some of her dreams can be categorized as "Turning Point Dreams," recently described by Warner (1986). These are dreams which clearly demonstrate that a therapeutic milestone has been reached. For example, in the dream where the ghost appeared outside the kitchen window and Carol felt sorry for it, a definite change in her relationship with her mother had taken place. She no longer felt as strongly influenced by her mother's pessimistic attitudes toward marriage, men and career. The terror and rage which her mother evoked had been tempered to the point where she felt compassion and pity for her. She had developed a closer relationship with her father and was not as threatened by her female friends and colleagues. The "dying" ghost represented the diminishing effect of those maternal introjects which promoted her fear of retaliation or failure if she were to have either a fulfilling relationship with a man or success at work. The dream in which she felt she could cross the lake without flippers indicated not only her desire to terminate treatment, but also a significant change in her self-concept. Although she did not see herself as problem-free, she could imagine herself functioning effectively without my active help. She had developed a more integrated sense of self, incorporating the positive qualities of both her "Mexican" and "Wasp" selves. Whereas she began treatment viewing herself as unattractive, unloveable, and creatively impaired, she now saw herself as attractive, worthwhile, and creatively productive.

Discussion:

I have attempted to demonstrate through these clinical illustrations how manifest and latent dream content can be employed to facilitate and document change during treatment. Representative dreams which were arbitrarily selected depicted psychopathology and subsequent change in the following areas: self-concept, defenses, core conflicts, transference, interpersonal relationships and feelings. Each patient reported numerous dreams over the course of treatment, many of which did not reflect significant clinical change even though they were dynamically informative and relevant. Nevertheless, there appeared to be an overall pattern to the content and outcome of certain dreams which correlated with progressive changes in dynamics and personality structure.

Initial dreams were of particular importance because they not only represented the yardstick by which subsequent dreams could be compared, but also because they provided data with predictive and therapeutic value. Tom's opening dream reflected his mortal fear of other men, it's crippling effects on his work and relationships, as well as his expectation of criticism and punishment from me. Carol's first dream (which she actually dreamt prior to treatment) portended the impact of her ambivalent relationship with her mother on her self-identity, career, perceptions of other women, and relationships with men. Sister Theresa's initial dream portrayed her alienation from her authentic self, her inability to communicate her feelings, as well as her defensive withdrawal. These early dreams indicated areas of dysfunction which might not otherwise have been recognized and dealt with so soon in treatment. For example, Sister Theresa's dream about bleeding from her vagina vividly presented her conflict, guilt and inhibitions connected with her sexual behavior. Carol's dream in which her mother interrupted her love-making emphasized the inhibiting influence of her mother and other women on her creativity and heterosexual relationships. These dreams and the associations derived from them helped both the patients and myself to become aware of conflicts and their ramifications which, without the aid of the dream material, might have taken us much longer to comprehend and work through. In effect, the associative work generated by dreams which occurred early in treatment often served as the first breach in the resistances connected to core conflicts and their derivative behaviors. In 1905, Freud pointed out the usefulness of dreams in dealing with resistance when he wrote: "The dream . . . is one of the detours by which repression can be evaded." Initial dreams and the associative work facilitated by them instituted a pattern of activity between the patient and myself which was repetitive throughout treatment; that is, identification and clarification of maladaptive functioning through the aid of dream content, followed by further exploration, insight and working through. This process promoted incremental changes in intrapsychic and interpersonal functioning, which was validated in the manifest and latent content of successive dreams, as well as clinically. For example, Sister Theresa's sequential dreams reflected her transition from a depressed, inhibited, guilt-ridden individual to a more gratified, emotionally expressive, sexually fulfilled person. The insights provided by Tom's dreams enabled him to work through his fear of injury by other men. His successive dreams documented his improved ability to compete effectively without fear of humiliation or annihilation. For example, his dream of enjoying the competitive intensity of the basketball game, even though his team lost, was evidence of his having successfully worked through his irrational fears connected with competition. In a similar vein, Carol's dream assisted her in resolving her conflicted relationship with her mother. As a result, she developed a more integrated sense of self, became less threatened by other women, increased her creative activity, and felt more secure in her relationships with men.

As Warner (1983) has previously observed, progress in treatment results in a change of self-perception in dream content. Themes of self-depreciation and self-destructiveness are replaced by those of self-gratification and self-satisfaction. Ornstein (1987) described a similar phenomenon in sequential self-state dreams. Sister Theresa, who originally viewed herself as estranged and emotionally empty in her dreams, evolved to where she experienced herself as worthwhile and vital. Tom's self-concept changed from one of vulnerability and ineffectiveness to a perception of himself as competent and secure. Whereas he fled from the devouring black fish in his first dream, he was able to remain in the thick of the basketball game and to genuinely enjoy the competition in a later dream in his analysis. Carol initially saw herself as a failure in her relationships with men, threatened by other women and incompetent at her work. Her successive dreams reflected a growing belief in her capacity to maintain a loving relationship with a man, to feel more secure with her female colleagues, and to write productively. In general, the successive dreams of these patients reflected the development of greater self-esteem and self-cohesiveness. Among the contributing factors were a reduction in superego demands, core conflict and transference resolution, as well as identification with and internalization of the empathic, organizing elements of my ego. Warner (1983) has referred to the latter process as internalization of the analyst as a "self-soothing agent."

Bonime's (1962, 1986) emphasis on exploring affects in dreams in order to promote insight and growth, was central to the treatment of these patients. Each of them developed an increased capacity for experiencing, tolerating, and expressing their feelings. Sister Theresa, who was emotionally inhibited at the beginning of treatment, became more comfortable in acknowledging and communicating a full range of feelings. The dream where she was asleep but then woke up, referred not only to her acquisition of insight, but also to how emotionally alive and free she had become. When Tom began treatment he was unable to derive pleasure from his relationships or career. His early dreams about the giant black fish and Hitler's violent temper vividly portrayed his terror of other men. However, his later dreams in which he felt "peaceful" with me and "enjoyed" playing basketball, conveyed his growing sense of trust in others and gratification from his work. Carol's initial dreams reflected her fear and intimidation by other women; (for example, her inability to even scream when the Japanese woman tried to kill her). Her subsequent dreams reflected her increasing confidence and diminished fear of female rivals. In the dream where she felt sorry for the dying ghost, it became clear that her fear, anger and guilt in connection with her mother had been replaced by compassion and acceptance of her mother's limitations. Moreover, she employed her acerbic wit, intellectualization and detachment less frequently for self-protection. Instead, she was able to express her genuine feelings more openly and spontaneously.

Dream content often signaled developing transference reactions and their resolutions before they were consciously acknowledged. For example, Sister Theresa's dream about Dave and his wife marked the beginning of a sexualized transference. It afforded us the opportunity to explore her masturbatory fantasies involving myself and other men. This, in turn, led to the Oedipal origin of her guilt and to her anxiety connected with sexual fantasies. Subsequent dreams indicated a gradual shift in her relationship with me to the point where she perceived me more realistically, and was less anxious over her sexual feelings toward me. Tom's initial dreams about the giant black fish and Hitler indicated his early fear and distrust of me. His later dreams revealed a more cooperative, trusting attitude toward me. His final dream in which he and his wife lived near my wife and myself reflected his emerging sense of equality with me and his gratefulness for my help. Carol related to me in a detached, often hostile manner at the beginning of treatment. Her dreams in which her mother, my wife and other women interrupted her sexual relationships enabled us to understand the defensive function which her distancing maneuvers with men served. The dream about my wedding signified a firmer resolution of her Oedipal conflict and was accompanied by a much warner, friendlier attitude toward me. Her last dream, in which she felt able to cross the lake without my assistance, indicated her readiness to separate from me, having sufficiently worked through the transference. It was also a termination dream which revealed her incorporation of my analyzing ability to the point where she felt confident enough to function autonomously. These observations are consistent with Carlson's (1986) study of "transference" dreams in a patient during and following treatment in which dream content reflected an increase in positive affects, along with greater independence from the analyst and more effective initiatives taken by the patient.

Summary:

In summary, there appears to be evidence for a correlation between manifest and latent dream content and evolving health over the course of treatment. Specific areas of change in personality structure and dynamics which are reflected in successive dreams include: self-concept, defenses, core conflicts, transference reactions, interpersonal relationships and affective communications. However, as Warner (1983) has observed, successive dreams during treatment may also indicate a therapeutic impasse or lack of progress. In this regard, dream content often provides evidence of regression, self-disintegration, psychotic decompensation, and potential suicidal or homicidal acting-out. However, these issues deserve separate and special attention.

In the Dora case, Freud (1905) analyzed two sequential dreams which provided insight into Dora's unconscious conflicts: namely, her wish to make love to Herr K., which articulated with her incestuous wishes for her father. In a postscript, Freud discussed the transferential implications of each dream. In retrospect, he realized that in the second dream Dora was telling him that they had only two more sessions before she would terminate the analysis. Freud concluded the postscript by commenting on the change in Dora's dynamics which the two dreams reflected: "Just as the first dream represented her turning away from the man she loved to her father-that is to say, her flight from life into disease-so the second dream announced that she was about to tear herself free from her father and had been reclaimed once more by the realities of life." In this paper, I have described what Freud observed almost a century ago: that successive dreams can be the royal road toward facilitating and documenting change during treatment.

References:

Alexander, F. (1961), *The Scope of Psychoanalysis*, Basic Books, New York, p. 256.

Bonime, W., with F. Bonime (1962), *The Clinical Use of Dreams*, Basic Books, New York and DeCapo Press, New York, 1982.

Bonime, W. (1986), Collaborative dream interpretation, *J. Am. Acad. Psychoanal.*, 14(l)\, 15-26; and in M. L. Glucksman and S. L. Warner (Eds.), *Dreams in New Perspective: The Royal Road Revisited*, Human Sciences, New York, 1987.

Bonime, W. (1985), Dreams, insight and functional change, presented at International Conference III, The Association for the Study of Dreams, Ottawa, Canada.

Carlson, R. (1986), After analysis: A study of Transference dreams following treatment, *J. of Consult. and Clin. Psychol.*, 54(2), 246 -252.

Dewald, P. (1972), Assessment of structural change, *J. Am. Psychoanal. Assn.*, 20,119-132.

Fosshage, J. L. (1987), New vistas on dream interpretation, in M. L. Glucksman and S. L. Warner (Eds.), *Dreams in New Perspective: The Royal Road Revisited*, Human Sciences, New York, 1987.

Freud, S. (1 905), *Fragment of an analysis of a case of hysteria, Standard Edition*, Vol. 7, Hogarth, London, 1953.

Greenberg, R. (1987), The dream problem and problems in dreams, in M. L. Glucksman and S. L. Warner (Eds.), *Dreams in New Perspective: The Royal Road Revisited*, Human Sciences, New York.

Ornstein, P. H. (1987), On self-state dreams in the psychoanalytic treatment process, in *The Significance of Interpretation in Clinical Work*, International Universities Press, New York, Chap. 7, in press.

Saul, L. (1972), *Psychodynamically Based Psychotherapy*, Science House, New York, p. 218.

Warner, S. L. (1983), Can psychoanalytic treatment change dreams? *J. Am. Acad. Psychoanal.*, 1 1 (2), 299-316.

Warner, S. L. (1987), Manifest dream analysis in contemporary practice, in M. L. Glucksman and S. L. Warner (Eds.), *Dreams in New Perspective: The Royal Road Revisited*, Human Sciences, New York.

Myron L. Glucksman is Associate Clinical Professor of Psychiatry, Yale University, School of Medicine; Associate Clinical Professor of Psychiatry, New York Medical College; Training and Supervising Analyst, Division of Psychoanalytic Training, New York Medical College.

Journal of the American Academy of Psychoanalysis, 16(1): 47-70 (1988).

USING DREAMS TO ASSESS CLINICAL CHANGE DURING
TREATMENT
MYRON L. GLUCKSMAN AND MILTON KRAMER

Abstract:

This article describes several studies that examine the relationship between the manifest content of selected dreams reported by patients and their clinical progress during psychoanalytic and psychodynamically oriented treatment. There are a number of elements that dreaming and psychotherapy have in common: affect regulation; conflict resolution; problem-solving; self-awareness; mastery and adaptation. Four different studies examined the relationship between the manifest content of selected dreams and clinical progress during treatment. In each study, the ratings of manifest content and clinical progress by independent observers were rank-ordered and compared. In three of the four studies there was a significant correlation between the rankings of manifest content and the rankings of clinical progress. This finding suggests that the manifest content of dreams can be used as an independent variable to assess clinical progress during psychoanalytic and psychodynamically oriented treatment.

Introduction:

This report describes several studies that examine the relationship between the manifest content of selected dreams reported by patients and their clinical progress during treatment. Previous attempts to correlate dream content and clinical change have been sparse and anecdotal. Freud (1905) commented on two sequential dreams in the Dora case that revealed her changing dynamics. Subsequent clinicians (Alexander, 1961; Dewald, 1972; Saul, 1972) noted changes in dream content over the course of analysis. Warner (1983, 1987) observed certain changes in the manifest content of successive dreams that corresponded with clinical improvement. These changes included increased self-esteem, greater self-soothing capability and less masochism. In addition, he described "turning point dreams" (1987) that reflected the achievement of a therapeutic milestone or a significant change in the patient's dynamics. On the other hand, he also described successive dreams that were unchanged and paralleled a lack of progress in treatment. Bonime (196211982, 1986) eloquently described how dreams reflect evolving health in patients. He illustrated in great detail the collaborative work between analyst and patient in understanding and using dream material to facilitate insight and to promote behavioral change. Glucksman (1988) described how the manifest and latent content of successive dreams can be used to document and facilitate clinical change during treatment. Specific areas of change included: self-concept, defenses, core conflicts, transference, interpersonal relationships, and affective communication. In recent years, investigators have increasingly emphasized the importance of understanding the manifest content of dreams (Fosshage, 1987; Greenberg and Pearlman, 1993; Kramer and Roth, 1977; Mendelsohn, 1990; Palombo, 1984; Wamer, 1983). Their observations suggest that rather than acting as a censorship mechanism to disguise underlying instinctual drives and wishes, the manifest content is a visual-auditory narrative that metaphorically expresses the dreamer's conflicts, problems, feelings, self-portrayals, and interpersonal relationships. Moreover, it may also serve a defensive function, including the neutralization of underlying wishes and instinctual drives. Greenberg and Pearlman (1993) suggest that the manifest dream may directly express the dreamer's problems and attempts at their resolution. Kramer et al. (1964, 1993) describe sleep laboratory observations that link manifest content with emotional problem-solving during a night's dreaming. Currently, the available evidence suggests that manifest content alone may serve as a reliable indicator of the dreamer's problems, conflicts and emotional state.

Despite the dream's central position as a source of information about the dreamer's intrapsychic functioning, it is noteworthy that studies evaluating the effectiveness of psychoanalytic treatment have paid little or no attention to it (Galatzer-Levy et al., 2000). Only the Boston Psychoanalytic Institute's prospective outcome study of patients in psychoanalysis (Kantrowitz et al., 1990) referred to the role of dreams. In that study, reference to dreams was included in the variable known as "self-analytic function". This variable included "the analysis of dreams, imaginary conversations with the former analyst, and the use of free association" (Kantrowitz et al., 1990). However, there was no further elaboration on the frequency or efficacy of dream analysis by analysands in that study. Geller's (1987) exploration of the role of internalization in the psychotherapeutic process examined the characteristic ways that psychotherapists are represented in the manifest content of patients' dreams. However, there was no attempt to correlate manifest content with clinical progress.

Numerous studies have examined patient variables exclusive of dream material that are relevant to therapeutic outcome in psychotherapy and psychoanalysis (Bachrach et al., 1985; Karasu, 1986; Kernberg et al, 1972; Luborsky et al., 1971; Waldinger and Gunderson, 1984). These include: ego strength, behavioral functioning, cognitive mastery, insight, affect regulation, object relations, self-representation, symptomatology, transference, defenses, patient-analyst match, motivation, problem-solving, and self-analytic function. Each of these variables significantly influences the outcome of psychotherapy. Coincidentally, many of these variables have been identified as an integral part of the dream process. For example, one of the primary functions of dreaming is problem-solving and conflict-resolution (Domhoff, 1993; French and Fromm, 1964; Greenberg et al., 1992; Greenberg and Pearlman, 1993). Another important function of dreaming is mood regulation; that is, emotionally relevant material is processed either successfully or unsuccessfully during dreaming (Kramer, 1993). Learning, memory-processing, mastery and adaptation have also been identified as significant functions of dreaming (Breger, et al., 1971; Cartwright, 1986; Hobson, 7999; Koulack, 1993; Palombo, 1978; Reiser, 2001; Smith, 1993). In addition, self-awareness and self-perception, both physical and psychological, have been demonstrated to be key elements in dreaming (Fiss, 1993; Purcell et al., 1993). Collectively, these functions of dreaming either compliment or are identical to those variables that significantly influence the outcome of psychotherapy. Recently, Glucksman (2001) classified dreams according to their functional and clinical significance. His categorization reflects some of the essential elements of the psychotherapeutic process (conflict, affect, self-representation, transference, relationships, resistance, problem-solving and decision making). In view of the close parallel between dream functions and the key components of the psychotherapeutic process that are predictive of therapeutic outcome, it seems logical to examine the relationship between dream content and clinical change during treatment. In particular, can dreams be utilized as an index to validate either progress or the lack of progress during psychotherapy and psychoanalysis? This type of study could have important clinical and practical ramifications. If dreams are a reliable index of clinical progress, then successive dreams selected during therapy may be an extremely useful tool for the clinician to evaluate the effectiveness of treatment. Furthermore, in the present era of demands for objective evidence of the effectiveness of psychoanalysis and psychodynamic psychotherapy, dreams may serve as a valid measure of clinical change. Manifest content, in particular, appears to reflect key elements of the psychotherapeutic process (conflicts, problem-solving, emotions, self-perception). Therefore, in order to systematically assess the relationship between manifest dreams and clinical progress, the following studies were carried out:

I: Comparison of the manifest content of dreams from the six most improved and six least improved Patients in the initial and later phases of treatment.

In an attempt to evaluate the relationship between clinical improvement and manifest dream content, 12 patients who had completed either psycho-analysis or psychodynamically oriented therapy were divided into two groups by the treating clinician (M.G.): (1) Six patients who demonstrated significant clinical improvement; (2) six patients who demonstrated limited or no clinical improvement. The manifest content of twelve dream pairs (24 dreams) was selected by M.G. (one from the initial and one from the later phase of treatment in each of the two groups). The dreams were selected on the basis of relevant clinical or psychodynamic issues portrayed in the manifest content. The 12 dream pairs were randomly presented to an independent observer (M.K.) who ranked them according to the six dream pairs that he believed demonstrated significant clinical improvement, and the six dream pairs that demonstrated little or no clinical change.

The six most clinically improved and six least clinically improved patients (rated by M.G.) were compared to the two similar groups of dream pairs (rated by M.K.). Both M.G. and M.K. independently placed exactly the same patients on the basis of clinical ratings and dream pair ratings into each group (Fisher's Exact Probability .001). The placement of both patients and manifest dreams into the two groups was done to a statistically highly significant degree. This study demonstrates that classifying manifest dream content is a highly reliable method of assessing clinical progress from the perspective of dividing patients into the most clinically improved and least clinically improved groups.

The following are examples of dream pairs from one of the six most clinically improved and one of the six least clinically improved patients.

Most Improved Patient:

Dream from Initial Phase of Treatment:
"I returned to teaching after a nervous breakdown. Another female teacher said: 'you just made it back in time or you would have been fired.' A choir director was trying to get me to sing alone. We were in an old Victorian house, and I saw a panther. I was frightened."

Dream from Later Phase of Treatment:
"I was at a beach resort where I won a beauty contest. I looked for my husband to tell him. I felt no urgency in finding him, and savored the experience."

Least Improved Patient:

Dream from Initial Phase of Treatment:
"I was with a group of college friends talking about having kids. I stayed out of the conversation, and someone asked why I was staying out of the discussion. I told them about the conflict between my husband and myself. I felt badly about telling them."

Dream from Later Phase of Treatment:
"I was on a sailboat with a man. He fell asleep. I tried to wake him up, but he wouldn't get up. I was totally on my own to sail the boat."

II: Utilizing the manifest Content of the First and Last Dream Report in Treatment to Assess Degree of Clinical Improvement

In view of the encouraging results of the previous study, a second one was designed using the same 12 patients. In this study, the manifest content of the first and last dream of treatment of each patient was selected by M.G. who rank ordered the patients according to clinical improvement based on the following criteria: (1) Symptom Reduction; (2) Resolution of Central Conflict(s); (3) Level of Functioning;(4) Ego Strength; (5) Interpersonal Relationships; (6) Transference Resolution; (7) Affect Regulation; and (8) Self-Analytic Capacity. The 12 dream pairs (24 dreams) were given to M.K. as randomly ordered pairs of dreams. M.K. evaluated and rank ordered the 12 dream pairs according to the following criteria: (1) Negative to Positive, or Positive to Negative Changes in Mood; (2) Positive or Negative Behavior;

(3) Positive or Negative Self-Image; and (4) Effective or Ineffective Problem-Solving. M.K.'s dream pair rankings were subsequently compared to M.G.'s clinical rankings.

The rationale for this study was based on the previous study's success in distinguishing clinically improved and unimproved groups of patients based on manifest dream pairs from the initial and later stages of treatment. In this study, an attempt was made to be more specific regarding clinical change. The treating clinician (M.G.) rank ordered the patients by degree of clinical improvement. Similarly, the manifest dream pairs were rank ordered by M.K. according to clinical improvement. However, in order to minimize the influence of psychodynamic content, the first and last manifest dreams of treatment were selected as dream pairs. This methodological approach focused on the manifest content of dreams at the beginning and end of treatment, exclusive of their psychodynamic meaning.

The correlation between M.G.'s clinical rankings and M.K.'s dream pair rankings was r = .45; p = .069; this correlation was significant almost at the .05 level of probability, and was very encouraging.

The following are examples of manifest dream pairs (first and last dreams of treatment) from one of the most improved and one of the least improved patients.

Most Improved Patient:

First Dream:
"I was put into a mental hospital."

Last Dream:
"I'm at an airport boarding a plane with a man. We climb up the stairs to the plane until there are no more rungs or stairs. I'm terrified. A little girl jumps off and is killed. But I climb to safety with the man and am glad that I survived. However, I'm angst-ridden over the little girl."

Least Improved Patient:

First Dream:
"I was trying to escape from a foreign country. It was a very repressive regime."

Last Dream:
"I was on a ship. It was fired on and I was hit by bullets in my back. I knew I was dying.

III: Assessing Degree of clinical improvement based on the manifest content of psychodynamically significant dreams from the initial and later phases of treatment

In view of the encouraging results from the second study, a third one was designed using the same 12 patients. It was hypothesized that the correlation between clinical rankings and manifest dreams might be greater if the dream pairs were selected according to psychodynamically meaningful content. Therefore, the manifest dream pairs were selected on the basis of their portrayal of a significant psychodynamic issue or conflict. One dream of the pair was selected from the initial phase of treatment, and the other was selected from a later stage of treatment. The 12 patients were rank ordered according to clinical improvement by M.G. using the same criteria as in Study II. The 12 dream pairs were randomly ordered and presented to M.K. who ranked ordered them according to the same criteria used in Study II.

The correlation between M.G.'s clinical rankings and M.K.'s dream pair rankings was r = .41; p = .09; this correlation was significant between the .05 and 0.1 level of probability, and encouraged us to further investigate the relationship between clinical progress and dream pair rankings.

The following are examples of two pairs of dreams (initial and later phases of treatment) from one of the most improved and one of the least improved patients.

Most Improved Patient:

Dream from Initial Phase of Treatment:
"My mother was in the hospital. I was with her doctor and we tried to get her into her room, but she jumped out the window before we could get to her."

Dream from Later Phase of Treatment:
"My mother was following me from room to room, screaming. I responded: " tough, but I'm getting out, anyhow."

Least Improved Patient:

Dream from Initial Phase of Treatment:
"I was going to take a civil service exam, but wasn't allowed to do it. I started crying".

Dream from Later Phase of Treatment:
"I was trying to go someplace, but was blocked in every direction. I was on my lunch break from work, and was lost. I couldn't get back to my office."

IV: Degree of clinical improvement assessed from multiple successive manifest dreams throughout treatment

In view of the promising results of the previous studies, a different group of 12 patients was evaluated in regard to their clinical progress and the manifest content of multiple successive dreams occurring over the course of treatment. It was hypothesized that a greater number of manifest dreams selected during treatment might improve the correlation between clinical rankings and manifest dream content ranking. 12 patients who had either completed treatment or who were in the termination phase of treatment were selected by M.G. who rated their clinical progress according to the same clinical criteria as in Studies II and III. The 12 patients were rank ordered according to their clinical progress based on those ratings. Manifest dream content was selected on the following basis: (1) initial dream of treatment; (2) subsequent dreams at equal intervals from the initial dream; and (3) final or most recent dream of treatment. The intervals between dreams ranged from two to five years, depending on the length of time the patient was in treatment. For example, the intervals between successive dreams for a patient who had been in treatment for six years were two years apart (four dreams). On the other hand, intervals between successive dreams for a patient who had been in treatment for 25 years were five years apart (six dreams). There was a range of four to six dreams per patient, occurring at intervals of two to five years apart.

The successive dreams of each of the 12 patients were randomly presented to M.K. who rank ordered each group of successive dreams according to clinical progress based on his rating criteria described in Studies II and III. M.K.'s rank ordering of the successive dreams of the 12 patients was correlated with M.G.'s rank ordering of the patients according to their clinical progress. The correlation between ratings of manifest dreams and clinical progress was $r = .377$; $p = .11$. This was not a statistically significant correlation.

The following are five successive dreams from a patient who had been in treatment for 15 years. This patient obtained one of the highest scores on the clinical ratings, and had demonstrated significant clinical improvement.

Dream 1 (Initial Dream of Treatment):
"My restaurant was in my father's apartment. It was Saturday night at 7:P.M. Nothing was set up and the kitchen was inadequate. I was very anxious about how I was going to cope with the crisis."

Dream 2:

"You were hosting a party for me in honor of my completing an outward-bound trip. It was at my son's fraternity house and it was a surprise. My old friends were there and you had photographed my life. You introduced me to your wife and she asked me how the restaurant was doing."

Dream 3:

"I was with a male robber. I tied him up and dialed 9l 1. However, I couldn't dial it right, and felt like a jerk."

Dream 4:

"I was in a parking lot. My wife was driving the car. A man was driving another car and almost hit us. I went over to his car and he put up his window. But he got out and I told him: That was really rude of you. I felt good about confronting him."

Dream 5

"A female teacher gave me an assignment under water. I didn't like it and protested to her. She gave me a failing grade. I expressed my frustration to her and felt good about it."

The following are four successive dreams from a patient who had been in treatment for nine years. This patient obtained one of the lowest clinical ratings, and was one of the least clinically improved patients.

Dream 1:

"A child was sick and throwing up. I helped it."

Dream 2:

"My mother was depressed and I tried to comfort her. She said she didn't love me."

Dream 3:

"I was defecating in a chair in the dining room. I looked and it disappeared. I left."

Dream 4:

"I was with my husband in our first apartment. I said: 'I don't want a divorce yet. I've changed my mind'. He said: 'no, I'm leaving.' I was scared."

Discussion:

In general, the results of Studies I, II and III strongly suggest that the manifest content of selected dreams during treatment reflects clinical change. Although this observation has been anecdotally reported previously (Bonime, 196211982; Glucksman, 1988; Warner, 1983,1987), this is the first study where clinical change and manifest dream content have been systematically rated as well as correlated between independent observers. The evidence provided by these studies supports the observation that the manifest content of dreams during treatment is a reliable indicator of clinical progress (or lack of progress). This conclusion is based on the significant correlations between ratings of clinical progress by the treating clinician (M.G.), and the ratings of manifest dream content by an independent observer (M.K.). This was particularly true for selected manifest dreams that included the first and last dreams of treatment, as well as dreams from the initial and later phases of treatment. These results are especially impressive in view of the fact that the correlations between clinical progress and manifest dream content were rank ordered. When clinical and dream rankings were grouped according to the most clinically and least clinically improved patients, the result was statistically highly significant. However, the correlation between clinical progress and multiple successive dreams over the course of treatment was less reliable and not statistically significant when patients were rank ordered. Paradoxically, the greater number of dream samples taken over the course of treatment, the less was the correlation between manifest content and clinical improvement. This may have been caused by the larger number of selected dream samples that included dreams reflecting situational or incidental problems, rather than central psychodynamic issues or conflicts. Nevertheless, the multiple successive dreams of those patients whose clinical progress was rank ordered by the treating clinician (M.G.) generally paralleled their clinical course, though not to a statistically significant degree. In fact, upon close examination, the manifest content of their successive dreams was complimented by the latent content, and corresponded to their clinical course.

The focus on manifest dream content in these studies does not necessarily diminish the value of latent content. It is still a widely held belief among clinicians that manifest content is the final common pathway of mental activity (latent content) that becomes condensed, symbolized and displaced. As a result, manifest content can be viewed as a metaphorical presentation of wishes, conflicts, feelings, perceptions, problems, and attempts at solutions. However, it would be difficult, if not impossible, for an independent observer to evaluate and rate the associative material derived from manifest content. The amount of data would be overwhelming, and the clinical information could bias the observer so that an evaluation of clinical progress might be less than objective. On the other hand, manifest dream content does lend itself to a more objective evaluation; such as, direct evidence of problem-solving, negative to positive or positive to negative feelings, positive or negative self-image and behavior. Nevertheless, an in-depth dynamic understanding of most dreams requires analysis of the latent content. Accordingly, the dreams in each of these studies were appropriately understood and interpreted by the treating clinician (M.G.) utilizing both manifest and latent content. A review of the relationship between manifest and latent content of some of these dreams may be of interest. For example, the latent content of the first and last dreams of treatment for the most improved patient in Study II revealed the following: in the initial dream, she associated being sent to a mental hospital with her sister (who had been hospitalized multiple times for psychotic episodes). She was afraid that treatment might uncover serious mental illness in herself. In the last dream, she identified the little girl who was killed to a schoolmate who was actually murdered. She also associated the girl to herself and her childhood fear of being killed by her violent father. She associated the man who was helping her up the ramp to safety with her therapist, who had helped her overcome severe phobias and anxiety stemming from her traumatic childhood. The latent content of the first and last dreams of the patient who was least improved in Study II revealed the following: in the initial dream, she associated the foreign country to therapy, as well as to that part of herself she was neither aware of nor understood. She identified the repressive regime with her job, marriage and parents, who were distant and unaffectionate. Moreover, she felt oppressed by her own rigidity, anger, and depression. In the last dream, she associated being hit in the back by bullets to the hurt and betrayal she felt when her husband neglected to give her a card or gift for Mother's Day. Moreover, she felt that she was emotionally dying in her marriage and at her job.

In Study I, the latent content of the dream from the initial phase of treatment reported by one of the most improved patients revealed the following: the patient was a teacher by profession, and her nervous breakdown referred to the symptoms that necessitated treatment. She associated the other female teacher to her sister, who was extremely competitive, and the choir director to her mother, who was domineering. The old Victorian house was her childhood home, and the panther that terrified her represented her mother's rage and warnings of dire consequences if she tried to become independent of her. The latent content of the dream from a later phase of treatment reflected her improved self-image and self-confidence. At this point in therapy, she was more assertive and less dependent on her husband and mother. The latent content of the dream in the initial phase of treatment reported by one of the least improved patients in Study I revealed the following: she had wanted children but her husband did not, and this was a source of conflict between them. Moreover, she subsequently developed breast cancer and had a mastectomy. Her husband's opposition and her medical condition prevented her from having children. The latent content of the dream in the later phase of her treatment revealed the following: the man in the sailboat was her therapist, whom she felt was inattentive and did not understand her. She felt abandoned and alone in the sailboat (therapy). Other important men in her life had also disappointed her, including her father, brother, and husband. They were emotionally unavailable and could not be trusted. The patient continued to be unhappy, resentful and bitter throughout treatment. Clearly, exploration of the latent content of the dreams reported by each of these patients provided a fuller dynamic understanding of the manifest content.

However, a close examination of the manifest content in and of itself also indicated objective changes in self-identity, feelings, and behavior. The most improved patient in Study II progressed from being sent to a mental hospital to climbing up stairs safely. On the other hand, the least improved patient in Study II went from escaping from a repressive regime to being shot in the back and dying. One of the most improved patients in Study I progressed from having a nervous breakdown and almost losing her job, to winning a beauty contest. On the other hand, one of the least improved patients in Study I went from being unable to participate in a conversation about having children, to finding herself sailing a boat alone without help from a man who fell asleep. Perhaps, clinical change is more clearly and objectively apparent in the manifest content of the successive dreams of Study IV, despite their lack of a statistically significant correlation with clinical progress. The patient who achieved one of the highest scores for clinical improvement feels anxious and inadequate about operating a restaurant in his father's apartment in Dream 1. In Dream 2, his therapist honors him for successfully completing an outward-bound trip. In Dream 3, he tries to apprehend a male robber unsuccessfully. However, in Dream 4, he is able to confront a male aggressor successfully. Finally, in Dream 5, he expresses his frustration to a female teacher who gives him a failing grade, and feels good about himself. This patient began treatment complaining of anxiety, feelings of inadequacy, and inability to assert himself, especially with other men. In fact, he did own a restaurant that was quite successful. His father was extremely critical and punitive, while his mother failed to protect him from his father's violence. He grew up believing that he could not rely on women, and that men would invariably hurt him. Consequently, he avoided confrontations with men and distrusted women. His clinical progress in treatment paralleled the manifest content of his dreams, in that he became more assertive with men and began to take more risks in his relationships with women.

On the other hand, the manifest content of the successive dreams of one of the least clinically improved patients in Study IV paralleled her clinical course. In Dream 1, she helps a sick child; in Dream 2, she comforts her depressed mother who doesn't love her; in Dream 3, she defecates in a chair; and in Dream 4, she tells her husband that she doesn't want a divorce, even though he's leaving her. This patient entered treatment because she was unhappily married, depressed, and suicidal. As a child, she felt she was ugly and a misfit. Her mother suffered from depression and was unaffectionate. She lacked self-esteem, and married an older man with whom she had a pathologically dependent relationship. Prior to and during treatment she exhibited self-destructive behavior, including suicide attempts, medication abuse, and sexual acting-out. Following her divorce, about which she was ambivalent, she began living with a man who was periodically verbally abusive.

Summary:

The results of the studies described in this report have important implications regarding the assessment of treatment progress and outcome for psychoanalytic and psychodynamically-oriented therapy, using manifest dream content as an index of clinical change. Of course, further methodological refinements may be necessary in regard to evaluating manifest dream content and correlating it with clinical progress. Hopefully, such refinements will provide us with greater reliability between manifest dreams and clinical change over the course of treatment. In summary, the manifest dream may not only be viewed as the royal road toward understanding the unconscious, but it may also serve as a reliable instrument for the validation of clinical progress during treatment.

References

Alexander, F. (1961), *The Scope of Psychoanalysis*, Basic Books, New York.

Bachrach, H., Weber, J., and Solomon, M. (1985), Factors associated with the outcome of psychoanalysis (clinical and methodological considerations) of the Columbia Psychoanalytic Center research project (IV). *International Review of Psychoanalysis*, 43, 161-174.

Bonime, W. (1986), Collaborative dream interpretation, *Journal of the American Academy of Psychoanalysis, 14* ((1), 15-26.

Bonime, W., with F. Bonime (1962), *The Clinical Use of Dreams*, Basic Books, New York, and DeCapo Press, New York, 1982.

Breger, L., Hunter, L, and Lane, R. (1971), *The effect of stress on dreams, Psychological issues Monograph, 27*, vol.7, no. 3, Interactional Universities Press, New York.

Cartwright, R. (1986), Affect and dream work from an information processing point of view, *Journal of Mind and Behavior, 7*, 411-428.

Dewald, P. (1972), Assessment of structural change, *Journal of the American Psychoanalytic Association, 20*, 119-132.

Domhoff, G. W. (1993), The repetition of dreams and dream elements: a possible clue to a function of dreams, in A. Moffitt, M. Kramer, and R. Hoffman (eds.), *The Functions of Dreaming*, State University of New York Press, Albany, pp. 293-320.

Fiss, H. (1993), The "royal road" to the unconscious revisited: a signal detection model of dream function, in A. Moffitt, M. Kramer, and R. Hoffman (eds.), *The Functions of Dreams*, State University of New York Press, Albany, pp. 381--4 I 8.

Fosshage, J. L. (1987), New vistas on dream interpretation, in M. L. Glucksman, and Wamer (eds.), *Dreams in New Perspective: The Royal Road Revisited*, Human Sciences Press, New York, pp.23-43.

French, T. M., and Fromm, E. (1964), *Dream Interpretation*, Basic Books, New York.

Freud, S. (1905), *Fragment of an analysis of a case of hysteria, Standard Edition*, Vol. 7, Hogarth Press, London, 1953.

Galatzer-Levy, R. M., Bachrach, H., Skolnikoff, A., and Waldron, S. (2000), *Does Psychoanalysis Work?* Yale University Press, New Haven and London.

Geller, J. D. (1987), The process of psychotherapy: Separation and the complex interplay among empathy, insight, and internalization, in *The Psychology of Separation and Loss*, J. Bloom-Feshbach, S. Bloom-Feshbach, and Associates (eds.), Jossey-Bass Publishers, pp. 459-513.

Glucksman, M. L. (1988), The use of successive dreams to facilitate and document change during treatment, *Journal of the American Academy of Psychoanalysis, 16*, 41-70.

Glucksman, M. L. (2001), The dream, a psychodynamically informative instrument, *Journal of Psychotherapy Practice and Research, 10*; 4, 223-230.

Greenberg, R., Katz, H., Schwartz, W., and Pearlman, C. (1992), A research based reconsideration of psychoanalytic dream theory, *Journal of the American Psychoanalytic Association, 40*, 531-550.

Greenberg, R., and Pearlman, C. (1993), An integrated approach to dream theory: contributions from sleep research and clinical practice, in A. Moffit, M. Kramer, and R. Hoffman, (eds.), *The Functions of Dreaming*, State University of New York Press, Albany, pp. 363-380.

Hobson, J. A. (1999), The new neuropsychology of sleep: Implications for psychoanalysis, *Neuro-Psychoanalysis*, 1, (2), 157-183.

Kantrowitz, J. L., Katz, A. L., and Paolitto, F. (1990), Followup of psychoanalysis five to ten years after termination: II. Development of the self-analytic function, *Journal of the American Psychoanalytic Association, 38*, (3), 637-654.

Karasu, T. B. (1986), The specificity versus nonspecificity dilemma: Toward identifying therapeutic change agents, *American Journal of Psychiatry, 143*, 6, 687-695.

Kernberg, O., Coyne, L., Horwitz, L., Appelbaum, A., and Burstein, E. (1972), Psychotherapy and psychoanalysis: final report of the Menninger Foundation psychotherapy research project, *Bulletin of the Menninger Clinic, 36*, 3-275.

Koulach, D. (1993), Dreams and adaptation to contemporary stress, in A. Moffitt, M. Kramer, and R. Hoffman, (eds.), *The Functions of Dreaming*, State University of New York Press, Albany, pp. 321-340.

Kramer, M. (1993), The selective mood regulatory function of dreaming; an update and revision, in A. Moffitt, M. Kramer, and R. Hoffman, (eds.), *The Functions of Dreaming*, State University of New York Press, Albany, pp. 139-195.

Kramer, M., and Roth, T. (1977), Dream translation, *Israel Annals of Psychiatry and Related Disciplines, 15*, 336-351.

Kramer, M., Whitman, R., Baldridge, B., and Lansky, L. (1964), Patterns of dreaming: the interrelationships of the dreams of the night, *Journal of Nervous and Mental Disorders, 139*, 426-439.

Luborsky, L., Chandler, M., Auerbach, A., Cohen, J., and Bachrach, H. M. (1971), Factors influencing the outcome of psychotherapy, *Psychological Bulletin, 75*, (3), 145-185.

Mendelsohn, R. M. (1990), *The Manifest Dream and Its Use in Therapy*, Jason Aronson, Northvale, NJ.

Palombo, S.R. (1978), *Dreaming and Memory*, Basic Books, New York.

Palombo, S. R. (1984), Deconstructing the manifest dream, *Journal of the American Psychoanalytic Association, 32*, (2), 405-420.

Purcell, S., Moffitt, A., Hoffman, R. (1993), Waking, dreaming, and self-regulation, in A. Moffitt, M. Kramer, and R. Hoffman, (eds.), *The Functions of Dreaming*, State University of New York Press, Albany, pp. 197-260.

Reiser, M. (2001), The dream in contemporary psychiatry, *American Journal of Psychiatry, 158*, 351-359.

Saul, L. (1972), *Psychodynamically Based Psychotherapy*, Science House, New York.

Smilh, C. (1993), REM sleep and learning: Some recent findings, in A. Moffitt, M. Kramer, and R. Hoffman, (eds.), *The Functions of Dreaming*, State University of New York, Albany, 341-362.

Waldinger, R. J., and Gunderson, J. G. (1984), Completed psychotherapies with borderline patients, *American Journal of Psychotherapy, 38*, (2), 190-202.

Warner, S. L. (1983), Can psychoanalytic treatment change dreams?, *Journal of the American Academy of Psychoanalysis, 11*, (2), 299-316.

Warner, S. L. (1987), Manifest dream analysis in contemporary practice, in M. L. Glucksman, S. L. Warner, (eds.), *Dreams in New Perspective: The Royal Road Revisited*, Human Sciences Press, New York, pp. 97-117.

Myron L. Glucksman, M.D., Clinical Professor of Psychiatry, New York Medical College; Supervising and Training Analyst, The Psychoanalytic Institute, New York Medical College.

Milton Kramer, M.D., Clinical Professor of Psychiatry, New York University School of Medicine; Staff Psychiatrist, Maimonides Medical Center, Brooklyn, N.Y.

Presented, in part, at the 47th Annual Meeting of the American Academy of Psychoanalysis, San Francisco, California, May 17, 2003.

Journal of the American Academy of Psychoanalysis and Dynamic Psychiatry, 32(2), 345-358, 2004.

THE CLINICAL AND PREDICTIVE VALUE OF THE INITIAL DREAM OF TREATMENT
MYRON L. GLUCKSMAN AND MILTON KRAMER

Abstract:

The authors collected the initial dreams of treatment from 63 patients and independently evaluated the manifest dream report (MDR). Variables included: Affect and Valence of Affect; Associations; Psychodynamic Theme; Psychodynamic Theme as Predictor of Core Psychodynamic Issues; Transference; Gender; Psychodynamic Theme Categories; Clinical Progress in relation to Psychodynamic Theme Categories and Transference.

The initial MDR invariably contains Affect that is frequently Negative. The Psychodynamic Themes of initial MDRs are dependable predictors of Core Psychodynamic Issues that emerge during treatment. Transference is evident in a significant number of initial MDRs and is often Negative. Gender of the majority of initial MDRs is predictable. The most frequent Psychodynamic Themes of initial MDRs fall into Relational and Injury Categories. Relational and Injury Themes, as well as Positive and Negative Transference, are associated with clinical progress. This study confirms that the initial MDR of treatment provides a significant amount of clinical and predictive information.

Introduction:

Historically, the initial dream of psychoanalytic treatment is considered to be of special significance. Stekel (1943) proposed that the first reported dream reveals the patient's entire life history. Saul (1940) concluded that early dreams reveal the patient's core psychodynamics, and are more revelatory because they are not yet influenced by interpretations and resistance. Bressler (1961) observed that the initial dream is similar to a Catholic confessional; it contains the basic elements of the patient's neurotic conflicts and magically absolves the patient of guilt for wishing to remain protected and gratified by the analyst. Franco and Levine (1969) concluded that the manifest content of initial dreams provides a relatively undisguised picture of the patient's central neurotic conflicts. Beratis (1984) stated that the initial dream communicates the patient's salient psychodynamic themes. In the clinical example he described, the patient's first dream introduced oral, oedipal, primal scene, voyeuristic, and self-destructive issues. Kradin (2006) terms the initial dream of treatment the "herald dream"; that is, it presents the major areas that concern the patient and anticipates the trajectory of the ensuing treatment. Similarly, Josef-Perelberg (2001) suggests that early dreams in analysis contain information about the transference that will unfold as treatment progresses. Some clinicians (Harris, 1962; Rappaport, 1959; Yazmajian, 1964) believe that the presence of the analyst undisguised in the first dream means that the dreamer cannot differentiate between analyst and parent. Accordingly, transference fantasies are not possible, while mistrust and difficulty with reality testing are likely, leading to unanalyzability. On the other hand, studies by Rosenbaum (1965) as well as Bradlow and Coen (1975) fail to demonstrate that the undisguised analyst in the initial dream is predictive of either unanalyzability or therapeutic outcome. They suggest that the undisguised analyst may reflect early object loss and unconscious denial of the analyst as the lost parent. These studies suggest that the initial dream of treatment offers a window into the patient's central psychodynamic conflicts, can predict the future course of therapy, and may or may not reflect a capacity for transference.

In two previous studies, the authors (Glucksman & Kramer, 2004; Kramer & Glucksman, 2006) noted the presence of affect in a majority (58%) of manifest dream reports (MDRs) of patients in psychoanalytic psychotherapy. Moreover, the manifest content of the initial dream in treatment contained significantly more negative than positive affect. On the other hand, substantially more positive than negative affect was observed in the manifest content of the final dream of treatment. In addition, the MDRs demonstrated significant clinical improvement between the first and last dreams, as well as from the early to the later dreams in treatment, according to specific criteria. The areas of clinical progress included: symptom reduction, resolution of central conflicts, improved level of functioning, greater ego strength, more satisfactory interpersonal relationships, transference resolution, improved affect regulation and self-analytic capacity. On the basis of these studies, we concluded that manifest dream content can be a reliable index of certain clinical variables and their direction of change during treatment. Nevertheless, we recognize that latent dream content is an important source of information in clinical work.

Since the literature on initial dreams emphasizes their clinical and prognostic importance, we decided to test this assertion by studying a group of patients who were either in ongoing treatment or had terminated; in particular, we focused on the manifest content of the initial dream report (MDR). Specifically, we evaluated the frequency and valence of affect in the initial MDR; psychodynamic themes in the initial MDR, as well as their predictability of core psychodynamic issues that emerged during treatment; the presence, absence, and type of transference found in the initial MDIR; whether or not clinical progress in treatment was associated with the type of transference in the initial MDR; gender of the patient suggested by the initial MDR; various psychodynamic theme categories of the initial MDRs, and their relationship to clinical progress. Wherever possible, the authors rated MDR variables independently of each other in order to establish reliability.

Method:

The initial dreams reported in treatment were collected from 63 patients (33 females, 30 males) who were currently in psychoanalytic or psychodynamically- oriented therapy, or had previously terminated treatment with one of the authors (MG). Their age ranged from 18 to 76years, and the mean length of treatment was 7.7 years. Diagnoses included a variety of Axis I and Axis II disorders, but excluded psychotic conditions. Some type of psychotropic medication was taken by 52/63 (82%) of the patients during treatment. Each initial manifest dream report (MDR) was assigned a number arbitrarily, and printed without any other identifiers, such as the name of the patient, age, gender, and associations. The MDR was rated according to the following variables by one or both authors (MG or MK): 1. *Affect and Affect Valence of manifest content* (MG and MK) and *Associations* (MG) in MDR; 2. *Psychodynamic Theme* of MDR (MG and MK); 3. *Psychodynamic Theme as Predictor of Core Psychodynamic Issues* (MG); 4. *Transference* in MDR (MG); 5. *Gender* suggested by MDR (MK); 6. *Psychodynamic Theme Category* of MDR (MG); 7. *Clinical Progress, Psychodynamic Theme Category and Transference* (MG). One or both authors rated the MDR depending on whether familiarity with the patient precluded both from doing so (e.g., gender), required the therapist's clinical knowledge (associations, transference, clinical progress), or required both authors for reliability (affect, affect valence, psychodynamic theme).

Results:

1. Affect and Affect Valence in Manifest Dream Report and Associations of MDRs (Table 1)

   The authors (MG and MK) had a high level of agreement (56/63 MDRs, 89%) on independent ratings of the presence or absence of Affect. They agreed that Affect occurred in 28/63 MDRs (44%). Of these, they agreed that Negative Affect occurred in 20 MDRs (32%); Positive Affect in 7 MDRs (11%); Mixed Affect in 1 MDR (2%); Affect was absent in 28 MDRs (44%). One author (MG), who treated all the patients, rated Affect in the Associations to MDRs (taken from therapy session notes). According to MG, Affect occurred in the manifest content of 33 (52%) manifest content, Affect occurred in 67/63 (97%) of MDRs. The same Affect Valence occurred in both the manifest content and Associations of 26 (41%) MDRs. Negative Affect occurred in either the manifest content or Associations, or both, in 47/63 MDRs (75%). Of 30 MDRs without Affect in the manifest content, 28/30 MDRs (93%) had Affect in the Associations. Of these, Negative Affect occurred in the Associations of 22/30 MDRs (73%).

TABLE 1. Affect and Affect Valence in MDR & Associations (Assoc.) (MG and MK)

Affect	# Patients	Agreement Between MK & MG on Affect (%)		Affect in MDR only (MG) in MDR (%)		Affect in Assoc. only (MG) (%)		Same Affect Valence in both MDR & Assoc. (MG) (%)		Affect Valence In either MDR or Assoc. or both (MG) (%)
Negative	20	(32)	25	(40)	44	(70)	22	(35)	47	(75)
Positive	7	(11)	7	(11)	4	(6)	3	(5)	8	(13)
Mixed	1	(2)	1	(2)	6	(9)	1	(2)	6	(9)
None	28	(44)	30	(48)	2	(3)	2	(3)	2	(3)
Total	56	(89)	33	(52)	54	(86)	26	(41)	61	(97)

2. Psychodynamic Theme of MDRs (Table 2)

   MK (who had no clinical knowledge of the patients) compared his understanding of the Psychodynamic Theme in the MDRs with MG's (who treated every patient). MK had close or partial agreement with MG in 57/63 (90%) of MDRs. This indicated a high level of agreement, and demonstrated that the authors conceptualized the Psychodynamic Themes in a very similar manner. The Psychodynamic Theme of the MDR was judged to be consistent with the core psychodynamic issues that emerged during treatment in 59/63 (94%) of MDRs by the patients' therapist (MG).

TABLE 2. Psychodynamic Theme of MDRs (MG and MK)

A. MK's comparison of Psychodynamic Themes to MG					
Agreement		Partial Agreement		Disagreement	
# Patients:	%		%		%
55/63	(88)	2/63	(3)	6/63	(9)

B. Psychodynamic Theme Predictive of Core Psychodynamic Issues (MG)			
Yes		No	
# Patients	%		%
59/63	(94)	4/63	(6)

3. Transference in MDRs (Table 3)

Transference was observed in 28/63 (44%) of MDRs by the patients' therapist (MG). When present, it was Negative in 17/28 (67%) of MDRs, Positive in 9/28 (32%) of MDRs, and Mixed in 2/28 (7%) of MDRs. The therapist as himself was not represented in any MDRs. More women 21/28 (75%) than men manifested Transference in MDRs. Of MDRs with Negative Transference, 12/17 (71%) were women; of MDRs with Positive Transference, 8/9 (89%) were women.

TABLE 3. Transference (MG)

A. Distribution					
# Patients:	%				
28/63	(44)				
B. Type of Transference					
Negative		Positive		Mixed	
# Patients	%		%		%
17	(61)	9	(32)	2	(7)
Female/Male					
12F/5M		8F/1M		(1F/1M)	

4. Gender Suggested by MDRs (Table 4)

The Gender of patients was correctly judged in 39/63 (62%) of MDRs by MK (who was not the patients' therapist). He judged incorrectly in 15/63 (24%) of MDRs, and was uncertain in 9/14 (74%) of MDRs.

TABLE 4. Gender (MK)

A. Distribution					
33 Females, 30 Males (Ages 18-76)					
B. MK's Judgments					
Correct		Incorrect		Uncertain	
# Patients	%		%		%
39	(62)	15	(24)	9	(14)

5. Psychodynamic Theme Categories of MDRs (Table 5)
MDRs were evaluated according to seven Psychodynamic Theme Categories by the patients' therapist (MG): 1. *Relational*: 27/63 MDRs (43%); 2. *Injury*: 23/63 MDRs (36%); *Others*: these categories contained too few patients to be of particular significance, but the dynamic themes were discrete enough to mention. (a) *Control*: 5/63 MDRs (8%); (b) *Self*: 3/63 MDRs (5%); (c) *Problem-Solving*: 2/63 MDRs (3%); (d) *Sexual*: 1/63 MDRs (2%); (e) *Loss*: 2/63 MDRs (3%). Relational Themes occurred from ages 21-73; Injury: ages 21-55; Control: ages 27-53; Self: ages 32-53; Problem-Solving: ages 42-48; Sexual: age 44; Loss: ages 65-76.

TABLE 5. Psychodynamic Theme Categories (MG)

Category	Patients	(%)	Female/Male	Age Range	Under Age 40	Over Age 40
Relational	27/63	(43)	13F/14M	21-73	12	15
Injury	23/63	(36)	16F/7M	21-55	11	12
Others:						
a. Control	5/63	(8)	1F/4M	27-53	2	3
b. Self	3/63	(5)	2F/1M	32-53	1	2
c. Problem-Solving	2/63	(3)	0F/2M	42-48	0	2
d. Sexual	1/63	(2)	0F/1M	44	0	1
e. Loss	2/63	(3)	1F/1M	65-76	0	2

6. Psychodynamic Theme, Transference and Clinical Progress (Table 5)
The range of duration of treatment for the 63 patients was from 3 weeks to 35 years. The mean duration of treatment was 7.7 years. Progress or lack of progress in treatment was globally rated by the patients' therapist (MG) according to the following criteria: symptom reduction, affective regulation, transference and conflict resolution, achievement of insight, improved self-image, more satisfactory interpersonal relationships, and a higher level of function. Significant progress in treatment occurred in 13/27 (48%) of patients with MDR Relational Themes and 13/23 (56%) of patients with MDR Injury Themes. Some type of progress was made by 27/27 (100%) of patients with Relational Themes, and 18/23 (78%) of patients with Injury Themes. Clinical progress in the Other

Psychodynamic Theme Categories was difficult to assess because of the small number of patients in each category, although 11/13 (85%) made some clinical progress. However, 56/63 (88%) of all the patients were judged by MG as significantly or partially improved. Of MDRs with Negative Transference, T4/17 (82%) of patients exhibited significant or partial progress in treatment; of MDRs with Positive Transference 9/9 (100%) of patients exhibited significant or partial clinical progress, according to MG.

TABLE 6. Psychodynamic Theme Category, Transference and Clinical progress (MG)

Category	Patients	Significant Progress	(%)	Partial Progress	(%)	No Progress	(%)
Relational	27	13/27	(48)	14/27	(52)		
Injury	23	13/23	(56)	5/23	(22)	5/23	(22)
Others	13	7/13	(54)	4/10	(40)	2/5	(40)
Transference	28	17/28	(61)	8/28	(29)	3/28	(11)
Negative	17	11/17	(65)	3/17	(18)	3/17	(18)
Positive	9	5/9	(56)	4/9	(44)		
Mixed	2	1/2	(50)	1/2	(50)		

Discussion:

Affect

The high level of agreement (89%) between the authors (MG and MK) who rated the presence, absence, and Valence of Affect indicated that their observations were reliable. The presence of Affect in 28/63 (44%) of initial MDRs was consistent with our previous study (Kramer & Glucksman, 2006) in which Affect was observed in 58% of dream reports. Negative Affect was the most predominant type in 20/63 (32%) of initial MDRs. This was also consistent with our previous finding that initial dreams contained significantly more Negative than Positive Affect. Positive Affect was present in only 7/63 (11%) of initial MDRs in this study. In addition, MDRs without Affect in the manifest content had a high occurrence of Affect in the Associative material (28/30 or 93%). Of these, 22/30 (73%) had Negative Affect in the Associative content. Altogether, 61/63 (97%) of initial MDRs had Affect in either the manifest content or the Associations, almost identical to our earlier study (98%). Moreover, Negative Affect was present in 47 /63 (75%) of initial MDRs, including either manifest content or Associations, or both. This finding was also similar to our previous study (Kramer & Glucksman, 2006) where Affect was Negative in 77% of initial MDRs. The presence of Affect in dreams, especially Negative Affect in the initial dream of treatment, is further confirmed by these observations.

Example of Initial MDR with Negative Affect:

"I went to a building where I used to work. I drove a Subaru coupe there. But nobody was there, and I felt alone and sad."

This patient entered treatment with symptoms of clinical depression, secondary to loss of his job and a recent myocardial infarction. Perhaps, the major reason for the preponderance of Negative Affect in the initial dream is because most patients are in a dysphoric state at the beginning of treatment, similar to this patient. One of the important functions of dreaming is to process and contain emotions, especially negative ones, according to the Mood Regulatory Theory of Dream Function (Kramer, 1993). In the later or final dreams of treatment, the Valence of Affect shifts from Negative to Positive, most likely because of the beneficial effects of treatment (Kramer & Glucksman, 2006).

Psychodynamic Theme of MDR

MK independently agreed with MG either closely or partially on the Psychodynamic Theme in 57/63 (90%) of initial MDRs. Since MG was aware of the psychodynamic issues of all the patients, and MK lacked clinical knowledge of any of the patients, this was an impressive level of agreement. It supported the conclusion that MG and MK conceptualized Psychodynamic Themes very similarly.

The following is an Initial MDR and the Psychodynamic Themes according to each author:

"I'm in the military and going off to war. I don't want to go and I try to figure out how to get out of it."

MG's *Psychodynamic Theme.* "This dream is about feeling trapped and wanting to escape. However, the dreamer is uncertain as to how he can accomplish this. He feels scared, vulnerable and unable to protect himself."

MK's *Psychodynamic Theme.* "The dreamer is in a situation where he has to go along with a group (work, social, religious) that can make him do things he doesn't want to do. It may be dangerous and he wants out. However, he could be punished or rejected if he tries to leave."

In actuality, the dreamer was in a power struggle with one of his peers at work. He felt very threatened and was afraid of being humiliated if his rival prevailed. He thought about leaving his job, but was uncertain about his future if he did so. He felt anxious, vulnerable, and stymied. Both authors conceptualized the Psychodynamic Theme of this MDR in a similar way. It is important to distinguish between dream interpretation and dream theme. Dream interpretation requires the participation of both the dreamer and the therapist in order to arrive at a mutually agreeable understanding of the dream. It requires the dreamer's associations to the manifest content in order to establish the latent content, as well as the therapist's clinical knowledge of the dreamer. This interpretation or understanding is ordinarily constructed using a psychodynamic model or system (e.g., Jungian, Freudian). Both manifest and latent content are utilized in forming an interpretation. On the other hand, the dream theme involves a phenomenological approach to the dream imagery without the dreamer's associations and exclusive of any one psychodynamic school of thought. It assumes that the manifest content is metaphorical or figurative, and reflects the dreamer's personal life experience. Kramer (1991, 1993) refers to this method of understanding the dream as "dream translation." The latter establishes the meaning or theme of the dream in a psychodynamically generic sense without the dreamer's input, We wish to emphasize, however, that the dreamer's associations to the manifest content are critical in order to arrive at a full understanding of the dream. Although a generic psychodynamic theme may be suggested by the MDR, it can only be reliably validated by the dreamer's associations in the context of therapy Psychodynamic Theme as Predictor of Core Psychodynamic Issues During Treatment MG examined the relationship between initial MDR Psychodynamic Themes and the essential or Core Psychodynamic Issues that emerged during the ensuing treatment. He observed that 59/63 (94%) of initial MDR Psychodynamic Themes predicted the major psychodynamic issues that arose during treatment. This finding corresponded to the observations of others (Beratis, 1984; Bressler, 1961; Kradin, 2006; Saul, 1940; Stekel, 1943) that the initial dream of treatment encapsulates the patient's central psychodynamic conflicts.

The following is an Initial MDR, the Psychodynamic Theme, and the salient psychodynamic issues that were identified during treatment:

> *"I was playing bridge with my wife and we were in a bidding sequence. I knew I was in a bad situation and was afraid I'd make a mistake with a bad result. I would be a failure and everyone would see it."*

Both MG and MK agreed that the generic Psychodynamic Theme or meaning of this MDR involved a sense of inadequacy, fear of being exposed, failing, and experiencing humiliation or shame.

The patient entered treatment after his wife threatened to leave him because of his controlling, perfectionistic behavior. His wife was a tournament bridge player and was trying to teach him how to play. Anticipating her criticism whenever he made a mistake in bidding, he would become extremely anxious and irritable. In reality, she was quite tolerant and generally very supportive of him. He maintained exceptionally high standards for himself at work, and was excessively competitive with others. While growing up, his mother was very critical and often did not speak to him for days when she was angry at him. His father was emotionally distant, and his occasional temper outbursts were frightening. He was in constant fear of making mistakes and feeling humiliated in public. Consequently, he was a compulsive perfectionist at work, socially, and even when he engaged in leisure activities. He was chronically anxious, drank excessively, and had no close male friends. He approached therapy as a challenge to his intellectual abilities, and was afraid of being criticized by his therapist. His feelings were strongly controlled, and he had great difficulty revealing his vulnerabilities. His early transference to the therapist was one of wariness and covert hostility; at times he viewed him as his critical mother, and at other times as his emotionally remote, potentially lethal father. Although he was overtly cooperative, he nevertheless remained fearful of exposing any psychological weaknesses. Over the course of therapy, it gradually became evident that he was terrified of emotional abandonment by his mother, and physical annihilation by his father. The latter was an army Ranger during WWII, and sometimes made oblique references to having killed enemy soldiers in hand-to-hand combat. It was only after several years of therapy that he developed a more trusting relationship with his therapist. In this context, he became less defensive and revealed his deepest fears of rejection, failure, and physical injury. This clinical example illustrates how the Psychodynamic Theme of the initial MDR was subsequently validated by the patient's psychodynamic issues that became evident during the course of treatment. According to MG (who treated every patient), the Psychodynamic Themes of the majority of initial MDRs (59/63 or 94%) in this study were, to a large degree, predictive of the Core Psychodynamic Issues characteristic of each patient.

Transference in MDR

Transference in the initial MDR was defined by the presence of the therapist (MG), a person, object, or situation serving as a projection and displacement of the therapist. According to these criteria, Transference was observed by MG in 28/63 (44%) of initial MDRs. When present, it was Negative in 17/28 (61%) of MDRs, Positive in 9/28 (32%) of MDRs, and Mixed in 2/28 (7%) of MDRs. The therapist as himself was not present in any MDRs. Some authors believe that transference dreams are ubiquitous because the therapeutic relationship is a template for all other relationships (Altman, 1979; Bonime, 1962; Sloane, 1990). Therefore, to the extent that manifest imagery often contains one or more individuals and objects, transference is almost omnipresent. Others point out that in order for a dream to be defined as transferential, the patient's associations must ultimately involve feelings and attitudes toward the analyst (Glucksman, 2007; Greenson, 1967). Initial dreams of treatment rarely contain the therapist undisguised in the manifest content (as was the case in the present study). Although controversy exists over the prognostic implications of the undisguised analyst in the initial dream (Bradlow & Coen, 1975; Harris, 1962; Rappaport, 1959; Rosenbaum, 1965; Yazmajian, 1964), the absence of such evidence in this study sheds no further light on this issue.

The type of Transference in the initial dream and its relationship to subsequent clinical progress was also examined by MG. Of initial MDRs exhibiting Negative Transference, 14/17 (82%) were associated with significant or partial clinical progress. Of initial MDRs manifesting Positive Transference, 9 /9 (100%) were associated with clinical improvement. On the basis of these findings, both Negative and Positive Transference in initial dreams were almost equally associated with clinical progress.

An example of Negative Transference in an initial MDR is the following:

"A man was attacking me and trying to cut my back with a knife. The cops couldn't catch him and he got away with it."

The patient was sexually abused by her father from childhood into adolescence. Her ex-husband also abused her physically and verbally. She was extremely distrustful of men, including the therapist, and had no further heterosexual relationships following her divorce. Self-mutilation (cutting) and depersonalization were her major presenting symptoms. She felt that her father had "gotten away with murder." Although she proceeded to have a stormy course of treatment, her transference gradually became more positive and she stopped cutting herself.

An example of Positive Transference in an initial MDR is the following:

"I went to the doctor and he did an MRI on my neck. He found something that explained all my symptoms. I felt relieved and happy."

The patient entered treatment with somatic symptoms associated with anxiety, including neck and back pain. A complete medical workup had failed to reveal an organic cause for her maladies. She was hopeful that the therapist could diagnose and treat her symptoms successfully. Her anxiety was connected to marital conflicts and job stress. Her transference remained positive throughout treatment, although her anxiety symptoms never completely abated despite satisfactory resolution of her marital difficulties and a change of jobs.

These clinical examples illustrate Negative and Positive Transference in the initial MDR, as well as the patients' expectations of treatment and their early perceptions of the therapist. Initial transference dreams can be extremely informative regarding patients' attitudes, expectations, and perceptions of the therapist. In this study, both Negative and Positive Transference in the initial MDRs were associated with clinical Progress.

Prediction of Gender in MDR

Previous studies (Hall & Van De Castle, 1966; Winget &Kramer, 1979; Winget, Kramer, & Whitman, 1972) have demonstrated male/female differences in dream content. Women have more dreams containing people, friendly social interactions, emotions, home and family references. Men have more aggression, hostility, sexual interactions, and striving for achievement in their dream content. Using these and other criteria, one of the authors (MK) who had no knowledge of the Gender of the patients in this study, judged initial MDRs for sexual identity. He correctly inferred the patient's Gender in 39/63 (62%) of MDRs. He incorrectly classified the patient's Gender in 15/63 (24%) of MDRs, and was uncertain in 9/63 (14%) of MDRs. Thus, he was able to correctly judge Gender in a majority of the patients based on the content of the initial MDR. His observations support the previous studies that report systematic differences in dream content between males and females.

Psychodynamic Theme Categories of MDR

Clinical investigators have previously categorized manifest and latent dream content according to psychodynamic meaning and function (Altman, 1975; Bonime, 1962; Glucksman, 1988; Glucksman, 2001; Glucksman, 2007; Glucksman & Kramer, 2004; Kramer, 2007; Warner, 1987). These psychodynamic categories include: transference, resistance, interpersonal relationships, self-identity, affect, trauma, sexual, wish-fulfillment, problem-solving, decision-making and turning-point dreams. Initially, the MDRs in this study were grouped according to 14 different Psychodynamic Theme Categories. Eventually, these were integrated into 7 categories: 1. *Relational*: primarily involves interpersonal relationships, including issues of rejection, reunion, attachment, intimacy, cooperation, conflict, abandonment, separation, exclusion, etc.; 2. *Injury*: primarily involves actual or feared emotional and physical injury or harm; includes being chased, shot, killed, robbed, beaten, mutilated, insulted, criticized, embarrassed, humiliated, abused, etc.; 3. *Control*: primarily involves situations or feelings of loss of control, including helplessness, submission, mastery, power, domination, etc. ; 4. *Self*: primarily involves physical or emotional aspects of self, including traits, qualities, attributes, physical appearance, etc.; 5. *Problem-Solving*: primarily includes resolving conflicts, dilemmas, problems, issues, decision-making, planning, deliberating, etc.; 6. *Sexual*: primarily involves actual or wished-for sexual activity and intimacy, including feelings, fantasies, lust, orgasm, etc.; 7. *Loss*: primarily involves actual or feared loss, including death, disappearance, absence or loss of spouse, relative, friend, job, position, status, money, possessions, physical or mental integrity, etc.

These Psychodynamic Theme Categories are somewhat arbitrary, and clearly overlap one another. Nevertheless, initial MDRs were rated in regard to the predominant theme of the dream imagery by the patients' therapist

(MG), who was intimately aware of their central psychodynamic issues and conflicts.

1. *Relational Themes* occurred in 27/63 (43%) of initial MDRs. They were almost equally divided between the sexes (13 females, 14 males). They occurred throughout the entire age spectrum (27-73), and were equally divided above and below age 40.

An example of a Relational Theme in an Initial MDR is the following:

"I saw Allan-his hair was longer and he was hosting people in the living room. He was handsome and greeting everyone, shaking their hands."

This female patient's son, Allan, had recently died subsequent to a drug overdose. She entered treatment with feelings of profound grief, guilt, and suicidal fantasies. Although she had made previous efforts to help him obtain treatment for his drug addiction, she felt remiss in not preventing his death. She fantasized rejoining him in death, and this was a dream about reunion. Much of her subsequent treatment revolved around her symbiotic attachment to him. Following her divorce when he was a child, she idealized him in order to partly compensate for her failed marriage as well as other unsatisfactory relationships with men.

Relationship or attachment issues are ubiquitous throughout the life cycle (Bowlby, 1969, 1973; Fairbairn, 1952; Guntrip, 1969; Kernberg, 1976; Ogden, 1990; Spitz, 1965; Sullivan, 1953; Winnicott, 1989). The occurrence of Relational MDRs over a wide age range in this study reflects this phenomenon; moreover, they were the most frequently observed of the initial MDRs. Since internal object representations are embedded unconsciously beginning at an early age, relational issues are inevitably present in dream content. Social interactions in dreams have been categorized as aggressive, friendly, or sexual (Hall & Van De Castle, 1966). Men have a higher frequency of aggressive interactions with other men in their dreams, while the amount of aggression decreases with age in both men and women (Hall & Domhoff, 1963). Friendly interactions are less frequent and less intense than aggressive ones for both men and women (Hall & Domhoff, 1964; Kramer et al., 1971). Wen social interactions occur in the initial MDR, they may inform the therapist about the nature of the patient's interpersonal relationships, conflicts, and the likely course of the therapeutic relationship.

2. *Injury Themes* occurred with slightly less frequency than Relational ones. They were observed in 23/63 (36%) of initial MDRs from ages 21-55. The majority, 16/23 (70%) were reported by females, and they were almost equally divided above and below age 40. Almost without exception, they were anxiety dreams, although anxiety was not always experienced by the dreamer in the manifest content. Since anxiety is the universal human response to threat or danger, these dreams were characterized by imagery involving actual or potential harm. Freud (1900) first described anxiety dreams, and believed that the function of dreaming was to censor or neutralize anxiety. Children begin to have anxiety dreams at an early age, consistent with their developmental phases (e.g., oedipal). Psychological or physical trauma, stress, and life crises facilitate anxiety dreams (Glucksman, 2007). Hall (1953) noted that the ratio of unpleasant to pleasant dreams increases with age, although anxiety dreams decrease with age. In this study, Injury Themes were not observed after age 55, in comparison to Relational Themes, which continued to age 73. Ward, Beck, and Roscoe (1961) found that the feeling of endangerment in dreams occurred in 57% of psychiatric patients. Harris (1948) observed imagery of being chased or attacked in72% of dreams of military subjects. Nightmares and repetitive anxiety dreams are characterized by extreme fear, and are frequently associated with trauma or PTSD (Hartmann, 1984; Kramer, 2007; Mack, 1970). Clearly, dreams with Injury Themes reflect the commonplace human experience of trauma, threat, or danger.

The following is an example of an Injury Theme in an initial MDR:

"An evil force enveloped me and followed me around. It stalked the family I lived with and it looked like a person. It killed one of the children in the family."

The patient entered treatment feeling anxious, depressed, and distrustful. She was divorced, lived alone, and was socially reclusive. Both parents were psychologically and physically abusive. She associated the evil force to them, and the murdered child to herself. Their abusive behavior "killed" her sense of trust and self-worth. She was wary of therapy, and expected the therapist to harm her in some fashion. It took several years before she could develop a trusting, therapeutic alliance. Initial MDRs with Injury Themes can alert the clinician to issues or conflicts that threaten the patient. They may also indicate the nature of the initial transference, which is often negative. In addition, the treatment situation itself may be viewed by the patient as potentially dangerous or harmful.

3. *Control Themes* were observed in 5/63 (8%) of initial MDRs, and were considered to be a special variant of Injury Themes, as well as a type of anxiety dream. Loss of control (e.g., falling) has been cited as a typical theme in anxiety dreams (Freud, 1900; Gahagan, 1936; Griffith, 1958; Harris, 1948,1951; Ward et al., 1961).

The following is an example of an initial MDR with a Control Theme:

"I was at work and was flooded with emails. I threw up my hands and walked away. I felt like I'd done all I could do."

The patient was a business executive who had an extremely stressful position, and entered treatment with symptoms of severe anxiety. He felt overwhelmed by the demands of his job, and unsupported by his boss. He entertained fantasies of quitting, but had a family to support. Consequently, he felt trapped and helpless. His father was alcoholic and prone to rages when drunk. The patient recalled feeling terrified and helpless when his father drank and became angry at him, for no apparent reason. His response was to run and hide.

4. *Self Themes* occurred in 3/63 (5%) of initial MDRs. In dreams that are primarily concerned with the self, the dreamer may appear undisguised, as an observer, or displaced by someone else in the manifest content (Glucksman, 2007). Although others may appear in dreams primarily about the self, there are certain dreams that are totally devoted to self-identity or self-experience, and exclude other individuals in the manifest content. These are termed "self-state" dreams (Kohut, 1971, 1977); however, none were observed in this study.

The following is an example of an initial MDR with a Self Theme:

"I was a teacher or medical advisor in an elementary school or high school. I didn't know which room I was supposed to be in and I felt estranged. I felt out of place, alone, and didn't know anyone."

This patient, a physician, entered treatment following the loss of his job in a hospital. He was depressed, feeling rejected and abandoned by his colleagues. While growing up, his father, a physician, favored his younger brother, leading to feelings of rejection and inadequacy. As a consequence, he looked for affirmation and acceptance from male mentors during his career, but was frequently disappointed. These experiences promoted his feelings of alienation and aloneness. Although this could be viewed as a Relational MDR because it reflected the patient's sense of estrangement from others, it was primarily about his self-experience; that is, he felt dislocated, alone and isolated.

5. *Problem-Solving Themes* were present in 2/63 (3%) of initial MDRs. Problem-Solving and decision-making are important functions

of dreaming (Domhoff, 1993; Greenberg, Katz, Schwartz, & Pearlman, 1992; Greenberg & Pearlman, 1993). Manifest content often expresses the dreamer's problems, including attempts to resolve them.

The following is an example of a Problem-Solving initial MDR:

"I was in a hotel room with Karen, and looking through her suitcase for something. I was fumbling and said: "I can't find it." I finally pulled something out of the suitcase and asked: "Is this it?" She replied: "yes," and I closed the suitcase."

The patient was an advertising executive who was in conflict with a female co-worker over the approach to marketing a product. The dream occurred the night before he was to attend a meeting about the issue. Karen was a friend in the same business whom he trusted and respected. One of his sisters with whom he had a good relationship was also named Karen. The following day, he discussed the problem with his friend, Karen, before the meeting, and was able to resolve the conflict with his co-worker.

6. *Sexual Themes* in initial MDRs were defined as explicit sexual behavior or experience in the manifest content. These occurred in only 1/63 (2%) of initial MDRs. Although Freud (1900) believed that sexual drives are a primary stimulus for dreaming, the frequency of overt sexual activity in dream manifest content is surprisingly low (Hall & van De Castle, 1966; Kramer et al., 1971). According to Freud, the dreamwork associated with the manifest content censors or neutralizes sexual impulses. As a result, actual sexual imagery is inhibited except when the underlying drive is too strong or the censorship mechanism fails. A more contemporary view is that the manifest content is less a censoring mechanism than a metaphorical presentation of the issues and conflicts addressed in the dream (Blechner, 2001; Bonime, 1962; Fosshage, 1987; Kramer, 2007).

Therefore, sexual impulses, cravings, activity, and conflicts can be symbolically incorporated into the manifest content without being necessarily explicit. This may explain why overt sexual imagery was almost totally absent in these MDRs.

An example of an initial MDR with a Sexual Theme is the following:

"I was on extraterrestrial terrain with a group of people, and we were looking out over a plain. There were alien figures, and one of the men in our group was supposed to have sex and procreate with one of the alien females. I picked out one of the women and had sex with her."

The patient, an engineer, worked on aerospace projects and was familiar with photos of the landscapes of other planets. He entered treatment for depression following a failure at his job. He felt socially isolated, and was always uncomfortable with women. His only sexual experience was with his wife, and he was impotent because of his depressed state. Extremely introverted, he felt alienated and cut off from others. The underlying wish in this dream was to be sexually potent and to connect with another person. Although it could be categorized as Relational, the dominant generic theme was Sexual.

7. *Loss Themes* occurred in 2/63 (3%) of initial MDRs. The two initial MDRs with Loss Themes were in older patients, ages 65 and 76. Older adults tend to dream about lost resources, death, helplessness, and weakness (Altshuler, Barad, & Goldfarb, 1963; Barad, Altshuler & Goldfarb, 1961; Kramer, 2010; Winget et al., 1972). Dream imagery involving death, vulnerability, and loss is positively correlated with age (Kramer, 2007).

The following is an example of an initial MDR with a Loss Theme:

"I was on a pier holding Ben in my arms. He was dying and we were the last two people alive in the world."

The patient was depressed when she entered treatment following the death of her brother. They were both physicians and practiced together for many years. Ben was another physician who was a friend and colleague. He had also died, and was the same age as her former husband whom she had divorced a few years prior to the dream. The deaths of her brother and Ben, as well as her divorce, were significant losses for her. She felt abandoned, alone, and vulnerable. Again, this MDR had Relational elements, but the predominant imagery was concerned with Loss. According to MG, patients made some type of clinical progress in treatment regardless of their initial MDR Psychodynamic Theme Category. In fact, all of those with Relational Themes made significant or partial progress in treatment. There was no specific Psychodynamic Theme Category that was associated with a significant lack of clinical progress.

Conclusion:

This study was a systematic attempt to evaluate the initial MDR of treatment according to a number of variables. It confirmed a previous observation (Kramer & Glucksman, 2006) that Affect is a significant component of the manifest content. Moreover, the previous finding that Negative Affect is present in a higher percentage of initial dreams than Positive Affect, was also validated. When manifest content as well as Associations (latent content) were included, initial MDRs contained a high percentage (75%) of Negative Affect. This observation was most likely a reflection of the dysphoria experienced by patients who are beginning treatment. Conversely, an earlier study revealed that later or final dreams of treatment contain more Positive than Negative Affect, most likely due to the beneficial effects of treatment (Kramer & Glucksman, 2006).

There was an impressive level of agreement between the authors regarding the generic Psychodynamic Themes of initial MDRs. The latter were highly predictive of Core Psychodynamic Issues that emerged during the ensuing treatment. Transference was evident in almost half of initial MDRs, and was more Negative than Positive. A higher percentage of women manifested both Positive and Negative Transference than men. However, there was no significant difference between Positive or Negative Transference in initial MDRs and clinical progress. Gender of patients was correctly judged for a majority of initial MDRs, supporting the fact that there are gender differences in manifest dream content.

When Psychodynamic Themes of initial MDRs were categorized, Relational and Injury Themes were the most frequently observed. The most likely explanation for this finding is that interpersonal and attachment issues, as well as threats of actual or potential harm, are part of developmental experience and ubiquitous throughout life. The majority of patients made significant or partial clinical progress in treatment, regardless of their initial MDR Psychodynamic Theme Category.

The findings of this study indicate that the initial MDR of treatment is a valuable source of clinical information in regard to the amount and Valence of Affect, Major Psychodynamic Theme, type of Transference, and Gender of the patient. In addition, the initial MDR is highly predictive of Core Psychodynamic Issues that emerge during the course of treatment. Both Positive and Negative Transference in initial MDRs are almost equally associated with clinical progress. Relational and Injury Psychodynamic Theme Categories occur most frequently in initial MDRs. Themes of Loss, although infrequent in this population, occur in older patients. Although this study has focused on manifest content in the initial dreams of treatment, we recognize the clinical importance of latent content in order to reach a fuller, psychodynamic understanding of initial dreams. Nevertheless, on the basis of this study, the initial MDR can be utilized as a reliable instrument for clinical and prognostic purposes.

References:

Altman, L.L. (1975). *The dream in psychoanalysis.* New York: International Universities Press.

Altshuler, K., Barad, M., & Goldfarb, A. (1963). A survey of dreams in the aged: Noninstitutionalized subjects. *Archives of General Psychiatry, 14,* 156-162.

Barad, M., Altshuler, K., & Goldfarb, A. (1961). A survey of dreams in aged persons. *Archives of General Psychiatry, 4,* 419-423.

Beratis, S. (1984). The first analytic dream: Mirror of the patient's neurotic conflicts and subsequent analytic process. *The International Journal of Psychoanalysis, 65,* 461-469.

Blechner, M. J. (2001). *The dream frontier.* Hillsdale, NJ: Analytic Press.

Bonime, W. (with F. Bonime). (1962). *The clinical use of dreams.* New York: Basic Books and DeCapo Press.

Bowlby, J. (1969). *Attachment: Vol. 1 of Attachment and loss.* New York: Basic Books.

Bowlby, J. (1973). *Separation: Anxiety and anger, Vol. 2 of Attachment and loss.* New York: Basic Books.

Bradlow, P. A., & Coen, S. J. (1975). The analyst undisguised in the initial dream of psychoanalysis. *The International Journal of Psychoanalysis, 56,* 415-425.

Bressler, B. (1961). First dreams in analysis: Their relationship to early memories and the pre-oedipal mother. *Psychoanalytic Review, 48D,* 60-82.

Domhoff, G. W. (1993). The repetition of dreams and dream elements: A possible clue to a function of dreams. In A. Moffitt, M. Kramer, & R. Hoffmann (Eds.), *The functions of dreaming* (pp. 293-320). Albany: State University of New York Press.

Fairbairn, W. R. D. (1952). *An object relations theory of personality.* New York: Basic Books.

Fosshage, J. (1987). New vistas in dream interpretation. In M. Glucksman & S. L. Wamer (Eds.), *Dreams in new perspective: The royal road revisited* (pp. 23-43). New York: Human Sciences Press.

Franco, D., & Levine, A. (1969). Psychic reality and psychic structure as predicted from the manifest content of first dreams. Proceedings 77th Annual Convention, APA, 4593-4594.

Freud, S. (1900). The interpretation of dreams. In J. Strachey (Ed. & Trans.), *The standard edition of the complete psychological works of Sigmund Freud* (Vols. 4 and 5). London: Hogarth Press.

Gahagan, L. (1936). Sex differences in the recall of stereotyped dreams, sleep-talking and sleep-walking. *Journal of General Psychology, 48,* 227 -236.

Glucksman, M. L. (1988). The use of successive dreams to facilitate and document change during treatment. *Journal of the American Academy of Psychoanalysis, 16,* 47-70.

Glucksman, M. L. (2001). The dream: A psychodynamically informative instrument. *Journal of Psychotherapy Practice and Research, 10*(4), 223-230.

Glucksman, M. L. (2007). *Dreaming: An opportunity for change.* Lanham, MD: Rowman and Littlefield.

Glucksman, M. L., & Kramer, M. (2004). Using dreams to assess clinical change during treatment. *Journal of the American Academy of Psychoanalysis and Dynamic Psychiatry, 32*(2), 345-358.

Greenberg, R., Katz, H., Schwartz, W., & Pearlman, C. (1992). A research based reconsideration of psychoanalytic dream theory. *Journal of the American Psychoanalytic Association, 40,* 531-550.

Greenberg, R., & Pearlman, C. (1993). An integrated approach to dream theory: Contributions from sleep research and clinical practice. In A. Moffitt, M. Kramer, and R. Hoffmann (Eds.), *The functions of dreaming* (pp. 363-380). Albany: State University of New York Press.

Greenson, R. R. (1967). *The technique and practice of psychoanalysis, vol. 1.* New York:

Griffith, R. (1958). The universality of typical dreams: Japanese versus Americans. *American Anthropologist, 60,* 1173-1179.

Guntrip, H. (1969). *Schizoid phenomena, object relations and the self.* New York: International Universities Press.

Hall, C. (1953). *The meaning of dreams.* New York: Harper Row.

Hall, C. & Domhoff, B. (1963). Aggression in dreams. *International Journal of Social Psychiatry, 10,* 259-267.

Hall, C., & Domhoff, B. (1964). Friendliness in dreams. *Journal of Social Psychology, 62,* 309-314.

Hall, C., & Van De Castle, R. (1966). *The content analysis of dreams.* New York: Appleton-Century-Crofts.

Harris, I. (1948). Observations concerning typical anxiety dreams. *Psychiatry, 11*, 301-309.

Harris, I. (1951). Characterological significance of the typical anxiety dreams. *Psychiatry, 14*(3), 279-294.

Harris, I. (1962). Dreams about the analyst. *International Journal of Psychoanalysis, 43*, 151-158.

Hartmann, E. (1984). *The nightmare: The psychology and biology of terrifying dreams.* New York: Basic Books.

Josef-Perelberg, R. (2001). The "oracle" in dreams: Past and future in the present. *Revue francaise de Psychoanalyse, 65*(3), 807-824.

Kernberg, O. (1976). *Object relations theory and clinical psychoanalysis.* New York: International Universities Press.

Kohut, H. (1971). *The analysis of the self.* New York: International Universities Press.

Kohut H. (1977). *The restoration of the self.* New York: International Universities Press.

Kradin, R. (2005). *The herald dream: An approach to the initial dream in psychotherapy.* London: Karnac Books.

Kramer, M. (1991). Dream translation: A non-associative method for understanding the dream. *Dreaming, 1*, 147-159.

Kramer, M. (1993). The selective mood regulatory function of dreaming: An update and revision. In A. Moffitt, M. Kramer, & R. Hoffmann (Eds.), *The functions of dreaming* (pp. 139-195). Albany: State University of New York Press.

Kramer, M. (2007). *The dream experience: A systematic exploration.* New York: Routledge.

Kramer, M. (2010). Dreaming and dreaming disorders in the elderly. In J. M. Monti & A. A. Monjan (Eds.), *Principles and practice of geriatric sleep medicine* (Chapter 29, pp. 307-318). London: Cambridge University Press.

Kramer, M., & Glucksman, M. L. (2006). Changes in manifest dream affect. *Journal of the American Academy of Psychoanalysis and Dynamic Psychiatry, 34*(2), 249-260.

Kramer, M., Winget, C., & Whitman, R. (1971). A city dreams: A survey approach to normative dream content. *American Journal of Psychiatry, 127*, 86-92.

Mack, J. (1970). *Nightmares and human conflict.* Boston: Little, Brown.

Ogden, T. H. (1990). *The matrix of the mind.* New York: Jason Aronson.

Rappaport, E. A. (1959). The first dream in an erotized transference. *The International Journal of Psychoanalysis, 40*, 240-245.

Rosenbaum, M. (1965). Dreams in which the analyst appears undisguised—A clinical and statistical study. *The International Journal of Psychoanalysis, 46*, 429-437.

Saul, L. J. (1940). Utilization of early current dreams in formulating psychoanalytic cases. *Psychoanalytic Quarterly, 9*(4), 453-469.

Sloane, P. (1990). *Psychoanalytic understanding of the dream.* New York: Jason Aronson.

Spitz, R. (1965). *The first year of life: A psychoanalytic study of normal and deviant development of object relations.* New York: International Universities Press.

Stekel, W. (1943). *The interpretation of dreams, vol. 1.* New York: Liverright Publishing.

Sullivan, H. S. (1953). *The interpersonal theory of psychiatry.* New York: Norton.

Ward, C., Beck, A., & Rascoe, E. (1961). Typical dreams: Incidence among psychiatric patients. *Archives of General Psychiatry, 5*, 606-615.

Warner, S. L. (1987). Manifest dream analysis in contemporary practice. In M. L. Glucksman & S. L. Warner (Eds.), *Dreams in new perspective: The royal road revisited* (pp. 97-117). New York: Human Sciences Press.

Winget, C., & Kramer, M. (1979). *Dimensions of dreams.* Gainsville: University Presses of Florida.

Winget, C., Kramer, M., & Whitman, R. (1972). Dreams and demography. *Canadian Psychiatric Association Journal, 17*(Suppl. 2), SS203-SS208.

Winnicott, D. W. (1989). *Psychoanalytic explorations.* C. Winnicott, R. Shepherd, & M. Davis (Eds.). Cambridge: Harvard University Press.

Yazmajian, R. V. (1964). First dreams directly representing the analyst. *Psychoanalytic Quarterly, 33*, 536-551.

Myron L. Glucksman, M.D. is Clinical Professor of Psychiatry, New York Medical College; Supervising and Training Analyst, The Psychoanalytic Institute, New York Medical College, Valhalla, NY.

Milton Kramer, M.D. is Emeritus Professor of Psychiatry, University of Cincinnati College of Medicine, Cincinnati, Ohio.

This article was presented, in part, at the 54th Annual Meeting of the American Academy of Psychoanalysis and Dynamic Psychiatry, New Orleans, LA, May 22, 2010.

Journal of the American Academy of Psychoanalysis and Dynamic Psychiatry, 39(2) 263-283, 2011.

INITIAL AND LAST MANIFEST DREAM REPORTS OF
PATIENTS IN PSYCHODYNAMIC PSYCHOTHERAPY AND
COMBINED PSYCHOTHERAPY/PHARMACOTHERAPY
MYRON L. GLUCKSMAN AND MILTON KRAMER

Abstract:

The initial and last manifest dream reports (MDRs) of 30 patients who had either successfully terminated, or continued to make satisfactory progress at an advanced stage of psychodynamic psychotherapy and combined psychotherapy/pharmacotherapy, were rated according to the following variables: Affect and Affect Valence; Affect Valence of Associations and Direction of Association Themes; Dream Narrative; Psychodynamic Formulation; Transference; and Dream Theme.

Similar to previous studies, the initial MDRs contained more negative than positive affect. Conversely, the last MDRs contained more positive than negative affect. Associations to initial MDRs contained more negative affect; on the other hand, associations to last MDRs contained more positive affect. Direction of association themes were more negative in initial MDRs and more positive in last MDRs. Dream narratives were more negative in initial MDRs and more positive in last MDRs. Psychodynamic formulations were more negative in initial MDRs and more positive in last MDRs. Transference was more negative in initial MDRs and more positive in last MDRs. Relational and injury dream themes occurred more frequently than others in both initial and last MDRs. Initial MDRs contained more injury dream themes than last MDRs. The findings of this study demonstrate that there is a correlation between MDR variables and clinical improvement during treatment. The patients in this study were selected by MG, the treating therapist, on the basis of satisfactory progress. The MDRs of patients who failed to progress or did poorly were not discussed in this report. The findings, therefore, must be taken as preliminary and indicate the need for further research on manifest dreams during psychotherapy and combined psychotherapy / pharmacotherapy.

Myron L. Glucksman, M.D.

Introduction:

Many clinicians have attempted to correlate dream content with clinical change during treatment (Alexander, 1961; Bonime, 1962/1982, 1986; Dewald, 1972; Glucksman, 1988; Saul, 1940; Warner, 1983, 1987). A number of clinical variables have been examined in connection with manifest and latent dream content; these included self-concept, self-soothing capacity, emotions, core conflicts, problems, defenses, relationships, and transference. However, most of these studies were anecdotal, not systematically rated by independent observers, and they lacked a sizeable number of patients.

In our previous studies using independent observers, we found a significant correlation between clinical improvement and changes in manifest imagery between the initial and final dreams of treatment (Glucksman & Kramer, 2004; Kramer & Glucksman, 2006). Conversely, we were able to identify the manifest dreams of those patients who had the least or no improvement in treatment (Glucksman& Kramer, 2004). Of those patients who made clinical progress, the initial dream of treatment contained significantly more negative than positive affect, while the final dream of treatment contained significantly more positive than negative affect. On the other hand, in those patients who did not make clinical progress, affect in the initial and final dreams remained negative.

In a recent study (Glucksman & Kramer, 2011), we examined the clinical and predictive value of the initial Manifest Dream Report (MDR) in 63 patients who were in psychoanalytic or psychodynamically oriented treatment with the lead author (MG). It confirmed our previous findings that initial MDRs contain a high percentage of negative affect, most likely due to the dysphoria experienced by patients in the beginning phase of treatment. Similar to previous anecdotal reports (Beratis, 1984; Franco & Levine, 1969; Kradin, 2006), the generic psychodynamic themes of initial MDRs were highly predictive of core psychodynamic issues that emerged during the ensuing treatment. Transference was evident in almost half of initial MDRs, and was more negative than positive. Also, psychodynamic themes involving relationships and perceived or actual injury occurred most frequently in initial MDRs. Clinical progress was almost equally associated with both negative and positive transference, as well as with relational and injury psychodynamic themes in initial MDRs.

On the basis of this in-depth study of initial MDRs (Glucksman & Kramer, 2011), we decided to examine the first and last MDRs of those patients in the study who had either successfully terminated or remained in treatment and were making satisfactory progress. We did so because we sought to replicate our previous findings with a larger group of patients. Our hypothesis was that the lead author's (MG) impression of clinical improvement would correlate with specific variables identified in the manifest content between the initial and last dreams of treatment.

Method:

The lead author (MG) selected 30 of the 63 patients (18 females, 12 males) from our previous study (Glucksman & Kramer, 2011). Five patients had already terminated treatment, and 25 remained at an advanced stage of treatment and were making satisfactory progress (Table 1). Active as well as terminated patients were combined in order to increase the size of the population under study. The other 33 patients either terminated treatment prematurely or failed to make satisfactory progress. The selected group of 30 patients was subjectively judged by the treating clinician (MG) to have made considerable clinical progress, using criteria employed by others to evaluate therapeutic outcome (Bachrach et al., 1985; Kantrowitz, Katz, & Paolitto, 1990; Kernberg et al., 1972; Luborsky et al., 1971; Waldinger & Gunderson, 1984). These included: 1. Symptom Reduction; 2. Resolution of Central Conflicts or Problems; 3. Affective Regulation; 4. Interpersonal Relationships; 5. Self-Image; 6. Transference Resolution; 7. Level of Functioning; and 8. Self-Analytic Capacity. Ages of the patients ranged from 35 to 76 years, and the mean length of treatment was 11.5 years. Median length of treatment was 10 years. The relatively long duration of treatment for many patients was due to the fact that they believed that on-going self-exploration and contact with the analyst was helpful (with which the analyst agreed). Diagnoses included Axis I and Axis II disorders, but excluded psychotic conditions (Table 2). Psychotropic medication was taken by 27 /30 (90%) of the patients at some point during treatment. These included anxiolytics, antidepressants, and mood stabilizers. Of the 25 patients who were on medication at the time of the last MDR, all had been receiving it for more than one year (Table 2). The initial and last Manifest Dream Reports (MDRs) of each patient were retrospectively collected verbatim from the treating clinician's (MG) therapy notes and were printed without any other identifiers such as name, age, or gender. The initial MDR was the first dream reported in treatment, while the last MDR was a dream reported just prior to successful termination, or the last dream reported during satisfactory ongoing treatment. The MDRs were rated according to the following variables by one or both authors.

1. Affect and Affect Valence of manifest content in MDR (MG and MK): Affect was rated according to the feeling, emotion, or mood reported by the patient in the manifest content. Affect valence denoted whether the affect was positive or negative; for example, happy or sad. 2. Affect Valence of Associations to MDR (MG): This variable assessed whether associations to the manifest content contained more positive or negative affect. 3. Direction of Associations (MG): This variable examined whether associations reflected a trend toward positive or negative feelings, memories, events, relationships, or behavior. 4. Narrative in MDR (MG and MK): Narrative was a non-psychodynamic, literal description of the imagery in the manifest content. 5. Psychodynamic Formulation of MDR (MG and MK): Psychodynamic Formulation was a generic psychodynamic interpretation of the manifest content. 6. Transference in MDR (MG): Transference was defined as the appearance of the actual therapist, another person, or object in the manifest imagery that represented a projection and displacement of the therapist. 7. Dream Theme in MDR (MG): Dream Theme was an overall characterization of the major theme of the manifest content according to specific categories. One or both authors rated the MDRs depending on whether clinical knowledge of the patient and confidentiality required the therapist (MG) to do so (Associations, Transference) or required both authors in order to establish significant inter-rater reliability (Affect, Affect Valence, Narrative, Psychodynamic Formulation).

TABLE 1.

Patient	Gender	Age	Status	Duration of Treatment	Frequency of Visits
1	Female	55	Active	4 years	1/week
2	Female	54	Active	2 years	1/week
3	Male	51	Terminated	5 years	3/week
4	Male	57	Terminated	6 years	1/week
5	Female	63	Active	13 years	1/week
6	Female	55	Active	5 years	1/2 weeks
7	Female	62	Active	26 years	1/week
8	Female	46	Active	12 years	1/2 week
9	Male	77	Active	3 years	1/2 week
10	Female	56	Active	11 years	1/2 week
11	Female	50	Active	6 years	1/week
12	Female	50	Active	2 years	1/week
13	Female	44	Active	6 years	1/2 week
14	Male	70	Terminated	22 years	1/2 week
15	Male	50	Active	7 years	1/month
16	Male	67	Active	9 years	2/week
17	Female	57	Active	9 years	1/month
18	Male	42	Active	9 years	1/month
19	Female	42	Active	11 years	1/month
20	Male	65	Active	22 years	1/month
21	Female	68	Active	15 years	2/week
22	Female	69	Active	35 years	1/month
23	Male	52	Active	2 years	1/2 week
24	Female	50	Active	13 years	1/2 week
25	Female	64	Active	10 years	1/week
26	Male	49	Active	7 years	1/month
27	Male	54	Active	22 years	1/week
28	Female	65	Terminated	12 years	1/week
29	Female	67	Active	17 years	1/month
30	Male	65	Terminated	21 years	1/month

TABLE 2.

Patient	Diagnosis	Medication at Time of Last MDR	Duration
1	Major Depression	Bupropion	>1 year
2	Recurrent Depression	Bupropion	>1 year
3	Anxiety Disorder	None	>1 year
4	Borderline Personality	Mirtazapine, Clonazepam	>1 year
5	Obsessive-Compulsive Personality	None	>1 year
6	Recurrent Depression	Fluoxetine, Buspirone	>1 year
7	Borderline Personality	Mirtazapine, Nefazodone, Buspirone, Clonazepam	>1 year
8	Major Depression	Mirtazapine, Buspirone, Alprazolam	>1 year
9	Major Depression	Fluoxetine, Bupropion	>1 year
10	Borderline Personality	Fluoxetine, Alprazolam	>1 year
11	Bipolar 1 Disorder	Venlafaxine, Fluoxetine, Lamotrigine	>1 year
12	Major Depression	Fluoxetine	>1 year
13	Bipolar 1 Disorder	Duloxetine HCL, Topiramate, Temazepam	>1 year
14	Recurrent Depression	Escitalopram	>1 year
15	Bipolar 1 Disorder	Divalproex, Quetiapine	>1 year
16	Recurrent Depression	Fluoxetine, Trazodone	>1 year
17	Anxiety Disorder	Alprazolam	>1 year
18	Obsessive-Compulsive Personality	None	>1 year
19	Recurrent Depression	Bupropion	>1 year
20	Recurrent Depression	Trazodone	>1 year
21	Dysthymic Disorder	Lorazepam	>1 year
22	Recurrent Depression	Venlafaxine, Amitriptyline	>1 year
23	Avoidant Personality Disorder	None	>1 year
24	Major Depression	Sertraline, Bupropion	>1 year
25	Major Depression	Venlafaxine	>1 year
26	Obsessive-Compulsive Personality	None	>1 year
27	Recurrent Depression	Sertraline	>1 year
28	Recurrent Depression	Venlafaxine, Amitriptyline, Trazodone	>1 year
29	Recurrent Depression	Fluoxetine, Bupropion	>1 year
30	Recurrent Depression	Mirtazapine	>1 year

TABLE 3.

AFFECT IN MDR: Rater Reliability (MG & MK)	AGREE		DISAGREE	
INITIAL	28		2	
LAST	25		5	
AFFECT VALENCE (MK)	NEGATIVE	POSITIVE	MIXED	ABSENT
INITIAL	13	1	0	16
LAST	11	7	1	11

Results:

1. Affect and Affect Valence in MDRs (Table 3)

   The authors had a high level of agreement on the Presence or absence of Affect, as well as the valence of Affect in 53 /60 (88%) of initial and last MDRs. In order to reduce rater bias, MK's ratings (MK had no clinical knowledge of the patients) were used for both the initial and last MDRs. Affect was present in 14/30 (47%) of initial MDRs and 19 /30 (63%) of last MDRs-. Negative affect occurred in 13/30 (43%) of initial MDRs, and. 11/30 (37%) of last MDRs. Positive affect occurred in 1/30 (3%) of initial MDRs and 7/30 (23%) of last MDRs. Affect was absent in 16/30 (53%) of initial MDRs and in 11/30 (37%) of last MDRs. There was a definite trend suggesting a difference in affect valence between the initial and last MDRs (p = .065, Fisher's exact probability test).

2. Affect and Affect Valence of Associations to MDRs

   Affect and Affect valence of Associations to MDRs were rated by the treating clinician (MG) who had direct knowledge from therapy notes of each patient's associations to the manifest content. Affect occurred in 50/60 (83%) of initial and last MDR associations. Negative affect occurred in 20/30 (67%) of initial MDR associations, and 12/30 (40%) of last MDR associations. On the other hand, positive affect was present in only 1/30 (3%) of initial MDR associations, and 9/30 (30%) of last MDR associations. There was a significant difference between the affect valence of initial and last MDR associations (*p* = .007, Fisher's exact probability test).

3. Direction of Association Themes to MDRs

   Direction of Association Themes to MDRs were also rated by the treating clinician (MG) according to whether they tended to be in a positive or negative direction. Their direction was negative in 26/30 (87%) of initial MDRs, and positive in 11/30 (3%) of initial MDRs. Conversely, they were negative in.17/30 (37%) of last MDRs, and positive in 14/30 (47%) of last

TABLE 4.

DREAM NARRATIVE: Rate Reliability (MG & MK)	AGREE	DISAGREE
INITIAL	28	2
LAST	25	2

DREAM NARRATIVE (MK)	NEGATIVE	POSITIVE	MIXED
INITIAL	13	1	0
LAST	11	7	1

MDRs. There was a significant difference between the direction of association themes of initial and last MDRs (p < .001, Fisher's exact probability test).

4. Dream Narrative in MDRs (Table 4)

   The Dream Narrative in the MDRs was a non-psychodynamic, phenomenological description of the manifest content, and was rated according to whether it reflected positive or negative imagery. The authors agreed on 56/60 (93%) of initial and last dream narratives. In view of their high level of agreement, and in order to reduce rater bias, MK's ratings were used for both the initial and last dream narratives. Initial MDRs had 23 /30 (77%) negative narratives and 4/30 (13%) positive narratives. Last MDRs had 18/30 (60%) negative narratives and 72/30 (40%) positive narratives. There was a statistically significant difference between the initial and last dream narratives (p = .076, Fisher's exact probability test).

TABLE 5. PSYCHODYNAMIC FORMULATION

Rater Reliability (MG & MK)	AGREE	DISAGREE	PARTIAL
INITIAL	28	1	1
LAST	27	0	3
PSYCHODYNAMIC FORMULATION (MK)	NEGATIVE	POSITIVE	MIXED
INITIAL	24	3	3
LAST	16	10	4

5. Psychodynamic Formulation of MDRs (Table 5)

   The Psychodynamic Formulation of the MDR was a generic psycho-dynamic interpretation based on the manifest content. It was rated according to a positive or negative quality. The authors agreed on 55/60 (92%) of the psychodynamic formulations of initial and last MDRs. As a result of this high level of agreement, MK's ratings were used for the psychodynamic formulations of the initial and last MDRs because of his lack of clinical information about the patients and likelihood of less bias. There were 24/30 (80%) negative and 3/30 (10%) positive psychodynamic formulations of the initial MDRS. Conversely, there were 16/30 (53%) negative and 10/30 (33%) positive psychodynamic formulations of the last MDRs. There was a statistically significant difference between the psychodynamic formulations of initial and last MDRs ($p = .054$, Fisher's exact probability test).

6. Transference in MDRs

   Transference was rated by the treating clinician (MG) on the basis of his clinical impression and familiarity with the patients. He observed transference in 16/30 (53%) of initial MDRs, and 12/30 (40%) of last MDRs. Negative Transference occurred in 13/30 (43%) of initial MDRs and 5/30 (17%) of last MDRs. Positive Transference occurred in 2/30 (7%) of initial MDRs, and 7/30 (23%) of last MDRs. Significantly more women than men manifested transference; 12/30 (40%) manifested transference in initial MDRs, and 8/30 (27%) in last MDRs. Men manifested transference in 4/30 (13%) of initial MDRs, and 4/30 (13%) of last MDRs. Negative transference was exhibited by 10/18 (56%) of women in initial MDRs, and 3/18 (17%) in last MDRs. On the other hand, women manifested positive transference in 2/18 (11%) of initial MDRs and 7/18 (39%) of last MDRs. There was a statistically significant difference in the type of transference exhibited between initial and last MDRs (p = .037, Fisher's exact probability test).

7. Dream Themes in MDRs

Dream Theme categories were rated by the treating clinician (MG) according to his impression of the predominant theme of the dream imagery. Overall, 28/60 (47%) of MDRs contained Relational Dream Themes, 17/60 (28%) of MDRs contained Injury Dream Themes, and 15/60 (25%) of MDRs contained the remainder of the dream theme categories. Initial MDRs contained 11/30 (37%) relational and14/30 (47%) injury dream themes. Other initial dream theme categories were too infrequent to enumerate (Control, Self, Problem-Solving, Sexual, Loss). Last MDRs contained 17/30 (57%) relational and 3/30 (10%) injury dream themes.

Discussion:

Affect and Affect Valence in MDRs

There was a high level of agreement between the authors, who rated the presence, absence, and Valence of Affect in MDRs (88%). This was almost identical (89%) to results of a previous study (Glucksman & Kramer, 2011) and indicated that our observations were reliable.

In view of the high inter-rater reliability MK's ratings for Affect and Affect Valence were used because he had no clinical contact with the patients and was therefore less biased. MK noted affect in 47% of initial MDRs, which was also nearly identical to the previous study (44%). Affect was present in 63% of last MDRs, which was virtually identical to the amount of affect (62%) in last MDRs of a previous study (Kramer & Glucksman, 2006). In this study, there was a decrease in Negative Affect from initial to last MDRs, and an increase in Positive Affect from initial to last MDRs. Although these changes were not statistically significant, a strong trend was clearly evident. The fact that a sizeable number of the patients in this study were still in active treatment and had not yet terminated therapy (as they had in the previous studies) might account for the less robust changes in affect valence than previously noted.

The following are the MDRs of a patient demonstrating negative affect in the initial MDR and positive affect in the last MDR:

Initial MDR: "I drove to a building where I used to work. Nobody was there and I felt alone and sad."

Last MDR: "My mother was in our kitchen and I called out to her. I was pleasantly surprised."

The patient was an older man who entered treatment with a major depression following a myocardial infarction and loss of his job. His depressive symptoms abated with antidepressant medication (Fluoxetine 40 mg./day and Bupropion 150 mg./day) as well as psychotherapy. He had a close, loving relationship with his mother and was still in active treatment when he reported the last MDR.

Affect and Affect Valence of Associations to MDRs

Affect and Affect Valence of Associations to MDRs were rated only by MG, who had direct access to this material from therapy notes. Similar to an earlier study (Glucksman & Kramer, 2011), affect was present in 77% of initial MDR associations and 90% of last MDR associations. Negative Affect occurred in significantly more initial MDR associations than Positive Affect (consistent with the earlier study). On the other hand, positive affect significantly increased in last MDR associations. The decrease in negative affect from initial to last MDR associations, and the increase in positive affect from initial to last MDR associations was statistically significant (p =.007), and it was consistent with findings of a previous study (Kramer & Glucksman, 2006). The change in affect valence of associations most likely reflected a shift from dysphoric feelings in the early stage of treatment to more normal ones in the later stage.

Direction of Association Themes to MDRs

The negative or positive Direction of Association Themes between initial and last MDRs was rated only by MG, who had access to this material from therapy notes. The direction of association themes depended on whether the content of associations reflected positive or negative memories, events, feelings, relationships, and behavior. The direction of association themes in initial MDRs was significantly more negative (87%) than positive (3%). Conversely, the direction of association themes was significantly more positive (47%) than negative (37%) in last MDRs. There was a highly significant change in the direction of association themes from the beginning to the later stages of treatment (p < .001). Once again, this shift more than likely represented an overall improvement in clinical status and life circumstances.

The following is an illustration of the change in direction of association themes from initial to last MDRs:

Initial MDR: "I was at work and was flooded with emails. I threw up my hands and walked away. I felt like I had done all I could do."

Associations: "My job is very stressful. I just had a review with my boss and it was a lower rating than I expected. I'm frustrated with the work, and I'm looking at other job possibilities."

Last MDR: "I'm driving my car and see a tornado coming. It hits me and the car is tossed around. Somehow, I get around it and ev6rything is OK."

Associations: "I just saw a tornado on a TV show-they're very dangerous and destructive. If you're in a car, you can get seriously hurt or killed. I was involved in a difficult situation at work that didn't seem proper. I told my boss to stop the transaction and he did. I felt relieved, and that it was a vote of confidence in me. Actually, it made me feel more confident."

The patient was a corporate executive who had entered treatment because of extreme anxiety and insomnia. He felt overwhelmed by his job and unappreciated by his boss. During treatment, he found a position with another firm where he felt more effective and validated.

Dream Narrative in MDRs

The Dream Narrative was a phenomenological, non-psychodynamic description of the MDR imagery. The authors rated the dream narrative as either positive or negative, depending on the nature of the imagery. In view of their high level of agreement, MK's ratings were used because of the likelihood of less bias. Initial MDRs had significantly more negative than positive narratives. On the other hand, there were significantly more positive than negative narratives in last MDRs. There was a statistically significant difference between initial and last MDR narratives (p = .01.6, Fishers exact probability test). The change from negative to positive dream narratives strongly indicated a beneficial response to treatment.

The following is an illustration of the difference between initial and last MDR narratives:

Initial MDR: "I'm in Iraq and the Iraqis are trying to kill me. I'm frightened and hiding."

Dream Narrative (Negative): The dreamer is in a combat setting and feels mortally threatened. She is frightened, and tries to hide in order to avoid being killed.

Last MDR: "I'm back at work and saving a co-worker, Dave. He was in trouble and I helped him. I made him look good."

Dream Narrative (Positive): The dreamer is in a work setting and helps a co-worker who is having difficulty. In doing so, she helps him improve his image. The patient began treatment because of a failing marriage and extreme financial problems. She was clinically depressed, felt extremely vulnerable, and had a poor self-image. In the course of treatment, she addressed her marital and financial difficulties. As a result, she felt less vulnerable and more effective.

Psychodynamic Formulation of MDRs

The Psychodynamic Formulation of the MDR was a generic, psychodynamic interpretation based on the manifest imagery. It was rated as either positive or negative, according to the type and quality of the psychodynamic elements. Because of their high level of agreement, MK's ratings were used to compare psychodynamic formulations between initial and last MDRs because his lack of clinical knowledge of the patients facilitated less bias. He observed significantly more negative than positive psychodynamic formulations in the initial MDRs. On the other hand, positive psychodynamic formulations significantly increased in the last MDRs and negative psychodynamic formulations significantly decreased. There was a statistically significant difference between psychodynamic formulations in the initial and last MDRs ($p = .054$, Fisher's exact probability test).

The following is an illustration of the difference between psychodynamic formulations of the initial and last MDRs:

Initial MDR: "An evil force enveloped me and followed me around. It stalked the family I lived with and it looked like a person. It killed one of the children in the family."

Psychodynamic Formulation (Negative): The dreamer is frightened of some type of injury or death. It may be part of the external surround or an externalization of an inner feeling. The evil may be within or a destructive force coming from others. The latter may or may not be her family.

Last MDR: "Some friends invited me to go ice skating. A very nice Asian man was also invited to meet me. We hit it off and skated around the pond together. I felt good."

Psychodynamic Formulation (Positive): The dreamer wishes to be accepted by others and to begin a romantic relationship with a man. The Asian man may represent her therapist with whom she feels secure and trusting.

This patient entered treatment with depressive and paranoid symptoms. She was alienated from both parents because they had abused her physically and emotionally as a child. At times, she believed her mother might kill her, and she identified with the child in the initial dream. She was distrustful and suspicious of others, including her therapist. As treatment progressed, she became more trusting and eventually began a romantic relationship with a man she met at work.

The shift from negative to positive psychodynamic formulations between the initial and last MDRs suggested that meaningful intrapsychic and interpersonal changes occurred during her treatment.

Transference in MDRs

Transference in the MDR was defined as the actual therapist, persons, or objects in the manifest imagery that represented projections or displacements of the therapist. MG rated the presence, absence, and type of transference because he had intimate knowledge of each therapeutic relationship. He observed the presence of transference in 53% of initial MDRs and 40% of last MDRs. The presence of transference in 53% of initial MDRs was similar to a previous study of initial MDRs (Glucksman & Kramer, 2011). In addition, identical with that study, there was no appearance of the therapist as himself in the MDRs. Negative transference was observed significantly more often in initial than last MDRs. Conversely, positive transference was observed significantly more often in last than initial MDRs. The observation that more women than men exhibited transference was also consistent with the previous study. However, this was not a statistically significant difference. In particular, women exhibited negative transference in more initial MDRs than last MDRs. on the other hand, they manifested positive transference in more last MDRs than initial MDRs. There was a statistically significant difference in the type of transference between initial and last MDRs (p - .037, Fisher's exact probability test). The following is an illustration of the presence and change in type of transference between the initial and last MDRs:

Initial MDR: "My father kissed me on the cheek. I wanted him to kiss me on the other one, but he didn't. It was a weak kiss."

Transference (Mixed or Ambivalent): The dreamer wishes to be loved and affirmed by a male authority. Instead, he is disappointed by the tepid show of affection. This is likely a transference dream and reflects the patient's ambivalent feelings for the therapist.

Last MDR: "I'm doing research at the maritime museum in Hyannis. The curator is surprised to see me, and he greets me enthusiastically."

Transference (Positive): The dreamer wishes to be recognized and praised for his work. He feels affirmed and supported by a male authority figure. This may also reflect a positive transference, and his feelings of acceptance by the therapist.

The patient entered treatment because he felt inadequate professionally and socially. He was afraid of being criticized and humiliated, particularly by male authority figures. His father was unaffectionate, while his mother was coercive and manipulative. He was initially guarded and ambivalent toward the therapist, but gradually became less defensive and more trusting.

Although transference in MDRs was observed by only one rater (MG) and therefore subject to countertransferential bias, his clinical knowledge of the patients was useful in identifying transference material. The term transference, as employed in this study, referred to any imagery that was judged to be connected to the therapist. The observation that more women than men manifested transference may have been due to the fact that the therapist was a man. This finding suggests that female patients may have had more intense reactions to a male therapist in the early phase of treatment. The shift from negative to positive transference, especially among women, suggested a resolution of transference issues during treatment. That is, the negative feelings and perceptions of the therapist by the patient in the early stage of treatment evolved into more positive ones at a later stage.

Dream Themes in MDRs

In a previous study (Glucksman & Kramer, 2011), MDRs were categorized according to seven different Dream Theme categories. These included: Relational, Injury, Control, Self, Problem-Solving, Sexual, and Loss. Relational themes were the most frequent and occurred in 43% of MDRs in that study, and in 47% of MDRs in this study. Injury themes were the second most frequent and occurred n 36% of MDRs in that study, and in 28% of MDRs in this study. The remaining themes occurred n 27% of MDRs in that study, and in 25% of MDRs in this study. Relational themes were observed in 37% of initial and 57% of last MDRs in this study. On the other hand, injury themes occurred in 47% of initial and 10% of last MDRs. The changes in other themes were too few to be of significance, although self themes increased from 0% in initial to 17% of last MDRs. The reduction in frequency of injury themes and increase in frequency of self themes between initial and last MDRs suggested a trend toward clinical improvement based on manifest dream imagery.

The effect of medication on the last MDR was most likely negligible because all patients had been receiving medication for a year or more before the last MDR. The subjective evaluation of clinical progress by only one observer (MG) was a methodological limitation; however, the private practice setting and retrospective nature of this study precluded the participation of other independent observers. MDRs were rated by an independent observer (MK) whenever possible, according to specific variables that measured relevant psychodynamic issues in the manifest imagery. Although dream content has been evaluated according to other rating scales (Winget & Kramer, 1979), we used a rater judgment approach that clinicians can apply directly without extensive training for the purpose of assessing relevant variables.

Summary:

Similar to previous studies, there was a decrease in negative affect between the initial and last MDRs of treatment. Conversely, there was an increase in positive affect between the initial and last MDRs of treatment. Although not statistically significant, these changes indicated a definite trend. This finding reinforced our hypothesis that the greater amount of negative affect in the initial dreams of patients reflected their dysphoric state upon entering treatment. On the other hand, the decrease in negative affect and increase in positive affect in last dreams indicated affective normalization. It is possible that some patients may have experienced an increase in negative affect as treatment progressed because of characterologic as well as transference issues. Indeed, increased evidence of negative affect may be viewed as clinical progress for certain patients, although it was not reflected in this study.

The presence of affect in associations to MDRs was also similar to a previous study (Kramer & Glucksman, 2006). Moreover, there was a significant decrease in negative affect and increase in positive affect between initial and last associations to MDRs. This observation underscored the importance of changes in affect from initial to last MDRs, since manifest content and associations (latent content) are both integral components of the dream.

The direction of association themes complemented the changes of affect in associations. There was a significant decrease in negative association themes, and increase in positive association themes between initial and last associations to MDRs. Of clinical relevance is the fact that associations not only contain affect, but also include cognitive and perceptual material. The change from a negative to a positive direction of association themes was another indication of clinical improvement during treatment.

Dream narratives, or the non-psychodynamic stories conveyed by the manifest imagery, changed significantly from negative to positive between initial and last MDRs. This observation provided further credence to the value of MDRs for the purpose of documenting clinical change. Moreover, this variable may be particularly important in assessing clinical improvement in those patients who are unable to articulate their feelings and internal psychic experience (e.g., Alexithymia).

Psychodynamic formulations, or generic psychodynamic interpretations of MDRs, mirrored the changes in dream narratives. There were significantly more negative psychodynamic formulations in initial MDRs. Conversely, there were significantly more positive psychodynamic formulations in final MDRs. Psychodynamic formulations were based on manifest imagery only, without the rater's knowledge of the patient or access to any other clinical information. Despite this handicap, the observed changes in psychodynamic formulations correctly reflected clinical improvement.

Evidence of transference appeared in almost half of the MDRs, and female patients reported the majority of these. Moreover, the therapist never appeared as himself, similar to a previous study (Glucksman & Kramer, 2011). There was a significant change from negative to positive transference between the initial and last MDRs, particularly among women. The change from negative to positive transference reflected the therapist's impression that resolution of transference occurred in a sizeable number of patients, especially women, who made clinical progress.

The frequency of relational and injury dream themes was consistent with a previous study (Glucksman & Kramer, 2011) in which both occurred more often than other dream themes. Of interest is that there was a decrease in injury dream themes from initial to last MDRs. This reduction in MDRs with threatening or injurious imagery appeared to correspond with clinical improvement.

In conclusion, this study demonstrated significant changes in clinically relevant variables between the initial and last MDRs of psychodynamic psychotherapy and combined psychotherapy/pharmacotherapy. These changes reflected the treating clinician's impression of clinical progress in a group of patients who either successfully terminated, or continued to make satisfactory progress at an advanced stage of treatment. Of note is that a large number of patients in this study received medication, and clinical improvement was most likely due to the synergistic action of medication and psychotherapy. Regardless of the mechanisms that facilitated clinical change, the findings of this study taken in conjunction with our previous reports suggest that manifest dream content may change during treatment in a manner consistent with changes in other areas of the patient's psychological functioning. Because a major limitation of this study was the lack of independent observers to evaluate clinical progress, further systematic investigation is needed to explore the role of manifest dream content as an index of change during treatment.

References:

Alexander, F. (1961). *The scope of psychoanalysis.* New York: Basic Books.

Bachrach, H., Weber, J., & Solomon, M. (1985). Factors associated with the outcome of psychoanalysis (clinical and methodological considerations) of the Columbia Psychoanalytic Center research project (IV). *International Review of psychoanalysis, 43,* 161-174.

Beratis, S. (1984). The first analytic dream: Mirror of the patient's neurotic conflicts and subsequent analytic process. *International Journal of Psychoanalysis, 65,* 461-469.

Bonime, W. (1986), Collaborative dream interpretation. *Journal of the American Academy of Psychoanalysis, 14*(1), 15-26.

Bonime, W., with F. Bonime. (1962). *The clinical use of dreams*. New York: Basic Books, and New York: DeCapo Press, 1982.

DeWald, P. (1972). Assessment of structural change. *Journal of the American psychoanalytic Association, 20*, 119-132.

Franco, D., & Levine, A. (1969). Psychic reality and psychic structure as predicted from the manifest content of first dreams. Proceedings of the 77th APA Annual Convention, 4593- 4594.

Glucksman, M. L. (1988). The use of successive dreams to facilitate and document change during treatment. *Journal of the American Academy of Psychoanalysis, 16*, 47-70.

Glucksman, M. L., & Kramer, M. (2004). Using dreams to assess clinical change during treatment. *Journal of the American Academy of Psychoanalysis & Dynamic Psychiatry, 32*(2), 345-358.

Glucksman, M. L., & Kramer, M. (2011). The clinical and predictive value of the initial dream of treatment. *Journal of the American Academy Psychoanalysis and Dynamic Psychiatry, 39*(2), 263-283.

Kantrowitz, J. L., Katz, A. L., & Paolitto, F. (1990). Follow-up of psycho-analysis five to ten years after termination: II. Development of the self-analytic function. *Journal of the American Psychoanalytic Association, 38*(3), 637-654.

Kernberg, O., Coyne, L., Horwitz, L., Appelbaum, A., & Burstein, E. (1972). Psychotherapy and psychoanalysis: Final report of the Menninger Foundation psychotherapy research project. *Bulletin of the Menninger Clinic, 36*, 3-275.

Kramer, M., & Glucksman, M. L. (2006). Changes in manifest dream affect. *Journal of the American Academy of Psychoanalysis and Dynamic Psychiatry, 34*(2), 249-260.

Kramer, M., Whitman, R., Baldridge, B., & Lansky, L. (1964). Patterns of dreaming: The inter-relationship of the dreams of the night. *Journal of Nervous and Mental Disease, 139*, 426-439.

Luborsky, L., Chandler, M., Auerbach, A., Cohen, J., & Bachrach, H. (1971). Factors influencing the outcome of psychotherapy. *Psychological Bulletin, 75*(3), 145-185.

Saul, L. J. (1940). Utilization of early current dreams in formulating psychoanalytic cases. *Psychoanalytic Quarterly, 9*(4), 453-469.

Waldinger, R. J., & Gunderson, J. G. (1984). Completed psychotherapies with borderline patients. *American Journal of Psychotherapy, 38*(2), 190-202.

Warner, S. L. (1983). Can psychoanalytic treatment change dreams? *Journal of the American Academy of Psychoanalysis, 11*(2), 299-316.

Warner, S. L. (1987). Manifest dream analysis in contemporary practice. In M. L. Glucksman & S. L. Warner (Eds.), *Dreams in new perspective: The royal road revisited* (pp. 97-117). New York: Human Sciences Press.

Winget, C., & Kramer, M. (1979). *Dimensions of the dream.* Gainesville: University of Florida Press.

Myron L. Glucksman, M.D., is Clinical Professor of Psychiatry, New York Medical College, and Supervising and Training Analyst, The Psychoanalytic Institute, New York Medical College, in Valhalla.

Milton Kramer, M.D., is Emeritus Professor of Psychiatry at the University of Cincinnati College of Medicine in Cincinnati, Ohio.

Psychodynamic Psychiatry, 40 (4) 617-634,. 2012

## Chapter 6

Psychodynamic and Psychoanalytic Education

Until the mid-twentieth century, psychoanalysis was the predominant type of outpatient intensive psychotherapy in the United States. Non-psychoanalytic therapies remained within the province of psychiatry and were carried out in outpatient, as well as mental hospital settings. The latter also routinely treated patients with electroshock, hydrotherapy, and sub-coma insulin therapy. For those psychiatrists who wished to become more proficient in psychotherapy, psychoanalytic training was the route most frequently taken. In order to become a psychoanalyst, it was necessary to undergo a personal analysis in addition to completing required courses at a psychoanalytic institute. The latter were freestanding institutions, apart from medical schools and organized medicine. These separate educational paths were instrumental in creating a divide between psychiatry and psychoanalysis that has persisted, and even widened, until the present. Nevertheless, many psychiatrists undertook psychoanalytic training; moreover, to become a psychiatrist and psychoanalyst was considered by many to be a mark of professional achievement.

Beginning in the mid-1950s, several major developments changed the course of psychiatry and psychoanalysis in the United States. These included

(1) the discovery of neurotransmitters (epinephrine, norepinephrine, dopamine) that led to the development of major tranquilizers and antidepressants; (2) the proliferation of various psychotherapies, partly influenced by the need for briefer forms of therapy during and after World War II; (3) the development of Community Mental Health Centers, encouraging the training of non-psychiatrists in various psychotherapeutic skills; (4) the expansion of knowledge in neuroscience, including neurochemistry, genetics, pharmacology, and neuroimaging; and (5) the emergence of managed care and its emphasis on briefer forms of inpatient and outpatient treatment. These developments profoundly changed both psychiatric as well as psychoanalytic education and practice. Residency training in psychiatry became more biologically oriented, emphasizing psychopharmacology and brief therapies. Psychiatric disorders were viewed more as a manifestation of brain disease or "chemical imbalance," rather than maladaptive mental functioning secondary to developmental, interpersonal, and sociocultural stressors. As a result, fewer psychiatrists pursued psychoanalytic training because it was perceived as archaic, time consuming, and financially less rewarding. On the other hand, psychologists, social workers, and others sought psychoanalytic training and increasingly filled the void left by psychiatrists.

In my opinion, the lack of knowledge of psychoanalytic/psychodynamic theories and treatment among contemporary psychiatrists threatens the humanistic foundation of psychiatry itself. The prevailing view that mental disorders are mainly a result of neurochemical dysfunction and can be cured by prescribing the correct psychotropic medication is, at best, naive, and, at worst, a disservice to patients. This approach fails to appreciate the complex interplay between biological, interpersonal, social, and cultural factors. Brain and mind are integrated phenomena, similar to computer hardware and software. Each requires understanding according to its unique mode of function. Exclusive focus on the brain fails to take into consideration the subjective experience of mind. On the other hand, emphasis on the latter may diminish appreciation of the interplay between mental phenomena and morphological as well as neurochemical changes in the brain. Unfortunately, many contemporary psychiatric residency training programs emphasize a "brain-centered" approach to mental disorders, rather than a biopsychosocial one. Diagnosis is arrived at by various algorithms of symptom clusters. Virtually ignored are the psychodynamic, interpersonal, and social factors that have promoted psychopathological symptoms. Two papers represent my thinking on ways to integrate psychodynamic/psychoanalytic theories and practice into residency training programs. By doing so, I believe that contemporary psychiatrists can be trained as psychodynamically oriented as well as neuroscientifically informed clinicians.

The first paper, "Integrating Psychoanalysis and Psychodynamic Psychotherapy into a Residency Training Program" (Glucksman, M.L., 1997), was motivated by a crisis within my own psychoanalytic institute. Our institute was facing a decline in candidates who were psychiatrists. Since its inception in 1944, The Psychoanalytic Institute has been an integral part of the Department of Psychiatry at New York Medical College. A guiding principle of the institute is to offer a doctrine-free, eclectic curriculum in order to train physician-psychiatrists to be psychoanalysts. I was director of The Psychoanalytic Institute from 1992 until 2002. Recognizing that fewer psychiatric residents were enrolling in The Psychoanalytic Institute, we offered a two-year course in psychodynamic psychotherapy for residents who were interested in psychoanalysis but unwilling to pursue formal psychoanalytic training. Termed the "Certification Course in Psychodynamic Psychotherapy," it proved to be popular not only with residents in our residency training program, but also with others in the New York area.

In view of the success of the Certification Course, we considered changing the curriculum of The Psychoanalytic Institute in order to make it more appealing to those residents who were interested in psychoanalytic training. Modifications to the curriculum included reducing the length of didactic coursework from four to three years. Another change was lowering the required number of supervised cases as well as the number of hours of case supervision. An even more radical proposal was to offer a Fellowship in Psychoanalytic and Psychodynamic Psychiatry. This would entail an additional two years of training beyond the PGY 3 year of residency. Unfortunately, these proposed changes never occurred, but the Certification Course has continued to be highly successful. The latter's popularity suggests that psychiatric residents continue to value an education in psychodynamic/psychoanalytic theory and practice.

A subsequent paper, "Psychoanalytic and Psychodynamic Education in the 21st Century" (Glucksman, M.L., 2006), complements and expands on the issues examined in the previous one. It focuses more specifically on the integration of psychodynamic theory and therapeutic technique into psychiatric residency training. Moreover, it proposes a model for providing psychoanalytic training within residency programs. Residents would have the option of taking courses in personality development, psychoanalytic theory, and psychodynamic psychotherapy in the PGY 3 and 4 years. Those who wished to continue psychoanalytic training could take didactic and clinical courses in psychoanalysis during the PGY 5 or 6 years (similar to fellowship years in other medical subspecialties). In addition, they would be required to undergo a personal analysis and control case supervision during that time frame. Emphasis would be given to understanding the interface between subjective and neurophysiological mechanisms that are associated with dreaming, cognition, affect regulation, learning, memory, consciousness, and unconsciousness. In my opinion, these proposed changes in psychiatric and psychoanalytic education could provide an optimal foundation for psychiatrists and psychoanalysts to practice in the twenty-first century. Moreover, it would help to preserve both the humanistic and neuroscientific components of psychiatry.

References:

Glucksman, M.L., "Integrating Psychoanalysis and Psychodynamic Psychotherapy into a Residency Training Program," *Journal of the American Academy of Psychoanalysis*, Vol. 25, No. 4 (1997): 655-662.

Glucksman, M.L., "Psychoanalytic and Psychodynamic Education in the 21st Century,", *Journal of the American Academy of Psychoanalysis and Dynamic Psychiatry*, Vol. 34, No. 1 (2006): 215-222.

COMMENTARY
INTEGRATINC PSYCHOANALYSIS AND PSYCHODYNAMIC
PSYCHOTHERAPY INTO A RESIDENCY TRAINING
PROGRAM
MYRON L. GLUCKSMAN, M.D.

The night of a recent faculty meeting at our psychoanalytic institute, I had the following dream:

"I was at some sort of meeting or seminar. The content of the meeting was unclear; when it ended, the participants had to find their way home. A group of us waited for a bus or train; none seemed to be going in the right direction. Finally, a bus came along that was going to New York. We got on it because it was going in the correct general direction, although not exactly where I wanted to go. When everyone was seated and the bus departed, various individuals made suggestions about how to raise funds and stimulate interest in our group. I looked around and saw that the majority of the passengers were not members of our group and not particularly interested in it, nor willing to give the amounts of money proposed. I became more and more frustrated, but was unable to make a sensible proposal of my own. The bus finally stopped at a station in a town where we had to transfer to another bus or train. I went to an information booth and asked directions to the place where we were supposed to transfer to another bus. However, the clerks at the booth were unable to give me an answer, and I was unable to provide them with the necessary information to help them out. I felt perplexed, lost, and uncertain. I awoke from the dream feeling very anxious".

When I reflected on this dream, it became apparent to me that, insofar as the previous night's experience was concerned, the dream was a metaphorical presentation of the current state of our psychoanalytic institute, psychoanalytic training, and my personal identity as a medical psycho-analyst. As with most dreams, there were additional themes of a more personal nature, but for purposes of this paper I shall focus on the former themes.

In general, the faculty meeting could be characterized as one of con-fusion, frustration, uncertainty, and conflicting opinions concerning the future direction of our institute. One faculty member suggested that we ought to stop training psychiatric residents to be psychoanalysts alto-gether, since so few were interested in obtaining psychoanalytic training, (like the majority of the passengers on the bus in my dream). Another suggested that if we are to continue training psychoanalysts we ought to focus on psychologists and social workers, since they constitute the ma-jority of those interested in psychoanalytic training. Yet another faculty member suggested that we ought to radically change our curriculum to one emphasizing the neurosciences. The meeting continued on in a simi-lar vein, with divergent opinions, a lack of consensus, and general uncer-tainty about the future of our discipline. I suspect that ours is not the only psychoanalytic institute entertaining such a wide range of options and experiencing so much confusion about our future direction. How did we arrive at such a state of affairs?

Perhaps, an historical overview of American psychiatry and psycho-analysis, as well a history of our own institute might be helpful. I have no doubt that for most psychoanalysts the following observations will seem redundant, but I believe that it is important to organize past events into a meaningful perspective in order to consider the problem under discussion; namely, how can we integrate psychoanalysis and psychoanalytically ori-ented psychotherapy into residency training? Moreover, why should we even consider teaching psychoanalysis to prospective psychiatrists? Historically, psychoanalysis and psychoanalytically oriented therapy were predominant modes of therapy in the United States from the early 1920s until the 1960s. The most talented psychiatric residents aspired to become psychoana-lysts and undertook psychoanalytic training. Many of those who did not, nevertheless, sought personal analysis and supervision by psychoanalysts.

Beginning in the mid-1950s, five major developments dramatically changed the course of American psychiatry and psychoanalysis:

1. The introduction of anti-psychotic, anxiolytic and anti-depressant medications;
2. The proliferation of various therapeutic modalities: marital, family, group, brief, behavioral, and cognitive;
3. The development of Community Mental Health Centers encouraging the training of non-psychiatrists (psychologists, social workers, nurses, etc.) in various psychotherapeutic skills;
4. An explosion of knowledge in the areas of brain neurochemistry, psychopharmacology, genetics, and neuroimaging;
5. The impact of the managed care industry on how psychiatric care is provided; in effect, an emphasis on ever briefer courses of treatment for inpatients and outpatients.

These changes have profoundly influenced how psychiatric residents are trained. There has been a general shift away from learning psychotherapeutic skills to becoming conversant with the actions and side effects of various psychotropic medications. There is less emphasis on understanding psychodynamics and more emphasis on acquiring knowledge in the neurosciences. Psychopathology is viewed as a manifestation of brain disease, rather than as a reflection of maladaptive functioning due to intrapsychic, interpersonal, and social stressors. As a result, psychiatric residents identify more with the biological or medical model and less with the psychodynamic or functional model of mental illness. They perceive psychotherapy as belonging in the domain of non-medical mental health professionals, and of less importance than psychopharmacological treat-ment. Moreover, because they attend medical school to become physicians, they do not identify with social workers and psychologists. They perceive psycho-analysis, in particular, as archaic, time-consuming, and generally not very ef-fective in treating most mental illnesses. As far as the residents are concerned, psychoanalytic training is expensive, takes too long, does not lead to financial rewards, and lacks the professional status it once had.

In my opinion, this trend in the training of psychiatric residents and their subsequent lack of knowledge about the psychotherapies is unfortunate, and threatens the humanistic foundation of psychiatry itself. There is an increasing belief among residents (and many psychiatrists) that most, if not all, mental suffering can be relieved by pharmacological intervention. The curative elements of human interaction, empathy, learning, and insight are either devalued or ignored. The causative factors of mental illness are assumed to be almost totally biological in origin, rather than presenting a complex interplay between biological, interpersonal, social, and cultural forces. In effect, mainstream psychiatry has fully embraced the medical/biological model of mental illness, and has distanced itself from the humanistic/experiential model.

The Psychoanalytic Institute, a division of the Department of Psychiatry and Behavioral Sciences at New York Medical College, has always sought to integrate psychoanalysis with psychiatry. It has the distinction of being this country's first psychoanalytic training program to be offered within the framework of a medical school and a department of psychiatry. The Institute was established within the context of another conflicted and difficult period in the history of American psychoanalysis.

At this time, an agonizing split was taking place within the New York Psychoanalytic Institute over differing theoretical points of view, as well as the issue of academic freedom. Several training analysts from the New York Psychoanalytic Institute approached Steven P. Jewett M.D., the chairman of psychiatry at New York Medical College at that time, and convinced him to form a division within the department called "The Comprehensive Course in Psychoanalysis." The year was 1944, and the analysts were Bernard Robbins, M.D. and William Silverberg, M.D. They were soon joined by others, and developed a doctrine-free, eclectic curriculum which recognized that psychoanalytic theories and technical approaches must be taught in complete academic freedom. Only psychiatric residents who are enrolled in, or who have graduated from an approved residency program are eligible for admission to the program. Graduation requirements include completion of four years of didactic courses, a personal analysis, and satisfactory treatment of three psychoanalytic cases under supervision.

Several years ago, the name of the division was changed to: "The Psychoanalytic Institute" (still within the Department of Psychiatry and Behavioral Sciences at New York Medical College). In the mid-1980s, the faculty became concerned with the decreasing number of psychiatric residents applying for admission to The Psychoanalytic Institute. Since most candidates come from the psychiatric residency consortium at New York Medical College, it seemed logical to make psychoanalytic training more attractive to them.

Several years ago, the faculty began considering various ways that the psychoanalytic curriculum could be integrated into the residency training program. One general principal agreed upon was that residents would receive credit for certain courses offered in the core curriculum of the residency training program, should they elect to pursue psychoanalytic training. It was decided that these would be required courses for all residents during the PGY 1 and PGY 2 years. They included the following: Child and Adolescent Personality Development; Psychopathology and Psychodynamic Formulation; and Introduction to Psychoanalytic Theory and Clinical Applications. These courses were to be taught entirely by faculty members of The Psychoanalytic Institute, and the integrated program was begun in the 1989-1990 academic year. All residents complete these courses by the end of the PGY 2 year. A resident can apply to be-come a candidate in The Psychoanalytic Institute either during the PGY 1 or PGY 2 years. Having successfully completed these courses, in addi-tion to a course offered only to those who are candidates (Introduction to Psychoanalysis: Theory and Technique), the resident is given credit for the first year of didactic psychoanalytic training. The psychoanalytic faculty are generous with their time in teaching these courses, and the residents accept this curriculum as an integral part of their psychiatric training. At the present time, candidates who progress to the second, third and fourth years of analytic training attend evening courses separate from their residency training program.

Despite these curriculum changes, there continues to be a declining interest by residents in psychoanalytic training. The most frequently cited reasons are: It is very time-consuming, too expensive, irrelevant to current psychiatric practice, which emphasizes shorter-term therapies and pharmacological intervention, and does not distinguish between psychiatrists and non-psychiatrists. (The majority of psychoanalytic candidates are now psychologists and social workers). In order to address this problem, the psychoanalytic faculty weighed possible solutions, including modification of the psychoanalytic curriculum. As a result, the second, third and fourth years of the psychoanalytic curriculum were revised; in addition, an entirely new program was developed to provide residents with further training in psychodynamic psychotherapy. In regard to modification of the psychoanalytic curriculum, the attention paid to Freudian theory was reduced, and further emphasis was placed on object relations, self-psychology, adaptational, interpersonal, culturalist, and post-modern theories. Courses were also introduced focusing on the psychoanalytic process and the relational aspects of treatment. In addition, a number of "interface" courses were offered, including time-limited therapies and psychoanalysis, female psychology and psychoanalysis, marital/family therapy and psychoanalysis, group therapy and psychoanalysis, as well as neurobiology and psychoanalysis.

However, the psychoanalytic training program continues to require four years of didactic courses, a personal training analysis, and satisfactory treatment of three supervised psychoanalytic cases. In 1995, an elective two-year course in psychodynamic psychotherapy, leading to Certification in Psychodynamic Psychotherapy was introduced. This course offers residents at the PGY 3 level or beyond additional training in psychodynamic psychotherapy, which they otherwise do not receive in their residency experience. It is taught entirely by members of the psychoanalytic faculty.

The first- year curriculum consists of semi-monthly evening seminars that consider the following topics: engaging and listening to the patient; basic principles of psychodynamics (unconscious mentation, defenses, symptom formation, resistance), and psychodynamic formulation; the therapeutic relationship (therapeutic alliance, transference, countertransference); social, cultural and gender issues; dreams; goals of therapy and termination issues. Evening seminars are augmented by clinical material relevant to the topic discussed. The second- year curriculum, also given on a semi-monthly basis, focuses primarily on the process and technique of psychodynamic psychotherapy, and is taught within the framework of continuous case-group supervision. Residents are also encouraged to obtain their personal psychotherapy.

At present, many more residents are enrolled in the Psychodynamic Psychotherapy Certification Course than in the full four-year psychoanalytic training program. It seems that a two-year commitment is more appealing and manageable than the longer and more arduous psychoanalytic curriculum. We plan to further modify the Psychodynamic Psychotherapy Certification Course, based on suggestions from both participating residents and faculty. For example, we are considering awarding additional credit to those residents who complete the course and then decide to pursue full psychoanalytic training. By doing so, we hope to make it easier for residents to enter psychoanalytic training.

Nevertheless, the apparent success of the Psychodynamic Psychotherapy Certification Course leads us to consider more radical changes in the psychoanalytic curriculum. Perhaps, we should reduce the length of didactic coursework from four to three years. By the same token, we might consider reducing either the required number of supervised cases or the total number of hours of supervision. Yet, we must remain cognizant of the risk of excessively diluting the psychoanalytic curriculum. Another option is to offer a Fellowship in Psychoanalytic and Psychodynamic Psychiatry, similar to Fellowships in Child or Geriatric Psychiatry. This might entail an additional two years of training beyond the PGY 3 year, including didactic courses, a personal analysis, and case supervision. Training in Psychoanalytic and Psychodynamic Psychiatry would be recognized as a subspecialty, perhaps with board certification. If the curriculum for such a fellowship included other theoretical and technical advances taking place in general psychiatry, I believe that residents would consider it relevant and useful for their future clinical, academic, and research careers.

Clearly, we are experiencing a period of dramatic and rapid change in the field of psychiatry. This has necessitated a re-examination of the role and functions of the contemporary psychiatrist. Residency training programs are undergoing constant modification in order to assimilate our expanding knowledge in various areas, including the neurosciences, genetics, psychopharmacology, epidemiology, and the psychotherapies. As medicine, including psychiatry, develops more sophisticated technological and biological interventions, there is an inherent danger of either de-emphasizing or even ignoring the therapeutic importance of the doctor-patient relationship.

The cornerstone of psychoanalytic treatment has always been its emphasis on the therapeutic relationship. Freud (1912) recognized the enormous power of that relationship when he described the phenomenon of transference. Despite all of the technological and biological advances we have made during the past century, nothing can substitute for the healing qualities of the therapeutic relationship and the curative influence of one empathically informed human being upon another. Psychoanalysis and psychodynamic psychotherapy specifically focus on understanding the subjective human experience, as well as the dynamics of communication between individuals. They have proven to be effective primary modes of treatment for personality disorders, adjustment disorders, post-traumatic stress disorders, and dysfunctional relationships. Moreover, they are therapeutically beneficial in combination with psychotropic medication in the treatment of depression, dysthymia, anxiety disorders, dissociative disorders, sexual dysfunctions, and eating disorders.

In view of this, I believe it is necessary for psychiatrists engaged in clinical practice to gain some expertise in either psychoanalysis or psychodynamic psychotherapy. Therefore, it is of vital importance that psychiatric residents are provided with the opportunity to learn these therapeutic modalities during and beyond their residency training. At the same time, training in psychoanalysis and psychodynamic psychotherapy must be integrated with advances in psychopharmacological and biological treatments. If this goal can be achieved, perhaps my dreams following future faculty meetings will be less confusing and more certain. Hopefully, they will reflect increased cohesiveness and direction in the development of our psychoanalytic and psychodynamic psychotherapy training programs, greater enthusiasm on the part of residents to participate in those programs, and a clearer identity for us as medical psychoanalysts.

References:

Babikian, H. M., Glucksman M. L., and Crewdson, F. R. (1993), A model for the integration of psychoanalytic and psychiatric training, unpublished.

Freud, S. (1912), The dynamics of transference, *Standard Edition*, Vol. 12, pp. 99-108, The Hogarth Press, London.

Gabbard, G. O., Lazar, S. G., Hornberger, J., and Spiegel D. (1997), The economic impact of psychotherapy: A review, *American Journal Psychiat*, 154, 2, 147-155.

Lazar, S. G., Hersh, E. K., and Hershberg, S. G. (1995), The long-term psychotherapy needs of psychiatric patients: Executive summary, in Psychoanalysis and long-term therapy work, presentation at the 39th Winter Meeting of the American Academy of Psychoanaysis December, 1995, Cambridge, Ma.

Presented, in part, at the Annual Meeting of the American Academy of Psychoanalysis, May 1997.

Journal of The American Academy of Psychoanalysis, 25(4), 655-662, 1997.

PSYCHOANALYTIC AND PSYCHODYNAMIC EDUCATION IN THE 21ST CENTURY

MYRON L. GLUCKSMAN, M.D.

Abstract:
Psychanalytic and psychodynamic education over the past 50 years is reviewed in the context of the author's personal experience, as well as the changes that have taken place in psychiatry and psychoanalysis over the same time span. Several key issues are identified, including (1) the increasing biological reductionism of psychiatry; (2) the gradual de-emphasis of subjective experience along with the biopsychosocial explanation of human behavior and psychopathology; and (3) the increasing attention paid to neuroscience, psychopharmacology, and brief therapies during residency training. In order to address these issues, it is suggested that education in psychodynamic and psychoanalytic psychiatry be integrated into residency training. This would take the form of subspecialty training in either psychodynamic psychiatry or neurobiology and psychodynamics, versatility with a variety of the dynamic psychotherapeutic techniques, and familiarity with research methodology. Psychiatrists educated in this type of integrated training program will be optimally equipped to advance psychodynamic and psychoanalytic treatment, theory and research in the 2lst century.

The purpose of this article is to provide a perspective on psychoanalytic and psychodynamic education over the past 50 years in order to make an informed judgment regarding its possible future direction in the 21st century. I shall limit the scope of this discussion to the education of medically trained psychiatrists and psychoanalysts, recognizing that psychodynamic and psychoanalytic training extends to nonmedically trained practitioners as well. I realize that this is an ambitious and perhaps impossible endeavor; nevertheless, I believe that we are at a critical juncture in the education and training of physicians who are interested in psychodynamic and psychoanalytic psychiatry. It is, therefore, imperative that we give serious thought to this issue in order to maintain the continuation of a vitally important discipline.

I wish to begin with some personal observations on my own journey in psychiatry and psychoanalysis over the past half-century. As I do so, I shall also make some general observations on the road that psychiatry and psychoanalysis have taken over the same time span. I began medical school in 1955 and became interested in psychiatry over the course of several summers when I worked at a state mental hospital. I recall the introduction of Chlorpromazine (Thorazine) during that time period, and the dramatic improvement in behavior of psychotic patients who were previously treated with electroshock, hydrotherapy, and sub-coma insulin. During my residency in psychiatry in the early 1960s, other major and minor tranquilizers were introduced along with the first antidepressants. Lithium was then still considered an experimental drug for bipolar patients. The supervisors who most impressed me were those who were psychoanalytically trained. They offered the most cohesive model of mental functioning and based their psychotherapy on specific psychodynamic principles. At that time, the epitome of psychiatry training (at least for me) was to become a psychoanalyst. I began my psychoanalytic training while I was in my last year of residency, deliberately choosing an institute that I felt was nondoctrinaire and eclectic in its theoretical orientation. That institute was then known as "The Comprehensive Course in Psychoanalysis," a division within the Department of Psychiatry at New York Medical College (currently known as The Psychoanalytic Institute at New York Medical College). Established in 1944, it was the first psychoanalytic institute in this country to exist within a department of psychiatry in a medical school (and still does to this day). It, too, began in the context of another critical point in the history of American psychoanalysis. I am referring to the momentous split that occurred at the New York Psychoanalytic Institute in the early 1940s over issues involving theoretical differences and academic freedom. That event was the beginning of the trend toward pluralism in psychoanalytic theory and practice in this country. Parenthetically, it also led to the founding of the American Academy of Psychoanalysis in 1956.

When I began my psychoanalytic training, the four-year curriculum was organized around the following areas: readings, theory, clinical case material, and psychoanalytic technique. The first year was devoted entirely to reading Freud's papers; the second to various psychoanalytic theories, including classical, neo-Freudian, adaptational, interpersonal, and ego-psychological. Objects relations, self-psychology, intersubjective, and postmodernist theories either did not exist or were not yet taught. The third and fourth years were largely clinical, including a continuous case seminar and clinical case presentations. Graduation required the approval or completion of a training analysis consisting of three or more sessions per week, completion of the didactic coursework, completion of at least 160 hours of control supervision on three different patients, and passing an oral exam based on one of the control cases. Of interest is that almost identical standards for psychoanalytic training were recently proposed by the Psychoanalytic Consortium (Gray, 2000). Although most psychoanalytic institutes have maintained a similar curriculum structure (with the exception of changes in course content), as well as training requirements over the past 50 years (Morris, 1992), there has been nothing short of a revolution in psychiatry over the same time span.

Federal legislation in 1963 ushered in the era of community mental health centers, along with the expanded training of non-medical mental health practitioners. Psychologists, social workers, nurses, and paraprofessionals began providing the bulk of clinical care over the succeeding decades. As a result, there was a proliferation of various types of therapies, including brief, supportive, group, family, marital, behavioral, cognitive, and self-help. The 1970s and 1980s brought the dismantling of state mental hospitals and greater emphasis on briefer inpatient stays. Our growing knowledge of brain chemistry resulted in a new generation of psychotropic medications that provided more effective treatment for psychosis, as well as for major affective and anxiety disorders. As third-party payers struggled with the rising costs of mental healthcare, the 1990s saw the introduction of managed care for both inpatient and outpatient treatment. Reimbursement and financial considerations increasingly dictated the type, length, and quality of treatment. As a consequence, greater emphasis was placed on pharmacological intervention and less attention was paid to the psychodynamic/developmental factors involved in psychopathology. Further discoveries in genetics, neurochemistry, and neuroimaging facilitated a biological orientation toward the etiology of psychiatric disorders rather than a balanced perspective of the complex interplay among developmental, interpersonal, social, and biological phenomena. As a result, mental illness came to be viewed by many psychiatrists, as well as the public, as a brain disorder or a "chemical imbalance." Moreover, managed care companies limited reimbursement or even refused to pay for psychodynamically oriented therapies and psychoanalysis. These changes have had a profound impact on psychiatric residency training programs. Corresponding to the expansion of knowledge in neuroscience, residents are currently required to devote a significant amount of their time toward acquiring skills in neurochemistry, psychopharmacology, neuropsychiatry, and genetics. The influence of managed care and the need for shorter lengths of treatment have led to an emphasis on learning supportive, brief, and cognitive-behavioral therapies. The time allotted to teaching psychodynamic psychotherapy has been gradually decreased. As a result, residents have less appreciation of intrapsychic and interpersonal psychodynamics in the genesis of normal and psychopathological behavior. They tend to identify psychiatric disorders with the biological or medical model of disease rather than with the biopsychosocial model. Moreover, they have less experience with the vicissitudes of the physician-patient relationship and less understanding of its importance in the healing process. As far as psychoanalysis is concerned, they view it an archaic, time-consuming, costly treatment, somehow connected to Freud. I believe that if this trend in psychiatric residency training continues, we are in danger of losing the very essence of psychiatry-its humanism. Less and less emphasis is being placed on an appreciation of subjective mental experience as well as the importance of connectedness between patient and therapist. Residents have less opportunity to learn the time-honored elements that facilitate clinical change: empathic listening, establishing a therapeutic alliance, working through resistances, understanding psychodynamics, recognizing and resolving transference, knowing when and how to make interpretations, and encouraging patients to act judiciously on their insights.

Where do these changes over the past several decades bring us at the beginning of the 21st century? First, psychiatry seems to be in the firm grip of neurobiological reductionism. An understanding of mind mechanisms and subjective experience seems to have a low priority, not only for residents, but also for many of those who train them. Self-introspection and psychotherapy are de-emphasized in a popular culture that expects quick cures provided by mind-altering drugs. The pharmaceutical industry, as well as the media, reinforce these attitudes and expectations. A recent article (Abboud, 2004) stated that 75% of all antidepressant prescriptions and 30% of all antipsychotic prescriptions are written by non-psychiatrists (family practitioners, internists, and others). Insurance and managed care companies no longer pay for long-term (or even medium-term) therapy; psychoanalysis and psychodynamic therapy are available to only a small percentage of patients who are either well-informed or who can afford it. Few researchers or clinicians are interested in exploring the bridge between mind phenomena (consciousness, affect, cognition, memory, dreaming) and brain mechanisms (the journal *Neuro-Psychoanalysis* is a notable exception). It has even been suggested that psychiatry be divided into two subspecialties: neurobiological and psychosocial. Those who oppose this type of division include Glen Gabbard, who stated: "the very essence of psychiatry as a unique medical specialty is that it integrates the biological and psychological in both diagnosis and treatment. To divide the two dimensions into subspecialties creates an artificial separation of mind and brain that would fragment the treatment of persons with psychiatric disorders" (cited in Lancet Criticized, 1994). Nobel Prize winner Eric Kandel adds: "I think psychoanalysis works because it creates changes in the brain" (cited in Lancet Criticized, 1994). He points out that functional as well as morphological changes in neuronal-synaptic networks are brought about by psychotherapy. Freud hoped and predicted that psychoanalysis and neurobiology would someday become integrated, with each discipline informing the other (Freud, 1932/ 1964). His "Project for a Scientific Psychology" (1895 /1966) was an attempt to explain mental phenomena in neurophysiological terms. Unfortunately, the lack of neuro-scientific knowledge available to him at that time forced him to abandon this endeavor, and instead he developed a metapsychological explanation of human behavior.

As a result, psychoanalytic theory and treatment evolved with little or no connection to the biological sciences. Most psychoanalytic institutes were established independently of medical schools and functioned outside the mainstream of medicine. The successful lawsuit against The American Psychoanalytic Association (Simons, 2003) has led to a significant increase in the number of non-medically trained psychoanalysts. If this trend continues, there is a realistic possibility that medical psychoanalysts as well as psychodynamically oriented psychiatrists will either continue to decrease in numbers or perhaps vanish altogether. In my view, a viable way to prevent this from occurring is to integrate psychoanalytic and psychodynamic education into residency training programs.

The Psychoanalytic Institute at New York Medical College has made an effort to integrate psychodynamic and psychoanalytic training into the psychiatric residency program over the past decade (Glucksman, 1997). A two-year elective course leading to Certification in Psychodynamic Psychotherapy was introduced in 1995. Residents are eligible to begin this course in the PGY-3 year, and classes are held in the evenings on a semimonthly basis. The first year consists of seminars on various topics, emphasizing psychodynamic theory and clinical material. The second year focuses on the technique of psychodynamic psychotherapy and is taught within the framework of group supervision of clinical cases. Students are strongly encouraged to seek their own psychotherapy (at least 40 hours) in order to experience and benefit from the therapeutic process. Graduates of the certification course who choose to continue on with psychoanalytic training are given credit for the first year of didactic courses in the psychoanalytic curriculum. The latter currently includes three years of didactic and clinical courses, some of which are aimed toward integrating psychoanalysis with neurobiology, psychopharmacology, medicine, cultural issues, and other types of therapy (brief, marital, family, group). So far, the Psychodynamic Psychotherapy Certification Course has proved to be far more popular with residents than the more arduous and time-consuming psychoanalytic training program. In view of this, I believe that more radical changes are needed in order to attract residents to psychodynamic psychiatry and psychoanalysis.

Training in other medical specialties could serve as a model; for example, residents might choose to take subspecialty or fellowship training in psychodynamic or psychoanalytic psychiatry, similar to medical residents who subspecialize in cardiology or gastroenterology. Residents interested in psychodynamic psychiatry could begin to take elective courses in the PGY-3 year (e.g., personality development, psychodynamic theory, introductory psychodynamic psychotherapy) and continue to do so in the PGY-4 year (e.g., psychodynamic formulation, psychodynamic psychotherapy technique). Those residents interested in psychoanalytic training would be required to take additional didactic and clinical courses beyond the PGY-4 year (perhaps a fifth year), as well as a personal analysis and control case supervision. An integral part of both psychodynamic and psychoanalytic training would be courses or seminars that interface with neurobiology, psychopharmacology, and neuroscience research. Clinically relevant areas that lend themselves to these kinds of interface or "bridging" courses include dreaming, cognition, affect regulation, learning, memory, perception, and conscious and unconscious mental mechanisms. Residents who complete their training in psychodynamic or psychoanalytic psychiatry would be knowledgeable about the connections between self-experience and neurobiological mechanisms, psychopharmacology, various psychotherapeutic modalities, the healing power of the therapist-patient relationship, and the relationship between conscious and unconscious mentation (especially as it pertains to symptom formation and psychopathology). Naturally, they would be skilled in conducting psychodynamically oriented and psychoanalytic treatment. In addition, they would also be required to have some understanding of research methodology and evidence-based medicine, especially as it relates to clinical and neuroscientific issues.

Research in the neurosciences requires cross-input between psychodynamically-oriented clinicians and basic science investigators. For example, during a 2003 meeting of the American Academy of Psychoanalysis and Dynamic Psychiatry, there was a demonstration at the Duke University Neuroimaging Laboratory of current MRI scanning techniques measuring brain responses under certain experimental conditions. One of the experiments evaluated brain metabolic changes in a subject who perceived either affirmation or rejection by another person. This kind of research has important implications for clinicians regarding idiosyncratic brain responses to various types of interpersonal interactions. It is not inconceivable that in the future, therapists may be able to use this kind of information to diagnose, plan, carry out, and evaluate the effects of treatment. By the same token, researchers may benefit from the observations and suggestions of psychodynamically informed clinicians regarding experimental designs that would be clinically relevant. This kind of collaboration between clinicians and research investigators could integrate rather than polarize psychodynamic psychiatry and neurobiology. However, it will require psychiatrists trained in both disciplines. The modifications in residency and post-residency training that I am proposing would facilitate the education of both neurobiologically and psychodynamically informed psychiatrists. I believe that the integration of neurobiological, psychodynamic, and psychoanalytic training within a residency program will offer the best foundation for those psychiatrists who choose to practice, teach, or do research in the 21st century. Naturally, it takes a professional lifetime to acquire the degree of experience and knowledge that is required for one to become a proficient clinician. However, in my opinion, individuals who have participated in the educational programs I have described will be the most optimally equipped psychiatrists capable of advancing psychodynamic and psychoanalytic theory, treatment and research in the coming century. If these educational goals can be accomplished, Freud's "Project" may once again be continued in a meaningful way, both theoretically and clinically, after a hiatus of over a century.

References:

Abboud, L. (2004, March 24). Should family doctors treat serious mental illness? *Wall Street Journal*, pp. D1-D4.

Freud, S. (1964). New introductory lectures on psychoanalysis. In J. Strachey (Ed. and Trans.), *The standard edition of the complete psychological works of Sigmund Freud* (Vol. 22, pp. 7-182) London: Hogarth Press. (Original work published 1932.)

Freud, S. (1966). Project for a scientific psychology. In J. Strachey (Ed. and Trans.), *The standard edition of the complete psychological works of Sigmund Freud* (Vol. 1, pp. 281-397). London: Hogarth Press. (Original work published 1895.)

Gabbard, G. (1994, May 6). "Lancet" criticized for suggesting that psychiatry be split along mind vs. brain lines (1994, May 6). *Psychiatric Times*, pp. 8-9.

Glucksman, M.L. (1997). Integrating psychoanalysis and psychodynamic psychiatry into a residency training program. *Journal of the American Academy of Psychoanalysis, 25*, 655-662.

Gray, S.H. (2000). Interim working draft, the Psychoanalytic Consortium, Accreditation Council for Psychoanalytic Education, standards for psychoanalytic education, pp. 1-8.

Myron L Glucksman, M.D., Clinical Professor of Psychiatry, New York Medical College; Supervising and Training Analyst, The Psychoanalytic Institute, New York Medical College.

Journal of the American Academy of Psychoanalysis and Dynamic Psychiatry, 34(1) 215-222, 2006.

## Chapter 7

Psychoanalysis and Neurobiology

As a discipline, psychoanalysis has diverged from mainstream psychiatry and medicine since its inception. However, Freud did attempt to integrate mental phenomena and brain mechanisms in his "Project for a Scientific Psychology" (1895). Because he lacked sufficient neurobiological information to successfully implement the "Project," he developed a metapsychology in order to explain personality structure, psychodynamics, and psychopathology. As a result, successive generations of psychoanalysts developed various theories describing normal and pathological mental functions. However, these schemata of the mind were not integrated with brain functions. Nevertheless, a number of psychoanalytic investigators attempted to link mental phenomena with other biological processes. In fact, the field of psychosomatic medicine originated with Franz Alexander (1950), who connected intrapsychic conflicts with peptic ulcer, hypertension, and asthma. Others explored the relationship between particular affective states and the onset of specific malignancies (Engel, G. L., and Schmale, A. H., 1967). Coronary atherosclerosis was correlated with Type A personality (Williams, R. B., et al; 1988), and bereavement, with changes in the immune system (Bartrop, R. W., et al., 1977). Accumulating evidence suggests that interactions between mother and infant influence the latter's self-regulatory affective, autonomic, hormonal, and neurochemical functions (Emde, R. N., and Robinson, J., 1979). However, it was not until the introduction of neuroimaging techniques that connections could be established between normal and pathological mental states. Schizophrenia, depression, OCD, and panic attacks have been correlated with morphological and neurotransmitter changes in the brain. In addition, the underlying neuronal-neurochemical mechanisms associated with cognition, memory, learning, and emotional regulation are now better understood. After more than a century, there is a real possibility that psychoanalytic theories of mental function can be not only tested, but also used to inform further neuroscientific investigation.

My first paper, "Psychodynamics and Neurobiology: An Integrated Approach" (Glucksman, M.L., 1995), initially reviews the relationship between psychoanalytic theories and psychosomatic medicine. Subsequently, it explores evidence of the dysregulation of neurotransmitter systems and specific psychopathological states, including schizophrenia, depression, OCD, and panic disorder. It also focuses on changes in neuronal-synaptic functioning associated with learning and experience. In that regard, it hypothesizes that current experience may articulate with previously stored memories, and activate a "sensitized" neuronal-synaptic network with associated affective and cognitive changes. As a result, a neurochemical "cascade" may develop, resulting in symptoms of a psychiatric disorder. Panic disorder is used as an example of a psychiatric illness with genetic, experiential, and neurochemical components. Panic attacks result from the synergistic interaction of magnified fears of abandonment or entrapment, accompanied by genetically and experientially sensitized noradrenergic-synaptic networks. The therapist may serve as a psycho-neurobiological regulator by teaching the patient coping skills to manage threatening affects and providing psychotropic medication for stabilization of dysregulated neuronal-synaptic networks.

Two clinical vignettes are presented in order to illustrate the psychodynamic-neurobiological model of a psychiatric disorder and its treatment.

The first patient was a young man with panic disorder who was sensitized by early frightening interactions within his family, as well as multiple geographic moves. His therapist taught him coping strategies to contain his overwhelming fear and prescribed medication. In addition, he internalized a sense of confidence and safety from his therapist that facilitated a regulating effect on his neuronal-synaptic functioning. Pharmacological intervention also stabilized his overreactive noradrenergic/serotoninergic systems. The second patient presented with depressive and dissociative symptoms connected to childhood sexual, verbal, and physical abuse. The loss of her previous therapist due to geographic relocation precipitated her depression and a suicide attempt. Intolerable feelings connected to her childhood abuse were defended against by depersonalization and multiple alters with distinct personalities. Psychotropic medication helped to restabilize her dysregulated dopaminergic/noradrenergic/serotoninergic systems. Moreover, an empathic self-object relationship with her therapist neutralized her negative parental introjects and improved her self-esteem. The neurobiological and neurochemical processes described in these case illustrations are, to some extent, speculative. Nevertheless, they represent an attempt to integrate psychodynamic and neurobiological factors associated with mind-brain phenomena.

My second paper, "Freud's 'Project': The Mind-Brain Connection Revisited" (Glucksman, M.L., 2016), examines the advances in our knowledge of the neurobiological substrate of mind that have occurred since Freud's (1895) publication more than a century ago. Although Freud was aware of the anatomical structure of the neuron when he wrote his monograph, he could only hypothesize about its neurophysiological function. Nevertheless, he took on the impossible task of explaining various mental mechanisms without the benefit of our current knowledge of neuronal-synaptic networks, neurotransmitters, hormones, genes, and epigenetic influences. This paper compares Freud's explanation of certain normal and pathological mental states with contemporary neurobiological knowledge of the same phenomena. Because his knowledge of brain biology was so severely limited, Freud abandoned the Project and devoted the remainder of his career to developing a metapsychology of the mind. Unfortunately, this led to a dualism between mind and brain that has persisted until the present.

Freud began his monograph postulating three types of neurons: "pi," "psi," and "omega." He hypothesized that neurons transmitted impulses from one to the other, but was unaware of the electro-chemical nature of the process. The latter was later described by the British neurophysiologist, Charles Sherrington (1906). Nevertheless, Freud used this neurological paradigm to explain a number of normal and pathological mental functions, including consciousness, memory, phobias, obsessions, compulsions, conversion disorders, affect, and cognition. Later in his career, he did predict the discovery of neurotransmitters and their role in brain function. The remainder of this paper summarizes what has been learned about the neurobiology of these mental functions since Freud's initial explanatory attempt.

The resting, conscious mental state is characterized by activation of the entire thalamic-cortical neuronal network. In contrast to other primates, humans have the capacity for self-reflection or introspection. During self-reflective consciousness, there is activation of the prefrontal cortex. Ongoing attention to external stimuli involves activation of the sensory cortex. However, the qualities of self-experience during consciousness, particularly feelings and fantasies, remain to be understood.

Memory is categorized as explicit, implicit, short-term, and long-term. It is mediated via the hippocampus, amygdala, prefrontal cortex, and temporal cortex. A number of neurotransmitter, molecular, genetic, and morphological changes are involved in memory processing. Memory and learning are interconnected phenomena. The most studied phenomenon of memory and learning is fear conditioning. The latter involves two major pathways: thalamic-amygdala and amygdala-prefrontal. The former is activated when a rapid response to an immediate threat is required; the latter becomes involved when there is time for a cognitive appraisal of the threat. Cognitive-behavioral and psychodynamic therapies utilize these pathways to develop cognitive as well as affective control via conditioning and insight.

Phobias are closely connected to anxiety, panic, and PTSD. Each of these conditions involves increased activation of the amygdala, hippocampus, insula, and orbitofrontal cortex. Certain individuals have a genetic predisposition for increased reactivity of the amygdala-cortical pathway when confronted with threat-relevant cues. Cognitive-behavioral and psychodynamic therapies, as well as pharmacotherapy, can regulate these dysfunctional neuronal pathways.

Freud grouped phobias, obsessions, compulsions, and conversion reactions under the rubric of "hysteria.". According to him, phobias are a manifestation of displaced ideas associated with anxiety, while obsessions are displaced ideas associated with various affects (anxiety, guilt, shame, anger, etc.). Conversion reactions occur when an affect associated with an unacceptable idea or event is displaced and "converted" to a somatic symptom. Recent evidence shows that individuals with OCD have hyperactivity of the caudate nucleus-orbitofrontal neuronal circuit when symptomatic (Baxter, et al., 1992). Treatment with SSRIs or cognitive-behavioral therapy can normalize this hyperactive neuronal circuit. Conversion symptoms often occur in conjunction with psychological trauma. Patients who exhibit conversion symptoms are typically unable to verbalize their conflicts and feelings. A recent study of functional motor paralysis revealed hyperactivation of the prefrontal cortex, precuneus, and other limbic structures, simultaneous with decreased activation of motor pathways at the cortical and subcortical levels (Vuilleumier, P., 2014). Similar neuronal dysfunction occurs with somatosensory, visual, and memory conversion symptoms. Nevertheless, the neuronal mechanisms mediating intrapsychic conflict, displaced affect, and symptom-formation remain a mystery.

Freud postulated that cognition was mediated via "psi" neurons, but focused more on primary process rather than secondary process mentation. The latter refers to conscious, logical thought and a linear sense of time. Primary process cognition is unconscious and characterized by timelessness, illogical thought, and symbolism. It is a major component of dreaming, and conveys metaphorical meaning. Freud never developed an integrated theory of cognition, although cognitive concepts are ubiquitous in contemporary psychoanalytic theory.

Freud viewed affect as a form of psychic energy that was divided into two components: pain and pleasure. Pain or unpleasure required inhibition by means of defense mechanisms. According to Freud's signal theory of anxiety, the ego utilizes defense mechanisms in order to avoid experiencing anxiety (or other painful affects). This psychodynamic model of containing dysphoric affects via defense mechanisms continues to be used as a clinical paradigm. However, the neurobiological substrate of affect regulation is now better understood. Anxiety and other affects are mediated through the amygdala, anterior cingulate, insular, and orbitofrontal cortex. A number of neurotransmitters are also involved, including norepinephrine, serotonin, acetylcholine, and glutamate. Focal awareness, or immediate attention to feelings, can be differentiated from reflective awareness of them by means of mentalization. The latter involves explicit and implicit awareness of feelings within the self and others. This process corresponds to activation of mirror neurons in the parietal and premotor cortex, as well as the limbic-mesial-frontal cortex. The mirror neuronal system is conjectured to mediate cognitive and emotional empathy. The latter is essential for interpersonal communication and, in particular, for psychotherapy. In fact, the mirror neuronal system may help us better understand the neurobiological correlates of introjection, projective identification, and transference.

A clinical illustration explores the possible role of mirror neurons between a male patient and his therapist during psychodynamic psychotherapy. Mirror neuronal activation in both patient and therapist may occur in the context of transferential and counter-transferential phenomena. The patient's improved capacity to experience and communicate his feelings may correspond to better regulation of his limbic-prefrontal cortical system. It is important to keep in mind that this is a speculative attempt to integrate mind-brain phenomena during psychotherapy. Interestingly, neuroimaging techniques employed pre- and post- psychotherapy demonstrate improvement in a number of conditions, including OCD, panic disorder, social phobia, depression, and borderline personality disorder. Nevertheless, certain phenomena remain to be more fully explained; for example, how are thoughts, feelings, and perceptions translated into neuronal and neurotransmitter activity? What are the neuronal-chemical changes that account for the different qualities of feelings? How do unconscious memories neuronal-chemically influence conscious mentation?

These and other mental functions remain to be further understood in terms of mind-brain interaction. However, in doing so, it is important to keep in mind the difference between subjective mental experience and corresponding neurobiological activity. Each provides valuable information in its unique way and can be described in its own language. Although considerable progress has been made toward understanding the neurobiology of the mental states Freud originally explored in the Project, much remains to be explained.

References:

Freud, S., "Project for a Scientific Psychology" in J. Strachey (ed. and trans.), *The Standard Edition of the Complete Psychological Works of Sigmund Freud, Vol. 1*, London: Hogarth Press, 1895, pp. 283-397.

Alexander, F., *Psychosomatic Medicine*, W.W. Norton, New York, 1950.

Engel, G. L., and Schmale, A. H., "Psychoanalytic Theory of Somatic Disorder: Conversion, Specificity, and the Disease Onset Situation," *Journal of the American Psychoanalytic Association*, Vol. 15 (1967): 34-365.

Williams, R. B., Barefoot, J. C., Haney, T. L., Harrell, F. E., Blumenthal, J. A., Pryor, D., and Peterson, B., "Type A Behavior and Angiographically Documented Coronary Atherosclerosis in a Sample of 2,289 Patients," *Psychosomatic Medicine*, Vol. 50 (1988): 139-152.

Bartrop, R. W., Luckhurst, E., Lazarus, L., Kiloh, L. G., and Penny, R., "Depressed Lymphocyte Function after Bereavement," *Lancet*, Vol. 1 (1977), 834-836.

Emde, R. N., and Robinson, J., "The First Two Months: Recent Research in Developmental Psychobiology and the Changing View of the Newborn, in J. D. Noshpitz (ed.), *Basic Handbook of Child Psychiatry*, Vol. 1. New York: Basic Books, 1979, 72-105..

Glucksman, M. L., "Psychodynamics and Neurobiology: An Integrated Approach," *Journal of the American Academy of Psychoanalysis*, Vol. 23, No. 2 (1995), 179-195.

Glucksman, M. L., "Freud's 'Project': The Mind-Brain Connection Revisited," *Psychodynamic Psychiatry*, Vol. 44, No. 1 (2016): 69-90.

Sherrington, C. S., *The Integrative Action of the Nervous System*, New Haven, CT: Yale University Press, 1906.

Baxter, L. R., Schwartz, J. M., Bergman, K. S., Szuba, M. P., Guze, B. H., Mazziotta, J. C., Alazraki A., Selin, C. E., Ferng, H. K., Munford, P., and Phelps, M. E., "Caudate Glucose Metabolic Rate Changes with Both Drug and Behavioral Therapy for Obsessive-Compulsive Disorder," *Archives of General Psychiatry*, Vol. 49 (1992), 681-689.

Vuilleumier, P., "Brain Circuits Implicated in Psychogenic Paralysis, in Conversion Disorders and Hypnosis," *Clinical Neurophysiology*, Vol. 44 (2014), 323-337.

PSYCHODYNAMICS AND NEUROBIOLOGY: AN INTEGRATED APPROACH
MYRON L. GLUCKSMAN, M.D.*

As a discipline, psychiatry has evolved along two major paths that reflect its concern with mind and brain. Unfortunately, this has promoted a Cartesian dualism dividing the psychological from the biological, leading to the conceptualization of behavior in unidimensional terms. There have been a number of reasons for this dichotomization, including differing philosophical orientations, limitations of knowledge, and difficulty integrating biological processes with psychodynamic phenomena. The psychodynamic approach to understanding mental activity focuses on subjective, experiential, nonquantifiable phenomena. The neurobiological approach attempts to explain the same phenomena in objective, measurable, neurochemical, or neuroanatomical terms. For example, an accepted psychodynamic theory of depression explains it as a prolonged disturbance of mood resulting from an anticipated or actual loss or disappointment. On the other hand, the current neurobiological theory holds that it is a dysregulation of noradrenergic and/or serotoninergic neurotransmitter systems. Both explanations may be correct, although from different vantage points. Freud (1895a) in his *Project for a Scientific Psychology* attempted an integrated neuropsychological explanation of mental events. His lack of adequate neurobiological information forced him to abandon this endeavor, and instead, he developed a metapsychology for personality development, psychopathology, and behavior. Although Freud never suggested neurophysiological or neuroanatomical correlates for different aspects of psychic functioning (e.g., unconscious, ego, id), he nevertheless based his theory on a biological substrate. For example, his dual drive theory depended on biologically determined instincts. Even the term "libido" was defined as a "somatic" sexual excitation (Freud, 1995). Freud repeatedly acknowledged the role of biological factors in the pathogenesis of mental illness; in fact, he predicted the central role of neurotransmitters: "It is here, indeed, that hope for the future lies: the possibility that our knowledge of the operations of the hormones may give us the means of successfully combating the quantitative factors of the illnesses" (Freud, 1932). Freud's metapsychological theories were further modified by subsequent generations of clinicians, resulting in various models of personality structure and functioning. Collectively, these represent attempts to explain intrapsychic and interpersonal phenomena in terms of subjective experience. For example, Kohut's (1971) "self-object" function signifies the gratification of subjective needs through another person. Commonly used terms such as transference, projective identification, empathy, introjection, and internal representation refer to subjectively experienced phenomena on an individual or dyadic level.

There is a lengthy and continuing history in which psychoanalytic as well as non-psychoanalytic investigators have attempted to link mental phenomena with biological processes; for example, Alexander (1950) and his colleagues developed the "Specificity Theory" of psychosomatic disorders; namely, that a specific intrapsychic conflict, including the drives, defenses, and affects connected with it, was the causative agent in the formation of such disorders as peptic ulcer, hypertension, and asthma. The Specificity Theory continued to be popular until Weiner et al. (1957) established the necessity for both intrapsychic and biological factors in the pathogenesis of peptic ulcer. A large number of investigators have subsequently studied somatic illnesses in order to determine the nature of the interaction between biological and psychological factors in the pathogenesis of disease. For example, Engel and Schmale (1967) observed a significant correlation between a hopeless/helpless state of mind and the onset of certain malignancies. Rosenman et al. (1964) and Williams et al. (1988) identified pathological hostility and competitiveness (cardinal features of Type A personality) as significant factors in the pathogenesis of coronary atherosclerosis. Bartrop et al. (1977) and Stein et al. (1985) associated bereavement with changes in the immune system, particularly T-cell suppression, leading to the onset of illness.

Other investigators, utilizing the technique of biofeedback (physiological monitoring), have explored the connection between autonomic as well as voluntary nervous system modalities and various psychophysiological disorders, including migraine, hypertension, cardiac arrhythmias, asthma, and so on. Physiological monitoring and operant conditioning techniques enable patients to alter certain autonomic and voluntary nervous system functions, such as heart rate, electrodermal activity, skin temperature, gastrointestinal motility, and muscle tension in order to prevent or modify symptoms. Biofeedback has demonstrated that physiologic changes (normal as well as pathological) may occur during psychotherapy in connection with significant conflicts, fantasies, memories, and feelings. For example, affective intensity, particularly negative affects such as anger and guilt, have been correlated with increased electrodermal activity; conversely, a sense of well-being and inner control or mastery have been associated with decreased electrodermal activity (Glucksman et al., 1985). Luborsky et al. (1973) observed that somatic symptoms occurring during therapy sessions are often preceded by transient feelings of helplessness, resentment, and frustration. Biofeedback can be especially helpful for patients who have difficulty connecting somatic sensations or symptoms with their feelings. A certain group of these individuals, whom Sifneos (1975) described as "alexithymic," are prone to have somatic disorders. They are characterized by an inability to identify and describe feelings; difficulty distinguishing between feelings and somatic sensations; concreteness and a limited fantasy life. Taylor (1992) suggests that the inability to identify and integrate affects with cognitive processing may amplify physiological arousal, leading to pathological physiological reactions and somatic disease.

Developmental studies indicate that alexithymia as well as other dysregulations of affect may result from a disturbed interaction between child and caregiver. Emde (1990) and Stern (1985) note that faulty parental affective responses may result in parent-child affective "misattunement." The child internalizes these faulty patterns of affective interaction, resulting in affective dysregulation. Hofer's (1983) experiments with rats indicate a similar regulating influence of the mother's behavior on the infant's internal physiological state. For example, it has been demonstrated that the body temperature of the mother determines the body temperature of the infant rat, which, in turn, regulates levels of brain amino acids and catecholamines

(Stone et al., 1976). If the infant rat is separated prematurely from the mother, its body temperature falls along with a reduction in brain protein (and most likely, a dysregulation of neurotransmitter systems). Thus, internal physiological processes are greatly influenced by the behavioral interaction between mother and infant. Similarly, the human infant's sleep/wake and feeding cycles are regulated by the mother's interaction with it (Emde and Robinson, 1979). Gross and Fligsten (1991) hypothesize that affective/physiologic rhythms in the mother-child relationship establish the basic cortical engrams for adult affective experience and corresponding physiological responses (e.g., blood pressure regulation). In general, there is accumulating evidence that the mother acts as an external psychoneurobiological regulator, enabling the infant to internalize various functions until they become autonomous. These internal self-regulatory functions most likely include affective, autonomic, hormonal, and neurochemical components.

Recent advances in neurobiology indicate a relationship between dysregulation of neurotransmitter systems and psychiatric illness. Schizophrenic patients appear to have dopamine system dysfunction, particularly in the limbic, cortical, and dopamine-projection fields (Michaels and Marzuk, 1993a). Neuroanatomical and imaging studies reveal enlarged ventricles, smaller amygdala/hippocampal, prefrontal cortical volumes, and diminished frontal lobe metabolic activity in some schizophrenic patients (Breier et al., 1992). Robbins (1992) speculates that the difficulty with integration and focus, as well as the tendency toward emotionless states in schizophrenic patients might be connected to frontal lobe hypometabolism. Affective blunting, anhedonia, and cognitive impairment have also been associated with decreased prefrontal cortical blood flow and glucose metabolism in schizophrenic patients (Andreason et al, 1992; Wolkin et al., 1992).

Neuroimaging studies indicate decreased metabolic function in the frontal-temporal cortex, caudate nucleus, hypothalamus, and limbic systems of depressed patients (Cummings, 1993; George et al., 1993). Both noradrenergic and serotoninergic neurotransmitter system dysregulation appears to be involved in depressive disorders. The cognitive, affective, and neurovegetative disturbances characteristic of depression (hopelessness, anhedonia, insomnia, dysphagia) may reflect these neuroanatomical-neurotransmitter areas of dysfunction. Most antidepressant drugs either reduce the breakdown of neurotansmitters (monoamine oxidase inhibitors) or block their synaptic reuptake (tricyclics, selective serotonin reuptake inhibitors); the net result is an increase in neurotransmitter concentrations at the synapse (Michaels and Marzuk, 1993b). Antidepressant medication alone is not always effective in curing depression, however, and there is evidence that psychotherapy following medication withdrawal significantly prolongs depression-free periods (Frank et al., 1990, 1991). This finding suggests that psychotherapy by itself may continue to stabilize a reconfiguration of the noradrenergic/serotoninergic neurotransmitter systems initially brought about by medication.

Studies of patients with obsessive-compulsive disorder (OCD) demonstrate that basal ganglia, limbic, thalamic, and cortical regions are involved in the mediation of OCD symptoms (Baxter et al., 1992). OCD was considered to be a disorder of serotoninergic dysregulation due to the beneficial response of patients to selective serotonin reuptake inhibitors; however, some patients respond to neuroleptic drugs, suggesting that the dopaminergic system is also involved (Michaels and Marzuk, 1993b). Baxter and his colleagues (1992) suggest that caudate nucleus dysfunction in OCD results in inadequate filtering of "worry" inputs from the orbital region of the brain. This disinhibition promotes a self-reinforcing excitation in the orbital-basal gangliathalamic neuronal circuit, which maintains OCD symptoms. From a psychodynamic viewpoint, significant intrapsychic or interpersonal threats (e.g., perceived psychological or physical injury; emergence of sexual or violent impulses, etc.) may not be adequately integrated and neutralized; instead, they are continuously reinforced because of this self-perpetuating excitatory circuit, leading to repetitive behaviors and obsessive ideation. The isolation, undoing, and displacement characteristic of OCD symptoms may reflect this maladaptive effort to control perceived external or internal danger. Recent evidence indicates that glucose metabolic rates in the right head of the caudate nucleus decrease significantly when OCD patients are treated successfully with either fluoxetine (a selective serotonin reuptake inhibitor) or behavior therapy (Baxter et al., 1992). This finding suggests that either neurochemical or psychotherapeutic intervention can effectively interrupt this self-sustaining circuit and restore normal neuronal-neurotransmitter functioning. In so far as psychotherapy is a learning experience, Kandel's (1979, 1983) experiments with the marine snail (*Aplysia californica*) seem relevant. Kandel demonstrated that the learning involved in habituation and sensitization in *Aplysia* results in corresponding decreases or increases of neurotransmitter release and calcium influx. Long-term habituation or sensitization can lead to prolonged functional synaptic inactivation or activation. Serotonin appears to be the neurotransmitter mediating these synaptic changes in *Aplysia*. Kandel (1983) points out that the learning of sensitization and habituation, similar to the learning and unlearning of anxiety, can result in "enduring changes in the structure and function of synapses." Thus, learning or experience can bring about both structural and functional synaptic alterations. Hyman and Nestler (1993) comment that it is probable that both psychotropic drugs and psychosocial interventions modify symptoms through identical processes, though from different avenues of approach. Both alter neurotransmitter-receptor systems and intracellular messenger pathways, resulting in long-lasting adaptive changes at the pre- and postsynaptic levels. Reiser (1984) notes that although the anatomical structure of neurons and synapses are genetically determined, it is experience and learning that shapes their functional effectiveness and stability. Learning, of course, is intimately connected to memory, which is a central component of adaptive and maladaptive behavior. Memory appears to be endowed with meaning and affective coloring when sensory percepts are processed through cortical-limbic pathways and stored in the cortex (Reiser, 1990). Dreaming appears to be one of the ways in which experience is stored as memory. An important function of dreaming is the integration and storage of current affect-laden experience with similar past events (Palombo, 1978). Cartwright (1986) and Greenberg et al. (1992) have demonstrated that this information-memory processing function of dreams serves to solve current waking problems or dilemmas. In this sense, dreaming can be viewed as a psychodynamically adaptive process subserved by rhythmic neuronal excitation that occurs during rapid-eye-movement (REM) sleep. Despite this adaptive role of dreaming, early traumatic experiences and their associated affects may form a network of interconnected memories maintained by strongly facilitated synapses. Edelman (1992) refers to such networks as "neuronal groups" in which synaptic connections are either strengthened or weakened through learning and memory. Olds (1994) suggests that these neuronal groups or "neural nets" may be facilitated or inhibited by affective experience. It is conceivable that meaningful current experience may articulate with previously stored memories and activate a "sensitized" neuronal-synaptic network with corresponding neurotransmitter release accompanied by affective and cognitive changes. If this neuronal-synaptic network is highly activated due to the nature of the current experience, a neurochemical cascade may develop along with overwhelming affects and cognitive disorganization, resulting in major psychiatric illness.

Panic and generalized anxiety disorders also appear to have a disordered neuroanatomical-neurochemical substrate. The locus coeruleus and pontine nucleus are implicated in the noradrenergic dysregulation of panic attacks. Pharmacological intervention with benzodiazepines facilitates binding of gamma-aminobutyric acid (GABA) to GABA receptors. GABA, in turn, activates the receptors' chlorine channel leading to inhibition of neurotransmission and reduction of anxiety (Hyman and Nestler, 1993). There is some evidence that benzodiazepines and GABA-mediated inhibition acts on noradrenergic and serotoninergic neurons in the limbic system, including the hippocampus and amygdala (Hyman and Nestler, 1993). The anti-panic efficacy of tricyclic antidepressants and selective serotonin reuptake inhibitors also implicate dysregulation of the noradrenergic/serotoninergic systems (Den-Boer et al., 1990; Klerman, 1992). Shear et al. (1993) have proposed a model of panic disorder that takes into account genetic neurophysiological vulnerability, disturbed parent-child interaction, and current triggering events. They postulate that patients susceptible to panic disorder have a genetic potential for "neurophysiologic irritability" (presumably, a potential for dysregulation of noradrenergic-serotoninergic systems). Moreover, they hypothesize that because these patients have been exposed during childhood to frightening or over-controlling parental behavior, they develop fragile self-representations as well as object representations composed of powerful others. Because of easily activated fantasies of being separated from or trapped by powerful others, they react with threatening affects (anxiety, guilt, anger) that generate superimposed anxiety, leading to panic. I would add that these overwhelming affects may result from a neuronal-synaptic network previously sensitized by both genetic factors and earlier traumatic interactions. According to this model, panic attacks result from the synergistic interaction of a vulnerable self, magnified fears of abandonment or entrapment by powerful others, and overwhelming negative affects (particularly anxiety) facilitated by genetically and experientially sensitized noradrenergic-serotoninergic neuronal groups. In terms of my clinical experience with such patients, this kind of psychodynamic-neurobiological model more closely fits the clinical data than the currently popular "spontaneous" neurophysiological-perturbation model. A major goal of treatment for patients with panic disorder is the development of a greater sense of internal control and less vulnerability to fantasies or events connected to separation and entrapment. This is conceptually similar to the achievement of mastery or control over inner feelings, thoughts, and impulses common to most psychotherapies (Frank, 1974; Liberman, 1978). Shear et al. (1993) suggest that the successful treatment of panic disorder entails a psychodynamically- oriented, empathic approach, which helps the patient develop a sense of inner safety as well as coping skills to manage threatening affects. Put another way, the therapist serves a "corrective" self-object function in place of earlier caregivers who failed in their role as external psychoneurobiological regulators during the patient's formative development. One hopes that internalization of certain qualities of the therapist leads to a stronger sense of self and inner safety, less fear of abandonment or entrapment, and more effective defense mechanisms for neutralizing threatening affects. An integral part of this process might be a recongifuration of previously dysregulated noradrenergic/serotoninergic neuronal groups. In this sense, the therapist acts as a new or different kind of external psychoneurobiological regulator for the patient. Of course, psychotropic medication might be necessary initially to stabilize an overreactive, dysregulated neuronal-synaptic network.

The following are two clinical vignettes that illustrate how this psychodynamic-neurobiological model might work in the pathogenesis of psychiatric disorders:

Clinical Vignette #1:

Tom was a 17-year-old male who entered treatment for panic attacks, agoraphobia, and disorganizing anxiety. His father's job as a corporate executive necessitated multiple geographic relocations during Tom's formative years. Tom recalled feeling anxiety, particularly gastrointestinal discomfort, with each move. In the context of his family's most recent move to another city, Tom became terrified, refused to leave the house or attend school, and was unable to think or speak coherently. Following a brief hospitalization, he began outpatient treatment including individual psychotherapy, and medication (a benzodiazepine and a tricyclic antidepressant). Although his acute symptomatology subsided, Tom was still unable to venture out in public or attend school. Initially, he could not articulate what it was that frightened him-only that it was a nameless, unbearable terror.

As treatment progressed and a positive therapeutic alliance was established, Tom gradually began to be more specific about some of his fears. He believed that if he left home without being in the physical presence of one or both parents he would "fall apart"-literally disintegrate physically and psychologically. He anticipated that if he attended school he would be ridiculed and humiliated by the other students. Tom's older brother frequently teased and criticized him. His father was a tall, heavily built man who physically intimidated Tom, and whose periodic temper outbursts terrified him. His mother was overprotective and "worried" over him; she suffered from migraine and backaches. Tom recalled that he was always shy and sensitive to the remarks or actions of others. His dreams vividly portrayed his inner world of fear and vulnerability. An example was the following dream:

> "I was at school in biology class. I didn't know any of the other kids. The teacher started yelling at us and one of the kids hit him. The teacher beat up the kid and began punching everybody, including me. Then he threw me out the window. I told my mother".

Tom associated his biology teacher to his father; both were big and powerful. Although they were ordinarily mild-mannered, he believed they had the capability of becoming violent when angry. His mother seemed incapable of protecting him from his father's destructive rage. It became clear that Tom's self-representation was extremely fragile and vulnerable. He perceived others as either powerful and dangerous, or indifferent and unsupportive. His mother, though protective, was incapable of saving him from injury or death. He realized that his panic attacks were often precipitated by fantasies of being abandoned or ridiculed by his family and friends. The following dream, which occurred about I year into treatment, reflected his transference to me and his relationships in general:

> "I was walking in a field where there were snakes that tried to bite me. I was on a boat with an older man. A huge snake came toward us in the water. A giant turtle appeared and the snake tried to eat it. But the turtle fought back and killed the snake".

Tom associated the snakes with his brother and others who could humiliate and reject him. The huge snake was his father who was capable of killing him. I was the giant turtle-slowly but constantly probing, invulnerable, yet protective. The therapeutic voyage with me (the older man in the boat) was his only hope of feeling safer and curing himself of his panic attacks. This dream was a good example of the problem-solving function of dreaming. Tom realized that his therapeutic collaboration with me offered him an opportunity to work through his fears and free himself of panic attacks. He gradually gained self-confidence and ventured out in public; eventually, he returned to school despite episodes of feeling anxious away from home.

Tom's personality structure resembled the profile of those panic disorder patients described by Shear et al. (1993). He viewed himself as powerless and vulnerable, unable to defend himself against the potential anger and violence of his father and brother. For several years prior to treatment, he experienced ever-increasing anxiety symptoms in social situations. The disorganizing panic, which required hospitalization, was precipitated by separation from familiar places, friends, and school. He felt trapped, helpless, and vulnerable in a strange city. Contrary to popular current theory, which hypothesizes a spontaneous neurochemical precipitation of panic disorder, his symptoms were clearly associated with his expectation of physical and psychological disintegration due to separation from familiar objects. One might speculate that the interaction of genetically determined overreactive noradrenergic/serotoninergic neuronal groups, self-fragility, and inadequate defense mechanisms contributed to the overwhelming anxiety evoked by his terrifying fantasies. Regardless of the mediating factors, a critical point of noradrenergic and/or serotoninergic dysregulation was reached resulting in cognitive and affective disorganization. Pharmacological intervention was necessary to bring about cognitive and affective stability. Once this occurred, Tom was able to engage in therapy and explore his inner fantasy life. Psychotherapy was directed toward helping him understand the conscious and unconscious sources of his anxiety, while at the same time providing him with specific coping strategies to contain it. For example, Tom learned that if he remained in a frightening situation rather than fleeing from it, his anxiety gradually subsided. His positive transference reflected a process of introjection of certain perceived qualities of mine (steadfastness, self-inquiry) that were internalized and contributed to an inner sense of confidence and safety. Our relationship represented a different kind of experience for Tom-one in which a male authority could be simultaneously strong and yet sensitive to his emotional needs. It is possible that as this self-object relationship continues, it will have a regulating effect on the neuronal-synaptic functioning of his noradrenergic/serotoninergic systems, which in turn, may become less reactive to future threatening experiences and fantasies.

Clinical Vignette #2:

Alice was a 42-year-old married woman who became depressed and attempted suicide by overdosing with antidepressant medication. Alice was sexually abused by her stepfather from ages 8-16. Her mother, who was verbally and physically abusive, frequently told Alice that she was worthless, stupid, clumsy, and unwanted. Alice recalled becoming suicidal around age 13 because of guilt and self-punitive feelings connected to the incest. She depersonalized whenever her stepfather abused her, thereby blocking out the accompanying feelings of shame, rage, and terror. In addition to her dissociative and depressive symptoms, she often "heard" her mother's voice inside her head criticizing and devaluing her. She became very attached to her first therapist, a woman, who was supportive and caring. When Alice's husband was transferred to another city by his employer, she was forced to leave her therapist, precipitating her depression and suicide attempt. While hospitalized, Alice was unable to distinguish whether her mother's voice was "real" or imaginary; it told her that she was evil, selfish, and that she should kill herself. During much of her hospitalization, she felt empty, unreal, and hopeless. She received psychotropic medication, including a major tranquilizer and an antidepressant.

Following her discharge from the hospital, Alice continued in individual psychotherapy. Her mother's voice became ego dystonic and her depression subsided. Nevertheless, she continued to struggle with a negative maternal introject. The following dream was illustrative of the unresolved conflict with her mother:

"I was watching a movie in which a big, brown horse was in a fenced-in area. A monkey kept landing on the horse's back. The horse couldn't get it off and the monkey wouldn't let go".

Alice associated the monkey to her mother and the horse to herself. The monkey on her back referred to her mother's constant criticism, which she was unable to disregard. Her mother often told her she was as "big as a horse" and as "clumsy as an ox." The fenced-in areas signified the extent to which her mother's criticism limited any positive feelings about herself. On the other hand, her identification with the horse indicated her potential for inner strength and the ability to free herself from her mother's destructive power over her. This dream pointedly illustrated the use of manifest imagery as a metaphorical presentation of Alice's relationship with her mother (Greenberg et al., 1992). As therapy progressed, Alice gradually began to experience the terror, shame, and rage associated with her earlier abuse. Whenever she recalled specific traumatic events and the feelings connected to them, she would invariably depersonalize. She revealed that around age 12 she began experiencing three distinct personalities. One was Ann, whom she described as confident, capable, and attractive. She often became Ann when her stepfather sexually abused her. Another alter was Jim, who was happy and fun loving. She became Jim when she felt guilty and self-punitive over her incestuous behavior. A third alter was a nameless girl with whom she closely identified: shy, sad, hurt, and unwanted. Alice experienced each of these alters as separate and external to herself. During the course of treatment, her feelings toward me vacillated between trust or fear of my disapproval. On one occasion, when she tentatively expressed annoyance over something I said, she was surprised and reassured over my acceptance of her criticism. As she gradually began to believe that I accepted all of her feelings, her negative maternal introject became less intrusive and critical. In addition, her guilt and self-punitiveness lessened, although her sense of self-worth remained tenuous.

Alice's clinical picture was one of dissociative phenomena (including multiple personality disorder and depersonalization), depression, ego fragmentation, and auditory hallucinations. She was the victim of profound sexual, emotional, and physical abuse. Her mother's introjected admonishments were continuous reminders of this abuse. Her dissociative defenses, including her multiple alters, helped to neutralize her unbearable feelings and compensated for an inner sense of worthlessness. During the process of internalizing a more positive maternal introject from her previous therapist, she was forced to leave her, and became depressed as well as suicidal. The loss of her therapist shattered her developing, though embryonic positive sense of self, leaving her feeling worthless, vulnerable, and empty. Arieti (1977) and Bemporad (1983) point out that depression may occur when an individual who empowers another to compensate for an essentially negative sense of self loses that powerful other. Without the availability of the important other (which may also be an institution or belief system), the individual feels hopeless, helpless, and worthless. Alice's loss of the healing self-object relationship with her therapist also resulted in a hallucinatory externalization of her introjected, rejecting, cruel mother. Her suicide attempt symbolized her mother's wish for her to die, her own wish to kill her bad, sinful self along with her introjected, hated mother and stepfather. As Alice began to believe that I accepted and understood her, a nascent sense of self-esteem emerged along with a diminution of her negative maternal introject. She continued to require a major tranquilizer, a tricyclic antidepressant, and a selective serotonin reuptake inhibitor.

The neurophysiological processes involved in dissociative phenomena, including multiple personality disorder, are poorly understood. One hypothesis is that dissociation is a form of epilepsy or temporal lobe dysfunction (Putnam, 1986). Another explanation is that it represents a complete or partial functional disconnection of the cerebral hemispheres (Putnam, 1991). This, in turn, results in a disruption of the sense of unity of the self. There is little evidence for either hypothesis, however. Demitrack et al. (1990) suggest a dysregulation of the serotoninergic and opiate systems in dissociative states. However, other neurotransmitters (dopamine) can also produce dissociative symptoms (depersonalization) in certain patients (Good, 1989). It is generally agreed that dissociative phenomena are an adaptation to intolerable experiences and affects. Identity, memory, cognition, emotions, and behavior are significantly altered by dissociation. Multiple personality is at the extreme end of the dissociative spectrum and is a result of severe childhood sexual, emotional, and physical abuse. The conditions of safety, soothing, and empathy necessary for the developing sense of self are non-existent. The emergence of alters as well as the ablation of overwhelmingly painful feelings serve to maintain ego organization and functioning. Alice's traumatic childhood, fragile ego, depersonalization, and multiple alters were consistent with the dissociative spectrum. Her hallucinatory maternal introject was characteristic of multiple personality patients (Kluft, 1991); it became ego syntonic in conjunction with the fragmentation of self and loss of reality testing in her depressed state. The combination of a major tran-quilizer, tricyclic antidepressant, and selective serotonin reuptake inhibitor ameliorated her depression and auditory hallucinations. This suggests that her dysregulated dopaminergic, noradrenergic, and serotoninergic systems were re-stabilized to some degree. The reorganization of her sense of self as well as the re-establishment of her reality testing enabled her to participate in a psychotherapeutic dialogue. Without medication, this would not have been possible. Her growing trust, as well as her solidifying belief that I accepted her, began to neutralize her negative maternal introject, providing her with greater self-esteem. It is conceivable that as her self-object needs continue to be met within the therapeutic relationship, her neurotransmitter systems will become more normally regulated and the requirement for medication will diminish.

In presenting these clinical vignettes I have attempted to integrate psychodynamic and neurobiological processes. Although our knowledge of each area is expanding, we know little of the bridging mechanisms between them. However, there is evidence from animal and human studies that developmental experiences affect neurobiological and psychophysiological regulation. In particular, the role of the caregiver as an external psychoneurobiological regulator exerts a powerful influence on the infant's development of autonomous, self-regulatory functions. Genetic endowment clearly plays an important role as well. Developmental emotional traumas (abuse, loss, abandonment) most likely sensitize neuronal-synaptic networks so that they are more easily dysregulated in the context of experiential stress later on. For example, the "kindling" phenomenon (Post et al., 1982) postulates that separations or losses earlier in life may precipitate depression and sensitize synaptic receptor sites and neurotransmitter systems. After repeated episodes of depression, however, it may require minimal or no psychological stress to trigger depression. Tom's vulnerability to panic disorder was most likely a result of early frightening experiences within his family as well as the fear connected to multiple geographic moves. These events may have led to sensitization of his noradrenergic-serotoninergic systems, making him more vulnerable and reactive to subsequent psychosocial stressors. Similarly, Alice's childhood abuse may have sensitized her dopaminergic-noradrenergic-serotoninergic systems, making her more likely to become dissociated, depressed, and fragmented in the context of subsequent emotional trauma. Psychopharmacological and psychotherapeutic intervention helped to reorganize and stabilize both patients. The continued use of medication served to maintain regulation of their neuronal-synaptic and neurotransmitter functioning. By the same token, psychotherapy provided them with improved self and object representations, more effective coping strategies, and healthier defenses through the internalization process (Geller et al., 1981-1982; Kantrowitz et al., 1989; Viederman, 1991). It is entirely possible that further internalization may lead to improved self-regulation of the previously sensitized neuronal-synaptic networks and neurotransmitter systems of both patients. This is in accordance with Kandel's (1983) suggestion that psychotherapy, which itself is a form of learning and unlearning, may result in "long-term functional and structural changes in the brain." Although my discussion of both patients is speculative to some degree, I have attempted to organize it around currently available psychodynamic and neurobiological information. I believe that we have entered into an era of exciting, new developments in genetics, neurochemistry, psychoanalytic theory, and treatment. One hopes the knowledge gained from these areas will facilitate a change from the dualistic approach involving mind and brain toward an integrated understanding of all mental phenomena.

References:

Alexander, F. (1950), *Psychosomatic Medicine*, W. W. Norton, New York.

Andreason, N. C., Rezai, K., Alliger, R., Swayze, V. W., Flaum, M., Kirchner, P., Cohen, G., and O'Leary, D. S. (1992), Hypofrontality in neuroleptic-naive patients and in patients with chronic schizophrenia, *Arch. Gen. Psychiat.*, *49*, 943-958.

Arieti, S. (1977), Psychotherapy of severe depression, *Am. J. Psychiat,*, *134*, 864-868.

Bartrop, R. W., Luckhurst, E., Lazarus, L., Kiloh, L. G., and Penny, R. (1977), Depressed lymphocyte function after bereavement, *Lancet, 1*, 834-836.

Baxter, L. R., Schwartz, J. M., Bergman, K. S., Szuba, M. P., Guze, B. H., Mazziotta, J. C., Alzraki, A., Selin, C. E., Ferng, H. K., Munford, P., and Phelps, M. E. (1992), Caudate glucose metabolic rate changes with both drug and behavior therapy for obsessive-compulsive disorder, *Arch. Gen. Psychiat.*, *49*, 681-689.

Bemporad, J. R. (1983), Cognitive, affective and physiologic changes in the depressive process, *J. Am. Acad. Psychoanal.*, *2*, 159-172.

Breier, A., Buchanan, R. W., Elkashef, A., Munson, R. C., Kirkpatrick, B., and Gellard, F. (1992), Brain morphology and schizophrenia, *Arch. Gen. Psychiat.*, *49*, 921-926.

Cartwright, R. (1986), Affect and dream work from an information processing point of view, *J. Mind and Behav.*, *7*, 411-427.

Cummings, J. L. (1993), The neuroanatomy of depression, *J. Clin. Psychiat.*, *54*, 14-20.

Demitrack, M. A., Putnam, F. W., Brewerton, T. D., Brandt, H. A., and Gold, P. W. (1990), Relation of clinical variables to dissociative phenomena in eating disorders, *Am. J. Psychiat.*, *147*, 1184-1188.

DenBoer, J. A., Westenberg, H. G. M., and Verhoeven, W. M. A. (1990), Biological aspects of panic anxiety. *Psychiat. Ann.*, *20*, 494-502.

Edelman, G. M. (1992), *Bright Air, Brilliant Fire*. Basic Books, New York.

Emde, R. N. (1990), Mobilizing fundamental modes of development: Empathic availability and therapeutic action, *J. Am. Psychoanal. Assoc.*, *38*, 881-913.

Emde, R. N., and Robinson, J. (1979), The first two months: Recent research in developmental psychobiology and the changing view of the newborn, in J. D. Noshpitz (Ed.), *Basic Handbook of Child Psychiatry*, Vol. 1, Basic Books, New York, pp. 72-105.

Engel, G. L., and Schmale, A. H. (1967), Psychoanalytic theory of somatic disorder: Conversion, specificity and the disease onset situation, *J. Am. Psvchoanal. Assoc.*, *15*, 34-365.

Frank, E., Kupfer, D. J., Perel, J. M., Cornes, C., Jarrett, D. B., Mallinger, A. G., Thase, M. E., McEachran, A. B., and Grochocinski, V. J. (1990), Three-year outcomes for maintenance therapies in recurrent depression, *Arch. Gen. Psychiat.*, *47*, 1093-1099.

Frank, E., Kupfer, D, J., Wagner, E. F., McEachran, A. B., and Cornes, C. (1991), Efficacy of Interpersonal psychotherapy as a maintenance treatment of recurrent depression, *Arch. Gen. Psychiat.*, *48*, 1053-1059.

Frank. J. D. (1974), How psychotherapy heals, *Henry Ford Hosp. Med. J.*, *22*(2), 71-81.

Freud, S. (1895a), Project for a scientific psychology, *Standard Edition*, pp. 295-397.

Freud, S. (1895b), On the grounds for detaching a particular syndrome from neurasthenia under the description anxiety neurosis. *Standard Edition*, Vol. 1, pp. 87-117.

Freud, S. (1932), New introductory lectures on psychoanalysis, *Standard Edition*, Vol. 3, pp. 7-182.

Geller, J. D., Cooley, R. S., and Hartley, D. (1981-1982), Images of the psychotherapist: A theoretical and methodological perspective, *Imagination, Cognition, and Personality*, *22*, 123-146.

George, M. S., Ketter, T. A., and Post, R. M. (1993), SPECT and PET imaging in mood disorders, *J. Clin. Psychiat.*, *54*, 6-13.

Glucksman, M. L., Quinlan, D. M., and Leigh, H. (1985), Skin conductance changes and psychotherapeutic content in the treatment of a phobic patient, *Br. J. Med. Psvchol., 58*, 155-163.

Good, M. I. (1989), Substance-induced dissociative disorders and psychiatric nosology, *J. Clin. Psychopharmacol., 9*, 88-93.

Greenberg, R., Katz, H., Schwartz, W., and Pearlman, C. (1992), A research-based reconsideration of the psychoanalytic theory of dreaming, *J. Am. Psvchoanal. Assoc., 40*, 531-550.

Gross, H. S., and Fligsten, K. (1991), A psychophysiologic perspective on affect and psychotherapy, *J. Am. Acad. Psychoanal., 19*, 189-212.

Hofer, M. A, (1983), The mother-infant interaction as a regulator of infant physiology and behavior, in L. Rosenblum and H. Moltz (Eds.), *Symbiosis in Parent-Offspring Interactions*, Plenum, New York, pp. 61-75.

Hyman, S. E., and Nestler, E. J. (1993), *The Molecular Foundations of Psychiatry*, American Psychiatric Press, Washington, DC.

Kandel, E. R. (1979), Psychotherapy and the single synapse, *N. Engl. J. Med., 301*, 1028-1037.

Kandel, E. R. (1983), From metapsychology to molecular biology: Explorations into the nature of anxiety, *Am. J. Psychiat., 140*, 1277-1293.

Kantrowitz, J. L., Katz, A. L., Greenman, D. A., Morris, H., Paolitto, F., Sashin, J., and Solomon, L. (1989), The patient-analyst match and the outcome of psychoanalysis: A pilot study, *J. Am. Psychoanal. Assoc., 37*, 893-919.

Klerman, G. L. (1992), Treatments for panic disorder, *J. Clin. Psychiat., 53*, 14-19.

Kluft, R. P. (1991), Multiple personality disorder in A. Tasman and S. M. Goldfinger (Eds.), *American Psychiatric Press Review of Psychiatry*, Vol. 10, American Psychiatric Press, Washington, DC, pp. 161-188.

Kohut, H. (1971), *The Analysis of the Self*, International University Press, New York.

Liberman, B. L. (1978), The role of mastery in psychotherapy: Maintenance of improvement and prescriptive change, in J. D. Frank, R. Hoehn-Saric, S. D. Imber, B. L. Liberman, and A. R. Stone

(Eds.), *Effective Ingredients of Successful Psychotherapy*, Brunner/ Mazel, New York, pp. 35-72.

Luborsky, L., Docherty, J. P., and Penick, S. (1973), Onset conditions for psychosomatic symptoms: A comparative review of immediate observation with retrospective research, *Psychosom. Med., 35*, 187-204.

Michels, R. and Marzuk, P. M. (1993a), Progress in psychiatry, *N. Engl. J. Med., 329*, 552-560.

Michels, R. and Marzuk, P. M. (1993b), Progress in psychiatry, *N. Engl. J. Med., 329*, 628-638.

Olds, D. D. (1994), Connectionism and psychoanalysis, *J. Am. Psychoanal. Assoc., 42*, 581-611.

Palombo, S. R. (1978), *Dreaming and Memory*, Basic Books, New York.

Post, R. M., Ballenger, J. C., Uhde, T. W, Putnam, F. W., and Bunney, W. E. (1982), Kindling and drug sensitization: Implications for the progressive development of psychopathology and treatment with carbamazepine, in M. Sandler (Ed.), *Psychopharmacology of Anticonvulsants*, Oxford University Press, Oxford.

Putnam, F. W. (1986), The scientific investigation of multiple personality, in J. M. Quen (Ed.), *Split Minds Split Brains*, New York University Press, New York, pp. 109-126.

Putnam, F. W. (1991), Dissociative phenomena, in A. Tasman and S. M. Goldfinger (Eds.), *American Psychiatric Press Review of Psychiatry*, Vol. 10, American Psychiatric Press, pp. 145-160.

Reiser, M. F. (1990), *Memory in Mind and Brain*, Basic Books, New York.

Robbins, M. (1992), Psychoanalytic and biological approaches to mental illness: Schizophrenia, *J. Am. Psychoanal. Assoc., 40*, 425-454.

Rosenman, R. H., Friedman, M., Straus, R., Wurm, M., Kositchek, R., and Werthessen, N. T. (1964), A predictive study of coronary heart disease: The Western Collaborative Group study, *JAMA, 189*, 113-120.

Shear, M. K., Cooper, A. M., Klerman, G. L., Busch, F. N., and Shapiro, T. (1993), A psychodynamic model of panic disorder, *Am. J. Psychiat., 150*, 859-866.

Sifneos, P. (1975), Problems of psychotherapy of patients with alexithymic characteristics and physical disease, *Psychother. Psychosom., 26*, 65-70.

Stein, M., Keller, S., and Schleifer, S. J. (1985), Stress and immunomodulation: The role of depression and neuroendocrine function, *J. Immunol., 135*, 827-833.

Stern, D. N. (1985), *The Interpersonal World of the Infant*, Basic Books, New York.

Stone, E. A., Bonnet, K. A., and Hofer, M. A. (1976), Survival and development of maternally deprived rats: Role of body temperature, *Psychosom. Med., 38*, 242-249.

Taylor, G. J. (1992), Psychoanalysis and psychosomatics: A new synthesis, *J. Am. Acad. Psychoanal., 20*, 251-275.

Viederman, M. (1991), The real person of the analyst and his role in the process of psychoanalytic cure, *J. Am. Psychoanal. Assoc., 39*, 451-489.

Weiner, H., Thaler, M., Reiser, M. F., and Mirsky, I. A. (1957), Etiology of duodenal ulcer: I. Relation of specific psychological characteristics to rate of gastric secretion (Serum Pepsinogen), *Psychosom. Med., 19*, 1-10.

Williams, R. B., Barefoot, J. C., Haney, T. L., Harrell, F. E., Blumenthal, J. A., Pryor, D. B., and Peterson, B. (1988), Type A behavior and angiographically documented coronary atherosclerosis in a sample of 2,289 patients, *Psychosom. Med., 50*, 139-152.

Wolkin, A., Sanfilipo, M, S., Woll, A. P., Angrist, B., Brodie, J. D., and Rotrosen, J. (1992), Negative symptoms and hypofrontality in chronic schizophrenia, *Arch. Gen. Psychiat., 49*, 959-965.

*Clinical Professor of Psychiatry, New York Medical College; Supervising and Training Analyst, The Psychoanalytic Institute, New York Medical College.

Presented, in part, at the Annual Meeting of the American Academy of Psychoanalysis, May 1994.

Journal of the American Academy of Psychoanalysis, 23(2), 179-195, 1995.

FREUD'S PROJECT: THE MIND-BRAIN CONNECTION REVISITED
MYRON L. GLUCKSMAN, M.D.

Abstract:

Freud's "Project for a Scientific Psychology" (1895) reflected his attempt to explain psychic phenomena in neurobiological terms. The recent discovery of the neuron motivated him to embark on this endeavor. His basic hypothesis was that neurons were vehicles for the conduction of "currents" or "excitations," and that they were connected to one another. Using this model, Freud attempted to describe a number of mental phenomena, including: consciousness, perception, affect, self, cognition, dreaming, memory and symptom formation. However, he was unable to complete his exploration of these mental processes because he lacked the information and technology that became available over the following century. Subsequent discoveries, including fMRIs, PET scans, EEGs, synapses, neural networks, genetic factors, neurotransmitters, and discrete brain circuits facilitated a significant expansion of our knowledge of mind-brain phenomena. As a result, effective pharmacological treatments have been developed for schizophrenia, mood and anxiety disorders. Moreover, changes in brain function can be measured that reflect successful pharmacologic and psychotherapeutic treatment. Despite these advances, there remain limitations in our understanding of the relationship between mind and brain functions. More than a century after Freud began the "Project," the neurobiology underlying the phenomena of consciousness, unconsciousness, qualities of subjective feelings, thoughts, and memories is still not fully understood. Can we expect to reach a more comprehensive integration of mind and its neurobiological substrate a century from now? The purpose of this article is to update our knowledge of the neurobiology associated with the specific mental functions that Freud examined in the "Project," and to pose questions concerning mind-brain phenomena that will hopefully be answered in the future.

Keywords: consciousness memory; hysteria; conversion; cognition; affect; mentalization; mirror neurons.

Introduction:

Over the span of a few weeks, Sigmund Freud (1895) wrote his "Project for a Scientific Psychology" in order to explain both normal and pathological psychic processes in neurobiological terms. He explored the following normal mental phenomena: memory, perception, consciousness, affect, cognition, self, sleep, and dreams. In addition, he examined the psychopathological processes involved in compulsions, obsessions, conversion reactions, and phobias. It was no coincidence that the neuron had already been described in 1888 by Santiago Ramon y Cajal (1899), and that Freud was most likely well aware of its anatomical structure (cell body, axis, and dendrites). However, he was still unaware of how impulses were transmitted from one neuron to the other by means of synapses. That process remained to be described by the English neurophysiologist, Charles Sherrington (1906). Nevertheless, Freud (1895) hypothesized that neurons conducted excitations from one to the other via "contact--barriers" (p. 298) that either resisted or facilitated excitations between neurons. According to Freud (1895), there were three types of neurons: "pi," "psi," and "omega" neurons. "Pi" neurons were permeable, offered no resistance and subserved perception; "psi" neurons were impermeable, offered resistance, and subserved memory; "omega" neurons transmitted the qualitative, subjective experiences of perception, memory, consciousness, and feelings. Affects were classified as either pleasurable or unpleasurable, and mediated through "psi" and "omega" neurons. Freud (1895) defined the ego as a network of neurons that maintained a balance between pleasure and unpleasure. It defended against psychic primary process, and facilitated secondary processes, as well as a sense of reality. Cognition was subserved by "psi" neurons, while "omega" neurons provided the quality of thought. Anticipating his later theory of dreaming, he hypothesized that it was characterized by primary process thought in the form of "psi" neuronal activation during sleep. He also noted that dreams were wish-fulfillments, hallucinatory, and that motor activity was inhibited during dreaming. In regard to psychopathology, Freud (1895) believed that symptoms were the result of the repression of disturbing affects and thoughts, although he was unable to describe their neuronal mediation. In his attempt to explain mental mechanisms using a neuronal paradigm, Freud basically laid the foundation for his theory of psychic function: conscious, unconscious, primary process, secondary process, ego, pleasure, unpleasure, affect, defenses, repression, and symptom formation. In the absence of neurobiological discoveries that were to come later, Freud was unable to pursue his "Project"; instead, he developed a metapsychology for personality structure, development, psychodynamics, and psychopathology. However, his emphasis on instincts, including libido and the death instinct, was biologically influenced (Sulloway, 1992). In fact, he continued to believe that mental functions would someday be explained by neurophysiology when he stated: "The deficiencies in our description would probably vanish if we were already in a position to replace the psychological terms by physiological or chemical ones" (Freud, 1920, p. 60). Serendipitously, he later predicted the central role of neurotransmitters when he stated, "It is here, indeed, that the hope for the future lies: the possibility that our knowledge of the operations of the hormones may give us the means of successfully combating the quantitative factors of the illnesses" (Freud, 1932, p. 154).

In this article, I intend to review some of the salient neurobiological discoveries that have been made in the succeeding 120 years since the "Project" (1895) was written. In particular, I shall focus on the neurobiology of those mental functions that Freud examined; namely, consciousness, memory, phobias, obsessions, compulsions, conversion disorders, affect, and cognition. Furthermore, I shall comment on the relevance of these discoveries in connection with our understanding of the mind, and speculate on how they might inform the psychodynamically oriented clinician.

Freud's (1932) prescience regarding the role of "hormones" in the brain was validated in the mid-20th century when Julius Axelrod (1957) discovered the neuronal-synaptic function of neurotransmitters, namely norepinephrine, epinephrine, and dopamine. The role of additional neurotransmitters soon followed, including acetylcholine, serotonin, GABA, glutamate, orexin, and other neuropeptides. Indeed, our understanding of the neuronal and neurochemical functioning of the brain has significantly expanded over the past half century (Kandel, Schwartz, Jessell, Siegelbaum, & Hudspeth, 2012). If Freud were to update the Project, he might include the following information that was unavailable when he attempted his synthesis of neurobiology and the mind.

Consciousness:

As far as consciousness is concerned, it is generally accepted that there is no specific location in the brain mediating conscious awareness (Farthing, 1992). Activation of the entire thalamo-cortical neuronal circuit occurs during the conscious state (Pally, 1998). A number of investigators (Baars, 2005; Crick & Koch, 1990, 2000; Pally, 1998) theorize that there is synchronized cortical neuronal oscillation in the gamma range between 30-70 Hz in the resting, conscious state. Humans, in contrast to other primates, are not only conscious of incoming sensory stimuli, but also have the capacity for self-reflection or introspection. Edelman (1989, 1992) makes the distinction between primary consciousness and self-reflective consciousness. According to him, primary consciousness is the awareness of current perceptions in the environment. Self-reflective consciousness involves the prefrontal cortex, and is concerned with internal experience. Neuroimaging studies demonstrate that during ongoing attention to external stimuli there is activation of the sensory cortex, while during introspection or self-reflective consciousness, there is activation of the prefrontal cortex (Tononi & Koch, 2008). Olds (1992) refers to a "self-awareness system" (p. 430) that involves inputs from cortical and inferior parietal areas. Panksepp (2005) speculates that an entity corresponding to self-awareness involves "the periaqueductal gray and surrounding collicular and tegmental zones...through many direct and indirect influences such as the strong two-way connections with frontal executive areas of the brain and...sensory cortices through the extended reticular and thalamic activating systems" (p. 21). Notwithstanding these descriptions of neuronal activity during consciousness and self-awareness, the qualities of self-experience, including the entire spectrum of emotions that Freud attributed to "omega" neurons, remain to be understood.

Memory:

In regard to memory, Freud (1895) postulated that it was mediated by "differences in the facilitations between the 'psi' neurons" (p. 300). Our current understanding of memory is far more complex and continues to evolve. In brief, memory is categorized as short-term, long-term, declarative (explicit), and procedural (implicit). Memory appears to be mediated by a hippocampal-cortical neuronal network; the hippocampus regulates recent memory and the cortex stores long-term memory (Pan & Tsukada, 2006). Explicit memory, or memory for people, places, facts, and events is mediated via the hippocampus and medial temporal lobe. On the other hand, implicit memory for automatic motor and perceptual skills is mediated through the amygdala, cerebellum, and cortex (Kandel, 2012). Both explicit and implicit memory are important components of interpersonal communication, including psychotherapy. Freud's (1900) concepts of "day residue" and "free association" involve short-term and long-term memory. Dreams juxtapose long-term and short-term memory; in essence, the unconscious does not distinguish between past and present. Brockman (2001) emphasizes the roles of explicit and implicit memory in the unconscious. Kandel (1999) points out that procedural or implicit memory is operative in both the unconscious and transference phenomena. However, elements of the preconscious unconscious are mediated by the prefrontal cortex and hippocampus. The latter facilitate the transfer of procedural or implicit memories into consciousness. Reiser (2001) theorizes that memories are stored and organized via nodal memory networks, according to their affective potential. Emotions that are either experienced or symbolized in dream manifest content may lead the dreamer to recall significant events in the recent or distant past. Moreover, feelings and percepts evoked in the therapeutic relationship may resonate with unconscious memories that can influence transference. Freud (1912) recognized the importance of unconscious memory when he first described transference: "unconscious impulses...reproduce themselves in accordance with the timelessness of the unconscious" (p. 108). Psychoanalytically oriented clinicians routinely question their patients about past experiences, relationships, and feelings in connection with manifestations of transference.

A cascade of neurotransmitter, molecular, genetic, and morphological changes are involved in memory processing. These include serotonin, GABA, glutamate, norepinephrine, dopamine, protein kinases, intracellular signaling events, and structural modifications of the synapse (Johansen, Cain, Ostroff, & LeDoux, 2011; Kandel, 2012). Memory and learning are interconnected, and are essential components of adaptive or maladaptive behavior. Perhaps, the most studied phenomenon of learning and memory is fear conditioning (Kandel, 1983; Kim et al., 2011; LeDoux, 1994). Kandel (1983) demonstrated that learning (habituation and sensitization) in Aplysia (sea snail) involves both neurotransmitter release and morphological changes in the synapse. He hypothesized that psychotherapy may bring about similar neuro-synaptic and neurotransmitter changes in the human brain. LeDoux (1994, 1996) notes that fear conditioning (learning to respond to a threat) is comprised of two major pathways; thalamic-amygdala and amygdala-prefrontal-cortical. The former is activated when a rapid response to an immediate threat is required; the latter becomes involved when there is time for a cognitive appraisal of the threat (Kim et al., 2011). Recent evidence reveals reciprocal functional connections between the amygdala and medial prefrontal cortex that regulate the fear response (Kim et al., 2011). Increased prefrontal cortical activity and simultaneous decreased amygdala activity occurs during successful fear regulation. The treatment of anxiety disorders, whether psychopharmacological or psychotherapeutic, is based on the suppression of thalamic-amygdala hyperactivity. Both cognitive-behavioral and psychodynamic therapies attempt to improve cognitive (prefrontal cortex) control by means of conditioning and insight.

Of interest, is that a group of individuals has been identified in childhood who have a genetically predisposed "anxious temperament" or AT (Shackman et al., 2013). They demonstrate increased amygdala and anterior hippocampal reactivity to threat-relevant cues, as well as weaker functional connections between the amygdala and medial-frontal cortex. This observation has important implications for the treatment of anxiety, social, phobic, and posttraumatic stress disorders. For example, a child with anxious temperament (AT) who is physically or emotionally abused might be more likely to develop generalized anxiety or posttraumatic stress disorder. Similarly, a child with AT who has overprotective, distrustful parents might become socially anxious and withdrawn. One of my patients developed a food phobia as an adult because her mother believed she had childhood allergies, and warned her that she could die from an anaphylactic reaction. Another patient developed free-floating anxiety in adulthood as a consequence of being traumatized by an alcoholic, violent father. Identification of children with AT is important so that early therapeutic interventions can be instituted if they are exposed to parental or environmental stress and trauma.

Hysteria:

Freud (1895) tentatively explored the mental mechanisms of "hysteria" in the Project. For him, hysteria included compulsions, obsessions, phobias, and conversion reactions. He attempted to correlate neuronal activity with such phenomena as repression, symbol formation and displacement. During this period, he also published papers devoted to the psychogenesis of conversion, obsessions, and phobias (Freud, 1894a, b). According to him, conversion symptoms result when the affect associated with an unacceptable idea or event is displaced and converted to a somatic symptom (e.g., paralysis). Phobias are displaced ideas associated with anxiety, while obsessions are displaced ideas associated with various emotional states, including anxiety, guilt, shame, anger etc. According to Freud (1895), the original idea or experience is usually connected to a sexual fantasy or activity. Although the exclusive sexual etiology of these disorders is no longer accepted, the role of repression, displacement, and symbol formation are still considered to be psychodynamically relevant in the genesis of phobias and obsessions. Recent evidence reveals that patients with OCD manifest hyperactivity of the caudate nucleus-orbitofrontal cortex neuronal circuit (Baxter et al., 1992; Saxena & Rauch, 2000; Whiteside, Port & Abramowitz, 2004). Gillan et al. (2015) demonstrated that excessive habit formation in OCD is associated with caudate nucleus hyperactivity. Baxter et al. (1992) suggest that caudate nucleus dysfunction is associated with inadequate filtering of "worry" inputs from the orbitofrontal cortex. In view of the fact that OCD appears to have a genetic component, similar to those individuals with AI, early identification and therapeutic intervention may be helpful (Browne, Gair, Scharf, & Grice, 2014; Mataix-Cols et al., 2013). Glucksman (1995) speculates that significant intrapsychic or interpersonal threats may not be adequately modulated or neutralized in patients with OCD; instead, threats are continuously reinforced by this self-perpetuating excitatory circuit, resulting in repetitive behaviors and obsessive ideation. Displacement, symbol-formation, isolation and undoing appear to be the psychodynamic manifestations of this dysfunctional neuronal pathway. However, treatment with either SSRIs or cognitive-behavioral therapy can normalize or interrupt this self-sustaining circuit (Baxter et al., 1992).

Conversion Disorders:

Conversion disorders remain a fascinating, yet puzzling clinical phenomenon. In DSM-5 (American Psychiatric Association, 2013), conversion disorder is termed "functional neurological symptom disorder," and involves the voluntary motor or sensory nervous systems. It is differentiated from "somatic symptom disorder"; the latter is mediated via the voluntary or involuntary nervous systems. According to Kaplan (2014), conversion disorders are precipitated when current life stressors resonate with childhood trauma. Patients with conversion symptoms are typically unable to verbally articulate their feelings and intrapsychic conflicts. They do not have the capacity to express their internal mental state through symbolic thought and language. The neuropsychological process of "conversion" is still poorly understood. A recent study (Vuilleumier, 2014) of functional motor paralysis reveals hyperactivation of the ventromedial prefrontal cortex, precuneus, and other limbic structures, simultaneous with decreased activation of motor pathways at the cortical and subcortical level. Similar dysfunction of neuronal pathways occurs with somatosensory, visual, and memory conversion symptoms. These findings suggest that Freud's (1894a) hypothesis regarding the conversion of disturbing affect to sensory-motor pathways may have some validity. In my practice, I continue to see conversion symptoms, including atypical pain, hypesthesia, and functional seizures. Conversion reactions are common in the context of traumatic events, including combat. As a military psychiatrist, I treated a helicopter pilot who developed conversion blindness after he realized that had accidentally attacked and killed his own soldiers. His feelings of guilt and remorse were repressed, displaced, and converted to his visual pathways and occipital cortex. Another patient was an army platoon leader who presented with bilateral upper extremity paralysis. His symptoms developed in the context of his repressed rage and murderous fantasies toward his commanding officer, whom he believed placed his men in mortal danger. His motor paralysis dramatically disappeared when he became consciously aware of his wish to strangle his superior. Recently, one of my patients presented with hypesthesia of his pubic and genital region during intercourse. In addition, he experienced either delayed or failed ejaculation. A neurological workup revealed no obvious organic cause for his symptoms. During psychotherapy, he revealed suppressed rage at his wife in connection with her manipulative, controlling behavior. As he became consciously aware of his feelings, sensation in his genitalia gradually normalized. Although current evidence demonstrates neuronal dysfunction in motor and sensory pathways associated with conversion symptoms (Black, Seritan, Taber, & Hurley, 2004; Bryant & Das, 2012; Vuilleumier, 2014), the inter-face between intrapsychic conflict, displaced affect, and neuronal activity remains a mystery.

Phobias:

Freud (1895) did not offer an explanation regarding neuronal activity associated with phobias in the Project, although he pointed out that phobias are always accompanied by anxiety (Freud, 1894b). However, his subsequent papers explored the etiology and psychodynamics of phobias and anxiety neurosis (Freud, 1909, 1917, 1926). In "The Introductory Lectures on Psychoanalysis" (Freud, 1917), he refers to his earlier research on the medulla oblongata, but then remarks, "I know nothing that could be of less interest to me for the psychological understanding of anxiety than a knowledge of the path of the nerves along which excitations pass" (Freud, 1917, p. 393). Ironically, almost a century since this statement, there is a growing body of data specifically concerned with the neuronal pathways and anatomic structures associated with anxiety, panic, phobias, and PTSD. As previously cited, certain anxiety prone children and adults exhibit increased activation of the amygdala, hippocampus, insula, and orbitofrontal cortex (Blackford et al., 2014; Fox & Kalin, 2014; Shackman et al., 2013). These individuals, identified as having a genetic predisposition for an anxious temperament (AT), are at higher risk for developing panic disorder and social anxiety. On the other hand, cognitive-behavioral and psychodynamic therapy can normalize their dysfunctional neuronal circuits (Kim et al., 2011; Lueken et al., 2013). Etkin and Wager (2007) note that social anxiety, specific phobias, and PTSD all have increased activation of the fear pathway that includes the amygdala and insula. In a PET scan study, Furmark et al. (2002) examined cerebral blood flow (CBF) in patients with social phobia before and after cognitive-behavior therapy or medication (citalopram). There were significant decreases in CBF of the amygdala, hippocampus, and adjacent cortical areas following successful treatment using both modalities.

Paquette et al. (2003) studied the effect of cognitive-behavioral therapy (CBT) on patients with spider phobia. Prior to CBT, he observed increased activation of the right inferior frontal gyrus, parahippocampal gyrus, and visual cortex. Following successful CBT, there was decreased activation of the right inferior frontal gyrus, parahippocampal gyrus, and prefrontal cortex. Almost 100 years after Freud dismissed the importance of understanding the neuronal and anatomic pathways of anxiety, there is clear evidence of dysfunctional circuits associated with anxiety, panic disorder, and phobias. Moreover, a specific population can be identified in early childhood that exhibits increased anxiety or anxious temperament (AI) and is more likely to develop anxiety disorders.

Effective treatment, including CBT, psychodynamic psychotherapy, or medication can now be monitored and documented using fMRIs and PET scans.

Cognition:

In his exploration of cognition, Freud (1895) was more concerned with primary process than secondary process thought. Primary process refers to unconscious mentation which is illogical, symbolic, and timeless. Secondary process is conscious mentation characterized by logical thought and a linear sense of time. Freud (1895) hypothesized that both types of cognition were mediated via "psi" neurons, although they differed according to the quantity of excitation. Prior to the publication of "The Interpretation of Dreams" (1900), he observed that there was a motor paralysis during dreaming, and that cognition in dreams was "non-sensical, partly feeble-minded, or even meaningless or strangely crazy" (Freud, 1895, p. 338). He attributed the hallucinatory experience and primary process thought in dreams to another neuronal excitation that he termed "Q" (Freud, 1895, p. 339). However, he did not pursue the nature of "Q" when he developed his later theory of dreaming; namely, that it is a form of censorship over instinctually driven wishes. Nor could he envision future discoveries about dreaming; first, that it is a biologically determined rhythmic activation of neuronal projections from the midbrain to the cortex during rapid eye movement (REM) sleep (although neuronal activation may also originate in the cortex); second, that its major function is not primarily to censor instinctual impulses, but rather to facilitate memory storage, learning, problem solving, and mood regulation; third, that primary process mentation in dreams often has metaphorical meaning and can be deciphered from the manifest content (Aserinsky & Kleitman, 1953; Dement & Kleitman, 1957; Glucksman, 2001; Greenberg & Pearlman, 1993; Hobson,1999; Kramer, 1993). Although Freud never developed an integrated theory of cognition, cognitive concepts are ubiquitous in psychoanalytic theories (Baars, 2005; Basch, 1997; Semenza, 2001). Included are such phenomena as mental representations, symbol formation, ideation, beliefs, rationalization, intellectualization, splitting, and insight.

Indeed, an entire field of cognitive neuropsychology has developed that is concerned with the neurobiology of cognitive processes.

Affect:

Similar to his observations on cognition, Freud never developed a comprehensive, systematic theory of affect. In "The Project" (1895), he described two categories of affect: satisfaction and pain (p. 321). While her viewed both as forms of psychic energy, pain or unpleasure required inhibition. In his signal theory of anxiety, Freud (7926) recognized affect (namely, anxiety) as a signal with cognitive meaning. In this model, an affect (anxiety) signals the ego to take evasive action and defend against it. Anxiety and fear are considered to be synonymous by neurobiologists, and mediated via the thalamo-amygdala-cortical neuronal axis (LeDoux, 1994, 1996; Panksepp, 1999, 2005). Other affects (joy, sadness, guilt, etc.) are regulated through the amygdala, anterior cingulate, insular, and orbito-frontal cortex (Pally, 2010; Panksepp, 2005). According to Panksepp (2005), all emotions involve neurotransmitters, including norepinephrine, serotonin, acetylcholine, and glutamate. However focal or discreet affects are thought to be mediated by specific neuropeptides; positive affects involve beta-endorphins and oxytocin, while negative affects involve CRF and cholecystokinin. Perhaps, the neurochemical, qualitative distinctions between feelings is analogous to Freud's (1895) "omega" neurons, but much more remains to be discovered in this area. Lane and coworkers (Lane & Garfield, 2005; Lane & Schwartz, 1987) describe five levels of emotional awareness: level one involves physiological arousal; level two involves action or motor tendencies; level three involves single emotions; level four involves blends of emotions; level five involves blends of blends of emotional experience. Levels one and two are implicit, and often out of conscious awareness. They are mediated via the thalamus, hypothalamus, amygdala, and basal ganglia. Levels three, four, and five are mediated by the anterior cingulate, insula, orbito-frontal cortex, and right parietal lobe. Maclean (1990) and Panksepp (1998) propose that activation of limbic and sub-cortical structures alone is sufficient for the conscious experience of emotion. However, others believe that cortical participation is necessary for emotional experience (Lane & Garfield, 2005; Mayberg, 2003). Focal awareness or immediate attention to feelings can be differentiated from reflective awareness of feelings (Farthing, 1992; Fonagy, Gergely, Jurist, & Target, 2002; Lane, Fink, Chua, & Dolan, 1997). Reflective awareness of feelings or mentalization, requires activation of the anterior cingulate and medial prefrontal cortex (Lane & Garfield, 2005). Mentalization refers to the process of explicit and implicit awareness of the feelings, thoughts, and behavior of self and others (Fonagy et al., 2002). Analogous to psychological-mindedness, it is necessary for participation in psychoanalytic or psychodynamic therapy. There is recent evidence that mentalizing corresponds to neuronal activation in the mesial frontal cortex and right temporo-parietal junction (Rizzolatti & Craighero, 2004; Rizolatti & Fogassi, 2014).

Mirror neurons appear to be a key mechanism for processing and re-creating in one's mind the intentions, actions, and feelings of another person. Mentalization most likely involves mirror neuron activation, and is necessary for normal interpersonal communication. Mirror neurons were first discovered in macaque monkeys who viewed and simulated the motor acts of other monkeys (Rizzolatti, 2001; Rizzolatti, Fadiga, Gallese, & Fogassi, 1996). During this activity, mirror neurons are activated in the ventral premotor cortex and inferior parietal lobe of macaque monkeys. In humans, mirror neurons consist of two major networks: (1) parietal lobe and premotor cortex; (2) insula and anterior-mesial frontal cortex or limbic mirror system (Cattaneo & Rizolatti, 2009). The mirror neuron system is involved with both visualized and auditory aspects of behavior (Keysers &. Gazzola, 2006). A number of investigators hypothesize that mirror neurons are involved in the mediation of emotional and cognitive empathy (Bernhardt & Stnger, 2012; Cattaneo & Rizolatti, 2009; Corradino & Antonietti, 2013; DeVignemont & Singer, 2006; Gallese, 2001, 2003; Gallese, Eagle, & Migone, 2007; Pally, 2010; Singer & Lamm, 2009; Singer et al., 2004). Using fMRIs, Broadbart, deGrauw, Perrett, Waiter, and Williams (2014) observed that empathy and facial imitation accuracy correspond with neuronal simulation of others' intentions in the insula, premotor, and somatosensory cortex. Specific emotions, including pain, disgust, anxiety, joy, pleasure, and distress evoke neuronal activation in the insular, cingulate, and medial prefrontal cortex (Morelli, Rameson, & Lieberman, 2014; Perry, Bentin, Bartal, Lamm, & Decety, 2010; Singer et al., 2004)' The neurochemical correlates of mirror neurons are not well understood, and remain to be delineated. Moreover, evidence that mirror neurons contribute to a specific and high level of interpersonal emotional understanding remains problematic (Lamm & Majdanzic, 2015). At the present time, evidence suggests that mirror neurons are associated with cognitive and emotional empathy, but further confirmation is necessary. Nevertheless, the more we learn about mirror neurons, the more we might understand the neurobiology of empathy, introjection, identification, projective identification, and transference. From a broader perspective, Whitehead (2009) optimistically points out that mirror neurons may facilitate two cardinal features of human evolution: empathy and interdependence.

Clinical Illustration:

Robert* is the only child of parents who were overprotective and strict. He attended private schools, but found himself unpopular and teased because of his awkwardness. As a result, he tended to be a loner and felt self-conscious in social situations. Following graduation from law school, he found a position with a prestigious firm and specialized in an arcane area of the law. He holds himself to extremely high standards at work, and expects others to do likewise. Married, without children, he is highly critical of his wife and others. Moreover, he is excessively self-critical at his job and in social situations. Despite years of therapy and psychotropic medication, he continues to feel dissatisfied with himself, professionally inadequate, and socially awkward. During therapy sessions, Robert avoids talking about his feelings and often brings up political or topical issues in order to avoid emotionally charged ones.

---

* Name and details have been changed to protect patient privacy

He is very deliberate in his choice of words and syntax. Preoccupied with potential criticism from others, he frequently misses social cues and is unable to react spontaneously. When I am with Robert, I often feel emotionally constricted, wary, and careful with my interventions. Periodically, I am the target of his anger or criticism, both of which can be withering.

What is transpiring psychodynamically between Robert and me? I know that he has an ambivalent transference that is connected to his father, who was emotionally aloof and critical. Furthermore, his mother was alcoholic, alternately seductive and volatile. Robert learned as a child to be obedient and emotionally controlled, in order to protect himself from his father's criticism and mother's manipulation. I transiently introject and identify with his frightened, emotionally inhibited, perfectionist self. Sometimes, I also feel inadequate, tentative, and reserved when I interact with him. At other times, I feel smoldering anger within myself and the potential for an eruption of rage (as Robert often feels toward others). Do these intrapsychic and interpersonal phenomena correspond to what is occurring neurobiologically within, as well as, between us? Are my mirror neurons resonating with Robert's inner cognitive-affective state? Is it reasonable to hypothesize that the projective identification and countertransference phenomena I have described are the psychodynamic correlates of mirror neuronal activation within and between us? Robert is intellectually well aware of the psychodynamic determinants for his need to be emotionally controlled and perfect. He realizes that I am neither his critical, distant father nor his unpredictably volatile mother. Multiple interpretive interventions on my part have helped him to cognitively appreciate the irrationality of his reflexive fear of criticism and rejection. Nevertheless, his amygdala-cingulate neuronal activation in the context of threatening interpersonal situations often negates his prefrontal cortical inhibition of an automatic fear response. When this occurs, he becomes symptomatic. At the beginning of treatment, Robert denied his feelings and placed paramount importance on his rational thought processes. Over time, he has developed the capacity to recognize and experience different emotional states without immediately shutting them off. Moreover, he is able to cognitively process his feelings and connect them to meaningful past and current experiences. Neurobiologically, he appears to have improved regulation of his limbic-prefrontal cortical system, as well as his mirror neuronal functioning. Anxiolytic and antidepressant medications have also helped with this regulatory process.

Does my knowledge of the neurobiological substrate of Robert's behavior facilitate his treatment? It definitely increases my awareness of the anatomical and physiological correlates of his thoughts, perceptions, and feelings. It also plays a role in whether or not I initiate specific psychotherapeutic interventions. For example, when I feel emotionally constricted, frightened, or angry, I suspect that my mirror neurons are simultaneously resonating with Robert's inner experience. Using that information, I can empathically suggest to him what I sense he might be feeling. If he concurs, we can jointly explore the proximate cause, as well as historical reasons for his emotional response. Repetitive interactions similar to this not only help Robert to identify his feelings, but also to understand their origin. His mirror neuronal response to me may also facilitate his ability to be more self-exploratory and self-aware. As a consequence, he is more likely able to identify with, and internalize my capacity to access my feelings and express them appropriately. Hopefully, this pattern of therapeutic interaction can help him become less self-critical and fearful of the disapproval of others. Neurobiologically, one might say that Robert and I are engaged in a process of mutual mentalization involving our mirror neurons, enabling him to better modulate his cingulate-prefrontal-right temporo-parietal cortex. In turn, he is sometimes, but not always, able to feel less threatened by others and more spontaneous in expressing his feelings.

Using this clinical vignette, I have speculatively synthesized mental processes and neurobiological phenomena based on our current knowledge. Freud (1895) attempted to do so in the Project, but lacked the information and technology that is now available. As a result, he developed a metapsychology in order to explain mental phenomena. The latter constitute what is commonly referred to as "mind" or "psyche." Brookes (2004) defines mind as a phenomenological entity that refers to the "totality of subjective experience." The substratum of mind is the brain, where the objective physical events that correspond to subjective experience occur. Mind and brain are at the same time separate, but indivisible, integrated entities. Freud's abandonment of the Project contributed to a century of dualism in psychiatry, one emphasizing subjective mental phenomena (mind), and the other concerned with objective, neurobiological processes (brain). In the recent past, there have been attempts to bridge the two entities (Beutel, Stern, & Silbersweig, 2003; Cooper, 1985; Gabbard, 2000, 2005; Glucksman, 1995; Kandel, 1998, 1999; Mundo, 2006; Pardes, 1986; Schore, 1997). Nevertheless, research into mental disorders still tends to be either mind-centered or neurobiologically focused. However, our current understanding of brain mechanisms associated with the mental phenomena addressed by Freud (1895) in the Project (consciousness, cognition, dreaming, memory, affect, anxiety, conversion, obsessions, and phobias) might pleasantly surprise him if he were alive today. Indeed, Freud (1913, p. 182) stated that "... after we have completed our psychoanalytic work we shall have to find a point of contact with biology, and we may rightly feel glad if that contact is already assured at one important point or another."

I wish to emphasize that the "point of contact" to which Freud (1913) referred, has been evolving, if not accelerating, over the past several decades. Kandel (1999) observes that there are significant areas where psychoanalysis and neurobiology converge, and can inform each other in terms of future research. First, the functions of unconscious mental processes can be further delineated utilizing information about the biology of procedural and declarative memory. Second, the neurobiology of learning and conditioning can help clarify the linkage between early experience, stress, threat, anxiety, and symptom formation. Third, the role of genetics needs to be further understood in the etiology of sexual orientation, anxiety, mood, and personality disorders. Fourth, psychotherapy outcomes need to be objectively measured in terms of structural and neurochemical changes in the brain. Schore (1997, 2003) emphasizes the importance of further exploration regarding the relationship between the orbitofrontal cortex-limbic system and affective regulation, mental representations, fantasy, and other cognitive functions. He points out that the orbitofrontal cortex undergoes critical growth during the first and second year of infancy. According to him, affective misattunement and disruptive attachment with the primary caregiver inhibits growth of the cortico-limbic system, and may result in autism, depression, and borderline personality disorder. Recent evidence suggests that parental maltreatment in early childhood may result in decreased serum oxytosin levels and the development of borderline personality disorder (Herpertz & Bertsch, 2015). They demonstrated in a placebo-controlled double-blind group design that oxytocin diminishes threat hypersensitivity in patients with borderline personality disorder. Gabbard (2000, 2005) describes a multiplicity of factors in the etiology of borderline personality disorder, including genes, environment, and interpersonal experience. He emphasizes the interplay between epigenetics and environmental influences in the etiology of borderline and other personality disorders. In addition, he points out that because neurobiology and psychodynamic phenomena utilize two separate languages, it is necessary to translate one to the other in order to more fully understand mental disorders. For example, there is accumulating evidence that major depression involves a complex interaction between genes, neurotransmitters, and experience. Caspi et al. (2003) report an alteration of the 5-HTT gene in those individuals vulnerable to depression. Beck (2008) speculates that genetic vulnerability as well as dysfunction of the amygdala-limbic-prefrontal cortex promotes cognitive distortions; namely, a focus on the negative aspects of experience and self that is characteristic of depression. Environmental factors and epigenetic mechanisms may also reduce or exacerbate the genetic expression of schizophrenia and bipolar disorder (Fass, Schroeder, Perlis, & Haggarty, 2014; Khare, Pal, & Petronis, 2011; Rivollier, Lotersztajn, Chaumette, Krebs, & Kebir, 2014; Shorter & Millea 2015).

Beutel et al. (2003) review the role of neuro-imaging techniques in evaluating the effects of both psychotherapy and medication on brain function associated with various disorders. A number of conditions, including OCD, panic disorder, social phobia, depression, and borderline personality have been studied pre- and post-treatment (Baxter et al., 1992; Furmark et al., 2002; Goldapple et al., 2004; Martin, Martin, Rai, Richardson, & Royall, 2001; Viinamaki, Kuikka, & Tiihonen, 1998).

Mayberg (2006) observed that both antidepressants-and-cognitive-behavioral therapy normalize prefrontal-cortical-cingulate dysfunction in depressed patients. Beutel, Stark, Pan, Silbersweig, and Dietrich (2010) examined brain function in patients with panic disorder before and after psychodynamic therapy; dysfunctional prefrontal-cortical-limbic activity normalized following treatment. Changes in brain function of these disorders before and after psychotherapeutic intervention appears to validate recent studies on the efficacy of psychotherapy (Leichsenring, Abbass, Luyten, Hilsenroth, & Rabung, 2013; Levy, Ehrenthal, Yeomans, & Caligor, 2014). Our knowledge of brain dysfunction in the disorders that Freud (1895) included under the rubric of hysteria is rapidly expanding. Moreover, there is accumulating evidence of normalization of brain function following successful treatment of these disorders. Paradoxically, more than a century after Freud abandoned the Project (1895), knowledge of the neurobiological substrate of mind is rapidly growing. The complex interaction of neuronal activity, neurotransmitter function, genetics, epigenetics, intrapsychic, and interpersonal experience is becoming increasingly apparent. It is clearly evident that mental and neurobiological processes are integrated phenomena that reflect our human experience. Nevertheless, certain phenomena remain to be more fully explained: for example, how do thoughts, feelings, or perceptions translate into neuronal activity and neurotransmitter secretion? How do neuronal-synaptic and neurochemical changes account for the different qualities of subjective emotional experience? How do unconscious memories neuronal-chemically influence conscious cognition and feelings? What are the neuronal-chemical substrates of defense mechanisms? These and other mental functions need to be further understood in terms of mind-brain interactivity. However, in doing so, it is important to respect the different languages used in describing subjective mental experiences and their corresponding neurobiological processes. Each provides valuable information connected to different facets of the same phenomena. Keeping in mind the unique nature of each, learning from one can provide us with knowledge about the other. Although Freud's (1895) Project may have been premature, it nevertheless addressed the central issue concerning human behavior: the relationship between mind and brain. In this article, I have attempted to highlight some of the significant advances made toward understanding the neurobiology of mind, with particular emphasis on those disorders Freud (1895) examined in the Project. Hopefully, the next 120 years will further enlighten us regarding the interrelated phenomena of mental experience and neurobiological function.

References:

American Psychiatric Association (2013). *American Psychiatric Association Desk Reference to the Diagnostic Criteria from DSM-5*. Arlington, VA: American Psychiatric Association.

Aserinsky, E., & Kleitman, N. (1953). Regularly occurring periods of eye motility and concomitant phenomena during sleep. *Science, 118*, 223-274.

Axelrod, J. (1957). O-methylation of epinephrine and other catechols in vitro and in vivo. *Science, 126*, 400-401.

Baars, B. J. (2005). Global workspace theory of consciousness. *Progress in Brain Research, 150*, 45-53.

Basch, M. F. (1997). Developmental psychology and explanatory theory in psychoanalysis. *Annals of Psychoanalysis, 5*, 229-263.

Baxter, L. R., Schwartz, J. M., Bergman, K. S., Szuba, M. P., Guze, B.H., Mazziotta, J. C., Alazraki, A., Selin, C. E., Ferng, H. K., Munford, P., & Phelps, M.E. (1992). Caudate glucose metabolic rate changes with both drug and behavior therapy for obsessive-compulsive disorder. *Archives of General Psychiatry, 49*, 969-977.

Beck, A. T. (2008). The evolution of the cognitive model of depression and its neurobiological correlates. *American Journal of Psychiatry, 165*, 969-977.

Bernhardt, B. C., & Singer, T. (2012). The neural basis of empathy. *Annual Review of Neuroscience, 35*, 1-23.

Beutel, M. E., Stark, R., Pan, H., Silbersweig, D., & Dietrich, S. (2010). Changes of brain activation pre-post short-term psychodynamic in-patient psychotherapy: An fMRI study of panic disorder patients. *Psychiatry Research, 184*, 96-104.

Beutel, M. E., Stern, E., & Silbersweig, D. A. (2003). The emerging dialogue between psychoanalysis and neuroscience: Neuroimaging perspectives. *Journal of the American Psychoanalytic Association, 51*, 773-801.

Black, D. N., Seritan, A. L., Taber, K. H., & Hurley, R. A. (2004). Conversion hysteria: Lessons from functional imaging. *Journal of Neuropsychiatry, 16*, 245-251.

Blackford, J. U., Clauss, J. A., Avery, S. N., Cowan, R. L., Benningfield, M. M., & VanDerKlok, R. M. (2014). Amygdala-cingulate intrinsic connectivity is associated with degree of social inhibition. *Biological Psychology, 99*, 15-25.

Broadbart, L., deGrauw, H., Perrett, D. I., Waiter, G. D., & Williams, J. H. G. (2014). The shared neural basis of empathy and facial imitation accuracy. *Neuroimage, 84*, 367-375.

Brockman, R. (2001). Toward a neurobiology of the unconscious. *Journal of the American Academy of Psychoanalysis, 29*(4), 601-615.

Brooks, C. E. (2004). Some comments on the nature and use of the concept of psyche in psychoanalysis and psychodynamic psychotherapy. *Journal of the American Academy of Psychoanalysis and Dynamic Psychiatry, 32*(2), 259-266.

Browne, H.A., Gair, S.L., Scharf, J.M., & Grice, D.E. (2014). Genetics of obsessive-compulsive disorder and related disorders, *Psychiatric Clinics of North America, 3*, 319-335.

Bryant, R. A., & Das, P. (2012). The neural circuitry of conversion disorder and its recovery. *Journal of Abnormal Psychology, 121*, 289-296.

Cajal, S. R. (1899). Textura del sistema nervioso del hombre y de los vertebrados. *Imprenta y Libreria de Nicolas Moya, 1*, 80-95, 106-110.

Caspi, A., Sugden, K., Moffitt, T. E., Taylor, A., Craig, I. W., & Harrington, H. L. (2003). Influence of life stress on depression moderation by a polymorphism in the 5-HTT gene. *Science, 301*, 386-389.

Cattaneo, L., & Rizzolatti, G. (2009). The mirror neuron system. *Archives of Neurology, 66*(5), 557-560.

Cooper, A. M. (1985). Will neurobiology influence psychoanalysis? *American Journal of Psychiatry, 142*(12), 1395-1402.

Corradini, A., & Antonietti, A. (2013). Mirror neurons and their function in cognitively understood empathy. *Conscious Cognition, 22*(3), 1152-1161.

Crick, F., & Koch, C. (1990). Towards a neurobiological theory of consciousness. *Sem. Neuroscientifica, 2,* 263-275.

Crick, F., & Koch C. (2000). The unconscious homunculus. *Neuro-Psychoanalysis, 2*(1), 3-11.

Dement, W., & Kleitman, N. (1957). The relation of eye movements during sleep to dream activity: An objective method for the study of dreaming. *Journal of Experimental Psychology, 53,* 89-97.

DeVignemont, F., & Singer T. (2006). The empathic brain: How, when and why. *Trends in Cognitive Sciences, 10,* 435-441.

Edelman, G. (1989). *The remembered present.* New York: Basic Books.

Edelman, G. (1992). *Bright air, brilliant fire.* New York: Basic Books.

Etkin, A., & Wager, T. D. (2007). Functional neuroimaging of anxiety: A meta-analysis of emotional processing in PTSD, social anxiety disorder, and specific phobia. *American Journal of Psychiatry, 164,* 1476-1488.

Farthing, G. W. (1992). *The psychology of consciousness.* Englewood Cliffs, NJ: Prentice-Hall.

Fass, D. M., Schroeder, F. A., Perlis, R. H., & Haggarty S. J. (2014). Epigenetic mechanisms in mood disorders: Targeting neuroplasticity. *Neuroscience, 264,* 112-130.

Fonagy, P., Gergely, G., Jurist, E. L., & Target, M. (2002). *Affect regulation, mentalization and the development of the self.* New York: Other Press.

Fox, A. S., & Kalin, N. H. (2014). A translational neuroscience approach to understanding the development of social anxiety disorder and its pathophysiology. *American Journal of Psychiatry, 171*(11), 1162-1173.

Freud, S. (1894a). The neuro-psychoses of defense. In J. Strachey (Ed. & Trans.), *The standard edition of the complete psychological works of Sigmund Freud* (Vol. 3, pp. 45-61). London: Hogarth Press.

Freud, S. (1894b). Obsessions and phobias. In J. Strachey (Ed. and Trans.), *The standard edition of the complete psychological works of Sigmund Freud* (Vol. 3, pp. 71-84). London: Hogarth Press.

Freud, S. (1895). Project for a scientific psychology. In J. Strachey (Ed. & Trans.), *The standard edition of the complete psychological works of Sigmund Freud* (Vol. 1, pp. 283-397). London: Hogarth Press.

Freud, S. (1900). The interpretation of dreams. In J. Strachey (Ed. & Trans.), *The standard edition of the complete psychological works of Sigmund Freud* (Vols. 4 and 5). London: Hogarth Press.

Freud, S. (1909). Analysis of a phobia in a five year old boy. In J. Strachey (Ed. & Trans.), *The standard edition of the complete psychological works of Sigmund Freud* (Vol. 10, pp. 5-147). London: Hogarth Press.

Freud, S. (1912). The dynamics of transference. In J. Strachey (Ed. & Trans.), *The standard edition of the complete psychological works of Sigmund Freud* (Vol. 12, p. 108). London: Hogarth Press.

Freud, S. (1913). The claims of psychoanalysis to scientific interest. In J. Strachey (Ed. & Trans.), *The standard edition of the complete psychological works of Sigmund Freud* (Vol. 13, p. 182). London: Hogarth Press.

Freud, S. (1917). Introductory lectures on psychoanalysis. In J. Strachey (Ed. & Trans.), *The standard edition of the complete psychological works of Sigmund Freud* (Vol. 16, p. 393). London: Hogarth Press.

Freud, S. (1920). Beyond the pleasure principal. In J. Strachey (Ed. & Trans.), *The standard edition of the complete psychological works of Sigmund Freud* (Vol. 18). London: Hogarth Press.

Freud, S. (1926). Inhibitions, symptoms and anxiety. In J. Strachey (Ed. & Trans.), *The standard edition of the complete psychological works of Sigmund Freud* (Vol. 20, pp. 87-174). London: Hogarth Press.

Freud, S. (1932). New introductory lectures on psychoanalysis. In J. Strachey (Ed. & Trans.), *The standard edition of the complete psychological works of Sigmund Freud* (Vol. 22, p. 154). London: Hogarth Press.

Furmark, T., Tillfors, M., Marteinsdottir, I., Fischer, H., Pissiota, A., Langstrom, B., & Frederickson, M. (2002). Common changes in cerebral blood flow in patients with social phobia treated with citalopram or cognitive-behavioral therapy. *Archives of Human Development, 3*, 30-61.

Gabbard, G. (2000). A neurobiologically informed perspective on psychotherapy. *British Journal of Psychiatry, 177*, 117-122.

Gabbard, G. (2005). Mind, brain, and personality disorders. *American Journal of Psychiatry, 162*, 648-655.

Gallese, V. (2001). The shared manifold hypothesis: From mirror neurons to empathy. *Journal of Consciousness Studies, 8*, 33-50.

Gallese, V. (2003). The roots of empathy: The shared manifold hypothesis and the neural basis of intersubjectivity. *Psychopathology, 36*, 171-180.

Gallese, V., Eagle, M. N., & Migone, P. (2007). Intentional attunement: Mirror neurons and the neural underpinnings of interpersonal relations. *Journal of the American Psychoanalytic Association, 55*(1), 131-176.

Gillan, C. M., Apergis-Schoute, A. M., Morein-Zamir, S., Urcelay, G.P., Sule, A., Fineberg, N. A., Sahakian, B. J., & Robbins, T. W. (2015). Functional neuroimaging of avoidance habits in obsessive-compulsive disorder. *American Journal of Psychiatry, 172*, 284-293.

Glucksman, M. L. (1995). Psychodynamics and neurobiology: An integrated approach. *Journal of the American Academy of Psychoanalysis, 23*(2), 179-195.

Glucksman, M. L. (2001). The dream, a psychodynamically informative instrument. *Journal of Psychotherapy Practice and Research, 10*(4), 223-230.

Goldapple, K., Zindel, S., Garson, C., Lau, M., Bieling, P., Kenney, S., & Mayberg, H. (2004). Modulation of cortical-limbic pathways in major depression. *Archives of General Psychiatry, 61*, 34-41.

Greenberg, R., & Pearlman, C. (1993). An integrated approach to dream theory: Contributions from sleep research and clinical practice. In A. Moffit, M. Kramer, & R. Hoffman (Eds.), *The functions of dreaming* (pp. 363-380). Albany, NY: State University of New York Press.

Herpertz, S. C., & Bertsch, K. (2015). A new perspective on the patho-physiology of borderline personality disorder: A model of the role of oxytocin. *American Journal of Psychiatry, 172*(9), 840-851.

Hobson, J. A. (1999). The new neuropsychology of sleep. *Neuro-Psychoanalysis, 1,* 157-183.

Johansen, J. P., Cain, C. K., Ostroff, L. E., & LeDoux, J. E. (2011). Molecular mechanisms of fear, learning, and memory. *Cell, 147* (3), 509-524.

Kandel, E. R. (1983). From metapsychology to molecular biology: Explorations into the nature of anxiety. *American Journal of Psychiatry,* 140, 1277-1293.

Kandel, E. R. (1998). A new intellectual framework for psychiatry. *American Journal of Psychiatry, 155,* 457-469.

Kandel, E. R. (1999). Biology and the future of psychoanalysis: A new intellectual framework for psychiatry revisited. *American Journal of Psychiatry, 156*(4), 505-524.

Kandel, E. R. (2012). The molecular biology of memory: cAMR, PKA, CRE, CREB-1, CREB-2, and CPEB. *Molecular Brain, 5*(14), 1-12.

Kandel, E. R., Schwartz, J. H., Jessell, T. M., Siegelbaum, S. A., & Hudspeth, A. J. (2012). *Principles of neural science.* New York: McGraw-Hill.

Kaplan, M. J. (2014). A psychodynamic perspective on treatment of pa-tients with conversion and other somatoform disorders. *Psychodynamic Psychiatry, 42*(4), 593-615.

Keysers, C., & Gazzola, V. (2006). Towards a unifying neural theory of social cognition. *Progress in Brain Research, 156,* 379-401.

Khare, T., Pal, M., & Petronis, A. (2011). Understanding bipolar disorder: The epigenetic perspective. *Current Topics in Behavioral Neurosciences, 5,* 31-49.

Kim, M. J., Loucks, R. A., Palmer, A. L., Brown, A. C., Solomon, K. M., Marchante, A. N., & Whalen, P. J. (2011). The structural and function-al connectivity of the amygdala: From normal emotion to pathological anxiety. *Behavior and Brain Research, 223*(2), 403-410.

Kramer, M. (1993). The selective mood regulatory function of dreaming: An update and revision. In A. Moffit, M. Kramer, & R. Hoffman (Eds.),

The functions of dreaming (pp. 139-195). Albany, NY: State University of New York Press.

Lamm, C., & Majdandzic, J. (2015). The role of shared neural activations, mirror neurons, and morality in empathy—A critical comment. *Neuroscience Research, 90,* 15-24.

Lane, R. D., Fink, G. R., Chua, P. M. L., & Dolan, R. J. (1997). Neural activation during selective attention to subjective emotional responses. *Neuroreport, 8*(18), 3969-3972.

Lane, R. D., & Garfield, D. A. S. (2005). Becoming aware of feelings: Integration of cognitive-developmental, neuroscientific, and psycho-analytic perspectives. *Neuro-Psychoanalysis, 7*(7), 5-30.

Lane, R. D., & Schwartz, G. E. (1987). Levels of emotional awareness: A cognitive-developmental theory and its application to psychopathology. *American Journal of Psychiatry, 144,* 133-143.

LeDoux, J. E. (1994). Emotion, memory and the brain. *Scientific American, 270*(6), 50-57.

LeDoux, J. E. (1996). *The emotional brain: The mysterious underpinnings of emotional life.* New York: Simon and Schuster.

Leichsenring, F., Abbass, A., Luyten, P., Hilsenroth, M., & Rabung, S. (2013). The emerging evidence for long-term psychodynamic therapy. *Psychodynamic Psychiatry, 41*(3), 361-384.

Levy, K. N., Ehrenthal, J. C., Yeomans, F. E., & Caligor, E. (2014). The efficacy of psychotherapy: Focus on psychodynamic psychotherapy as an example. *Psychodynamic Psychiatry, 42*(3), 377-421.

Lueken, U., Straube, B., Konrad, C., Wittchen, H.-U., Strohle, A., Wittmann, A., Pfleiderer, B., Uhlmann, C., Arolt, V., Jansen, A., & Kircher, T. (2013). Neural substrates of treatment response to cognitive-behavioral therapy in panic disorder with agoraphobia. *American Journal of Psychiatry, 170,* 1345-1355.

MacLean, P. D. (1990). *The triune brain in evolution: Role in paleocerebral functions.* New York: Plenum.

Martin, S. D., Martin, E., Rai, S. S., Richardson, M. A., & Royall, R. (2001). Brain blood flow changes in depressed patients treated with interpersonal psychotherapy or venlafaxine hydrochloride: Preliminary findings. *Archives of General Psychiatry, 58*, 641-648.

Mataix-Cols, D., Boman, M., Monzani, B., Ruck, C., Serlachius, E., Langstrom, N., & Lichtenstein, P. (2013). Population-based multi-generational family clustering study of obsessive-compulsive disorder. *JAMA Psychiatry, 70*(7), 709-717.

Mayberg, H. S. (2003). Modulating dysfunctional limbic-cortical circuits in depression: Towards development of brain-based algorithms for diagnosis and optimized treatment. *British Medical Bulletin, 65*, 193-207.

Mayberg, H. S. (2006). Defining neurocircuits in depression: Insights from functional neuroimaging studies of diverse treatments. *Psychiatric Annals, 4*, 258-267.

Morelli, S. A., Rameson, L. T., & Lieberman, M. D. (2014). The neural components of empathy: Predicting daily prosocial behavior. *Cognitive, Affective, and Behavioral Neuroscience, 4*, 270-278.

Mundo, E. (2006). Neurobiology of dynamic psychotherapy: An integration possible? *Journal of the American Academy of Psychoanalysis and Dynamic Psychiatry, 34*(4), 679-691.

Olds, D. D. (1992). Consciousness: A brain-centered, informational approach. *Psychoanalytic Inquiry, 12*, 419-444.

Pally, R. (1998). Consciousness: A neuroscience perspective. *International Journal of Psychoanalysis, 79*, 971-989.

Pally, R. (2010). The brain's shared circuits of interpersonal understanding: Implications for psychoanalysis and psychodynamic psychotherapy. *Journal of the American Academy of Psychoanalysis and Dynamic Psychiatry, 38*(3), 381-471.

Pan, X., & Tsukada, M. (2006). A model of the hippocampal-cortical memory system. *Biological Cybernetics, 95*, 159-167.

Panksepp, J. (1998). *Affective neuroscience: The foundation of human and animal emotions.* New York: Oxford University Press.

Panksepp, J. (1999). Emotions as viewed by psychoanalysis and neuroscience: An exercise in consilience. *Neuropsychoanalysis, 1*, 15-38.

Panksepp, J. (2005). Commentary on becoming aware of feelings. *Neuropsychoanalysis, 7,* 40-55

Paquette, V., Levesque, J., Mensour, B., Leroux, J. M., Beaudoin, G., Bourgouin, P., & Beauregard, M. (2003). Change the mind and you change the brain: Effects of cognitive-behavioral therapy on the neural correlates of spider phobia. *NeuroImage, 18,* 401-419.

Pardes, H. (1986). Neuroscience and psychiatry: Marriage or coexistence? *American Journal of Psychiatry, 143,* 1205-1212.

Perry, A., Bentin, S., Bartal, I. B., Lamm, C., & Decety, J. (2010). Feeling the pain of those who are different from us: Modulation of EEG in the mu/alpha range. *Cognitive, Affective, and Behavioral Neuroscience, 10*(4), 493-504.

Reiser, M. F. (2001). The dream in contemporary psychiatry. *American Journal of Psychiatry, 158,* 351-359.

Rivollier, F., Lotersztajn, L., Chaumette, B., Krebs, M. O., & Kebir, O. (2014). Epigenetics of schizophrenia: *A review. L'Encéphale, 40*(5), 380-386.

Rizzolatti, G. (2001). Reafferent copies of initiated actions in the right superior temporal cortex. *Proceedings of the National Academy of Sciences, 98,* 13995-13999.

Rizzolatti, G., & Craighero, L. (2004). The mirror neuron system. *Annual Review of Neuroscience, 27,* 169-192.

Rizzolatti, G., Fadiga, L., Gallese, V., Fogassi, L. (1996). Premotor cortex and the recognition of motor actions. *Cognitive Brain Research, 3,* 131-141.

Rizzolatti, G., & Fogassi, L. (2014). The mirror mechanism: Recent findings and perspectives. *Philosophical Transactions of the Royal Society B: Biological, 369*(1644), 20130420.

Saxena, S., & Rauch, S. L. (2000). Functional neuroimaging and the neuroanatomy of obsessive-compulsive disorder. *Psychiatric Clinics of North America, 23,* 563-586.

Schore, A. N. (1997). A century after Freud's project: Is a rapprochement between psychoanalysis and neurobiology at hand? *Journal of the American Psychoanalytic Association, 45*(3), 807-840.

Schore, A. N. (2003). *Affective dysregulation and disorders of the self.* New York: Erlbaum.

Semenza, C. (2001). Psychoanalysis and cognitive neuropsychology: Theoretical and methodological affinities. *Neuropsychoanalysis, 3*, 3-10.

Shackman, A. J., Fox, A. S., Oler, J. A., Shelton, S. E., Davidson, R. J., & Kalin, N. H. (2013). Neural mechanisms underlying heterogeneity in the presentation of anxious temperament. *Proceedings of the National Academy of Sciences, 110*, 6145-6150.

Sherrington, C. S. (1906). *The integrative action of the nervous system.* New Haven, CT: Yale University Press.

Shorter, K. R., & Miller, B. H. (2015). Epigenetic mechanisms in schizophrenia. *Progress in Biophysics and Molecular Biology, 118*(1-2), 1-7.

Singer, T., & Lamm, C. (2009). The social neuroscience of empathy. *Annals of the New York Academy of Sciences, 1150*, 81-96.

Singer, T., Seymour, B., O'Doherty, J., Kaube, H., Dolan, R. J., & Frith, C. D. (2004). Empathy for pain involves the affective but not the sensory components of pain. *Science, 303*, 1157-1161.

Sulloway, F. J. (1992). *Freud, biologist of the mind.* Cambridge: Harvard University Press.

Tononi, G., & Koch, C. (2008). The neural correlates of consciousness: An update. *Annals of the New York Academy of Sciences, 1124*, 239-261.

Viinamaki, H., Kuikka, J., & Tiihonen, J. (1998). Change in monoamine transporter density related to clinical recovery: A case-control study. *Nordic Journal of Psychiatry, 52*, 39-44.

Vuilleumier, P. (2014). Brain circuits implicated in psychogenic paralysis, in conversion disorders and hypnosis. *Clinical Neurophysiology, 44*, 323-337.

Whitehead, C. C. (2009). Brief communication-mirror neurons, the self, and culture: An essay in neopsychoanalysis. *Journal of the American Academy of Psychoanalysis and Dynamic Psychiatry, 37*, 701.-712.

Whiteside, S. P., Port, J. D., & Abramowitz, J. S. (2004). A meta-analysis of functional neuroimaging in obsessive-compulsive disorder. *Psychiatry Research, 132*, 69-79.

Myron L. Glucksman, M.D., Clinical Professor of Psychiatry, New York Medical College, Valhalla, NY; Supervising and Training Analyst, The Psychoanalytic Institute, New York Medical College.
Psychodynamic Psychiatry, 44(1) 69-90, 2016.

## Chapter 8

Animal Assisted Therapy

My dog, Joe, a Labrador retriever, was my faithful companion and co-therapist for twelve years. Patients still talk about him even though he's no longer with us. I often think of him when I'm in the middle of a difficult interaction with a patient and wonder how he would react. Most probably, he would facilitate a positive outcome in his usual wise, nonverbal way. The following paper, "The Dog's Role in the Analyst's Consulting Room" (Glucksman, M. L., 2005), is in honor of the ways he enriched my life and the lives of my patients. Parenthetically, this paper received more comments from readers than any previous ones that I have published.

Freud was the first psychoanalyst to have a dog in the consulting room. Consequently, he may have also been the father of "Animal Assisted Therapy" (Lipton, 2001). The latter refers to the use of domesticated animals (usually dogs) for the purpose of helping or healing the ill, disabled, and elderly. Joe began accompanying me to my office when he was three years old. He possessed the ideal nonverbal qualities of a good therapist: even tempered, nonjudgmental, empathic, and friendly. Joe facilitated the therapeutic alliance by promoting the patient's feelings of safety and trust in a potentially threatening situation.

He also functioned as a transitional object and a transference displacement. Patients appreciated his soothing presence and often felt safer communicating either their angry or affectionate feelings toward him rather than directly to me. Sometimes, he functioned as an introject of qualities they desired, such as confidence, strength, and self-esteem. On other occasions, he became a countertransference displacement of my feelings; for example, I sometimes petted him when I required support or felt discouraged in treating a challenging patient. Occasionally, I displaced and projected my annoyance with a patient by giving him a curt command, e.g. "Lie down, Joe." At other times, I was playful and affectionate with him in a manner that would be inappropriate with a patient.

Three clinical examples demonstrate how Joe functioned as a soothing introject and transitional object, as well as an object of both positive and negative transference displacements. On several occasions, displaced positive transference to Joe enabled patients to avoid self-destructive or suicidal acts. As a displacement of me, he facilitated their identification and internalization of my healing qualities, including empathy, constancy, and affirmation. Moreover, his interaction with patients encouraged them to express themselves more spontaneously and openly, both inside and outside the treatment setting. Lastly, he served as a non-judgmental, loyal, co-therapist who was a constant source of support. Not only is a dog man's best friend, but a dog is also a therapist's and patient's best friend in the consulting room. Joe certainly fulfilled all the criteria required of an ideal co-therapist.

References:

Glucksman, M.L., "The Dog's Role in the Analyst's Consulting Room," *Journal of the American Academy of Psychoanalysis and Dynamic Psychiatry*, Vol. 33, No. 4 (2005): 611-618.

Lipton, L., "Some Patients Petting Their Way Toward Improved Mental Health," *Psychiatric News*, Vol. 36, No. 3 (2001): 17.

Editor's Note: Many analysts—Freud, most famously—have had dogs in their consulting rooms. Yet none to our knowledge have described the psychodynamic role of dogs or other pets that may be present during the treatment process. At the Journal's *request, the author of the following article agreed to briefly explore this matter.*

THE DOG'S ROLE IN THE ANALYST'S CONSULTING ROOM
MYRON L. GLUCKSMAN, M.D.

Joe, a Labrador retriever, has accompanied an analyst in the consulting room since the dog was age three. Patients uniformly find him soothing and reassuring. In this capacity, he facilitates the therapeutic alliance and the holding environment. In addition, he often functions as a transitional object and transference displacement. Patients frequently use him as an introject for certain qualities they desire, such as security, strength, and confidence. Sometimes he promotes enactments between the patient and the analyst. At other times, he functions as a countertransference displacement for the analyst. On occasion, he is incorporated into the patient's defensive maneuvers and resistance. In each of these roles, he facilitates key elements of the therapeutic process, including exploration, understanding, interpretation, and working- through. Perhaps his most important role is that of a nonjudgmental, supportive, loyal co-therapist. Case illustrations highlight Joe's various functions in the analyst's consulting room.

Predictably, Freud, the preeminent groundbreaker in our field, was the first analyst to have a dog in the consulting room (Gay, 1988). As a consequence, he may have also been the father of "Animal Assisted Therapy" (AAT). The latter is a rapidly developing field centered on the use of domesticated animals (usually dogs) for the purpose of aiding and healing those who are ill, elderly, or alone (Lipton, 2001). Studies have demonstrated that AAI helps decrease anxiety, depression, anger/ and aggression. It also increases social interaction and encourages patients to discuss painful material by reducing the threat of the treatment setting (Barker,1999). The first published report of a psychiatrist using a dog in therapy sessions was by Levinson (1962). He reported that the dog facilitated communication and provided a sense of security to his child patients. Freud was given his first dog, a German shepherd, by his daughter, Anna, in 1928. Later he had several chows, the best known of whom was Jo-Fi. The traditional 50-minute hour is allegedly attributed to Jo-Fi, who used to get up at ten minutes to the hour, thereby allowing Freud to end the session in order to let her out. Freud believed that dogs possess qualities that humans often lack; they express their feelings directly, are incapable of deception, and remain fiercely loyal (Roazen, 1975).

Since Freud, many analysts have had dogs in their consulting room, but none have written explicitly about the role of the dog in the analytic setting. Although I have owned several dogs, I never had one stay with me in the consulting room until I moved my office adjacent to my house. When my Labrador retriever, Joe, was about age 3, he began accompanying me into my office. Patients did not seem to mind having him sleep quietly through sessions (better him than me), and his presence became habitual. Joe possesses the ideal nonverbal qualities of a good therapist. He is even-tempered, nonjudgmental, empathic, friendly, and not easily provoked. Confidentiality is his forte, and I have never known him to betray a secret.

I always ask new patients if they mind having a dog in the consulting room before I allow him to be present. The majority of them do not object; in fact, they express eagerness for his company. The few who decline or express reservations about his presence usually reveal a pathological source. They are phobic of dogs, allergic, or narcissistically resent having someone else in the same room who might demand my attention. After greeting each patient with a wag of his tail and a cursory identifying sniff, Joe usually lies down somewhere between the patient and me. He invariably sleeps during the session, and is awakened only if a voice is raised or if he becomes aware of intense emotion (e.g., crying, laughing). If a patient exhibits emotional distress, Joe often goes over and offers a paw or whimpers in an empathetic tone. Otherwise, he is respectful of boundaries and is never intrusive unless the patient asks him to come over for some reason. The only exception is when he hears an extraneous noise outside the office that disturbs him. On those occasions, he might go toward the door and bark. However, he will quickly stop on my command unless I cannot control the outside disturbance (e.g., a delivery person knocking at the door).

On the whole, patients find Joe soothing and comforting. They often pet him when they first enter the room as a way of calming and reassuring themselves. In that sense, he facilitates the holding environment and is a positive influence on the therapeutic alliance. In effect, he promotes the patient's feelings of safety and security in a potentially threatening situation. He also functions as a transitional object and a transference displacement. Patients often feel less threatened communicating disturbed feelings and fantasies to him rather than directly to me. For example, a patient may begin the session by saying, "Oh, Joe, it's been a tough day," or "I'm an unhappy camper today, Joe." By the same token, they are frequently less inhibited about expressing both positive and negative transference feelings to him instead of toward me. Examples are: "You're such a good boy, Joe"; "I love you, Joe"; "bad boy, Joe"; or "mean dog." Generally speaking, he functions as an available, benign object for the projection of threatening and nonthreatening feelings. Evidence of this is the following: "Joe looks mad today"; "Joe acts bored"; "Joe seems happy") or "Joe's relaxed and peaceful." On the other hand, he also functions as an introject of qualities and feelings that patients desire. He is looked at, spoken to, or touched for solace, affection, reassurance, strength, confidence, and protection. For example, patients say, "I'd love to have Joe's peace of mind" or "I wish I had Joe's determination." Either as an object for projection or as an introject, Joe frequently serves as a displacement of me that patients find more tolerable and less threatening. Sometimes he becomes an unwitting ally in the patient's defensive or resistance maneuvers. For example, talking and playing with him may divert patients from focusing on themselves. Silence and withdrawal are more easily camouflaged when the time is spent petting Joe. He may also act as a facilitator of enactments between patients and me. For example, a patient may point out a sore on his body that has escaped my notice. In turn, I become involved in examining it and discussing possible remedies. The entire interaction between patient, dog, and me may be a repetition of the physical or emotional neglect the patient experienced with her parents. Simultaneously, it may be a transference displacement signifying the patient's dissatisfaction with my therapeutic efforts.

Joe occasionally functions as a countertransference displacement for my feelings. I sometimes stroke him for reassurance and support when I am attacked or devalued by a patient. When I feel uncertain or discouraged, his soulful eyes will often communicate an understanding of my discomfort and affirm my purpose as a therapist. At times, I project my frustration and anger onto him with a curt command such as "lie down" or "stop doing that." At other times, I can be affectionate and playful with him in a manner that would be totally inappropriate with a patient. As an object for transference and countertransference displacement, he is also helpful in maintaining boundaries while simultaneously promoting continuity and spontaneity.

The following clinical vignettes may serve to illustrate Joe's functions in the treatment situation:

I:

A divorced woman was in treatment for recurrent depression, depersonalization, self-mutilation, and suicidal behavior. She was sexually and physically abused by her father from age 6 to 13. Her ex-husband, an alcoholic, was verbally and physically abusive. Her mother, who failed to protect her from her father, nevertheless loved and cared for her. Following an initial idealizing transference, she began to view me as abusive (e.g., insensitive and indifferent). On the other hand, she perceived Joe as friendly and affectionate. She often brought him biscuits and petted him during sessions. As this split transference evolved, she withheld critical information from me, but confided in Joe. She would frequently arrive early and ask if Joe could stay with her in the waiting room. While alone with Joe, she often whispered to him her urges to cut or kill herself. When I became aware of this, I would ask Joe in a play-acting mode whether she was feeling self-destructive. Sometimes it took an entire session before she begrudgingly acknowledged that she had told Joe about cutting herself, or that she was planning to overdose on medication. Once, she reported that she was feeling suicidal at home and was about to cut herself when she noticed a photo of Joe that I had previously given her at her request. She began stroking it, soothing herself until her self-destructive urge subsided. In that instance, she stated that Joe "saved my life." While critical of me during sessions, she would sometimes motion to the dog and say, "He would never hurt me." Over a period of time, I interpreted to her how she perceived Joe as the good, loving father she wished for, while selectively focusing on my shortcomings. Ever so gradually, she began to express negative feelings for Joe (e.g., "he's not friendly today"; "he almost bit me when I fed him a biscuit"). Paradoxically, I became the recipient of more positive feelings (e.g.," I can always rely on you"; "I believe you really do care about me"). Increasingly, she began telling me directly about her feelings and fantasies rather than communicating them through Joe. It became clear that her self-mutilating behavior was connected to intense guilt and anger over her incestuous relationship with her father. Cutting herself was also a way to acquire feelings, albeit painful ones, in order to overcome the inner numbness of her depersonalization. Over the course of treatment, she has become much less self-destructive and sees both Joe and me more realistically (although she still maintains a special affection for the dog). In my opinion, Joe served as a benign, transitional object for her that she could trust, and in whom she was able to confide. He became the recipient of a displaced positive transference while I was the object of her negative transference. As treatment progressed, she introjected the positive aspects of her relationship with Joe (trust, safety, affection) while simultaneously identifying them with me. For example, her capacity to control her suicidal impulses when she looked at Joe's photo represented an internalization of my self-regulatory function. Gradually, her relationship with me was transformed and internalized from an abusing one into a protective, caring one. Correspondingly, the guilt and anger connected to her father diminished. Although all of these changes would most likely have occurred without the dog's presence, I believe that he facilitated and perhaps even accelerated them.

II:

A young man entered treatment for impulsive, acting-out behavior, temper outbursts, and disturbed interpersonal relationships. He frequently lost jobs because of quarrels with fellow employees and supervisors. On several occasions, he was arrested by the police for using abusive language after being stopped for traffic violations. He also had a dog and initially behaved toward Joe as if he owned him. For example, he would command Joe to "sit down" or to "come over to me," as though I were not in the room. As I explored this interaction with the dog, his sense of entitlement and grandiosity became apparent. Born into a wealthy family, his parents failed to set limits for him and catered to his every demand. During sessions, he often became enraged, yelled, used profanity, and became agitated as he reported an encounter with someone who disturbed him. When these episodes occurred, Joe would become startled, get up, and follow him around the room. Finally noticing the dog, he would begin petting him, calm down, and lower his voice. This allowed me the opportunity to explore the particular interaction he was describing in a more rational way. With his rage and aggression contained by his physical contact with Joe, we were able to examine the situation in question from different perspectives. Sometimes he was able to realize how his actions had been irrational and provoked the other person. Although it was relatively easy for him to openly express his hostility and aggression, he was only able to communicate his tender, loving feelings to Joe (e.g., "I love you, Joe; "I'll take good care of you, boy"). Negative transference was the hallmark of a substantial part of therapy, and the following statements were typical: "You're just like the cops"; "I don't care what you think." Conversely, his positive transference was displaced onto Joe by bringing him biscuits, or comments such as "you're a good boy, Joe." His pattern of interpersonal boundary violations was manifested within our relationship when he would sometimes insist that he take Joe home with him for a weekend. On another occasion, he announced that he was bringing me a puppy so that Joe would have company. These occurrences provided me with an opportunity to explore the origins of his fantasies, and to point out how his statements and behavior could be threatening to others. We gradually discovered that a good deal of his anger and sense of entitlement were connected to his inner feelings of inadequacy and failure. His educational history revealed ample evidence of a learning disability and attention-deficit disorder. With appropriate medication and therapy, his anger and aggressive behavior diminished. However, it was Joe's presence that soothed and helped him to contain his rage, permitting me to engage him in a rational, calmer exploration of his behavior.

III:

A divorced woman entered treatment for depression, social isolation, and paranoid ideation. Since her divorce, she totally avoided relationships with men. She lived alone with two cats, and rarely socialized. Her mother was physically and verbally abusive toward her, while her father was remote and indifferent. At the beginning of therapy, she was wary of Joe and avoided petting him. Curiously, he positioned himself at her feet as though he were protecting her, forming a barrier between her and the outside world. Slowly and hesitantly, she told me about her profound distrust of others, including me. Her mother, who made her feel unwanted and useless, was the target of enormous rage. Her ex-husband, similar to her father, was inattentive and enmeshed within his own family. Therapy was punctuated by long periods of silence, during which she would look away from me and stare at Joe. Gradually, she began petting him, simultaneously telling me how sad, frightened, and lonely she felt. As she petted Joe, she began making references to him (e.g., "he's always here for me"; "there's not a mean bone in his body"). At the same time, she expressed her distrust of me. In particular, she was afraid that I might betray her by revealing a confidence to someone else (as she believed a previous therapist had), or that I might abandon her. Her split transference continued for several years, complicated by medication noncompliance and several attempts to end treatment. In the meantime, her father died, she changed jobs several times, and she sustained a fractured wrist and leg in separate falls. Throughout each of these events, Joe remained steadfastly beside her, and I maintained my empathic stance. Ever so gradually, she began commenting on my availability and reliability.

Eventually, she revealed that in spite of herself, she was feeling affectionate toward me. However, she acknowledged that any romantic or sexual fantasies about me would be too frightening and inappropriate. Nevertheless, she allowed herself to begin imagining the possibility of an intimate relationship with another man again. Her social life gradually expanded, and she finally began a relationship with a man she met at work. In this case, Joe served as a soothing, protective transitional object. He was also a transference displacement, facilitating a gradual shift in the patient's feelings of distrust and fear to affection and trust toward me.

Discussion:

In each of these clinical examples, Joe was available to the patient as a soothing introject. In this capacity, he facilitated the therapeutic alliance and helped the patient feel less threatened in the treatment setting. Moreover, he fostered transference displacement, particularly positive transference, thereby allowing negative feelings to be more easily directed toward me. Over the course of treatment, he often became the foil for negative transference when patients shifted their positive feelings more consciously toward me. As a non-threatening object, he also served as a repository for painful feelings and fantasies. He was frequently a patient's initial confidant for feelings of sadness, loneliness, and despair. On more than one occasion, it was communication through Joe that alerted me to self-destructive and suicidal fantasies. By the same token, it was easier for patients to project positive feelings and fantasies onto him rather than me (e.g., affection, love, trust). As an object of displacement, Joe helped me to make transference interpretations more understandable and acceptable. Enactments and boundary violations were more effectively managed and interpreted with Joe playing the role of intermediary. Because he was a convenient displacement of me, he helped to reinforce patients' identification and internalization of my healing qualities, including constancy, containment, and affirmation. In particular, I believe that the bond of mutual love and loyalty that patients observed between Joe and me encouraged them to replicate it in their relationships with significant others (at the very least, with their pets). Moreover, his presence encouraged patients to express themselves more spontaneously and playfully inside and outside the treatment setting.

Lastly, and perhaps most importantly, Joe provided me with a companion who was always available for self-soothing and narcissistic reinforcement. The work of therapy can be demanding, frustrating, and emotionally depleting. A nonjudgmental, loyal co-therapist is a reassuring source of support. Furthermore, an idealizing, loving dog is an additional bonus that makes up for the many hours that often go unrewarded during the therapeutic journey. Some might argue that a dog's presence in therapy is more of a distraction and a potential source of resistance than it is beneficial. This may be true in certain instances, but more often than not, I have found that Joe's usefulness in the therapeutic process outweighs his liabilities. Perhaps, the outcome of each treatment I have described would have been the same without Joe's presence. And there is no doubt that I have engaged in a certain degree of idealization and projection regarding Joe's role in therapy. However, keeping in mind that a dog is known to be man's best friend, I would emphatically add that a dog can also function as both a therapist's and a patient's best friend in the consulting room.

References:

Barker, S. B. (1999). Therapeutic aspects of the human-companion animal interaction. *Psychiatric Times*, 1 6(2), 43-45.

Gay, P. (1988). *Freud: A life for our time.* New York: Norton.

Levinson, B.M. (1962). The dog as co-therapist. *Mental Hygiene*, 46, 59-65.

Lipton, L. (2001). Some patients petting their way toward improved mental health. *Psychiatric News*, 36(3), 77.

Roazen, P. (1975). *Freud and his followers.* New York: Knopf.

Journal of the American Academy of Psychoanalysis and Dynamic Psychiatry, 33(4) 611-618, 2005.

On Being A Psychiatrist and Psychoanalyst

The preceding papers and commentaries are meant to provide a perspective on my personal journey as a psychiatrist and psychoanalyst. Hopefully, they reflect the arc of my professional evolution from psychiatric resident to seasoned clinician. My medical training heavily influenced my earlier research in obesity and biofeedback. In addition, my involvement in consultation-liaison psychiatry was facilitated by my training as a physician. The latter also motivated my interest in psychosomatic disorders. Moreover, it gave rise to my ongoing exploration of the connections between mind, brain, and body phenomena.

In retrospect, as I gained more experience as a clinician, I became increasingly interested in the psychotherapeutic process. In particular, I was intrigued with the relationship between therapist and patient. It became apparent to me that the emotional communication between patient and therapist is of singular importance. In this regard, I was greatly influenced by one of my psychoanalytic mentors, Ian Alger, M.D. Ian was a pioneer of videotherapy, and widely known for his work in group and family therapy. Exquisitely sensitive to the nuances of feelings communicated between patient and therapist, he encouraged me to pay more attention to both the verbal and nonverbal feelings expressed by my patients. In doing so, I also became more aware of my internal emotional states. As a result, I began to understand that the interplay between the subjective feelings of both patient and therapist are fundamental to the development of an empathic relationship. In the absence of feeling understood at an emotional level, it is difficult, if not impossible, for a patient to fully trust his or her therapist. Moreover, the experience of being emotionally understood provides a sense of validation and acceptance, as well as a feeling of self-authenticity for the patient. Equally important is a cognitive explanation, or insight into the reasons for the development of symptoms and pathological behavior. The latter enables the patient to have a degree of internal mastery or control over previously unexplained feelings, thoughts, and behavior. As far as I am concerned, the acquisition of a cognitive-affective schema of one's internal mental landscape is essential for change to occur. A prerequisite for accomplishing this is the ability to access unconscious mentation.

One of Freud's major contributions was his appreciation of the role of unconscious factors in the development of psychopathology. He emphasized the important role that repressed affects and memories play in the evolution of various symptoms, including phobias, obsessions, and conversion reactions. I might add that the same is also true for delusions and hallucinations. Of course, maladaptive defense mechanisms, compromise formation, genetic, and neurochemical factors also play a role in symptom formation. Of interest, current imaging technology (e.g., fMRIs, PET scans) can identify areas of the brain that are activated when certain symptoms occur. However, the salient psychodynamic phenomena involved in the development of such symptoms cannot be understood by viewing brain scans alone.

For example, recent evidence demonstrates that in the case of functional motor paralysis there is activation of the prefrontal cortex and limbic area, but an absence of activation in the motor cortex. I suggest that a meaningful explanation for this finding may exist in the realm of the mind, specifically psychodynamic processes. When I was an army psychiatrist, a career sergeant was referred to me with bilateral upper extremity paralysis. In the course of eliciting his history, it became apparent that he was enraged with his commanding officer for issuing orders that he believed would endanger the lives of the soldiers in his platoon. With his paralyzed arms dangling beside him, I asked him what he felt like doing to his superior. Without hesitation, he suddenly lifted up both arms with clenched hands and said, "I wanted to strangle him." To my astonishment, as well as his, it was apparent that his repressed murderous rage was a key factor in the development of this conversion symptom. Clearly, there was a functional inhibition of the neuronal connections between his prefrontal, limbic, and motor cortex. Neither brain scans nor neurochemical theories can explain the remarkable intrapsychic phenomenon that "converted" his unconscious rage into an upper-extremity motor paralysis.

In teaching medical students and residents, I emphasize the importance of unconscious feelings, memories, and conflicts, as well as the defenses to contain them, in the development of psychopathology. In addition, I stress the role of conscious experience in one's life, including traumatic events such as the illness or death of a loved one, divorce, a ruptured romantic relationship, loss of job, geographic move, financial duress, physical injury or illness, etc. I also emphasize the impact of positive experiences, including marriage, birth of a child, job promotion, graduation, financial success, new romantic relationship, etc. These events have both conscious and unconscious meanings based on past experience in a person's life. Although the *DSM-V* describes mental disorders and the symptom clusters that characterize them in great detail, it omits the life circumstances and psychodynamic processes involved. While diagnostic criteria may help students to recognize and diagnose psychopathology, they do not inform them of the precipitating factors and life events that facilitate symptom occurrence. One might ask, why is the latter is so important? In my opinion, viewing mental disorders primarily as symptom complexes and diagnostic categories may facilitate the excessive, or even exclusive, use of psychotropic medication without an adequate exploration or understanding of their psychodynamic etiology and meaning. Psychopathology is viewed as arising de novo, instead of occurring in a particular life context. Genetic and neurochemical factors notwithstanding, current and past experiences may alter brain function and the corresponding subjective perceptions that we term "mind". If life circumstances are ignored, symptom complexes can be misinterpreted and diagnoses mistaken. For example, a female patient who presented with symptoms of agitation, irritability, obsessive thoughts, insomnia, and pressured speech was initially diagnosed with a hypomanic episode, Bipolar II Disorder. A careful evaluation revealed that she was raped in adolescence, was subsequently involved in abusive relationships, and recently experienced a traumatic incident with her current boyfriend. In view of her psychodynamic history, the diagnosis was revised to PTSD with anxiety symptoms. As a consequence, her medication regimen was changed and her psychotherapy became focused on her experience of emotional as well as physical abuse. The foregoing clinical examples underscore the importance of considering the influence of subjective experience and psychodynamic processes on brain function. Indeed, several generations of analysts have conceptualized various psychodynamic theories of mind for the purpose of understanding symptom formation and maladaptive behavior.

Almost without exception, individuals who develop psychological symptoms are able to provide a narrative or story that precedes their appearance. Novels, plays, movies, and TV dramas are replete with portrayals of the human condition. Patients seek help for a myriad of reasons: conflicted relationships, emotional or physical abuse, marital discord, loss of a loved one, career disappointments, financial setbacks, physical illness, low self-esteem, self-destructive behavior, etc. I always stress the importance of obtaining a comprehensive psychiatric evaluation that addresses the individual's developmental experiences from early childhood through adolescence and adulthood. Invariably, a narrative evolves that suggests the nature of a person's character structure, defenses, adaptive capacity, cognitive patterns, self-image, gender identity, sexual orientation, as well as the capacity to express feelings and form emotionally intimate attachments.

Information from a careful history usually provides a psychodynamic explanation for the development of symptoms and maladaptive behavior. For example, a middle-aged woman sought treatment for recurrent depression. A detailed history revealed that her mother was psychologically abusive throughout her childhood. She repeatedly devalued and rejected the patient until the latter moved out at age nineteen. Shortly before she died, her mother told her, "I don't understand why I never wanted to hold or kiss you." The patient's father was kind but not affectionate; he died when she was sixteen. An older sister was prone to temper tantrums and violent behavior. At age twelve, the patient was sexually molested by a camp counselor. She totally repressed this event until she was in her mid-forties. During her early twenties, she engaged in multiple affairs and prostitution. Depressive symptoms and suicidal ideation prompted her to enter psychiatric treatment. At age twenty-seven, she married a much older man who was widowed. Increasing jealousy of his deceased wife as well as feelings of rejection by his family resulted in uncontrolled rage and violent behavior. As a result, she was hospitalized and received both antidepressant and antipsychotic medication. Following discharge from the hospital, she continued in outpatient treatment. Of interest, she worked for many years as an executive assistant to a verbally abusive employer. She remained in treatment with several successive male psychiatrists. Invariably, she developed an erotic transference toward each one. In retrospect, it became evident that the patient's sexualization of her therapeutic relationships was a way of searching for the love she never received from her mother. Whenever she felt rejected or slighted by her psychiatrist, she became depressed and sometimes suicidal. Her self-representation was extremely fragile, characterized by feelings of being unlovable and worthless.

The foregoing case presentation illustrates how symptoms develop in a life context. The recurrent themes in this patient's life were emotional abuse, feeling unloved, and a lack of self-worth. Her promiscuity and eroticized therapeutic relationships were misguided attempts to obtain the love she never received in childhood. Viewing her symptoms only as diagnostic entities (e.g. "recurrent depression" or "borderline personality"), without taking into account her salient psychodynamic issues would have facilitated a limited approach to her treatment. In addition to medication, she also required an empathic, stable therapeutic relationship. Within the secure setting of this relationship, she was able to understand the reasons why she repetitively sought romantic love from her therapists. Over the course of treatment, she felt increasingly validated, worthwhile, and even loveable. Moreover, she no longer eroticized her relationship with her therapist. The manifest content of the following dream that occurred after several years of treatment reflected a non-eroticized transference: "You (the therapist) were lying beside me. Your fingers curled around mine and vice versa. It was a loving connection without an erotic element." Her associations to the dream validated her sense of mutual caring and trust with her therapist, as well as the apparent absence of erotic fantasies or feelings.

Narratives or themes also unfold during, as well as across, successive therapy sessions. For example, an eighty-year-old married man entered treatment with symptoms of fatigue, insomnia, and depression. His internist had already prescribed an antidepressant. The latter improved his sleep and lessened his fatigue, but he continued to feel despondent. The patient was a retired college professor who spent much of his time taking care of his chronically ill wife. His younger brother was terminally ill with cancer. Therapy sessions centered around ageing, declining health, deaths of friends, and perceived failures in his past career. At the beginning of one session, he reported the following dream: "My brother and I were on an island in the middle of San Francisco Bay. It was bleak and uninhabited. I escaped, and floated back to the mainland on a raft." He associated to his dying brother with whom he had never had a close relationship. His brother lived near San Francisco, and the patient deliberated about traveling there to visit him before he died. He interpreted his escape from the island as avoiding death and a wish to continue living. It may also have symbolized his need to deny feelings of loss, sadness, and aloneness. At his next session, he announced that his brother had died. Moreover, he wondered why he did not feel a sense of grief. His brother was to be buried in the family plot at a cemetery close to their hometown. The remainder of the session was devoted to reminiscences of his childhood and parents. In the following session, he reported that he had been hospitalized for several days with a severe case of influenza. While in the hospital, he had the following dream: "Superman lost his kryptonite, and was without his usual powers. However, he eventually found it and was his strong self again." The patient associated Superman's loss of his powers with his recent illness. Prior to his hospitalization, he felt energetic and worked out at a gym several times a week. During his hospitalization, he felt "haggard," weak, and helpless.

Nevertheless, he was determined to regain his strength and resume his usual activities. At a subsequent session, he reported the following dream: "I was looking at two inverted parentheses with lakes or bodies of water on either side. I watched and counted people moving from one body of water to the other. My family was gathered on a green lawn having a picnic as I sat on a hill above them observing." The patient felt that the people moving from one body of water to the other represented those who were either ill, dying, or dead. He associated sitting on a hill above them to his wish to keep illness and death at a distance from himself and his immediate family. In addition, he always considered himself to be a loner and "apart" from others. He often found himself holding an opinion different from the majority at work and socially.

The foregoing case illustration demonstrates how a narrative or theme continues from one session to another. Illness, death, and vulnerability are recurrent issues from one session to the next. The patient's dreams reflect his internal struggle to defend against these threats and to continue a meaningful life. They also portray his defensive maneuvers, including avoidance, denial, and reaction formation. Despite his ongoing confrontation with illness and death, the patient exhibited a resilience and deep desire to continue living. Perhaps his own words in one of his therapy sessions describe this struggle best: "I'm not done with the making of me."

In my opinion, dreams are the sine qua non toward understanding our deepest wishes, fears, feelings, perceptions, and conflicts. It is as though we maintain a nighttime diary of our daily activities and experiences. Instead of presenting us with a written commentary, the dream focuses our attention on a motion picture drama taking place while we sleep. Dream imagery is symbolic, often bizarre, without regard to logic or sequential time. Other sensory modalities may accompany the visual imagery, including auditory, tactile, olfactory, and proprioceptive stimuli. Freud believed that the dream is a censoring mechanism that prevents unconscious aggressive and sexual impulses from reaching consciousness. On the basis of clinical research, it is now widely accepted that dreams are metaphorical presentations of our conflicts, emotions, relationships, and self-representations. In addition, they are integral to memory processing, learning, problem-solving, and affective regulation.

Dream imagery, or manifest dream content, often conveys a theme or narrative. For example, a woman dreams that she is walking up a hill carrying two heavy suitcases. She feels weighed down with a burdensome load. Her associations to the dream revolve around the recent loss of a loved one, and feeling weighed down with grief. Her associations to the manifest dream imagery constitute the latent content, or underlying meaning of the dream. Although latent dream content may facilitate a fuller understanding of the manifest dream imagery, the latter often conveys a meaningful theme or narrative of its own accord. For example, a self-employed man in his seventies is considering retirement. He is experiencing health problems related to ageing and wants to spend more time with his wife and grandchildren. However, he is ambivalent about not working anymore and wonders if he will become bored after he retires. In this context, he reports the following dream: "I was standing in front of my brother's house and watched it being torn down. I couldn't understand why it was being destroyed." The major theme of the manifest dream content involves the dismantling of a house without a reasonable explanation. The context in which this dream occurs is sufficient to infer the probable meaning of the manifest dream imagery: the dreamer is not sure of his motives for retiring and believes it may have adverse consequences. Incidentally, his older brother is in poor health and recently retired.

Dream narratives often focus on relationships, self-identity, feelings, crises, conflicts, and wishes. For example, a married man dreams that he and his wife are at a party to which they were not invited. He feels inhibited and uncomfortable, but his wife engages with others in superficial conversation. The central theme of the manifest dream imagery is that the dreamer feels out of place, but his wife is socially adept. In fact, he does feel anxious in social settings and has no close friends. On the other hand, his wife engages with others easily, but is sometimes insensitive to emotional cues in conversation.

An older man dreams that he is walking in a farm pasture with a male friend. It is a peaceful, pastoral setting. A farmer approaches them and as he comes closer, his face appears to be part bovine and part human. The dreamer recently underwent open heart surgery to replace an aortic valve. He was informed that his prosthetic valve contained tissue from a cow's valve. His friend had also undergone valve replacement surgery. This dream reflects a change in self-identity (internalization of a bovine valve) subsequent to his surgery. The peaceful landscape suggests that he feels reassured and secure with his new heart valve.

A woman with a history of bipolar disorder dreams that she is tied to multi-colored balloons filled with helium. The balloons lift her off the ground, and she feels elated as she rises into the air. The imagery in this dream indicates an incipient manic episode. Indeed, a short time after having this dream she began to manifest symptoms of mania.

Another woman who is in an emotionally abusive marriage dreams that she is swimming in a vast ocean. She feels totally alone, helpless, and about to drown. At the time of this dream, she was in such a state of hopelessness that she considered suicide. Her husband was opposed to marital therapy and refused to give her a divorce. The dream imagery graphically portrays the crisis in her life, and her sense of despair.

A divorced female executive is dissatisfied with her job, and is in an unfulfilling relationship with a man. She dreams that she boards a bus in California that is heading east. However, she realizes that she is traveling in the wrong direction and gets off. She rents a car, heads west again, and feels relieved. The main theme of the dream is that she is going in the wrong direction and changes her mind. Following the dream, she decided to quit her job and ended the unsatisfactory relationship. Of interest, is that she lived and worked in California after her divorce and enjoyed her life there. This is an example of a problem-solving or decision-making dream.

A man with a history of alcoholism recently joined Alcoholics Anonymous. He dreams that he is at a party and someone offers him a drink. He refuses to take it. This is a transparent wish-fulfillment that occurs in the context of his attempt to give up drinking.

All of the foregoing dreams contain narratives in their manifest imagery that are substantiated by the latent content. They dramatically portray the dreamers' relationships, self-identity, feelings, crises, conflicts, and wishes. Of course, the information provided by these dreams might have been elicited from the patients' conscious productions, but it probably would not have been presented in such a poignant or dramatic fashion.

Human experience consists of both conscious and unconscious narratives. Self-identity is defined by shifting as well as consistent narratives. These involve both self and others, including family and friends. Self-worth and self-authenticity are dependent on feedback from others. The concept of the "self-object" is based on an empathic response from another individual. We need others to validate our perceptions of self and relationships. Moreover, our sense of meaningful continuity in life is largely based on shared memories with others. The empathic substrate of the "self-other" experience begins during the early attachment process. If parenting provides sufficient love and security during childhood, there is a greater likelihood that the individual will be able to appropriately receive and give love as an adult. If not, there will be a greater probability of deficiencies of self-worth and trust. As a consequence, the capacity for empathy, intimacy, and love with others will be impaired. Character pathology in particular, including borderline and narcissistic personality disorders, is often the result of inadequate or disturbed childhood attachment. In addition, the capacity to experience and express feelings depends on appropriate affective "mirroring" or attunement between parent and child. Impaired or inadequate emotional resonance between parent and child may result in a condition known as "alexithymia." Although the latter condition is diagnosed infrequently, difficulty in identifying and communicating feelings is not uncommon. In fact, misunderstandings and ruptures of interpersonal relationships are frequent outcomes of limitations in the ability to access and express emotions. The therapeutic relationship offers an opportunity to repair a damaged sense of self. The process of identification and internalization of the therapist's empathic understanding can build trust, intimacy, and self-worth. It may also facilitate learning how to identify, modulate, and communicate feelings. At best, it can result in the experience of mature love; that is, the capacity to engage in mutual trust, caring, and respect.

Changes in self-identity occur in the context of the therapist-patient relationship, and are often reflected in dreams. For example, a female patient who was physically and psychologically abused as a child viewed herself as unloveable and unwanted. After several years of treatment, she reported the following dream: "I found myself in my childhood apartment. It was under renovation, and seemed better and brighter than when I lived there. I saw the table under which I used to hide as a child in order to escape my mother's wrath. However, I did not feel frightened or unworthy; instead, I felt hopeful". The patient felt that the renovated apartment represented the changes in her self-identity over the course of therapy. Rather than feeling frightened and unworthy, as she did when she was a child, she felt more valued and optimistic about the future. Moreover, she felt that her therapist understood her, was not judgmental, and made her feel more acceptable. Although she could not erase her past, she felt that she could tolerate it with less emotional distress.

Another married female professional entered treatment because she experienced an inner sense of emptiness. Her husband was emotionally abusive and controlling. She found it difficult, if not impossible, to identify and express her internal emotional state. She was raised in a family where feelings were rarely communicated. Instead, conversation centered around facts and activities. After many months of therapy, she recognized how unhappy she felt in her marriage. Following several years of treatment, she was able to identify, as well as express, her inner feelings of sadness and anger. Despite her requests, her husband refused to engage in marital therapy. In fact, he suspected that she was having an affair with her psychiatrist (myself) and even threatened to kill me. Nevertheless, she was finally able to leave him and obtained a divorce. With continued therapy, she was gradually able to recognize various emotions, including anxiety, guilt, embarrassment, joy, and happiness. Ultimately, she acknowledged her sexual urges and romantic feelings for me. After further treatment, she was able to distinguish between her erotic fantasies and her mature, loving feelings for me. During this lengthy process, she came to view herself as increasingly worthwhile and loveable. Throughout her treatment, I maintained an empathic, non-judgmental, validating attitude. This patient began treatment in a depressive state and most likely had a variant form of alexithymia.

The foregoing clinical example illustrates the value of long-term, psychodynamically oriented psychotherapy. The patient had an impaired attachment experience in childhood, specifically a deficient emotional attunement between her parents and herself. As a consequence, she was unable to identify and express her inner feelings. There was little, if any, emotional communication with her husband. The latter was also emotionally limited, although he also exhibited severe character pathology. Therapy consisted largely of learning how to identify her inner feelings and communicating them to others. Simultaneously, she identified with and internalized my emotional availability, unconditional acceptance, and validation. An emerging erotic transference reflected a growing awareness of her sexual feelings and idealization of me. However, she was gradually able to distinguish between her romantic, sexual feelings and her mature, loving feelings for me. Our relationship was characterized by mutual feelings of caring, trust, and respect. This is often referred to as a "special friendship," or "transformative relationship." Ideally, it facilitates the patient's capacity to form other loving relationships. Unfortunately, in this case, a terminal physical illness precluded the patient from fulfilling a loving relationship with another person. However, she was able to experience much deeper attachments to her children, grandchildren, and friends prior to her untimely death.

My career in the mental health field has spanned almost sixty years. During that time, I have witnessed significant changes in our knowledge of brain functioning, pharmacological interventions, and psychotherapeutic techniques. I have no doubt that future discoveries involving the genetic factors that contribute to mental disorders will help to either prevent or modify their occurrence. Likewise, I believe that further understanding of the neurophysiological and neurochemical functions of the brain will lead to more effective pharmacological interventions. I have already observed the beneficial effects of the major antipsychotics, antidepressants, and anxiolytics on the psychoses, mood, and anxiety disorders. However, I remain doubtful that these future advances will enable us to fully comprehend the subjective experience of mind. The capacity to self-observe and communicate mind phenomena is uniquely human. The progress of human civilization has been, and continues to be, recorded by means of the written and spoken word. Interpersonal dialogue as well as other means of communication (books, movies, television, internet) are the vehicles that provide meaning within and between minds. Individual and collective narratives also provide perspective and meaning for the human species. They are transmitted between minds from one generation to the next, and promote the evolution of mankind.

The psychotherapeutic endeavor, in particular, remains an effective way to communicate thoughts, feelings, perceptions, and memories. In doing so, it enables us to understand the meaning of symptoms and dysfunctional behavior. Understanding and insight provide a measure of control or mastery over what is often puzzling and incomprehensible. To share our innermost thoughts and feelings with another empathic individual is both comforting and reassuring. Ideally, it can also help us to change maladaptive cognition, emotions, and behavior. Historically, psychiatry has utilized various psychotherapies to treat those suffering from mental disorders. These include psychoanalysis, psychodynamically-oriented psychotherapy, cognitive-behavioral therapy, group, marital and family therapy. There is substantial evidence that almost all forms of psychotherapy may be helpful. Indeed, the nature of the relationship between therapist and patient appears to be the common curative factor. In recent decades, psychiatry has paid increasing attention to normal and pathological brain processes in order to understand and treat mental disorders. Without doubt, the more we understand normal and pathological brain function, the more enlightened we will become regarding mind phenomena. Unfortunately, there appears to be a reductionist trend toward explaining mental functions. Subjective experience appears to be of lesser importance than objective measurements of brain activity. As a consequence, less emphasis seems to be placed on the subjective response to verbal and nonverbal communication between individuals. Nevertheless, interpersonal communication undoubtedly affects brain function and vice versa. For example, a reassuring comment by a therapist can instantaneously reduce the subjective feeling of apprehension in a patient. By the same token, a well-timed, illuminating interpretation can free one from a troublesome symptom. Yet we still do not understand how words from one person can alter neuronal circuits in the brain of another. Nor do we know how nonverbal behavior or unarticulated feelings can activate the mirror neurons of an observer, resulting in an empathic response. The subjective experience of verbal or nonverbal communication and associated brain activity is still poorly understood. Likewise, the incorporation of a previous day's experience into dream imagery that articulates with meaningful past and current issues in the dreamer's life remains a mystery. The subjective perception of ideas, feelings, and memories, as well as their associated brain changes, are still beyond our comprehension. Therefore, I believe it is essential to pay attention to the subjective phenomena of mind, as well as to corresponding brain activity. Mind and brain are analogous to computer software and hardware. Each can be described in its own language, according to its unique functions. Without doubt, the interaction between mind and brain is one of the most important challenges facing psychiatry.

During my career, I have always tried to integrate the subjective experience of mind with neurobiological and physiological phenomena. In the course of doing so, I believe that I have helped many of my patients to reduce their mental or physical suffering, and to improve their lives. In addition to the use of medication, I believe that an empathic understanding of another's mental anguish is a fundamental curative factor. In essence, an empathic attitude promotes a deep emotional resonance between patient and therapist. It is a prerequisite for the acquisition of insight and change. Emotional and cognitive understanding between patient and therapist reflect an optimally functioning empathic therapeutic relationship. As far as I am concerned, empathy and the mutuality of communication between two or more minds are among the fundamental healing factors common to all psychotherapies. In my opinion, they are vitally necessary for the maintenance of a civilized society. Perhaps Freud's greatest contribution was to make us aware of both conscious and unconscious mind phenomena. Unfortunately, he did not have the benefit of contemporary technology to identify and measure corresponding brain functions. We currently have the technological potential to further explore the relationship between mind and brain activity. It is my fondest hope that we will someday understand the mind-brain phenomena associated with empathic communication, including emotional and cognitive resonance between individuals. In doing so, we may discover important mind-brain alterations that are associated with psychodynamic mechanisms and various mental disorders. In particular, we may also learn how mind-brain activity can be beneficially altered in the context of an empathic therapist-patient relationship. As a physician, psychiatrist and psychoanalyst, I have had the good fortune to participate in the ongoing search for mind-brain-body connections. I hope the papers and commentaries in this volume reflect the arc of that journey.

Board-certified psychiatrist and psychoanalyst Myron L. Glucksman, MD, maintains a practice in Redding, Connecticut, and serves as a Clinical Professor of Psychiatry at New York Medical College. Glucksman earned his medical degree at the University of Washington School of Medicine and completed his psychiatric training at the Payne Whitney Clinic, New York Hospital–Cornell Medical Center.

The author of multiple peer-reviewed papers in psychiatric and psychoanalytic literature, Glucksman is the author of *Dreaming: An Opportunity for Change*. He is the coeditor of several other books related to dreams and affect. Glucksman is a Training and Supervising Analyst at The Psychoanalytic Institute, New York Medical College, and a Past President of the American Academy of Psychoanalysis and Dynamic Psychiatry. He resides in Redding, and is married with three daughters and six grandchildren.

Index

Abandonment 22, 50, 74, 75, 92, 130, 131, 206, 248, 310, 324, 331, 354

Acetylcholine 104, 314, 340, 349

Acting-out 3, 74, 76, 119, 130, 140, 144, 232, 375

Adaptational 296, 302

Addictive 19, 20, 36, 38

Adipose 1, 2, 17, 38

Affect 18; biofeedback 41-44, 62-68; conversion; introject 126; manifest dream content 187-285; neurotransmitters 349; obsessions phobias, 313-347, 380; regulation 306; symptom context 71-78; therapeutic relationship 81-110; weight loss 20-22

Agape 158

Aggression animal assisted therapy 370-375; biofeedback therapy 47; gender 250-252; obesity 22; therapeutic relationship 142-145, 160

Agoraphobia xiv, 325

Alexithymia 82, affective attunement 388-390; affective dysregulation 100-107; 283, 319

Alliance animal assisted therapy 368, 372; curriculum 296, 303; manifest dream content 254; therapeutic relationship 23, 82, 144, 155, 173, 179; 377; treatment 325

Alpha elements 86, 91, 99, 102

Amino acid xi, 319

Amygdala affect 83, 349; anxiety 104-106, 314, 323, 344, 352; depression 355; memory 312, 342-343; phobias 313, 347; schizophrenia 320

Anger biofeedback therapy 47-75; affect 88, 90, 98, 123, 193-194, 313, 319, 324, 389; defense 118; dreams 199-203, 213, 230; obsessions 344; overeating 19, 26, 31; therapy 172,

327, 373-376; transference 119, 122,
155-160, 352

Anhedonia 320, 321

Annihilation 211, 248

Animal assisted therapy 368, 370

Anxiety xii; affect 81, 91-98, 118, 314,
324, 349, 351, 354, 389; biofeedback
therapy 41-46; 57; disorder 323,
343-344, 390; dreams 182-184,
197, 230-231, 253-254; medication
302, 338; oedipal 27-28, 159, 213;
overeating 18-20, 31-32; phobia
313, 346-347; sexual 30; symptom-
context 71-77; symptom 56, 63-68,
97, 127-133, 149, 198, 250, 277, 325,
327, 370, 382; 354, 389; therapy
180, 298; weight loss 3

Anxiolytic 268, 293, 353, 390

As-if personality 99-104; 144, 158, 160

Associations dreams 28, 32, 66, 74-76,
102, 128, 134, 169, 181-198, 211, 219,
237, 241-249, 258, 265-282, 384;
therapy 91-94

Attachment 20, 25, 105, 140, 157, 160,
251-252, 259, 355, 382, 388, 390

Attunement 19, 37, affect 90-99, 102-107,
124, 148, 151-157, 388, 390

Autonomic nervous system biofeedback
therapy 41-45, 63

Basal ganglia 321, 349

Behavioral affect 81, 97-98, 104. 124;
attachment 320; biofeedback 62-64;
dreams 191, 218-219; identification

126; therapy 6, 56, 84, 178, 185, 293,
302-303, 312-313, 343-347, 356, 391;
residency training 294, weight loss
xiv, 1-3, 6

Benzodiazepine 323, 325

Beta elements 86-87, 91, 99, 102

Beta endorphins 349

Biofeedback therapy xiv, 41-43, 64-65,
318-319; 379

Biological xvi, mental processes 317-318;
obesity 1-2, 17, 33-37; residency training 288-309

Bipolar disorder xii, 301, 355, 382; affect
97; dreams 387

Blood pressure biofeedback therapy 41-
42, 63-68; 78, 320

Body image biofeedback therapy 46;
obesity xii, 2-6, 17-21, 31-36; weight
loss 22

Borderline personality disorder 65, 167,
177, 314, 355, 383, 388

Brain xi, xvi, xvii,; affect 105-106;
mind 309-393; obesity 2-6, 42-43;
residency training 288-307; therapy
91-94; tumor 87

Broad context biofeedback therapy 71-76

Cardiac arrhythmia 41, 64, 319

Caudate nucleus 313, 320-321, 344-345

Cell adipose xii, 1-2; neuron 339; T-cell
318

Cerebellum 342

Cingulate affect 83, 104, 349-353; anxiety 314; depression 356

Cognitive xvi, 65; affect 93-98, 104-107, 319-327; change 310; consciousness 82-84; dreams 219, 283; empathy 123-124, 314, 350-352; insight 380-382; love 141; memory 312; theory 348-354; therapy 117, 135, 178, 293, 302-303, 313, 345-347, 356, 391-393; threat 343

Conflict xii; biofeedback therapy 41-76; dreams 181-186, 191-199, 210-266, 328; obesity 19-34; relationship 382; symptoms 313, 345-346; theory 118-120, 309, 318-319, 381, 388; therapeutic relationship 94, 121; therapy 116, 148-153; transference 159

Conversion 380-381; disorder 312-313, 339-345, 354; symptom 42, 62, 69, 346

Compulsion eating 30; symptom 312-313, 339-344

Condensation 181

Cortical affect 349-350; attachment 320; consciousness 312, 341; conversion 313, 346; depression 356; fear 104; memory 322, 342; OCD 321; phobia 313, 347; threat 343; transference 314, 347, 352-353

Culturalist 296

Decompensation 214

Defense anxiety 314, 327; affect 82-106, 324, 329; biofeedback therapy 49, 56, 69-77; conflict 318, 381; dreams 191-194, 202-218, 266, 296; neurochemical substrate 356; overeating 26, 32; symptoms 340, 380, 382; therapy 113-119, 168, 175, 332

Deficit affect 82-83, 90, 97-99, 100, 105; attention 376; self 86, 93, 106-107, 119-121; love 140

Depersonalization defense 106-107, 114, 168, 175; neurotransmitter 330; self 82-89, 91-100; symptom 103, 249, 311, 329-331, 373-374

Depression animal assisted therapy 370, 373, 376; biofeedback therapy 43, 46. 57, 68, 70; disorder 88, 91, 102, 118, 121, 130-132, 167, 168, 177-178, 193-194, 230-232, 245, 257, 275, 328, 355, 382-384; dreams 182; medication 321, 331; neurotransmitters 310-311, 320, 332; theory 317, 330; therapy 298, 314; weight loss 22, 33-34

Deprivation affect 85, 93; self 70; transference 156; weight loss 3, 19-20

Desensitization biofeedback therapy 42, 46-47, 63-64

Developmental xiv; affect 99-107, 319, 331; countertransference 94; danger 97; disorders 288, 303; dreams 253, 259; empathy 123; love 145; obesity 17-21, 31-37; psychodynamics 303; psychopathology 119-120; symptoms 382; transference 139, 142, 149; 156-159

Disintegration panic disorder 327; self
127, 214

Displacement defense 114, 168; dreamwork 181; neuronal activity 344;
obsessions 321; transference 25, 248,
268, 279, 369-377; transference love
141-142, 152, 156

Dissociation consciousness 84; defense 91-
94; self 100; temporal lobe 330

Dog co-therapist 368-378; therapy 114,
177; transference 172, 372-375; transitional object 168, 174

Dopamine memory 343; neurotransmitter 288, 311, 320-321, 330-332, 340

Dreamwork dreams (condensation,
displacement, symbolism) 181-182;
manifest content 256

Drive instinct 191, 218; theory 118, 120,
317-318; sexual 256

Dysphoria affect 20, 92, 103; treatment
186, 258

Dysregulation affect 82, 97, 104-107, 319;
mood 178; neurotransmitters 310,
317, 320-330

Education psychodynamic psychoanalytic
xvi, 287-290, 300-307

Ego anxiety 82, 97, 118, 314, 349; biofeedback therapy 77; development
126; love 141, 158; strength 186,
219, 222, 239; theory 317, 339, 340;
therapy 116, 120, 125, 144, 190, 212,
328-331

Electrical Skin Conductance biofeedback
therapy 41

Electroshock treatment 287, 301

Emotional affect feeling 50, 81-82, 97;
abandonment; abuse 100, 119, 124,
329-331, 344, 382-383; arousal 68,
72, 99; attunement 37, 90, 103-107,
148, 151, 157, 390; awareness 349;
closeness 25; communication 93, 103,
192, 379, 390; connectedness xxi,
114; constriction inhibition 89, 352;
control 352; cues 99, 386; deprivation 33; discomfort distress, 18, 20,
153, 371, 389; distance 89-91; empathy 314, 350; emptiness 28, 91, 100;
experience 98; expression 89, 124;
feedback 98, 102; gratification 33-34;
hunger 18; injury 251; intimacy 146,
151-154, 160; learning 104; mastery
56; medication 2, 327; neglect 373;
numbness 170; painful 20-22;
regulation 83, 98, 310; resonance xv,
388, 392-393; response 46, 101, 103,
353; state xv, 19, 82, 141, 182, 218,
344, 352, 380, 389; trauma 119, 332;
understanding 351, 392

Empathy affect 124; attachment 388;
love 140, 146, 157-159 314,
350-351; therapeutic relationship
xv, 63, 82, 84, 114, 369; therapy
32, 113, 116, 120, 123, 127, 175,
294, 318, 331, 392

Enactment therapeutic relationship 114, 377; therapy 130, 370-372; transference 89, 91; countertransference 145

Epigenetic xvi, 311, 355, 356

Epinephrine xi, 288, 340

Erotic transference 113, 139-142, 152, 160, 179, 383-390; countertransference 122, 140-145; gratification 150

Family biofeedback therapy 46, 67; dreams 185, 192-209, 250, 254, 278-279, 326; obesity 5, 24, 26; therapy 121, 132, 147, 293-296, 302-305, 311, 325, 332, 375-391

Fantasy affect 86, 103, 354; alexithymia 319; dreams 195-197; obesity 24-32; phobia 344; therapy 130-131, 154, 171-173, 327

Feeling acting-out 175; affect 81-134, 311-331, 351-353, 379-390; ambivalent 173; animal assisted therapy 368-377; anxiety 325-327; biofeedback therapy 41-76; consciousness 312-314, 350; conversion 313, 345-346; countertransference 171; dreams 181-197; empathy 123, 380; guilt 167-174; loving 113-114, 139-161; manifest content 218, 229, 231, 241, 248-255, 274-291; mastery 324; memory 342-343; mirror neurons 391-392; neurobiology neurotransmitters 315, 338-339, 349, 356; obesity overeating 2-32

sexual 328, 384; suicidal 172; 215, 385-388

Fluoxetine 101, 275, 321

Fixation oral 17-18

Galvanic skin response 48, 57

Gender identity 282; manifest dream content 186-187, 237-242, 250-259, 268; residency training 297

Genetic xvi, anxiety 313, 347; depression 355; learning 322; memory 312, 343; mind brain 338, 356, 381, 390; obesity 3, 23, 35-37; OCD 345; panic disorder 210, 323-327; residency training 288-303; schizophrenia 355; self-regulation 331-332; sexual orientation 354; symptoms 380

Geriatric 297

Ghrelin 2

Glutamate affect 104, 314; emotions 349; memory 343; neurotransmitter 340

Gratification dreams 212-213; giving-up, given-up complex 70; love 160; obesity 22, 34; 75-76; oral 17; overeating 20, 33; self-object 318; sexual 114, 140, 146, 150

Guilt affect 57, 66-68, 73-74, 168, 173-175, 199-208, 319, 324, 349, 389; conversion 346; dreams 213, 237, 252; obesity overeating 19-33; obsessions 313, 344; sexual 88, 114, 128, 131, 154, 168-172, 184, 192-197, 211-213, 328-329, 374

Headache migraine 71; muscle tension 41-
     42, 64-66; symptom 72, 121, 147

Heart biofeedback therapy 41-48, 62-68,
     319; dream 24; surgery 387

Hemisphere affect emotion 105-106; dis-
     sociation 330

Hippocampus affect 83, 104; anxi-
     ety. panic 313, 323, 347; fear 105;
     memory 312, 342

Hormone obesity 2; mind brain 311, 317, 340

Hunger obesity 2, 18-19; weight loss 3

Hyperplasia adipose cells 35

Hypertrophy adipose cells 2, 35

Hypertension biofeedback therapy 41-42,
     62-69, 78; psychosomatic disorder
     309, 318-319

Hysteria 117, 313, 339, 344, 356

Idealization animal assisted therapy 378;
     love 141; therapist 113, 122, 148-149,
     152, 155, 390

Ideation affect 97-98; cognition 348;
     delusional 156; empathy 124, 167-
     168, 173; obsessive 321, 345; paranoid
     376; phobic 56, 68; suicidal 101, 383;
     therapeutic relationship 84, 93

Identification anxious temperament
     344-345; biofeedback therapy 47;
     counter-identification 91, 94, 102,
     113; counter-projective identifica-
     tion 156; countertransference 84, 87;
     dreams 211-212, 329; empathy 123,
     388; internalization 125-126, 135;

introjective 85-94 102-103; mirror
     neurons 351; projective xv, 85, 94,
     113, 119, 141, 156, 171, 314, 318, 352;
     transference 369, 377

Image body xii, 2-5, 17-36, 46; body size
     3-8, 13-14; empathy 123; memory
     153; self 25-34, 47, 159, 175, 189,
     223, 229-230, 243, 267, 278, 282;
     self-object 124, 132-133

Immediate Context symptoms 71, 75

Injury counter-projective 154; dreams
     185-188, 200, 211, 237, 243, 248,
     251-259, 265-266, 274, 278,
     281-284; interpersonal 21; OCD
     321; panic 326; physical 381

Insight xv, clinical change 113-120, 127-
     135, 209, 294, 304, 391; cognition
     348, 380; dreams 191, 211-219, 243;
     empathy 392; free association 183,
     196; learning 312, 343; masochism
     167-168; transference 118, 156

Interpersonal communication 82, 314,
     342, 350-351, 391; dreams 184-188,
     259, 279; empathy 123, 157; injury
     21; mirroring 352; model 120;
     psychodynamics 303; relationships
     22, 65-66, 91, 116-118, 190-191,
     210-222, 239, 243, 251-253, 267,
     307, 375, 388; stress 288; symptoms
     289, 293-294; theory 296, 302-303,
     318, 355-366; threat 321, 345;
     transference 157

Instinct affect 81; impulses drives 118,
120, 218, 317, 340, 348; wishes 182,
191, 218, 348

Insula affect 349; anxiety 314, 347; mirror
neurons 350-351; phobias 313

Internalization affect 104; attunement 19;
clinical change 113, 127, 132, 212,
219, 332; love 158; self-identity 387;
therapeutic relationship 126, 129,
134-135, 161, 167, 172, 175, 324, 369,
374, 377, 388; transmuting identification 126

Interpretation clinical change 113-117;
despair 92; dreams 181-188, 237, 246,
268, 273, 278, 283, 348; insight
118-120, 134; therapy 175, 304, 370;
transference 118, 156, 377; well-timed
392

Intersubjective theory 302; transference
love 144

Intimacy attachment 388; dreams 251;
emotional 151, 154; empathy 388;
love 113-114, 154, 160-161; sexual
150-152; special friendship 146;
therapy 152; transference 158

Intrapsychic change 116, 190; conflict 116, 309, 313, 318, 345-346;
conversion 381; countertransference
85; dreams 184, 191, 211, 218, 279;
empathy 123; experience 356; latent
dream content 182-183, 187-190,
210-218, 229-231, 239, 246, 251, 259,

266, 258, 282, 386-387; mastery 56;
mirror neurons 352; psychodynamics
303; stressors 293; theory 318; threat
321, 345

Leptin 2

Libido instinct 340; sexual 97, 317

Limbic conversion 345, 380-381; emotion
83, 104, 106, 349, 353-356; emotional attunement 355; feelings 313-314,
322; mirror neurons 359; OCD 321;
panic 323; schizophrenia 320

Loss abandonment 92, 139; defense 77,
145; depression 72, 104, 311, 317,
330-331; dream 206, 243-245, 251-
259, 274-275, 281, 382, 386; feeling
384; mastery 77; object 70-77, 238;
relationship 209; symptom 71, 382;
weight xii, 1-14, 22-35

Love affect 98; countertransference
144-156; curative 142; idealistic
140; maternal 18; mature 140-141,
161, 158, 388; object 20, 27, 73,
142; paternal 29, 154, 157, 388;
relationship 113, 114, 139, 377;
sexual 103, 156; therapeutic
relationship xv, 25-32, 113, 129,
139-146, 151-158, 383; transference
139-148, 153-156, 160, 375

Manifest dream content report xv, 77,
151, 173, 182-191, 205, 210-283, 342,
348, 383, 386; imagery 183, 329,
386-387

Masochism 218

Mastery autonomic nervous system 63; behavior 157; cognitive 219; ego 77; feelings 324, 380; manifest dream content 251; overeating 20; skin conductance response 42-49, 54-57, 68, 319; symptoms 391; therapy 217; transference-countertransference 156

Maternal attunement soothing nurturing 18-20, 34-36, 156; introject 104; love 18; transference 27, 145; 131, 210, 328-331

Memory affect 97, 106-107; conscious 105; dissociation 330; dreams 182, 198, 219, 322, 348, 386; evocative 123; explicit declarative 106, 312, 342, 354; implicit procedural 106, 312, 342; learning 322; neuronal neurochemical 310-313, 323, 338-346; short-term 312, 342; skin conductance 66; long-term 312, 342; traces 124; unconscious 105, 342; vivid 153; working 105-106

Mentalization 314, 339, 350; mirror neurons 350, 353

Mentation xvi; conscious 315, 348; primary process 313; unconscious 181, 296, 306, 348, 380

Metabolic brain 307, 320-321; obesity 3, 23, 35-37

Migraine biofeedback therapy 41-42, 64-69, 319; symptom 71, 147, 325

Mind brain xvi, xvii, 43, 288, 304-317, 332-341, 353-357, 379, 392-393; affect 90; conscious unconscious 183, 392; dream 387; hopeless helpless 318; introject 126, 392; medica-tion 304; mental phenomena 353; metapsychology 312; mirror neurons 350; peace of 372; psychodynamic processes 380-382; subjective experience 304, 354, 381, 391-392; therapy 392; transference 132, 160

Mirror body image 5; mirroring affective attunement 82, 98-99, 124, 388; empathy 129, 191; love 141-142; neurons 314, 350-353, 392; self-object 124-125; 157

Mood affect 22, 50, 81; biofeedback therapy 43; depression 317; disorder xii, 338, 354, 390; dream 222, 245; medication 114, 168, 268; overeating hyperphagia 24, 33, 36; regulation dysregulation 178, 219, 348

MRI brain function activity 42, 307, 338, 380; empathy 350; treatment 348

Morphology adipose cell 1, 35

Murderous impulses fantasies 346; feelings 73-74; rage 206, 381; wishes 118

Muscle contraction headache 64-66; tension 41-42, 48, 62-68, 78, 319

Narcissistic depletion 85; injury 142, 156; 378; needs 85, 148-149, 152, 160; patients 86, 145; personality disorder 388; reinforcement 378

Narrative dream imagery xv, 188, 283;
individual collective 391; manifest
dream content report 183, 187, 218,
265-278, 283, 386-387; self-identity
388; symptoms 382; therapy 385

Network memories 323, 342; mirror
neurons 350; neuronal 83, 104, 304,
310-312, 323-339

Neurobiological affective regulation dysregulation 83, 97-100, 104-107, 310,
314, 331; brain 309-311, 317, 331-332,
338-340, 353-354; mind 311, 339,
356-357, 392; mirror neurons 314,
352-353; model 310; panic 324; reductionism 304; theory 317, 325

Neuronal affect feelings 315, 323-324,
340; anxiety 327; consciousness 312,
315, 341; conversion 346; defenses
344; dreams 322, 339; excitations
182; 314; medication 325; memory
learning 323, 342; mirror 314; neurochemical 310, 341; neurotransmitter
340; OCD 313, 321-322, 344-345;
phobia 313; regulation dysregulation
328, 331-332; synaptic 83, 104, 107,
304, 310-311

Neurotransmitter acetylcholine, affect
83, 97, 104, 349; anxiety 314; brain
338; depression 310, 317, 320-321,
332, 355; dissociation 330; dysregulation 320; epinephrine norepinephrine xi, 288, 340; GABA, glutamate
340-343; learning 322; memory 312,

323, 343; mentation 311, 315, 356;
OCD 310, 322; orexin 340-341;
panic 310; schizophrenia 310; self-
regulation 332; serotonin 36, 104,
314, 321-323, 330-331, 340-343,
349; therapy 331, 347

Object constancy 19, 119; dreams 249;
good 135; gratification 70; loss 70-
76, 97, 233; lost 125; love 20, 27,
141; new 121-123, 129-130, 153-160,
175; old 120-122, 129, 135, 175;
oedipal 139, 155; pre-oedipal 155;
relations 18, 85, 114, 119-121, 142-
143, 219, 296, 302; representation
94, 119, 124, 252, 324; self 18-19,
33, 70, 75-76, 86, 123-125, 145,
157, 311, 318, 324, 328-332, 388;
transference 248, 268, 279, 370;
transitional 18, 28, 32, 34, 99, 114,
168, 174, 369, 372-374, 377

Obsessive-compulsive 65, 321

OCD 43, 310, 313-314, 321, 344-345,
355

Oedipal conflict 34, 118, 201, 207, 213;
dreams 32, 238, 253; fantasies 32;
guilt 213; love 140, 141, 145; needs
141; object relations 139; pre-oedipal
26, 28, 32, 36, 139-141, 155-156;
rivalry 184; sexual 27, 73, 149, 161;
themes 25, 185, 205; transference-
countertransference 155; triumph 32,
130; wishes 28, 32, 130

Omega neurons 312, 339, 342, 349

Oral behavior 17; dreams 238; erotogenic zone 17; fixation 1; gratification 17; needs 2; pre-oral 20; sex
178; stage phase 1, 17, 20, 34, 37;
stimulation 17

Overeating defense 77; obesity 2, 19-20,
24; oedipal wishes 28; oral 17; retaliation 32; self-soothing 20; weight gain
22, 32

Oxytosin affects 349; borderline personality 355

Orexin 341

Orbitofrontal affect 354; anxiety panic
347; cortex 313-314, 344-345; OCD
313

Panic 31 47, 127; disorder 310-314,
323-327, 332, 347, 355-356

Parietal lobe 349-350

Personality analyst's 119-120; as-if 99,
103-104, 107; borderline 355, 383;
development 290, 295, 306, 317;
318; disorder 97, 167, 177, 298, 314,
329-330, 354-355; factors 62; integration 178; multiple 330-331; narcissistic 388; structure 85, 116, 190, 210,
214, 309, 318, 312, 341; Type A 309

PET scan anxiety disorder 348; brain
function 43, 338; social phobia 347;
symptoms 380

Pharmacotherapy 167-168, 187, 265, 284,
313

Philein 140

Pi neuron 312

Post-traumatic stress disorder 298; PTSD
253, 313, 347, 382

Process analytic 134, 296; attachment
157, 388; biological 37, 309, 317-318;
clinical change 83; cognitive thought
99, 117, 352; defensive 98; developmental 123; dream 219; empathic
82, 84, 92, 112, 124; feeding 37; free
association 183; internalization 332;
neurobiological neurochemical 311,
331, 354; neurophysiological 330;
primary 181, 313, 339-340, 348;
projective introjective 95; psychic
339; psychodynamic 37, 62; regulatory 353; secondary 313, 340, 348;
therapeutic xv, 55, 58, 64, 77-78, 85;
transference-countertransference 85,
94; treatment 112, 122, 129, 139,
141, 145-146, 155, 186, 219-220, 305,
370, 378-379

Psi neuron 312

Psychoanalysis American Academy of xiv,
21, 81, 307; clinical change 116, 190;
cognitive process 117; dreams 220;
education 289-306; Freud 347; neurobiology 354; theory practice xvi, xvii,
119, 309; treatment 56, 72, 185, 218,
287, 303-304, 391

Psychodynamics affect dysregulation 97,
102, 107, 314; anxiety 347-348;
biofeedback therapy 41-42, 64-69;
body image xii, 3, 13-14, 19, 22, 23;
compulsive overeating 3, 20-23,
31-37;

conflicts 65, 77; dreams xv, 182-189, 221-237, 290, 301; education 290-306; formulation 187-188, 265-283, 296; Freud 340; love 141; manifest dream content 223-224, 266; mentalization 350; metapsychology 309; mirror neurons 352; narrative 268, 272, 277, 283; neurobiology 310-311, 317, 324-332, 355; obesity 17, 21, 23; obsessions 344; OCD 321, 345; 340; panic disorder 356; phobias 344, 347; psychiatry 307; PTSD 313, 347, 382; somatic symptoms xii, xiv, 2, 19, 62-69, 70-77, 82, 90-93, 99-101, 250, 313, 319, 345, 280-289, 383; themes 186-187, 237-259, 267, 382; theory 288-290, 303, 309, 340; therapy xvi, 112-114, 167-168, 177, 188, 217-220, 232, 265, 284-298, 304-313, 343, 390-391, 322; weight gain 3, 22, 31-37; weight loss x11, 1-3, 5-6, 11-14, 22-29, 31-35

Psychotherapy xi; affect dysregulation 82, 106-107; anxiety 348; biofeedback 41-45, 319; clinical change xv, 112; conversion 346; depression 321; dreams 217, 238; individual 325-328; internalization 332; learning 322; long-term 114, 167-168; manifest dream content 265, 275, 284; mastery 56, 78, 390; memory 342; mirror neurons; 314; neurotransmitter changes 343, 354-356; obesity xiv, 3, 36;

physiological monitoring 62-69; psychodynamic 112, 187, 287, 306, 391; 177-179, 390; PTSD 342; residency training 289-305; symptoms 69, 72-77; therapeutic outcome 219-220

Psychopathology xii; brain disease 293, 300; developmental-arrest model 119; dreams 191, 210; metapsychology 309, 317, 340; psychodynamic formulation 295, 303; relational-conflict model 121; skin conductance 45; somatic symptoms 62; sexual abuse 167; symptom formation 306, 340; unconscious factors 380-381

Psychotic xii; biofeedback therapy 63; diagnosis 239, 268; manifest dream content 214, 229; medication 293, 301; psychotherapy 74, 130; symptoms 63; weight loss 1

Psychotropic medication 114, 168-169, 239, 268, 288, 293, 298, 302, 310-311, 322, 325, 328, 351, 381

Reaction formation 99, 385

Relational manifest dream content 187-188, 237, 243, 251-258, 265-267, 274, 281-283; relational-conflict model 120; transference 142, 296

REM sleep 182, 323, 348

Repression defense 76-77, 99, 114, 168, 175, 340; dreams 211; symptoms 340, 344

Residency training xii, xiii, 1, 112-113, 288-307

Resistance autonomic nervous system
63; dreams 211, 237; manifest dream
content 251; neurons 339; obesity
34; psychodynamics 296;
psychotherapy 33, 73, 126, 132,
220, 370, 372, 378; transference love
139, 142, 155; working-through 303
Satiation obesity 2, 19
Schizophrenia 43, 130, 310, 338, 355
Self analytic 134, 186, 219, 222, 239,
267; assertive 26, 46; authentic 380,
388; awareness 217, 232, 353; body
size 9, 14, 36; cohesion 19, 119, 190;
concept 209-210, 214; confident
125, 151; conscious 5, 47, 351; deficit
90, 93; dependence 197; depreciation
212; destructive 172-174, 212, 232,
369, 373-377, 382; disclosure 159;
238, 369, 373-374, 377, 382;
disintegration 127, 214; esteem 23,
112, 119, 145, 197, 212, 218, 331,
369, 382; experience 84, 124, 306,
342; fragmentation 21, 127; function 119; genetic 355; gratifying 190,
212; identity 101, 183-185, 203, 211,
231, 251, 255, 386-389; image 20-27,
33-36, 47, 159, 189, 222; imaging
43; integration 116; loathing 88, 170;
manifest dream content 231, 243,
251, 255, 267, 278; medication 338;
mutilation 88, 114, 167-175, 249,
373-374; neurotransmitters 310;
object 33, 70-76, 86, 94, 123-125,
142-145, 157,

311, 318, 324, 328, 331; observation
xvi; other 388; perception 12-13, 212;
psychology 302; punishment 19, 168,
174, 178, 329; reflection xvi, 312,
341; regulatory 175, 310, 320, 331-
332; representation 21-36, 70, 83-93,
99-107, 114, 127-129, 175, 182, 191,
219-220, 324-326, 383; reward 19;
18; sabotage 206; 266; self-soothing
2, 19-20, 31-34, 99, 190, 212, 266,
378; self-state dream 212, 255; worth
383, 388
Separation 18-19, 22, 49, 70, 132-133,
304; abuse 88, 102, 114, 119, 167,
170, 174-177, 328-331; acting-out 74,
119, 232; anxiety 81; depression 332;
manifest dream content 251; memory
343; panic 324, 327
Serotonin emotions 36, 349; neurotransmitter 104, 311-332, 340
Sexual arousal excitation 97, 103, 155,
317; boundaries 140; conflict 22, 193,
19; dreams 122; drive impulse 66,
77, 114, 118, 140, 146, 160, 181, 257,
321, 385; dysfunction 298; fantasies
3, 27, 75-76, 113, 122, 148-158, 161,
184, 192, 196, 213, 344, 377; feelings
113, 128, 130-131, 141; gratification
114, 146; harassment 156; hetero-
sexuality 26, 30, 204, 211; homo-
sexuality 26, 149-154, 249; identity
151; imagery 257; inhibition 32, 76,
151; intercourse 27, 170, 178, 184,

193, 197, 205; intimacy 151-152; love 140; manifest dream content 243, 251, 256-257, 274-281; oral zone 17; orientation 354, 382; pleasure 31; projections 145; promiscuity 88, 145, 151-153, 159, 193, 201, 390; relationship 21-26, 66, 73, 146, 149, 154, 195, 198; transference-countertransference 159-160, 213

Skin conductance response biofeedback therapy 42-48, 52-55, 64-68

Splitting defense 119, 348

Stress affect 98; anxiety 77; conflict 76; chronic 178; experiential 331; life 250, 345; oral behavior 17; psychosocial 72, 293, 332; PTSD xiii, 167, 183, 298, 344; symptoms 354; trauma 253; work 149

Suicidal 88, 114, 167; acting-out 214; acts 369; behavior xv, 167, 175, 373; fantasies ideation 101, 167-173, 252, 377, 383; impulses 169, 172-173, 374; threats 156

Symbiotic attachment 252, bliss 141; unity 123

Symptom anxiety 45-48, 63-68, 184, 197-198, 250, 254, 327; alexithymic 103; biofeedback therapy 42-44, 50-56, 65-69, 319; bipolar 382; conversion 313, 344-346, 381; defenses 118; depressive 72, 90, 100-104, 168, 177, 245, 275, 328, 383-384; deperson-alization dissociation 249, 328-330;

DSM V 381; formation 296, 306, 338-340, 354, 380; interpretation 392; mania 387; manifest dream content 222, 238; medication 114, 168, 322; mood dysregulation 178; neurochemical cascade 310; OCD 321; onset 71; paranoid 279; psycho-therapy 116-117, 243, 267; psychotic 1, 63; self-mutilation 249; somatic xiii, xiv, 62-64, 73-77, 82, 90-101, 250, 319, 344; symptom context 70-72; transference 139; weight loss 3

Synaptic connections 323; functioning 328; inactivation 322; network 323-325; neuronal 304, 310-311, 321-322. 331-332, 340, 343, 356; receptor 332

Thalamic amygdala 105-106, 312, 343; activating system 341 cortical 312; hippocampal 105; OCD 321

Theme abandonment loss 130, 206, 257; associations 188, 265, 272, 276, 283; control 254; dreams 127, 204, 207, 212, 246, 274, 387; gratifying 190; injury 237, 253-259, 265-267, 281-284; manifest dream content xv, 173, 183-188, 268, 281, 386; narrative 384-385; oedipal 25, 205; pre-oedipal 26; psychodynamic 186-187; 237-259, 266; relational 252-253, 258-259, 265-267, 281-283; self 255, 281, 383; separation isolation 49; sexual 256

Transference xv, 3, 116-122, 127-134, 144-147, 155, 159, 184, 199, 248,

296-298, 304, 314, 318; affectionate
157, 161; ambivalent 25, 32; countertransference 33, 84-85, 93-94,
119-122, 144-147, 152-159, 352, 369-
370; cure 31; 375; displacement 172,
369-377; dreams 150, 186-187, 191,
197, 205, 210, 213, 220, 237-238,
249, 326; enactment 89-91; erotic
sexual 113, 141, 151, 160, 179, 213,
383, 390;   fantasies 171; idealized
129, 373; manifest dream content
186-188, 239-282; love 113, 139-160;
maternal 145; memory 342-343;
mirror neurons 351; mixed 172, 200;
negative 114, 128, 168, 172, 249,
250, 259, 267, 273-274, 280-283,
372-375; old object 135; positive 23,
31, 47, 170, 244, 249-250, 259, 267,
273-274, 280-283, 327, 372, 375;
psychotherapy 21, 73, 112-113,
218-219, 352; resolution 118, 203,
212, 222, 239, 267; split 373, 376;
working-through 157, 214
Transformative friendship relationship
114, 139, 155-161, 390; love 146

Transmuting internalization 125
Tryptophan brain 36
Turning-point dream 209, 218, 251;
therapy 28, 154, 170
Unconscious dreams 183, 190, 214, 232,
238, 252; Freud 317; impulses motivation wishes 152-153, 343, 381, 385;
interpretation 34; love 140; meanings
159, 327, 381; memory 105, 315, 340,
356; mentation 181, 290, 296, 306,
380, 392; narrative 388; needs 25;
neurobiology 338; oedipal wishes 73;
primary process 116, 313, 340, 348,
354; transference 84, 120, 134, 139;
symptoms 117, 381
Weight average normal 8, 22-28; fluctua-
tion 23, 31, 34-37; gain 2, 22, 25-26,
35; loss xii, xiv, 1-9, 12-14, 22-35;
maintenance 6, 11, 14; obesity 17, 20;
overweight xiv; watchers 23
Wish-fulfillment dreams 251, 239, 387
Working-through oedipal conflict 207;
therapeutic process 370; transference-countertransference 146,
155, 157, 160